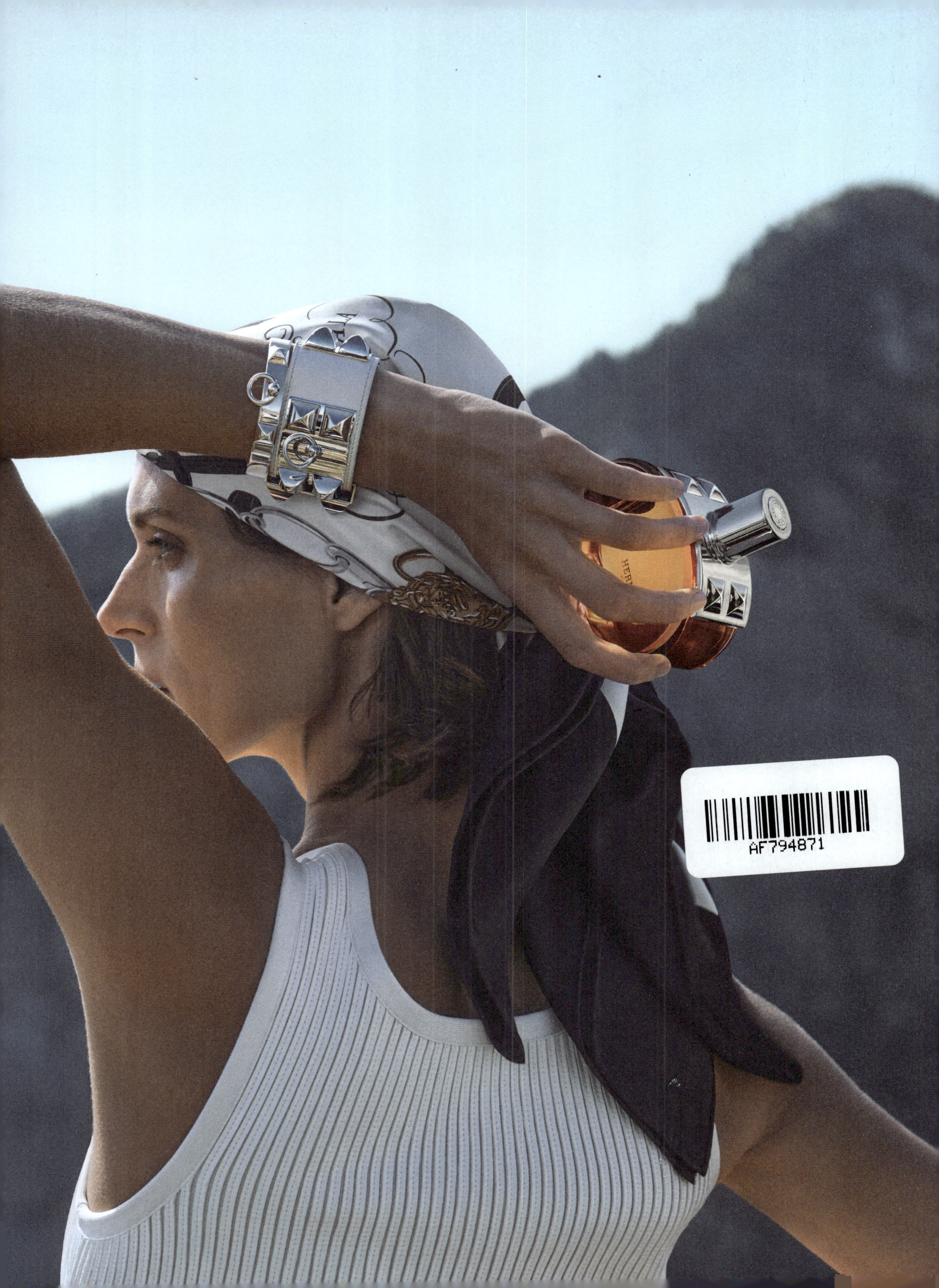

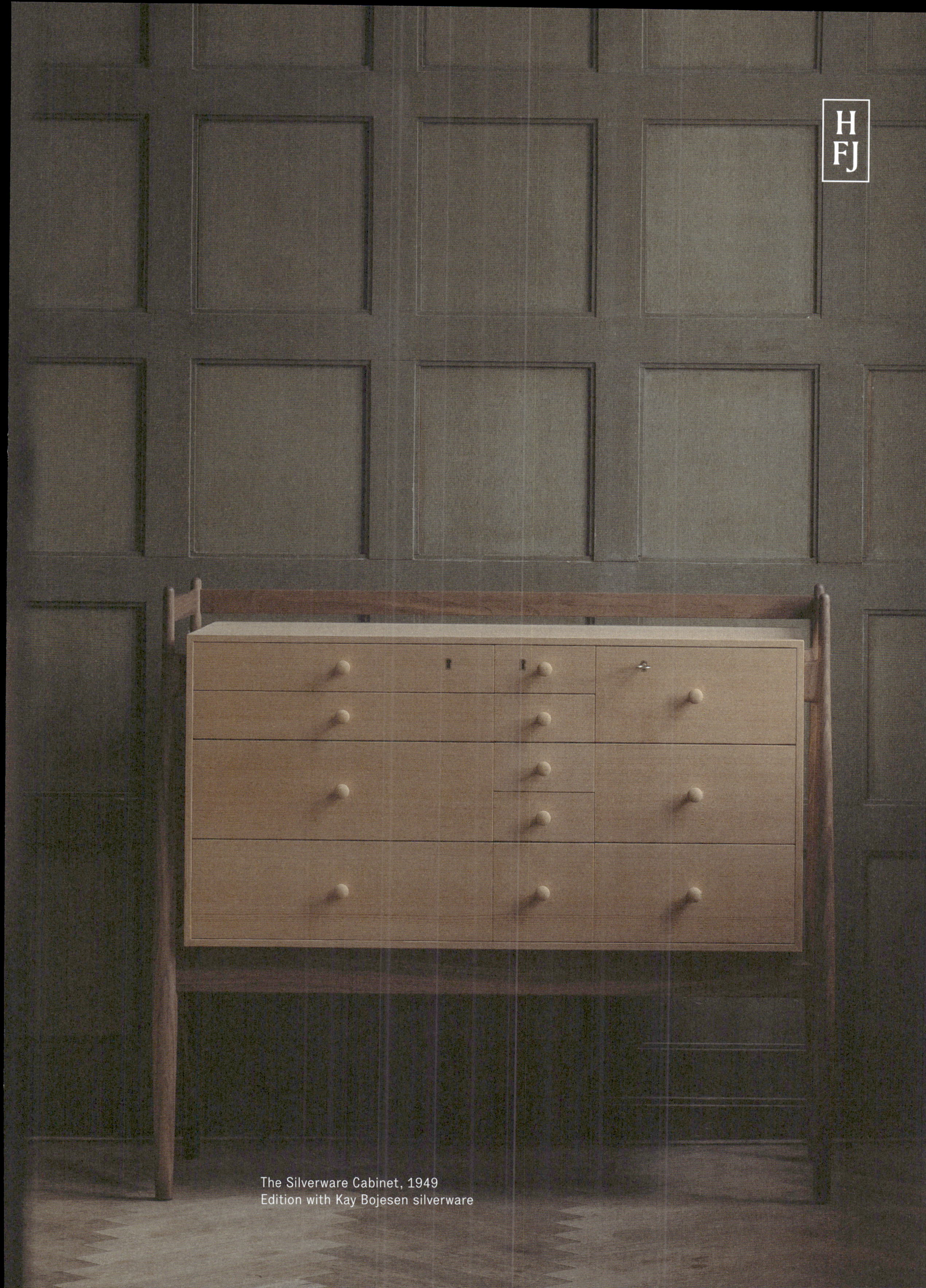

The Silverware Cabinet, 1949
Edition with Kay Bojesen silverware

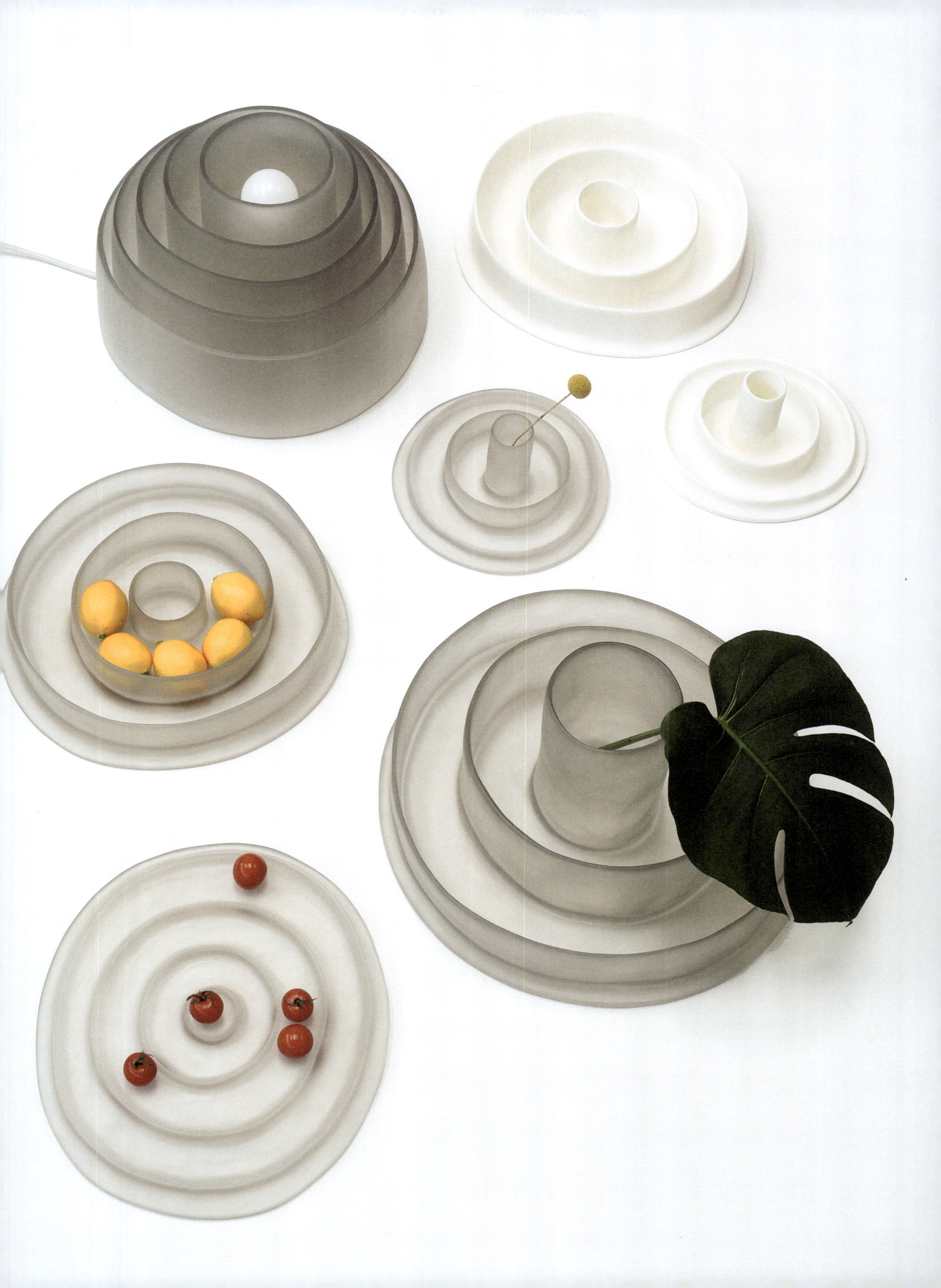

KINFOLK

TEAM

—

EDITOR IN CHIEF	John Burns
DEPUTY EDITOR	George Upton
ART DIRECTOR	Isabel Lea
DESIGN DIRECTOR	Alex Hunting
COPY EDITOR	Rachel Holzman
PUBLISHING DIRECTOR	Edward Mannering
DIGITAL MANAGER	Cecilie Jegsen
ENGAGEMENT EDITOR	Rachel Ellison
STUDIO MANAGER	Victoria Benfeldt

—

CROSSWORD	Mark Halpin
PUBLICATION DESIGN	Alex Hunting Studio
COVER PHOTOGRAPH	Alejandro Arrias & David Bravo

WORDS

—

Julia Webster Ayuso
Benjamin Dane
Gabriele Dellisanti
Daphnée Denis
Tom Faber
James Greig
Simran Hans
Sandy Ho
Elle Hunt
Robert Ito
Tal Janner-Klausner
Rebecca May Johnson
Tara Joshi
Haeryun Kang
Hannah Marriott
Kyla Marshell
Emily May
Emma Moore
Ali Morris
Emily Nathan
Celine Nguyen
Okechukwu Nzelu
Poppy Okotcha
Ellen Peirson-Hagger
Agnish Ray
Asher Ross
Laura Rysman
Natasha Stallard
Fiona Sturges
Ruby Tandoh
Annick Weber
Tom Whyman
Sumiko Wilson

STYLING, SET DESIGN, HAIR & MAKEUP

—

Jhonson Camilo
Sarah Carlier
Tim Ferro
Alisa Hirvonen
Hwayoung Kim
Judy Kim
Mari Kuno
Victor Maresco
Laura Meijueiro
Manu Mendi
Mahito Ohtani
Madeline Rouge
Martin Tournebize

ARTWORK & PHOTOGRAPHY

—

Nikolai Ahn
Alejandro Arrias & David Bravo
Aaron Bernstein
Yuhao Chang
Cristina Coral
Sean Davidson
James O Davies
Joyce and Andres de Lange
DSL Studio
Anselm Ebulue
William Elliot
James Emmerman
Tim Evans
Raphaël Gaultier
Nathan Wolf Grace
Camilla Greenwell
Eugenio Intini
Edouard Jacquinet
Cecilie Jegsen
Hugh Kretschmer
Vera Lair
Weiyu Lin & Fei Yang
Liam MacRae
Andrew B. Myers
Joshua Monaghan
Silvia Conde Oliván
Adriana Parrilla
Ben Rollins
Lewis Ronald
Phil Sayer
Beowulf Sheehan
Christopher Simpson
Aaron Tilley
The Voorhes
Paul Westlake
Magdalena Wosinska

PUBLISHER

—

Chul-Joon Park

The views expressed in *Kinfolk* magazine are those of the respective contributors and are not necessarily shared by the company or its staff. *Kinfolk* (ISSN 2596-6154) is published quarterly by Ouur ApS, Amagertorv 14B, 2, 1160 Copenhagen, Denmark. Printed by Park Communications Ltd in London, United Kingdom. Color reproduction by Park Communications Ltd in London, United Kingdom. The US annual subscription price is $80 USD. Airfreight and mailing in the USA by WN Shipping USA, 156-15, 146th Avenue, 2nd Floor, Jamaica, NY 11434, USA. Application to mail at periodicals postage prices is pending at Jamaica NY 11431. US Postmaster: Send address changes to *Kinfolk*, WN Shipping USA, 156-15, 146th Avenue, 2nd Floor, Jamaica, NY 11434, USA. Subscription records are maintained at Ouur ApS, Amagertorv 14B, 2, 1160 Copenhagen, Denmark. SUBSCRIBE: *Kinfolk* is published four times a year. To subscribe, visit kinfolk.com/subscribe or email us at info@kinfolk.com. CONTACT US: If you have questions or comments, please write to us at info@kinfolk.com. For advertising and partnership inquiries, get in touch at advertising@kinfolk.com.

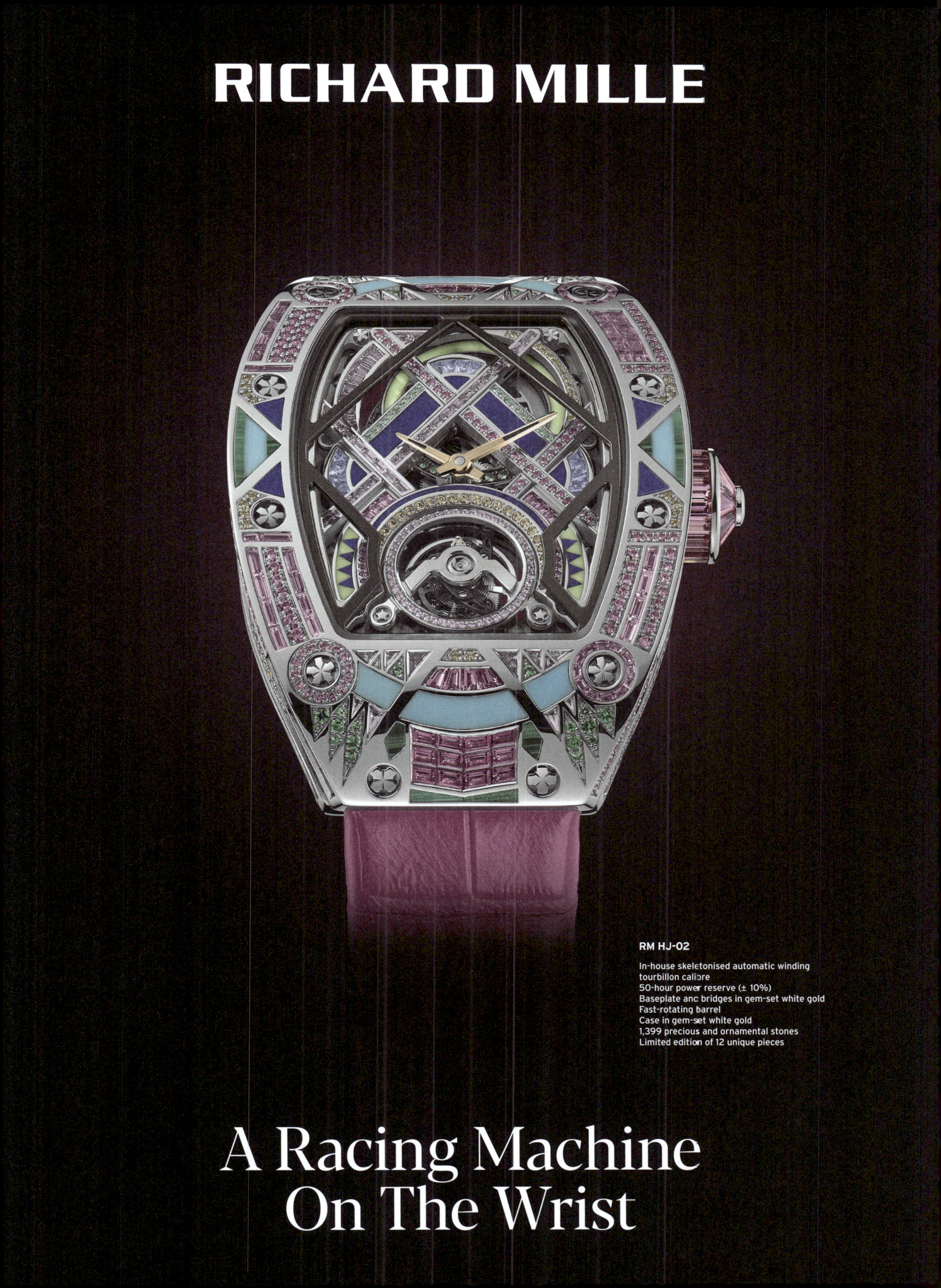
RICHARD MILLE
RM HJ-02
In-house skeletonised automatic winding
tourbillon calibre
50-hour power reserve (± 10%)
Baseplate and bridges in gem-set white gold
Fast-rotating barrel
Case in gem-set white gold
1,399 precious and ornamental stones
Limited edition of 12 unique pieces
A Racing Machine
On The Wrist

WELCOME
The Play Issue

In the 1980s, the term "Peter Pan Syndrome" was coined by psychologist Dr. Dan Kiley to describe adults—primarily men—who exhibit chronic immaturity, avoid adult responsibilities and struggle with emotional commitment. A red flag, in other words, and perhaps also the reason why getting in touch with our inner child rarely feels welcome outside the therapist's office.

There is, however, a significant difference between being childish and being childlike. Where *childishness* implies regression, to be childlike is something else entirely: to remain open, imaginative and willing to experiment without knowing the outcome. That distinction matters because inviting adults to play—as we do throughout this issue—can collapse the two together and shut play down before it even begins.

In this issue, play is presented as a prism through which we might recover some of that openness again—a way to move through adulthood with greater joy, curiosity and wonder. "We don't ever lose the desire to play; we're just socialized to stop playing in certain ways," Mia Sundstrom, who leads the National Institute for Play, explains to us on page 154.

In the right context or company, however, we can all find ways to play. We see this most clearly among people whose work depends on imagination. In a study of architects, psychologist Donald MacKinnon found that those considered most creative by their peers were often those who knew how to play; this is certainly true of John Outram, whose over the top masterpiece Sphinx Hill we visit on page 70. Painters play with color and line, a type of immersive flow state our fashion editorial explores on page 60. And musicians improvise and experiment, a process familiar to the band Balming Tiger (interviewed on page 78), whose alternative approach to K-pop subverts the genre's perfectly synchronized image.

Of course, losing ourselves in play has benefits far beyond outcomes like making art, or designing beautiful buildings. Play can build communities and inspire connection—as with the thousands of adult furries we meet in Atlanta on page 136—and help us slow down, reconnect and become more present with one another. Throughout the issue, we explore pathways into play, including expert advice on rediscovering your own play type as a busy adult and, failing that, five games devised and demonstrated by artist Carsten Höller for those who don't know where to begin.

As Sundstrom points out, adults need only 30 seconds to build play into their day. It's a small investment for something that, she says, "fundamentally makes us human."

WORDS
JOHN BURNS

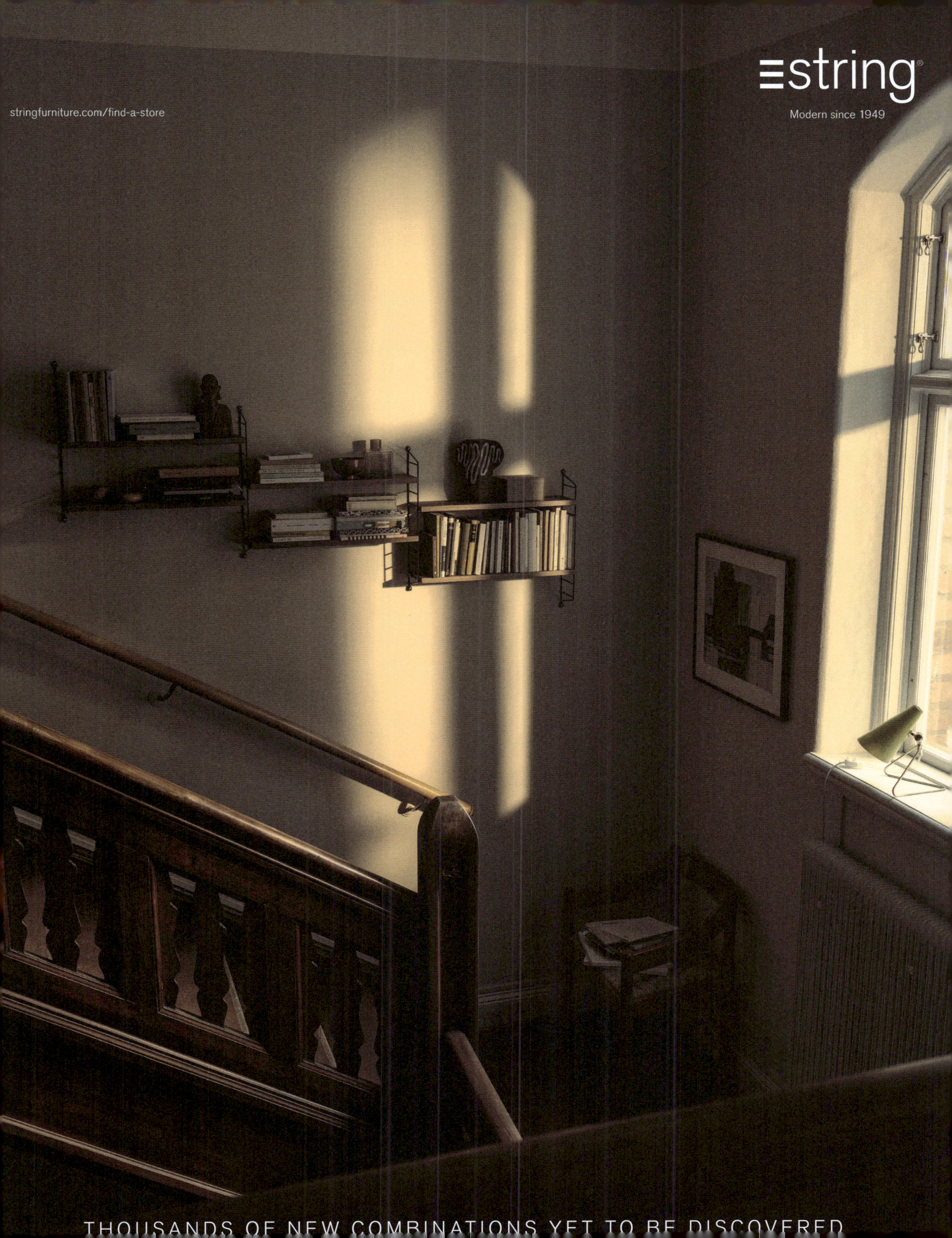
string
Modern since 1949
stringfurniture.com/find-a-store
THOUSANDS OF NEW COMBINATIONS YET TO BE DISCOVERED

14 — 44

STARTERS
On duty, snacks and Pulitzer Prizes.

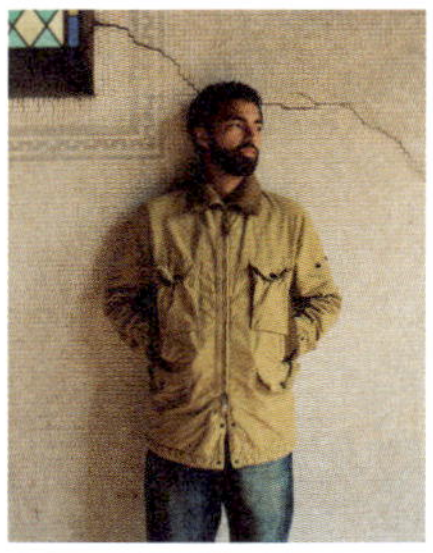

45 — 96

FEATURES
From K-pop to Egyptian Revival.

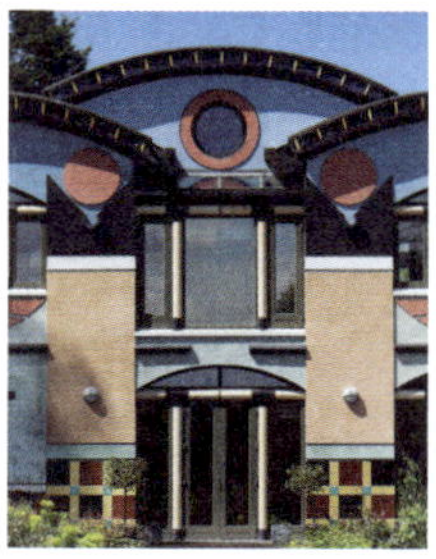

"Design for me is an act of nurturing care." (Faye Toogood – P. 52)

Photograph: Alejandro Arrias & David Bravo

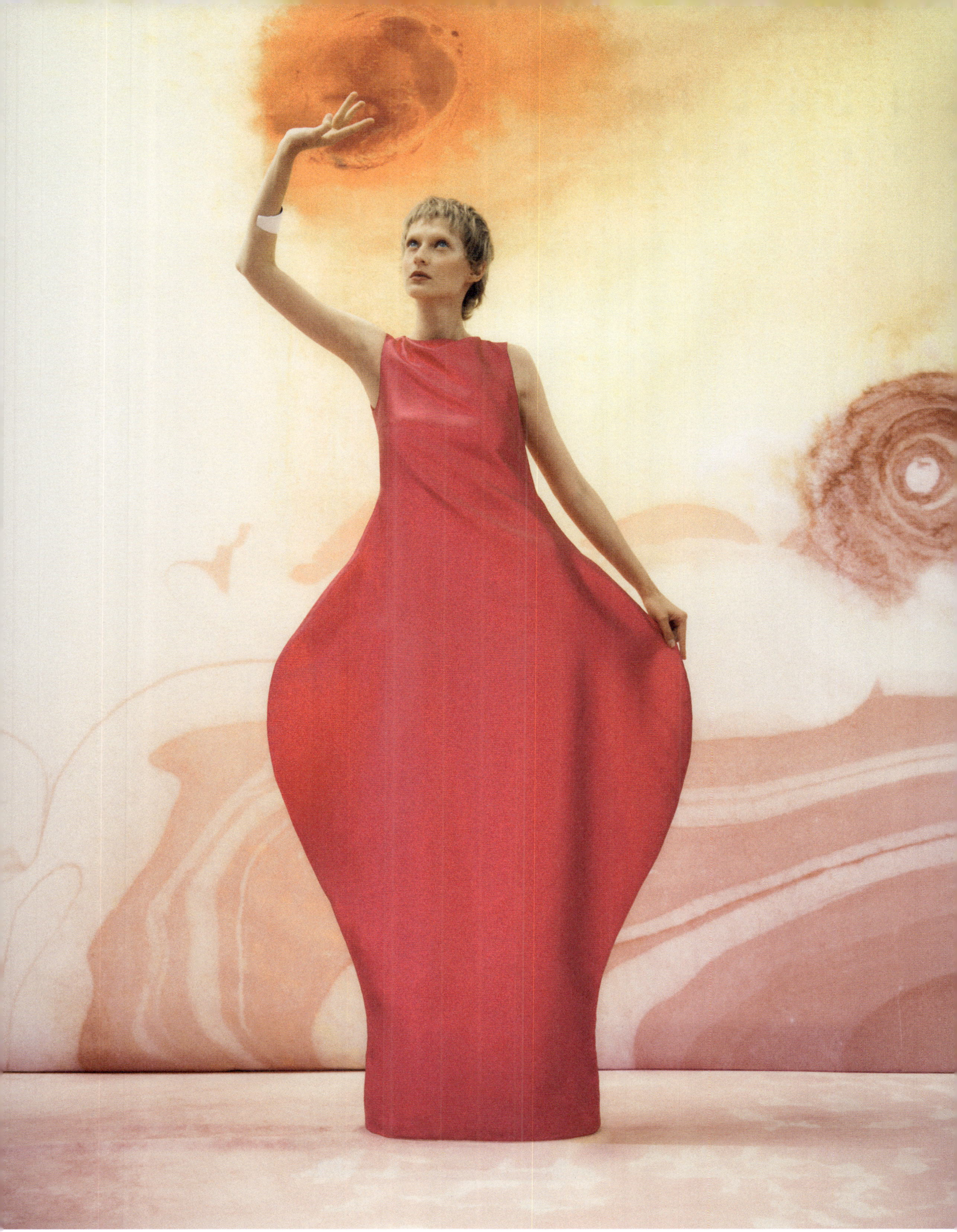

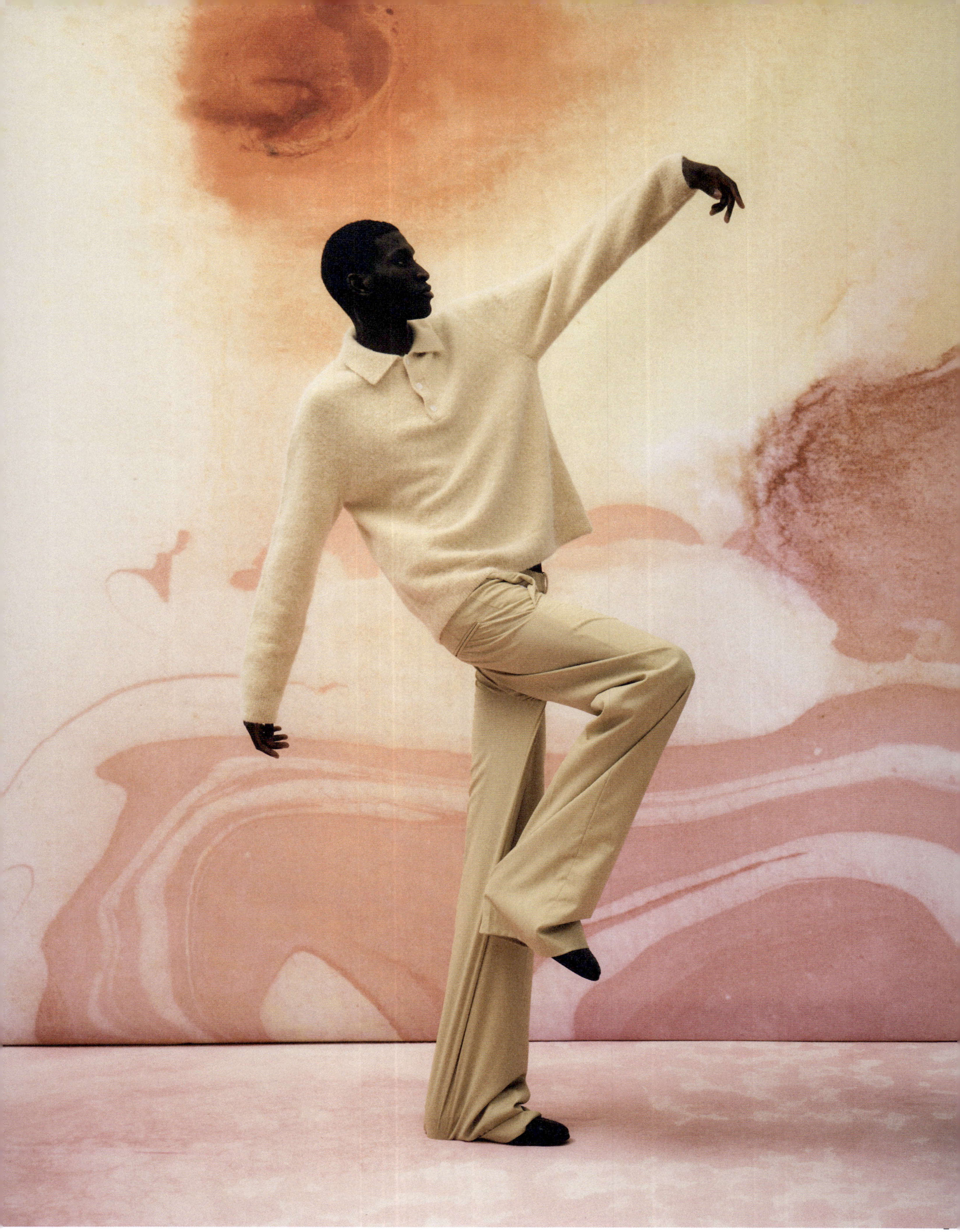

97 — 160

PLAY
De-stress, connect and find joy.

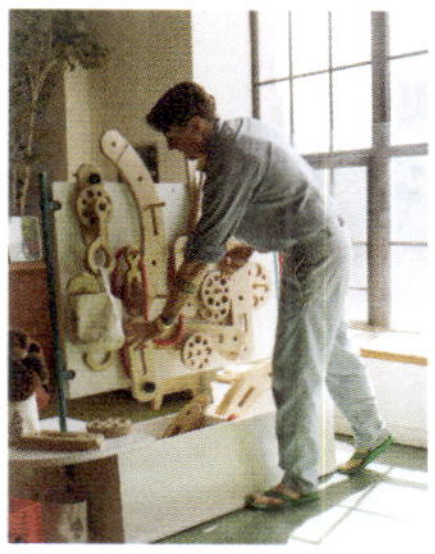

161 — 176

DIRECTORY
A fresh take on fall.

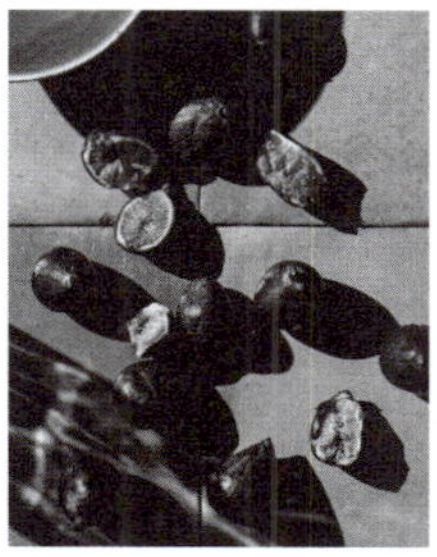

Photograph: Alejandro Arrias & David Bravo

I

Starters

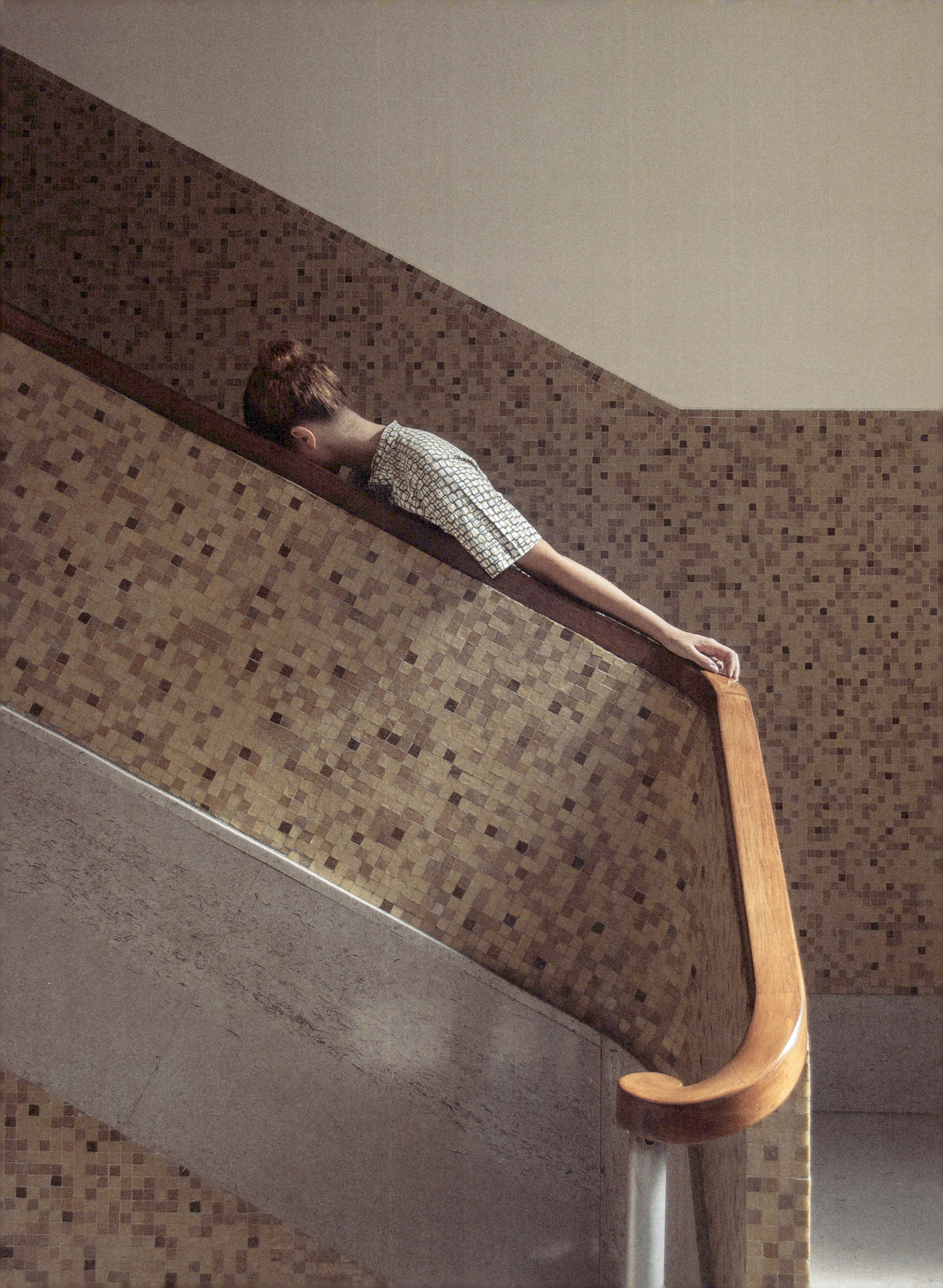

ALWAYS GO TO THE FUNERAL
The case for doing the difficult thing.

WORDS
TAL JANNER-KLAUSNER
PHOTO
CRISTINA CORAL

In the Jewish tradition, a "mitzvah" refers to something you're supposed to do. Socially oriented mitzvahs include visiting the sick, comforting the bereaved and avoiding causing embarrassment to others. It is often considered to be akin to a good deed—a benevolent act of kindness—though the literal translation is different: a mitzvah is a commandment, something you are obligated to do, even if it is hard.

We can take this framing—the positive value of doing the things you *should* do—into secular life. Quoting her father, writer and lawyer Deirdre Sullivan titled her widely read 2005 essay "Always Go to the Funeral."[1] Her point was: Do it. Do the hard, responsible thing, even if it is inconvenient or uncomfortable, or you just don't feel like it.

Making yourself do the difficult thing can be a little like plunging into a cold body of water. It would be easier to stay warm and dry, but you know that you'll thank yourself later when you're enjoying the post-dip dopamine. Overriding your instinctive desire to avoid discomfort requires self-knowledge and conscious decision-making: You take a deep breath and jump in.

But why? Fundamentally, this can be seen as reciprocity and social solidarity, not altruism. This is not about being a good person; rather, it is about duty—and perhaps wanting to live in a world where other people will also go out of their way to look after you or your loved ones when you need it. In today's discourse of self-care and boundaries, collective responsibility can too easily be left behind.

There is, of course, a risk of giving too much or spreading yourself too thin. If you take every possible opportunity to look after others and act responsibly, you will find yourself depleted of time and emotional resources; remember, you're no use to anyone if you're drained or exhausted. But beyond the benefit of living in a society where people make the effort to care for each other, there is a personal benefit to doing the difficult thing, regardless of what it is. Pushing yourself through discomfort and inconvenience is a training in resilience. It is the real work that makes us grow as people, and for which we can be most proud.

So: Go to your colleague's parent's funeral, visit your friend in the hospital after their operation, help your neighbor search for their cat who hasn't come home. Years from now, you won't remember how busy or tired you were that day, but they will remember that you were by their side when they needed it, and you will feel confident in knowing that they will be there for you in turn.

(1) The need to attend funerals has only increased in recent years. The number of direct cremations—those without a ceremony—grew from roughly a third of all cremations in 2015 to 41% by 2022, according to the National Funeral Directors Association. This is despite many people later expressing regret: the NFDA also found that 29% of Americans whose loved one was cremated or buried without a service wished they had held one.

We have long been fascinated by images of decline. From the intellectuals of the Italian Renaissance to 19th-century Romantic painters and 18th-century English architects, scenes of decay and ruin have served as reminders that, no matter how great our civilization, like Ancient Rome, Greece or Egypt, it too will one day end—a kind of memento mori for society. In the 19th century, architect John Soane even celebrated the completion of his design for the Bank Of England by commissioning a painting that rendered the building as a Roman ruin.

The tradition continues today in the age of social media, with popular accounts juxtaposing images of war-damaged European cities with their present-day appearance, or sharing slideshows assembled from Google Street View images showing houses gradually becoming overrun by nature. But while such depictions have traditionally invited reflections on mortality and impermanence, a newer genre of online content revels in decline itself—and in the anger it provokes.

One of the most infamous examples of "decline porn," as it has come to be known, is a video purporting to show a squalid, "taxpayer-funded" water park in Croydon, a borough in south London. No such park exists; the video is entirely fake, having been generated using AI; and when the BBC's disinformation specialist, Marianna Spring, reached out to the creator, she learned that he had never even been to Croydon. He explained that the video was purely for entertainment.

As Spring observes, however, there is often a "political undertone" to this type of content. The deepfaked Croydon video, which shows mostly gangs of young men wearing balaclavas and padded jackets, plays into narratives promoted by far-right figures such as Elon Musk and JD Vance, who have decried the "civilizational erasure" of the West. The reality is quite different: A report published in early 2026 found that 63% of Londoners believed the city was a safe place to live.

Where Romantic painters once transformed collapse into melancholy beauty, social media turns it into an endless stream of reactionary fantasy—images of cities supposedly unraveling through social decay. The imagery may be fake, but judging by the vitriolic and divisive responses it provokes, its political impact is all too real.

—

A CIVIL QUESTION
What's up with decline porn?

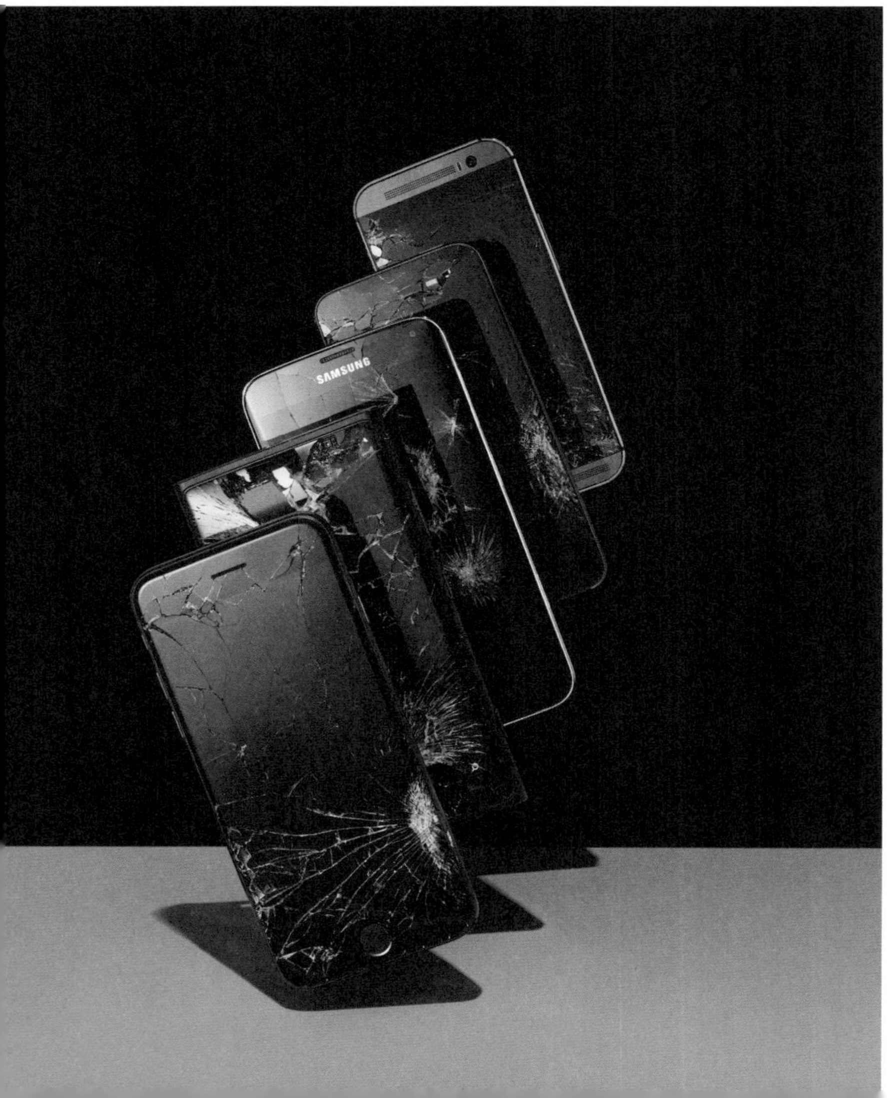

WORDS
CELINE NGUYEN
PHOTO
THE VOORHES

IF DESTROYED, STILL TRUE
A short history of the love lock.

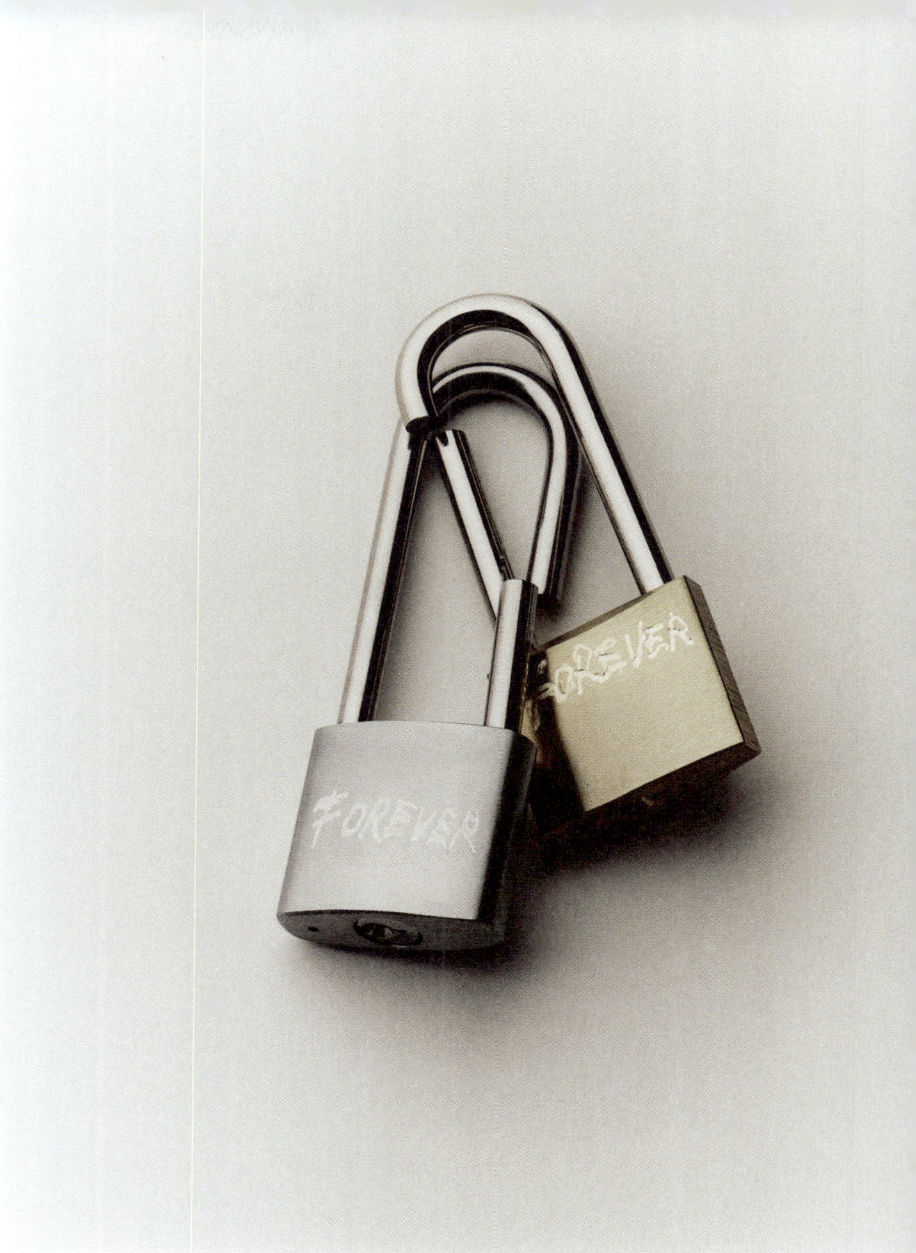

WORDS
OKECHUKWU NZELU
PHOTO
WEIYU LIN & FEI YANG

It might sound like a romantic gesture—securing a padlock engraved with your paramour's name to a bridge and throwing the key into the water—but today it's unlikely to be a lasting declaration. In 2014, there were enough padlocks fastened to Paris' Pont des Arts to cause a railing to collapse, leading to the removal of an estimated one million locks and the installation of plexiglass to prevent more from being added. Similarly, on the Brooklyn Bridge, municipal workers and volunteers now patrol the famous walkway with angle grinders. What was once a charming custom—a symbol of unbreakable connection—has buckled under the weight of mass tourism.

The practice is thought to have begun in Vrnjačka Banja, Serbia in 1914, when a teacher named Nada became engaged to an officer named Relja. They would meet one another on Most Ljubavi, the Bridge of Love, but when the First World War broke out, Relja was deployed overseas and never returned; Nada is said to have died of grief. Moved by her story, local women began writing their names and their lovers' on padlocks, fastening them to the railings of Most Ljubavi and throwing the keys in the river below.

The practice remained largely forgotten until 2006, when the protagonist of Italian novelist Federico Moccia's *I Want You* declared his eternal love by securing a padlock to a lamppost on Ponte Milvio in Rome. Shortly after its publication, love locks started appearing on the real-life bridge, and the tradition spread across Italy and the wider world.

Moccia believes the popularity of love locks was due to a lack of opportunities for young people to express their feelings; a padlock, he suggested, is "a promise." But while the future of the practice looks uncertain, some innovative solutions have emerged. On the Luzhkov Bridge in Moscow, officials installed dedicated "lock trees" that provide a more structurally sound home for love locks. Virtual love locks are also available online, as are, for a fee, NFTs of some 37,000 love locks that were photographed before their removal from the Pont des Arts. If the tradition now feels diminished, it may be because the fantasy at its center has become harder to sustain: the idea that love can be fixed permanently in place, unchanged by time, repetition or reality.

"A room within a room." This is how the Italian architect and designer Ettore Sottsass described the innovative solution he devised in 1963 for the Milan apartment of his friend Giovanni Lana, a printer, lithographer and art collector. In order to maximize the 668 square feet, Sottsass compressed typically separate rooms into a single, fluid space, dividing different zones with perforated ash panels that let in light and allowed for shifting perspectives: an outer perimeter accommodated a study and dining area, while the inner section featured the main living area, with three sofas in a "U" shape.

Sottsass is considered one of Italy's most important architects and designers and is celebrated for, among other things, his design of the Olivetti Valentine typewriter and for founding the Memphis Group in 1980, when he was 63. But his design of Casa Lana came earlier, and it shows his gradual move away from modernism. He was rejecting the functionalist idea of the home as a rational, efficient system in favor of a belief that it was a social stage, where design and objects encourage interaction and foster personal, everyday rituals.

Following Lana's death in 2019, the apartment's central room was carefully dismantled and rebuilt at a dedicated space in the Triennale di Milano museum. Today, more than six decades after it was designed, Casa Lana feels just as groundbreaking as ever. "[In Casa Lana] one always has a complete sense of one's life," Sottsass wrote in 1967, "because everything is there, in a small square where one moves around and encounters others."

WORDS
GABRIELE DELLISANTI
PHOTO
DSL STUDIO

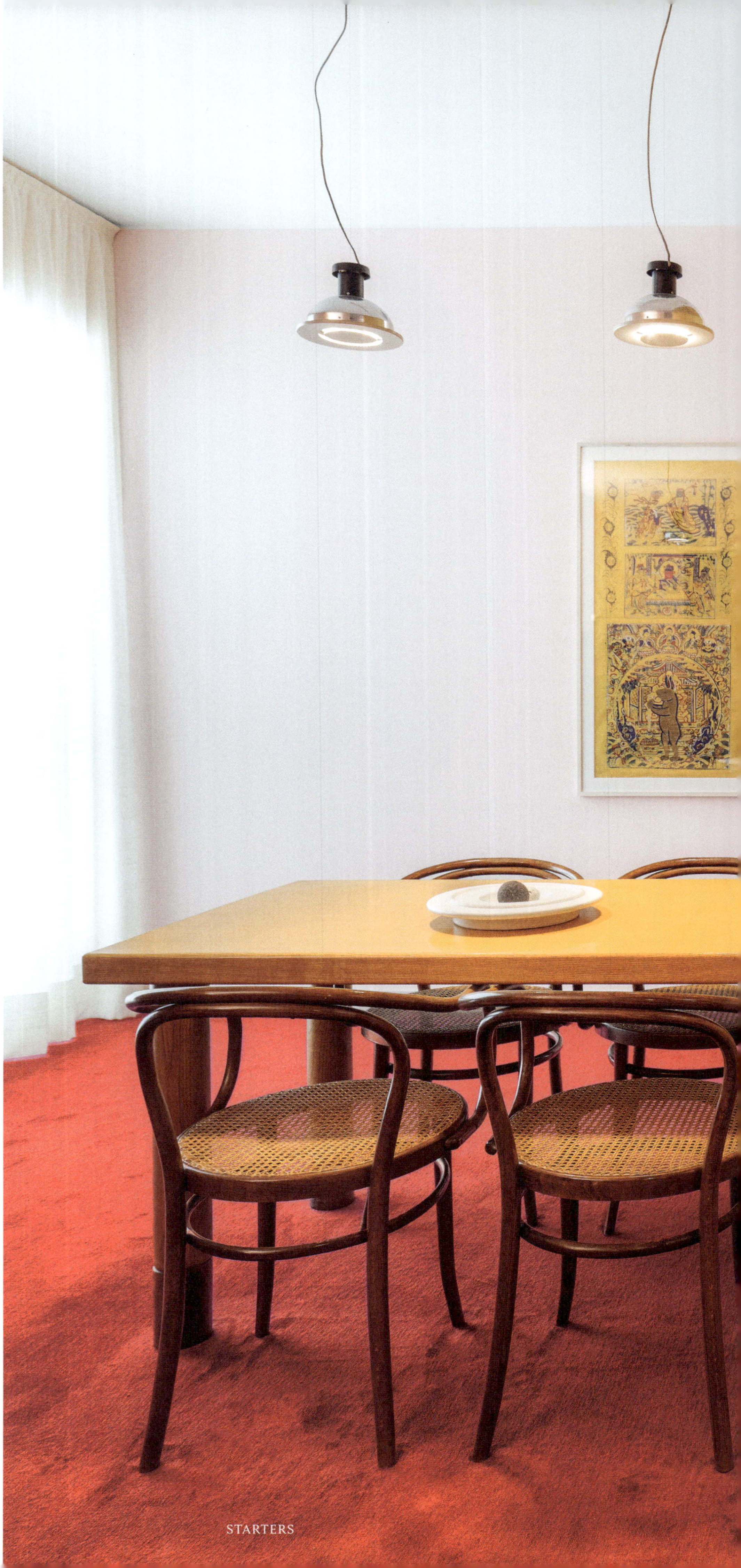

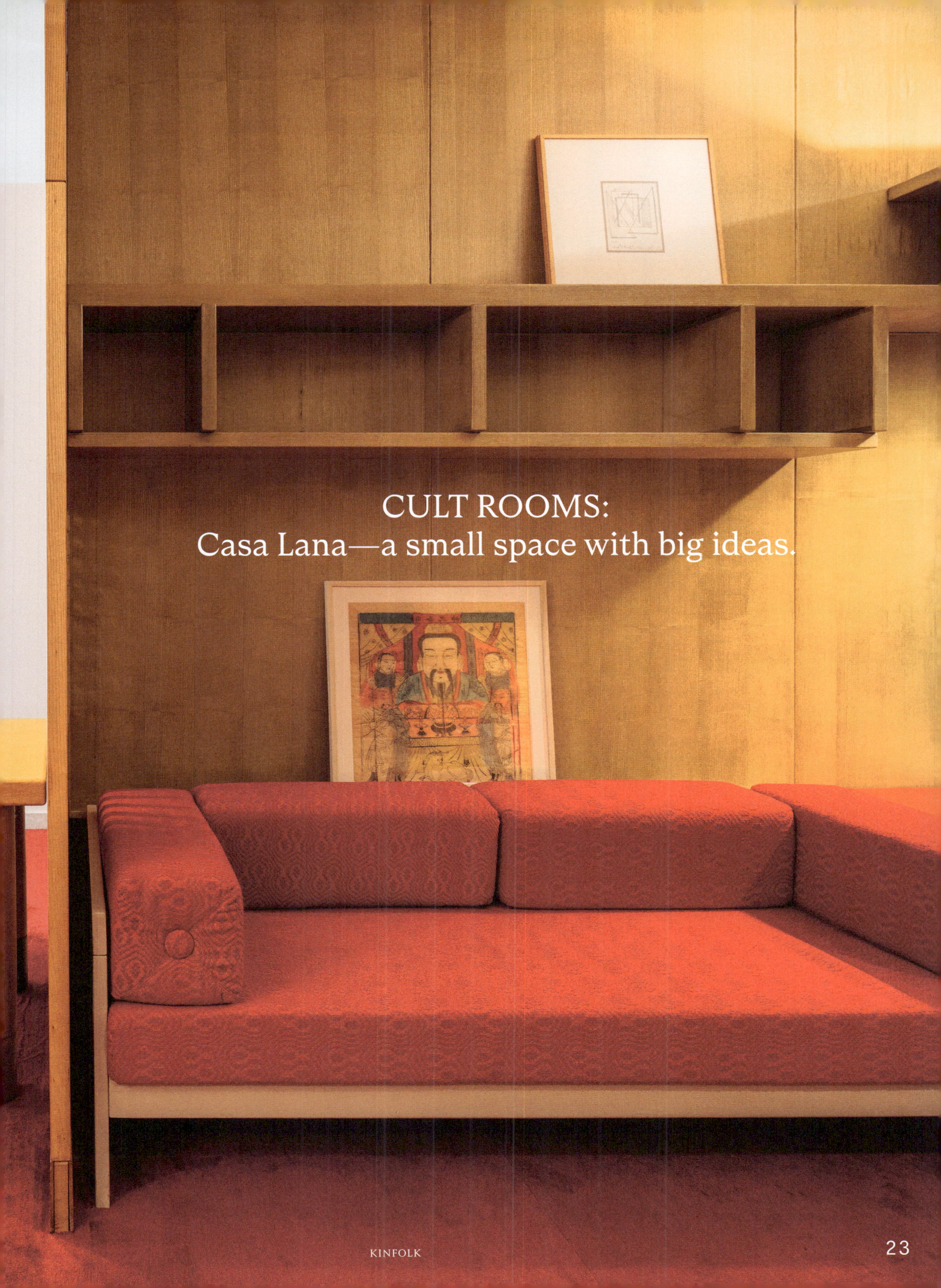

CULT ROOMS:
Casa Lana—a small space with big ideas.

PLAYING IT BY EAR
Should podcasting be regulated?

When Steven Bartlett launched his podcast, *The Diary of a CEO*, in 2017, the aim was to provide insight and tips for people in business. As a successful entrepreneur who would later be featured on the *Forbes* "30 Under 30" list, Bartlett came from a place of knowledge and expertise. But then the podcast branched out into health and wellness, and Bartlett began platforming guests whose opinions veered between the unorthodox and the downright dangerous.

To look at *The Diary of a CEO*'s YouTube page today is to be assailed by alarmist, clickbait headlines, including "In three months, we'll enter a famine," and "95% of your mind is controlled!" When the BBC World Service investigated the podcast 18 months ago, it found 15 health-related episodes in which guests shared misinformation, including discredited anti-vaccine theories and a claim that cancer can be treated by following a keto diet.

Bartlett's defense has long been that he is open to hearing all viewpoints on his show and that he doesn't believe in censorship. It's an approach that certainly hasn't dented the popularity of his podcast—last year it reported 50 million monthly downloads and views. That's a lot of people being exposed to inaccurate and potentially dangerous ideas.

Unfortunately, *The Diary of a CEO* is simply one example of how little production companies and platforms seem to care about accusations of misinformation. Spotify was more than happy to go into business with Joe Rogan, who has given airtime to climate change deniers and anti-vaxxers via his chart-busting podcast *The Joe Rogan Experience* (the latest Spotify–Rogan deal is alleged to be worth $250 million). In 2022, medical and science experts wrote an open letter to Spotify asking the company to crack down on COVID misinformation, specifically referencing Rogan's podcast. Two years later, CNN reported that Donald Trump made 32 false claims during his appearance on the same show.

If podcast creators and networks are declining to do the basic checks and balances before publishing, then surely some sort of outside regulation is required. In the US, the Federal Communications Commission oversees broadcast radio along with TV and on-demand services, while Ofcom does the same in the UK. But those regulators were established at a time when mainstream broadcasters and legacy media reigned supreme, long before new technology enabled everyone and their dog to launch a podcast.[1] For these regulators to now extend their authority to take in the entire audioverse would require a huge overhaul: there are currently around 4.58 million podcasts, and the sector is still rapidly growing.

A further complication is that the definition of a podcast has become fuzzy. With YouTube having leapfrogged Spotify and Apple as the platform of choice for podcast lovers, video podcasts—shows that can be watched as well as listened to—are on the rise. The result is a medium that now sits somewhere between radio, television and social media, making questions of accountability even harder to navigate.

At the same time, carefully reported, narrative, audio-first series are proving harder to fund, commission and produce, and draw only a fraction of the audience commanded by celebrity-led interview podcasts, which translate more easily to video. None of this, of course, suggests that watching a podcast makes for a better experience than listening to one. Often, the opposite is true. As Roman Mars, host of *99% Invisible*, noted recently: "I just think it's way more interesting to make the best possible audio show than the shittiest television show."

That truth and accuracy are seen as optional in podcasting is, of course, part of a wider malaise across politics, tech and media. And as long as there is no single platform to hold podcasts accountable, there can be no single solution. The only possible answer at present is for all in the industry—from hosts and producers to network heads and platforms—to grow a conscience and apply editorial standards for the greater good. But we'll probably be waiting some time for that.

(1) The word "podcast" was coined in 2004 by journalist Ben Hammersley in *The Guardian* as one of several throwaway suggestions, combining "iPod" and "broadcast." He later expressed embarrassment at how thoroughly the term stuck.

WORDS
FIONA STURGES
PHOTO
HUGH KRETSCHMER

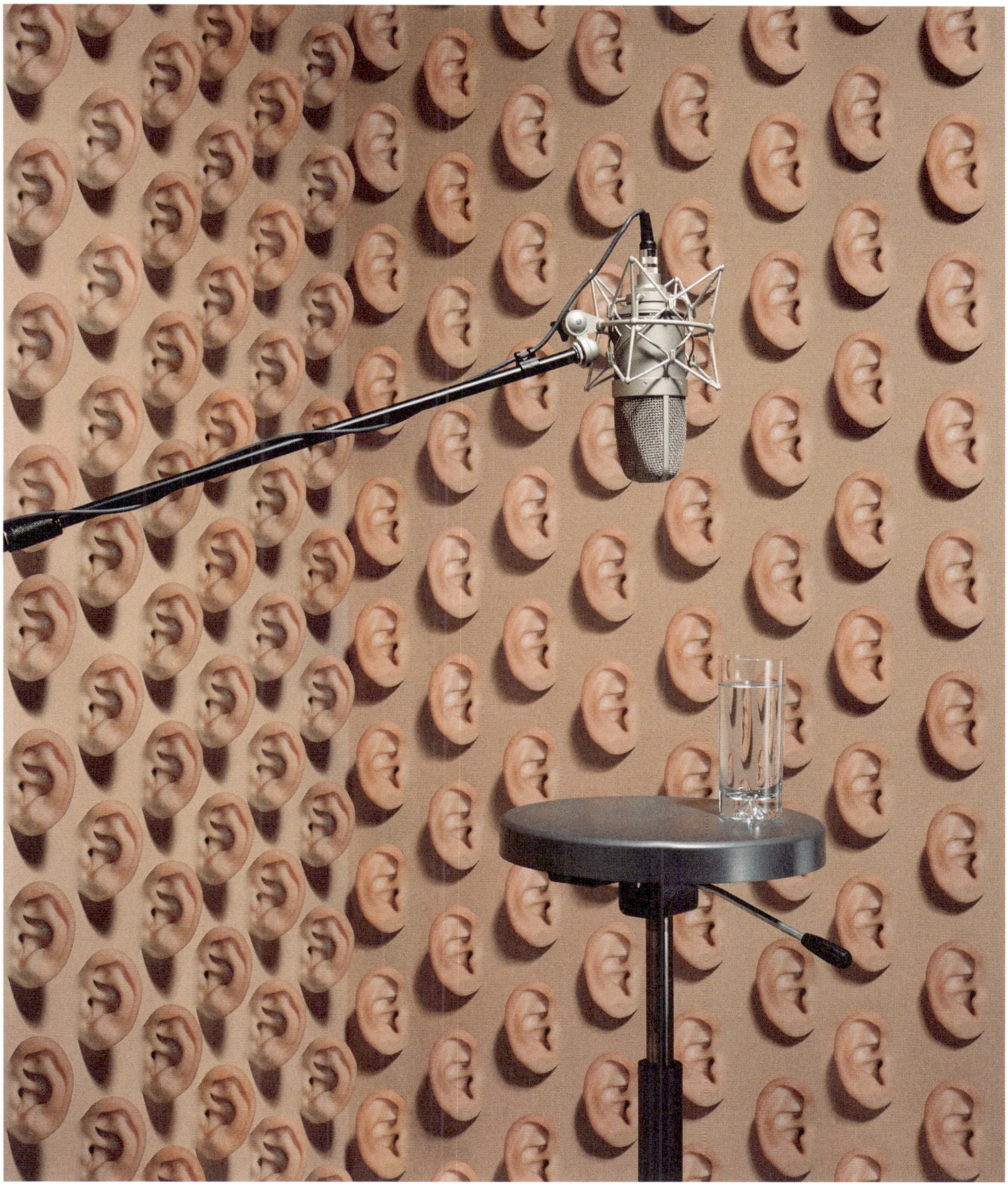

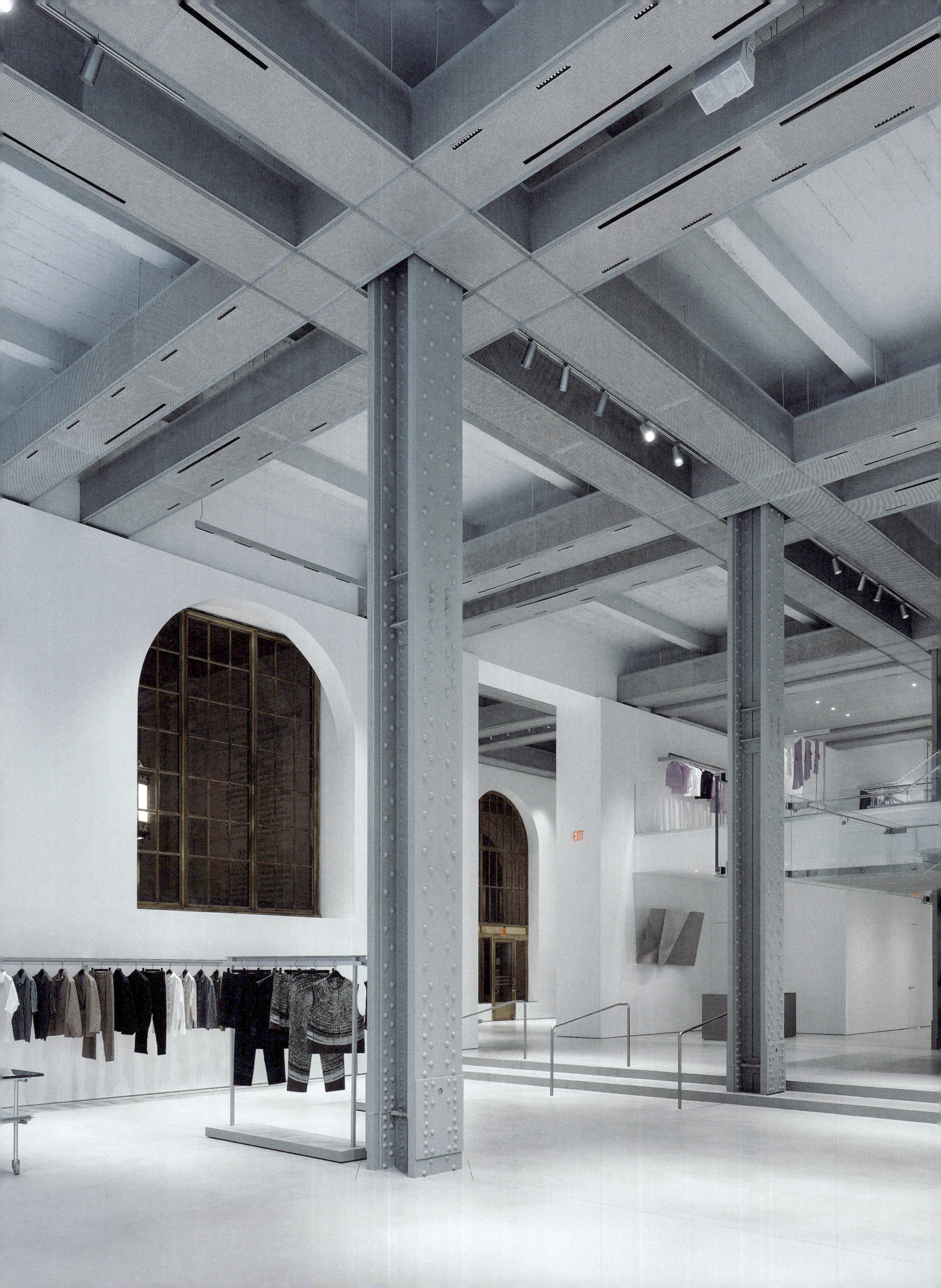
EXIT

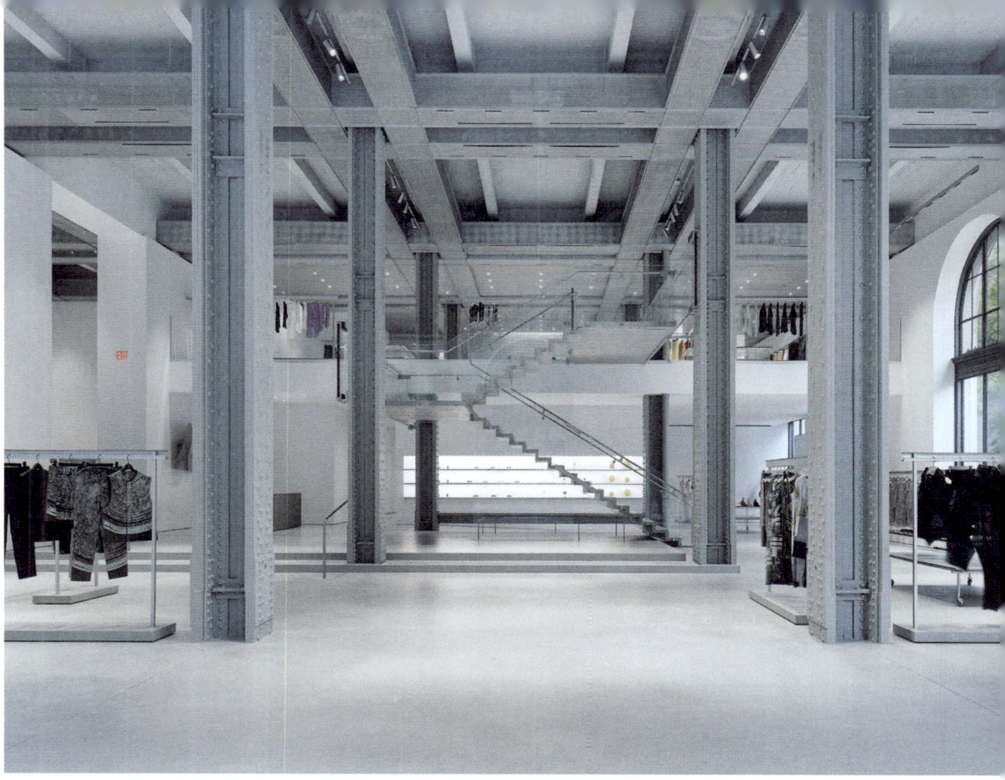

MULTIPLE DIMENSIONS
ISSEY MIYAKE's new Manhattan flagship.

WORDS
HANNAH MARRIOTT
PHOTOS
SEAN DAVIDSON

"Are you ready? Some people get nervous." Jing Liu is guiding me onto the floating staircase at the center of ISSEY MIYAKE's new flagship store in the New York Life Building. Liu's Brooklyn-based firm, SO–IL, is known for its use of unexpected materials and it's an approach that's also evident here. The new 13,000-square-foot store houses eight ISSEY MIYAKE lines and the company's first dedicated gallery space outside of Japan in a commanding, light-filled space overlooking Madison Square Park. The high ceilings, vast arched windows, exposed steel pillars, aluminum mesh ducts—and that staircase—form a striking response to the 1928 landmark it sits within.

HANNAH MARRIOTT: How did the historic building inform your design?

JING LIU: We wanted to emphasize the height of the space and its light—there's a Gothic pursuit of light that feels very present here. We also wanted to highlight how urban it is with the park outside and people moving constantly through the area. When we first arrived, it was a mess; there was dust everywhere. We stripped everything back, exposed the steel beams and pushed the ceiling as high as possible.

HM: To what extent did you look to incorporate ISSEY MIYAKE's brand identity?

JL: Our early ideas incorporated a lot of textiles, which we often work with, but we realized the architecture shouldn't mimic the clothing. Instead, we thought it should share the ethos behind it: craft, precision, engineering and innovation. We also wanted the architecture to disappear as much as possible. The garment rails, for example, are made from extrusions. You can't see the supports, so the shadows remain continuous. It's highly architectural but also practical—even heavy winter coats won't make them sag.

HM: What else has come to characterize your approach?

JL: The store is very functional and minimal. We knew we needed a staircase to the second floor, for example, but anything too solid would block the space behind it, so we proposed glass. We'd designed a 32-foot glass staircase for a museum in Hong Kong, so I already understood what the material could do.

HM: Who inspires your work?

JL: Frank Gehry, who designed the previous ISSEY MIYAKE store in Tribeca, because of his boldness and focus on materials. Some elements from that store have been recycled here, including a titanium wall piece. I admire designers who are smart with materials and who take risks. It's easy to do the "nice" thing; it's much harder to do the thing that might fail.

This story was produced in partnership with ISSEY MIYAKE.

DUA SALEH

WORDS
TARA JOSHI
PHOTOS
MAGDALENA WOSINSKA

On AI, activism and their sophomore album.

Dua Saleh left Sudan during the Darfur War, when the artist, actor, poet and activist was just one. The family moved to Eritrea, and then to the US, when Saleh was six, where they grew up in a political household, learning the value of speaking up and using art as a means of nourishment.

It's a grounding that's evident in Saleh's multifaceted career. Perhaps best known for their role as Cal Bowman on the Netflix hit series *Sex Education*, they are also a celebrated musician; when we speak, they've just released their stirring, silky second album, *Of Earth & Wires*, a postapocalyptic queer love story imbued with grief, nods to their ancestral Sudanese musicality and, of course, hope.

TARA JOSHI: How's life following the release of the new album?

DUA SALEH: I'm doing some shows, but one actually just got canceled—I think the universe is giving me some rest; there's a lot going on. Later on, I'm going to go on tour and do a writing camp for some other artists. So I'm using this time as a resting period, letting my creativity out on social media. I've been dressing up and doing a "choose your own adventure" thing on my [Instagram] Story.

TJ: Is it ever strange that people have a parasocial relationship with you through social media?

DS: Oh my God, for sure. It startled me a little bit, because the way that people are engaging with me, it's like I'm not actually a person, they think I'm AI or something—which is funny, because the new album is so anti-AI.

TJ: To what extent do people assume you're the same as your *Sex Education* character, Cal?

DS: I've seen it happen to Kedar [Williams-Stirling, who played Jackson]—we were getting dinner with another cast member, Alex [James, who played Aisha], and the server refused to engage with me because she thought I was dating him. It made me realize that, Okay, people are actually going to see me as Cal. Also, Cal is politically active, and I'm doing that myself.

I'm scared about the Earth coming to ruin. I'm scared about AI drone bombing. I'm scared about any surveillance. As an artist, I'm scared about AI, as well. And that bleeds out into supporting other movements—the Palestine movement, talking to people from different nation-states, Syria, Yemen. All of us are going through a lot.

I know that because of how I'm perceived by the media, it's beneficial to me to speak up, and that's a relief in and of itself, because not that many actors can say the same. I know all my co-stars on the show are politically active, at least on

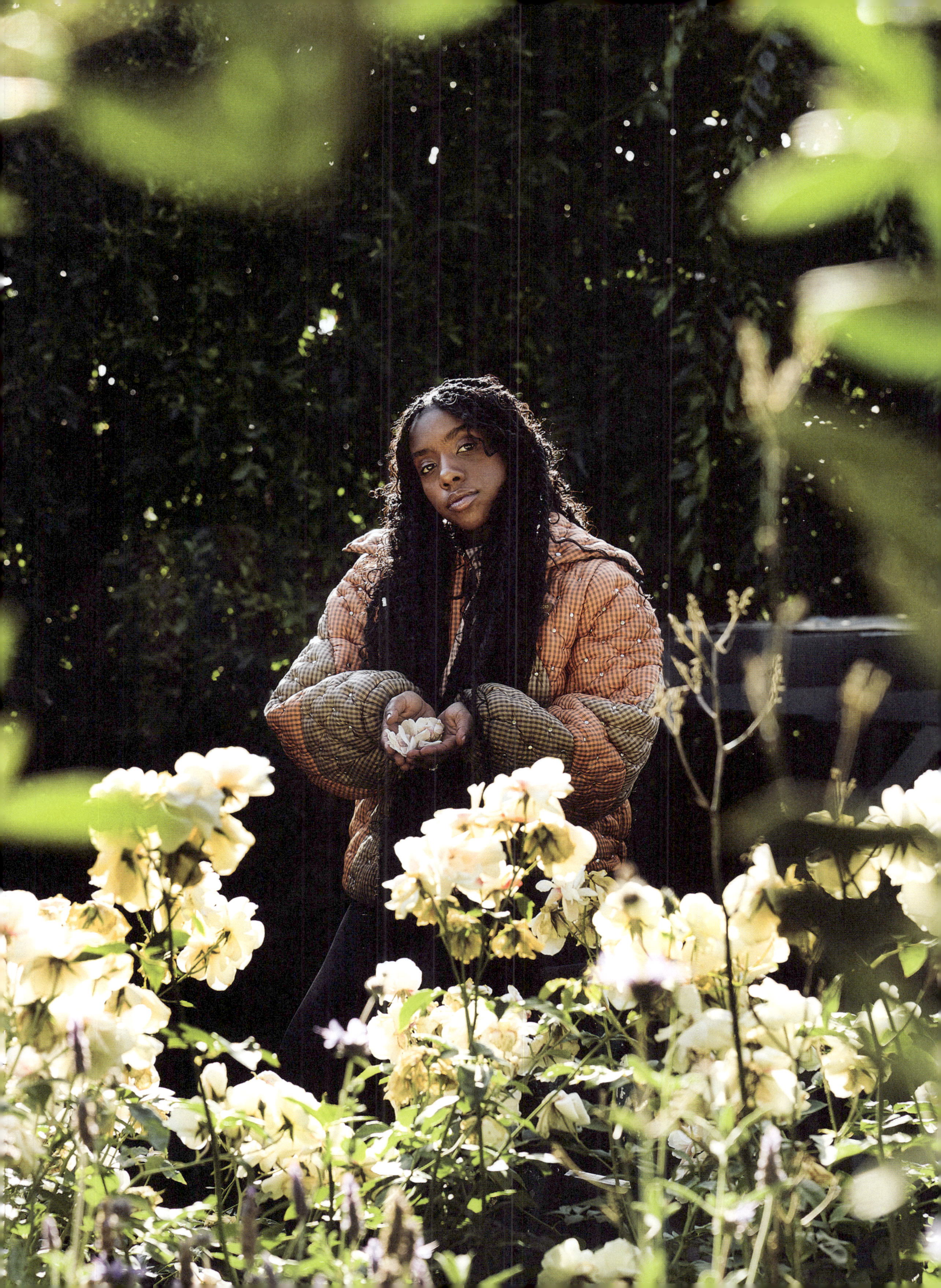

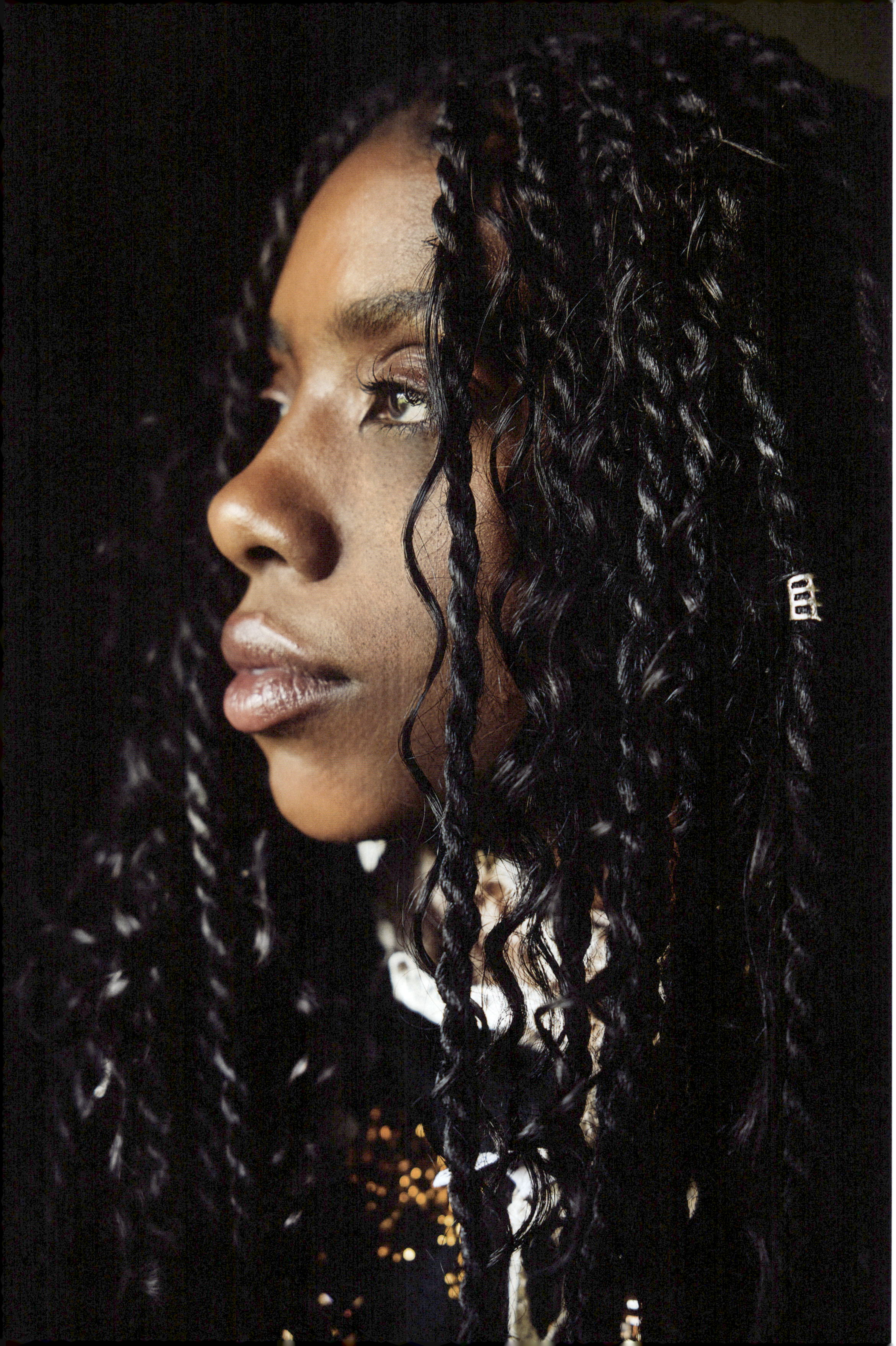

their stories or posting, but it's better for me to speak up often, because it's reflective of Cal, and that's how people are going to see me...which is not bad.

TJ: There are definitely worse characters to be associated with.

DS: The character is an implication of a shift in culture. You know, people are DMing me, being like, "My parents finally get it." I can't say that I'm anything other than blessed to be able to create art and just be myself, honestly. Alhamdulillah.

TJ: Is it ever tiring or frustrating to be a voice for trans rights at a time when those rights are actively being rolled back?

DS: I don't think of it as a problem, because I can just put a Band-Aid on it, and I know it'll heal. I know I need to engage with it, regardless. But I also get this euphoria from talking about gender, just thinking about transness. Maybe it's childish, but it's hard for me to not be happy when talking about transness, and not be happy when I'm in community with queer folk and with trans folk. So even if it hurts for a little bit, it's just a scrape, you know? I'll take some rest, I'll bed rot, go on TikTok, I'll go to a café and drink some chamomile tea.

TJ: How does your Sudanese heritage come through on the record?

DS: The song "Anemic" featuring Gaidaa is an homage to what's happening with the war in Sudan right now, but then we also brought some of the joy from the country. When my family visited Sudan, my sister sent me a video of all the women within their neighborhood, singing together. I was like, I need to usher in some of that joy. I also brought in Sudanese oud to the song "I Do, I Do," and I did a vocal reference—not exact, because I'm not a thief!—to Mohammed Wardi who is a famous pop star. He's our Michael Jackson, basically.

TJ: There are several collaborations on this record. Is working with other artists a way of embodying community in a time of upheaval?

DS: Our hearts are feeling so tumultuous, and I'm very grateful to have people like Bon Iver, who was actively talking about ICE raids in the midst of the Grammys. Aja Monet, she just is active in general, talking about Palestine, talking about the ICE raids that were happening in LA, and organizing around that. Just having those people that I knew are already in the family, it feels more comforting. But I know this is not forever. Things will be better. There's always a cycle, that's just how human society works. It'll get better.

TJ: Do you feel like we need hope and optimism to help make things better?

DS: I think it's better if you do have optimism; you don't need to, but I think it's beneficial. I believe there's divine essence in being hopeful. And I have to be checked in that way, because I don't necessarily come from the most positive mind-set. I am bubbly, which is confusing, but I'm also from Minneapolis and St. Paul, Minnesota, and it's very cold and desolate, and there's a lot of racial issues. I have an Afropessimistic mindset, which makes sense, because Afropessimism—the term, not the concept—was coined in Minnesota by Frank B. Wilderson III, and so I come to life with a punk mentality: "F the system, this is so messed up, I'm here for y'all, let's party it out."

But I needed that grounding Mother Gaia energy for this album, and that hope. I needed "All Is Love," which features Aja Monet; it was necessary to hear that hopeful, joyful, bliss-induced messaging, because there's a chance that things might turn around in the end. I needed to be reminded of that. We need the next generation to be hopeful that they'll be able to live and actually sit with joy.

"They think I'm AI or something—which is funny, because the new album is so anti-AI."

(opposite)
Avant-pop musician, actor, activist and poet Dua Saleh was photographed in Los Angeles while preparing for an international tour through Europe and North America.

WORD: YES, AND...
An invitation to improvise.

Etymology: Developed by a troupe of actors in Chicago in the 1950s, and a cornerstone of improvisational comedy ever since, the concept of "Yes, and..." is about fostering a collaborative spirit and maintaining momentum in a discussion.[1] "Yes"—accepting the idea; "and..."—expanding on it and adding something relevant.

Definition: "Yes, and..." makes perfect sense in the world of improv comedy, where sketches depend on performers building upon one another's ideas. A scene would quickly fall apart if one actor announced, "Captain, our spaceship is heading straight toward that asteroid field!" and their partner replies, "That's odd, given we're actually in a 1950s diner...." But the method is not without its critics: Actor (and acting coach) Gary Schwartz, for example, has argued that "yes, and..." can add *too* much information, leading to performances that are "uninspired, 'talky' and not very theatrical."

In the corporate world, "yes, and..." has taken off as a management ethos. But here the phrase runs into an obvious problem: Some ideas are just bad. And agreeing with everything everyone says can be counterproductive. Of course, no one should be pelted with tomatoes for speaking their mind at a meeting, but there's a hint of noblesse oblige—an illusory sense of democracy—about "yes, and...." It's often about making people *feel* as though they're being listened to, rather than actually listening to them, or being bound by any obligation that listening to them might entail.

A 2017 article in *Forbes*, for example, suggests that if an employee asks for a pay raise, answering "Yes, I hear that you need to make more money, *and* that's not possible right now" is more productive than "Yes, I hear that you need to make more money, *but* that's not possible right now." In this case, the argument for "yes, and..." is that it opens up the space for further communication. But if that dialogue ends with the request being denied—in a more drawn out and roundabout way—is it really any better than "Sorry, but no"?

In encouraging a gentler corporate environment, "yes, and..." is preferable to a model where bosses ignore their employees. But the pursuit of frictionless communication misses the important fact that disagreement can be productive, particularly if both sides are open-minded and willing to listen. Sometimes it is more respectful to tell someone "no" and "but"—to take their idea seriously by arguing why it doesn't work, and allowing them either to accept that assessment or fight their case. Better that than fobbing them off with a linguistic trick and steamrolling them anyway.

(1) Two members of the troupe would go on to found the Second City, the legendary comedy theater in Chicago which helped launch the careers of John Belushi, Bill Murray, Catherine O'Hara, Tina Fey, Amy Poehler and Steve Carell.

WORDS
JAMES GREIG
PHOTO
VERA LAIR

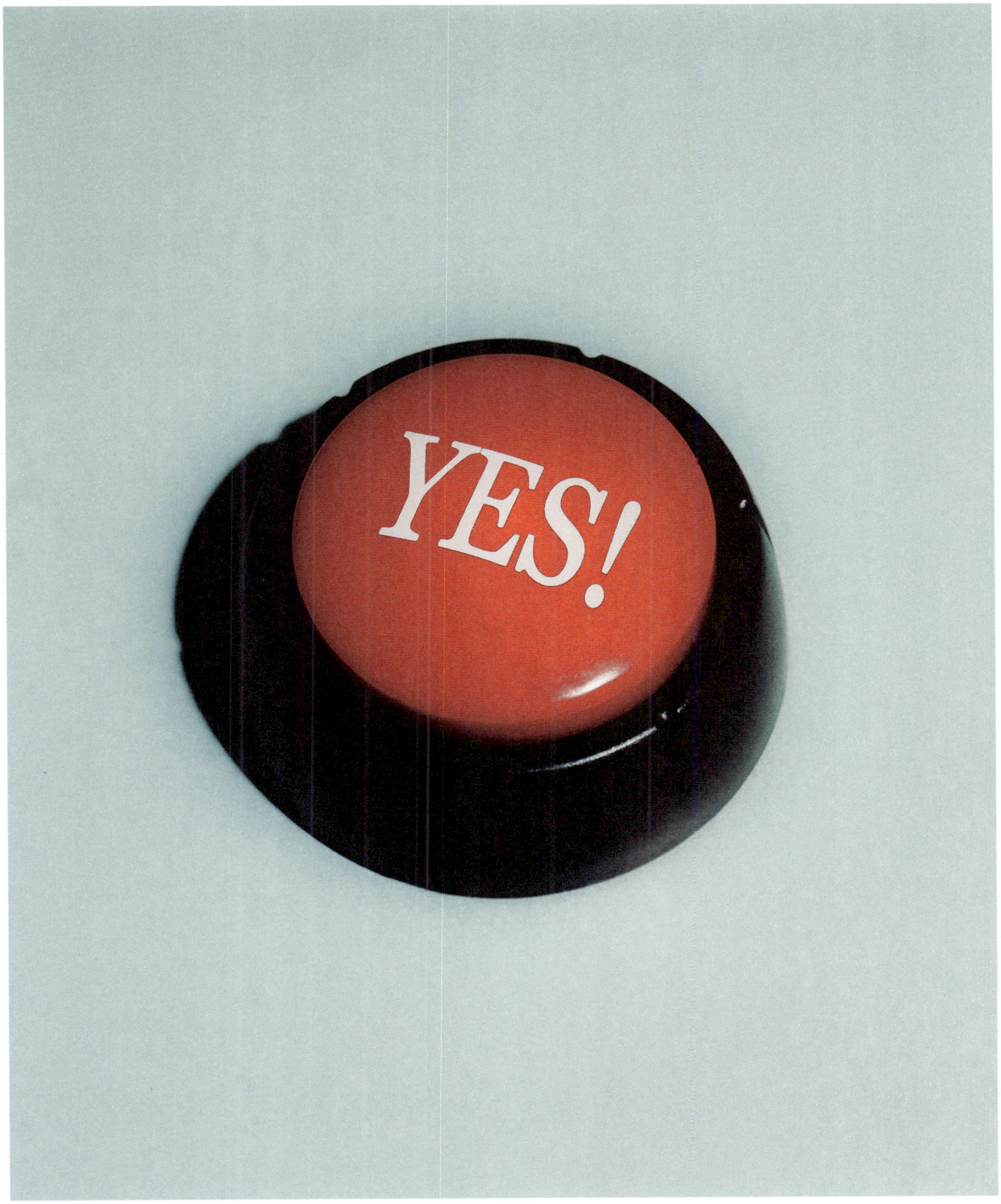

33

ODD JOBS
Cole Wehrle, board game designer.

WORDS
ELLE HUNT
PHOTO
TIM EVANS

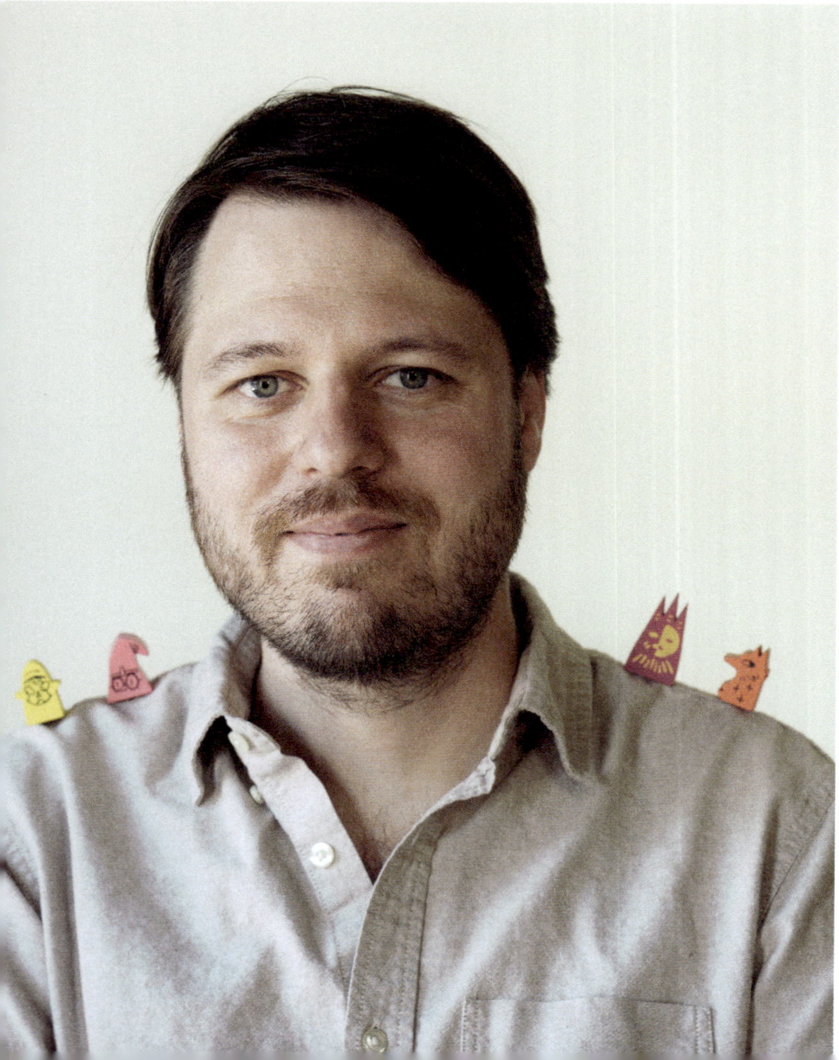

Cole Wehrle was in graduate school in Austin, Texas, when he chanced upon a board game about the Mexican Revolution. At the time, Wehrle was working toward his PhD on the British Empire in the 19th century—a dark and bloody period of history that was often shaped by mundane, personal motivations. Maybe, Wehrle thought, there could be a game in that too.

Ten years later, he is the designer behind popular games like Root, Oath and John Company, one of the tentpole projects of Wehrlegig Games, the company he now heads with his brother, Drew. He continues to design and publish historical tabletop games that, as Wehrle puts it, "help us understand our world."[1]

ELLE HUNT: How did you come to be a board game designer?

COLE WEHRLE: By accident. No one studies this—the industry is filled with people who have stumbled into it. When I found Pax Porfiriana, a board game about the Mexican Revolution and the geopolitical currents that shaped it, I wrote to its publisher telling them how much I liked it. Pretty soon, I found myself play-testing, teaching myself graphic design and learning some basic components of production.

I then got a job at a small studio in Minnesota, where I learned about all the other parts of the board game industry, like how to work with larger factories and charter a shipping container. I was making these little history games, basically for fun. When they did well, my brother and I decided to start our own company. That was eight years ago, and our audience has been consistently growing.

EH: Why do you think board games have become so popular?

CW: So much of the media we consume, and the systems we engage with, are completely opaque. To play a board game, you have to understand how it works, and I think that leads to deeper engagement. We're playful creatures; to be able to sit down, understand and explore a game together can be a real balm in times like these.

EH: What does a game need in order to be effective and rewarding?

CW: Players need to be able to feel like the choices they make have consequences—that they can trace their successes and failures. I think aiming for fun, as a design principle, is vastly overrated. What you're trying to do is intrigue players. Usually there's an element of puzzle and interaction: If you and I sit down to play a game, our relationship is being reconfigured in some way. As a designer, I want to bring out those ambiguities and treat the player not just as a participant but as a partner, who is creating the game with me.

(1) Wehrle's games shed light on lesser-known histories, such as Molly House, which is named after and based on the taverns where gay men would meet in secret in 18th-century London.

WORDS
REBECCA MAY JOHNSON
PHOTO
ANDREW B. MYERS

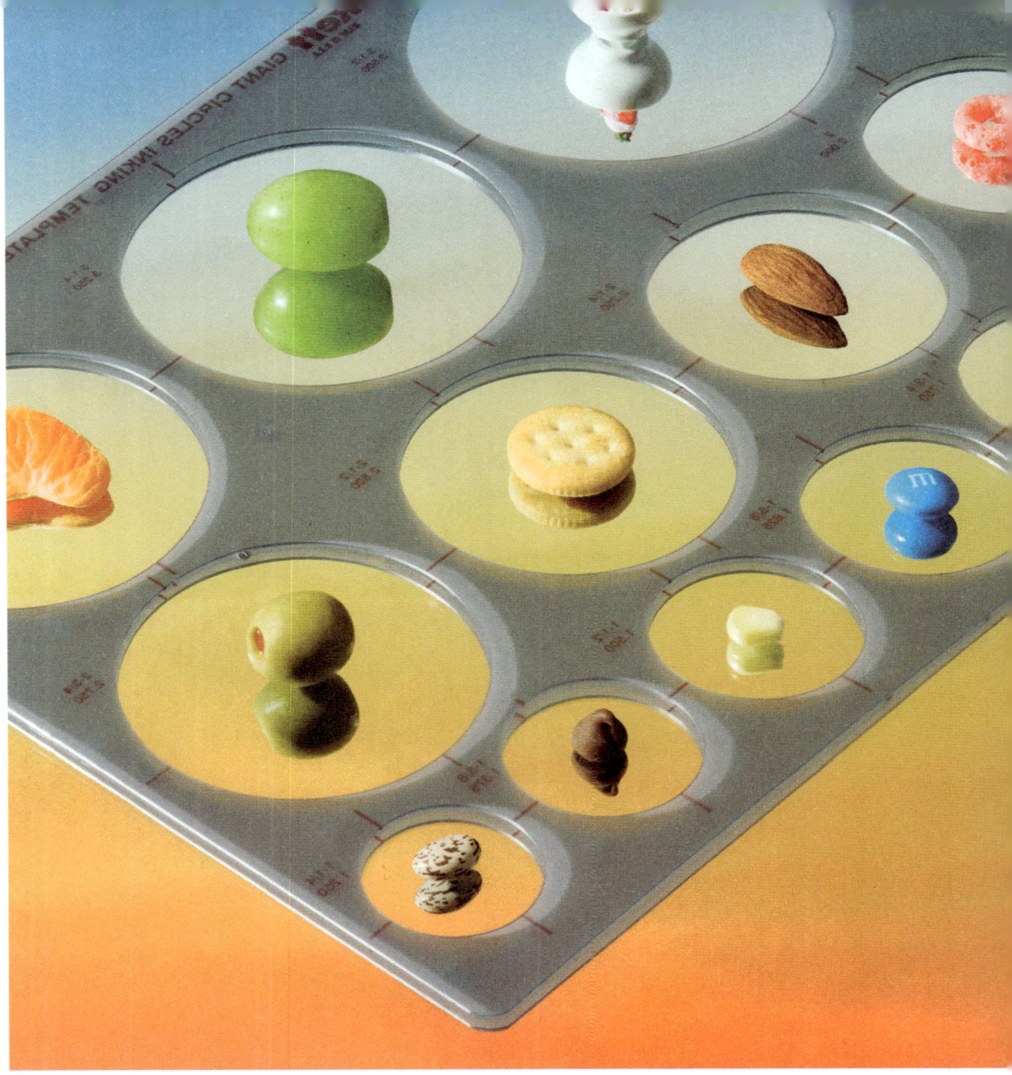

HOW TO: SNACK
A bite-size guide to informal eating.

Shockingly, there is no entry for "snack" or "snacking" in Alan Davidson's 1999 *Oxford Companion to Food*, the much-celebrated encyclopedia of culinary knowledge. It does however receive a fleeting reference in the entry for "lunch," where "a light snack" is suggested as an alternative to a "proper lunch" as a form of eating that will not interrupt the day's activity.

This does at least hint at what it is to snack: to eat between meals, at a time that is not formally allocated to it; in other words, a moment of stolen pleasure. Eating a snack can thus bestow a feeling of rebellion, of briefly absconding from your obligations at work, your responsibilities as a parent, your spring cleaning (something advertisements for chocolate bars and chips often enthusiastically play into).

However, in a significant way, the snack actually facilitates these commitments by making them bearable without requiring you to stop what you're doing. After all, one cannot fully relax during snack time; you can't run to the post office or conduct an extramarital affair, as you can during a lunch hour (see for reference, the 1961 film *Lunch Hour*).

The use of the word "snack" accelerated exponentially from the 1960s onward, tracking both the rise of consumer culture in late capitalism and the decline of the sacred lunch break. Today lunch increasingly resembles a snack—that is, food eaten during a moment snatched from the day, without interrupting the activity at hand... at our desks, in the car, on the go.

The natural evolution of this idea is, of course, the meal replacement drink. Once the preserve of dystopian science fiction, these multihyphenate drinks offer a full program of nutrition without the need for cutlery, or even mastication. An Iced Vanilla Protein Matcha Latte can slip down a straw in seconds, never requiring you to look away from your screen. At least it doesn't leave any crumbs.

—

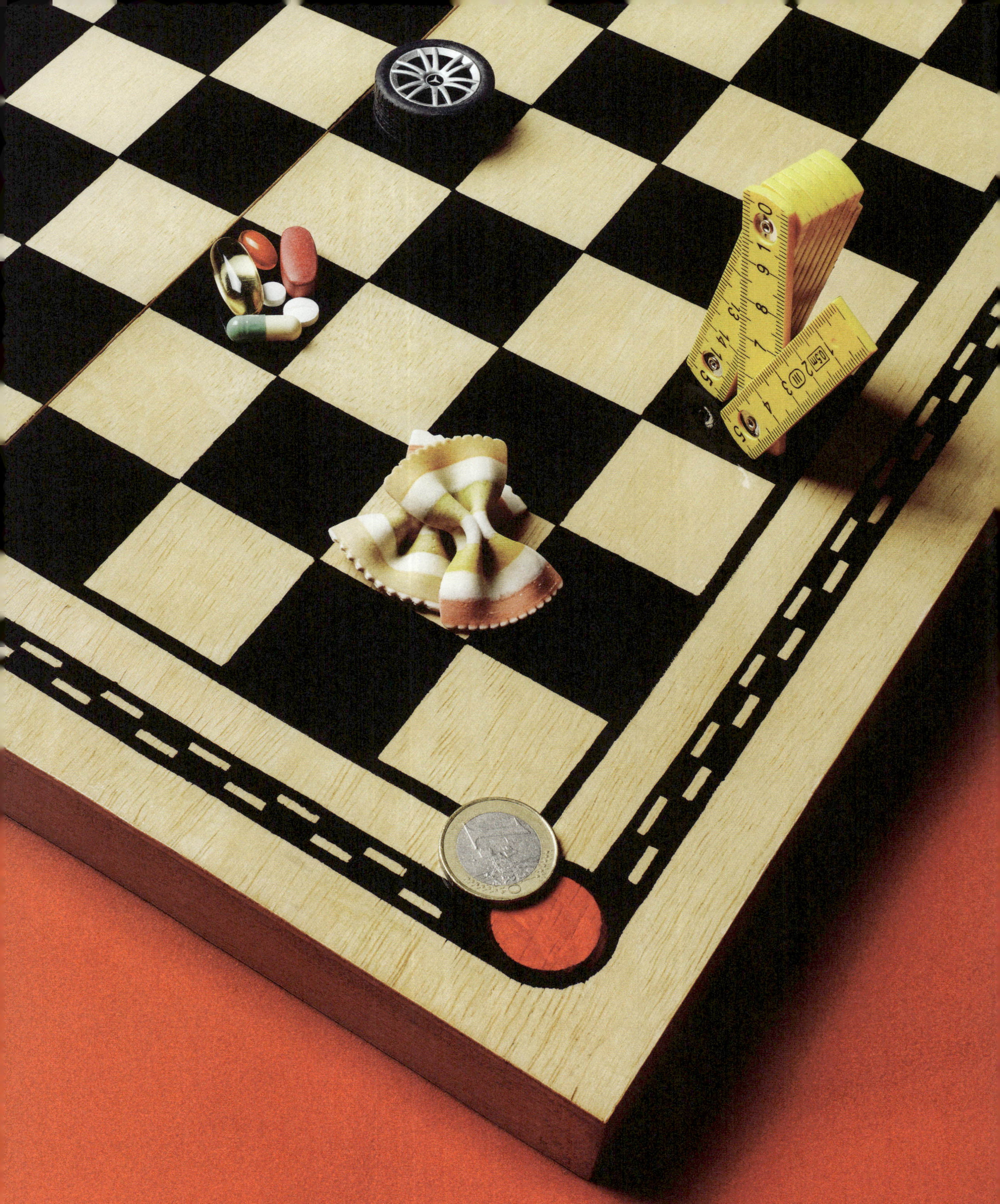

MIND GAMES

Why keeping score doesn't work.

WORDS
TOM WHYMAN
PHOTO
WEIYU LIN & FEI YANG

Philosophers, scientists and other intellectuals have defined the human being as a rational animal, a tool-using animal, a spiritual animal, an animal that uses language. But in many ways, it might be more accurate to say that we are an animal that likes to earn points.

As the philosopher C. Thi Nguyen notes in his recent book *The Score*, metrics have gradually come to dominate our attempts to understand the world—from how to tell if we're healthy, to how to tell if a university is any good at teaching students. Thanks to industrialization, the Enlightenment and the invention of double-entry bookkeeping, we have come to think of disinterested, quantitative data as the gold standard of truth. But whenever we carve the world into metrics, as Nguyen points out, we place a value—witting or otherwise—on the things we find important; we make a choice about the ideals we wish to foster. And when we pursue these metrics at the expense of all else, we can end up sacrificing autonomy; finding ourselves, as Nguyen says, "playing someone else's game."[1]

It's why "gamified" systems can have such a hold over us: We points-getting animals are horribly capable of dedicating ourselves to the pursuit of the same empty goal all day: I might log into Duolingo with an aim to learn Spanish, but then spend the whole time repeatedly playing the same lessons, because that's a more reliable way to rack up points. Or I might, as Nguyen claims he once did, set out on a philosophical career hoping to think deeply about the intellectual mysteries that bother me the most, only to spend my time working on topics that will get me published in prestigious journals.

Luckily, as Nguyen argues, our very love of games can also offer us a way out of this trap. Games, after all, are in their truest sense things we *play*. And in play, we not only chase points but switch between roles: We try out different goals, different ways of seeing and understanding. When I play a board game, for example, I might suggest an alteration to the rules to encourage more cooperation between players. In doing so, Nguyen seems to hope, I might learn how to adopt different roles at, say, my job, and internalize something deep about the arbitrariness of metrics. To escape an increasingly gamified world, then, we must foster a more playful spirit in ourselves—starting with taking the rules less seriously.

(1) Nguyen's book explores the idea of gamification: the use of points, rankings and rewards to motivate behavior in non-game contexts. One example is the streak feature in Duolingo, which the company has said is its most effective tool for keeping users coming back. The term was coined by British programmer Nick Pelling in 2002, originally in reference to making ATM interfaces more enjoyable to use.

WHAT ARE YOU WORKING ON?

WORDS
ROBERT ITO
PHOTO
RAPHAËL GAULTIER

Playwright Sanaz Toossi's next productions.

Sanaz Toossi wrote *English* as her final thesis project for an MFA degree at New York University. The story of a small group of students of varying ages preparing for the Test of English as a Foreign Language in Iran, the play went on to receive five Tony Award nominations, including one for Best Play, as well as a Pulitzer Prize for Drama in 2023. It was Toossi's first theatrical work.

Toossi was born and raised in the Orange County town of Irvine, California, the only child of Iranian immigrants. "I hated Irvine when I was growing up, because everything is really safe there," she says. "But now that I'm an adult, I realize how lucky I was, not only to grow up somewhere safe, but to grow up in a huge Iranian diaspora, with the musicality of people slipping between Farsi and English. It's probably why I became a playwright."

ROBERT ITO: What inspired you to write *English*?

SANAZ TOOSSI: I wrote it as a response to the first travel ban—more colloquially called the Muslim ban—at a time of heightened xenophobia in the United States. I was wounded by the anti-immigrant rhetoric that I felt, and do feel, is poisoning our country. The idea was born out of seeing my parents condescended to because they spoke with accents.

RI: At the heart of *English* is language, and the struggles of learning a second one. Do you struggle with language?

ST: Oh, my God, yes. I harbor great insecurity over my command of language. Verbal communication, interviews like this, are really hard for me. I feel like I'm always making a fool of myself on panels. I think that's why I'm a writer. I arrive at words too late.

RI: How did you find out that you had won the Pulitzer?

ST: I found out at the same time as everybody else. They give you no warning beforehand. I was at an airport, which is not the most ideal place to be upon receiving big news as a Middle Easterner. I had just passed through security, and when I heard, I screamed into my arm, so as not to alarm anyone.

RI: What are you working on now?

ST: I'm working on two plays. The first is my crack at the American family drama. I want my *August: Osage County*, my *A Raisin in the Sun*. And the other play is my version of *The Seagull*. I think both are an attempt to look at a truth. I don't always have the spine to tell the truth, and I think for a lot of my life, I felt I was playing chicken with the truth. But I'm trying in these plays to look hard questions in the eye.

The family drama is asking some questions that have arisen since the war started, like: Does Iranian trauma excuse our more difficult or harmful viewpoints? Is the mythology of the Iranian American family built on something fragile or false? And *The Seagull*–inspired piece is asking: Who would I be if I couldn't be an artist anymore? And should we be expanding our definition of artistry at a moment when a lot of people are leaving art?

RI: Do you have a dream project?

ST: I think I'm doing them already. What I'm really trying to do now is to build a body of work for the actors I work with, Marjan Neshat and Tala Ashe. I hoped the Pulitzer would set me free. It hasn't. But I have to forget that and behave like it did.

RI: What do you mean that the Pulitzer didn't set you free?

ST: I still want people... I'll just say the crass, gross thing: I still want to be loved.

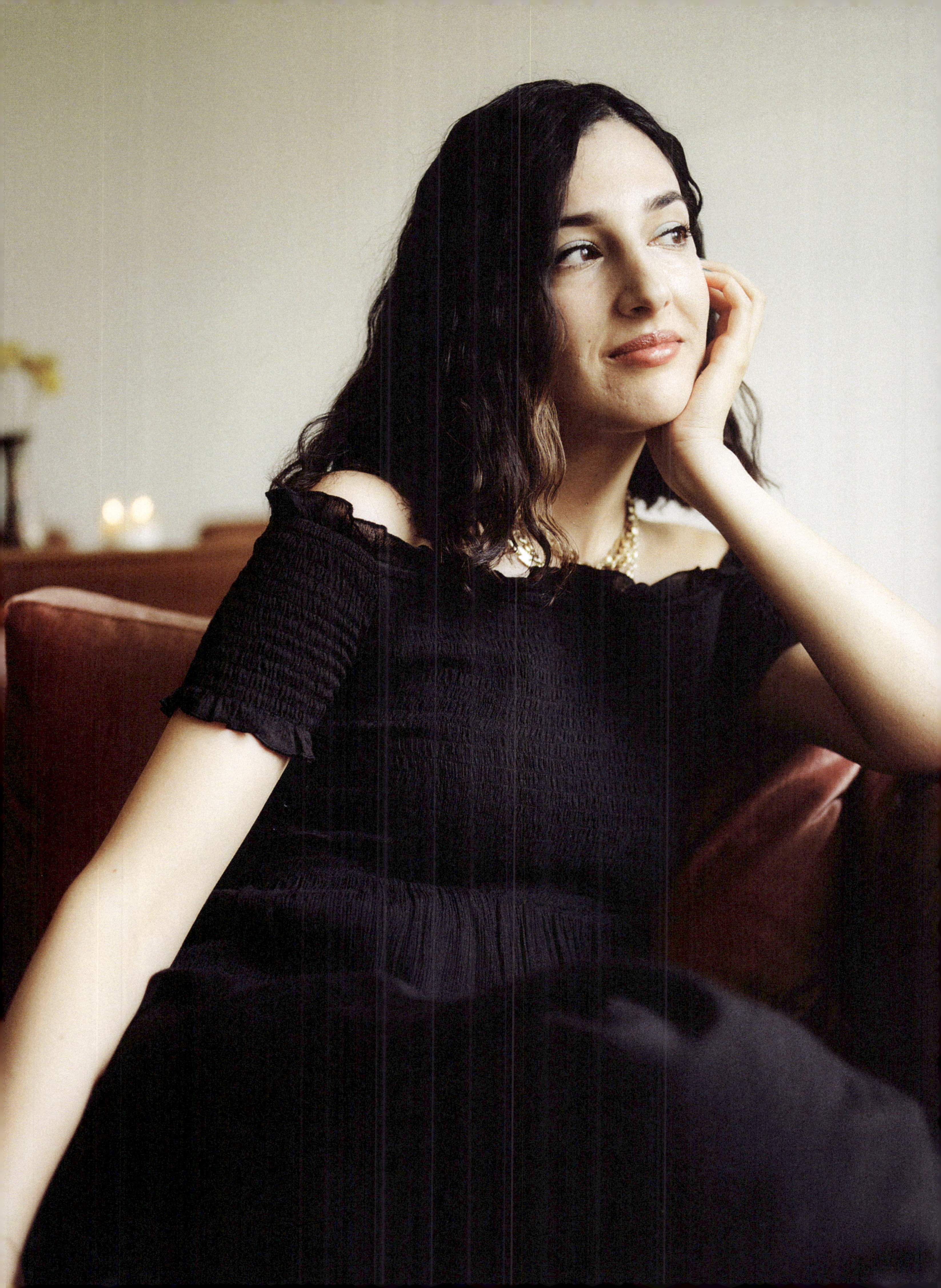

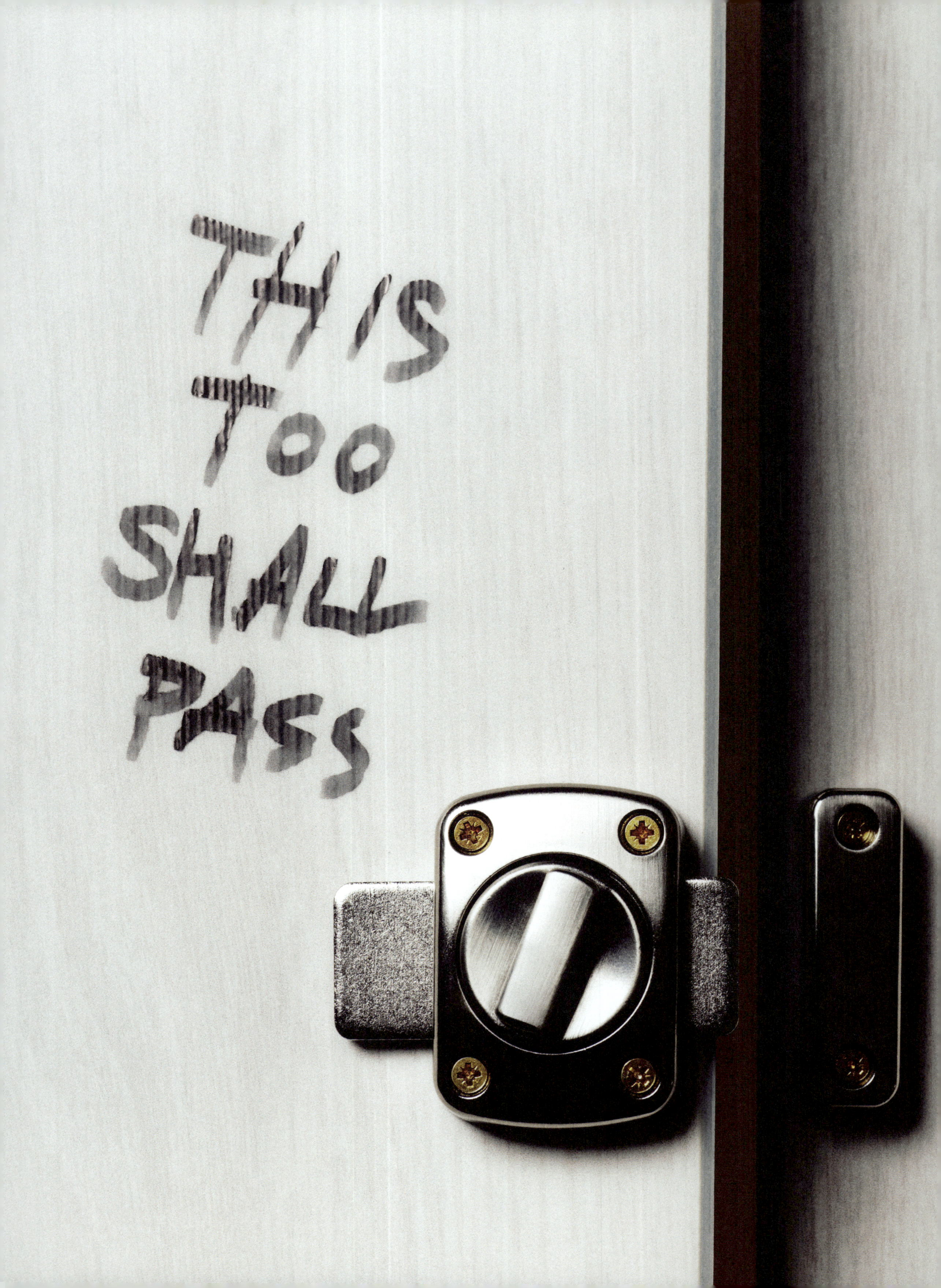
THIS
TOO
SHALL
PASS

BATHROOM BREAK
The ancient art of *latrinalia.*

WORDS
EMILY NATHAN
PHOTO
WEIYU LIN & FEI YANG

Confessions. Accusations. Propositions. Declarations of love and heartbreak. Jokes, insults, warnings, crude drawings and emotional outpourings scribbled and etched into tile and partition with whatever happens to be on hand: keys, a bobby pin, even eyeliner.

Toilet graffiti, or *latrinalia*—as the American folklorist Alan Dundes termed it in 1966—exists in a peculiar space between confession and performance: private in the moment, public in its afterlife. It is at once intimate and exhibitionistic, anonymous and unaccountable: a message left for no one in particular, and therefore, in a sense, for everyone.

Such graffiti can be encountered in today's bar bathrooms and public conveniences the world over—but the impulse to create it is, in fact, far older than the bathroom stall itself. The walls of Pompeii's communal latrines, for example, are filled with first-century insults, flirtations and crude drawings, while medieval pilgrims carved names and messages into nooks throughout roadside inns across Europe.[1]

Today, the bathroom stall offers something increasingly rare in modern life: a brief withdrawal from surveillance and consequence. Behind a locked door, out of sight of cameras and prying eyes, people confess things they might never admit elsewhere. There's cruelty, certainly, but also tenderness, absurdity, insecurity and longing. In this sense, toilet graffiti offers an unusually candid portrait of collective interior life: less polished than social media and less guarded than public speech.

At a moment when so much of modern existence is tracked, archived and made permanently attributable—our deepest desires and secret opinions logged by our messaging apps or anticipated by advertising algorithms—the bathroom stall remains one of the last forums where we can express ourselves anonymously. No audience metrics, no profile, no performance of the self. Just a wall, a thought and the fleeting freedom to leave something behind without being caught in the act.

In many cases, these markings come to reflect the establishments in which they sit, charting tendencies and thresholds of tolerance, eventually coalescing into an illegible but harmonious chorus. In others, it is simply a record of someone's presence, their state of mind, the person they were at that particular moment in time.

Toilet graffiti is, undeniably, a relatively minor form of expression, but it persists; and history will attest to the fact that if we're given a closed door, a wall and a moment alone, we will write what we cannot say.

(1) The word "graffiti" was coined in 1851 to describe the inscriptions archaeologists found scratched into the walls of Pompeii. It derives from the Italian *graffiare*, meaning "to scratch," and ultimately from the Greek *graphein*: "to write," "draw" or "scratch."

OVER AND OVER
The appeal of pointless pursuits.

WORDS
ELLE HUNT
PHOTO
WILLIAM ELLIOT

In mid-November 2022, a University of Connecticut student named Luke Lorraine was walking to class when his toe clipped a rock. There was nothing remarkable about the smallish gray-green pebble, but Lorraine ended up kicking it all the way to class, a little over a mile, then pocketed it for later. He had remembered something his bandmate told him a few weeks prior: that a rock rolled consistently on a hard surface would eventually become a sphere.

Lorraine resolved to find out if that was true. He set up a TikTok account, @guykickingrock, and began posting daily updates until, after 11 months and three rocks, his mission was achieved. Rock #3, if not a perfect sphere, was certainly an easy-rolling ball. In the process, @guykickingrock gained close to a million followers.

It's hard to say which is more remarkable: that Lorraine saw his somewhat random, low-reward goal through to the end, or that so many people wanted to follow his attempt. Yet social media is full of people committed to similarly arbitrary, repetitive projects—activities with no greater purpose or meaning, that are carried out simply for their own sake.

Noah Kalina, for example, has taken a photograph of himself every day for more than 25 years. Michael Carmichael has been painting a baseball since 1977; after more than 30,000 coats, the ball now has a circumference of more than 19 feet and is a tourist attraction in Indiana. And on TikTok, Matt Brockman has gained more than 2 million followers for his impressive trick shots—like tossing a playing card between two coins, or stacking cups in mid-air—while also documenting the hours of tedious repetition it can take to succeed. It took Brockman two hours to roll a coin into a bottle cap, for example, and nearly two days to land a playing card in a rotating plastic sleeve.

What is it that makes people invest so much time in such low-stakes endeavors—and why do others love to watch them? After all, these are not objectively meaningful achievements like running a marathon or picking up trash from a beach. Yet this only underscores the "intrinsic motivation," as psychologists term it, that fuels these odd undertakings. It's not simply obsessiveness: People are driven to engage in these activities purely for their personal satisfaction, curiosity or enjoyment.[1]

They may bring benefits associated with hobbies, such as relaxation and pleasure, as well as reduced anxiety, depression and stress, but in a culture so focused on outcomes, returns on investment and achievements, the apparent pointlessness *is* the point. They are expressions, in many ways, of free will.

Perhaps that is why these projects are so irresistible to their online followers. Amid frenetic social media feeds and doomsaying headlines, it is a balm—and even oddly inspiring—to be reminded that people are still pursuing pointless goals. As Lorraine said, reflecting on his endeavor a few weeks into kicking a rock: "It's good to get moving, clear the mind, and there's no limit to it."

(1) In 1975, Hungarian American psychologist Mihaly Csikszentmihalyi popularized the term "autotelic" to describe activities pursued purely for their own sake. He found that people who regularly sought out autotelic experiences reported significantly higher levels of well-being than those driven by external rewards.

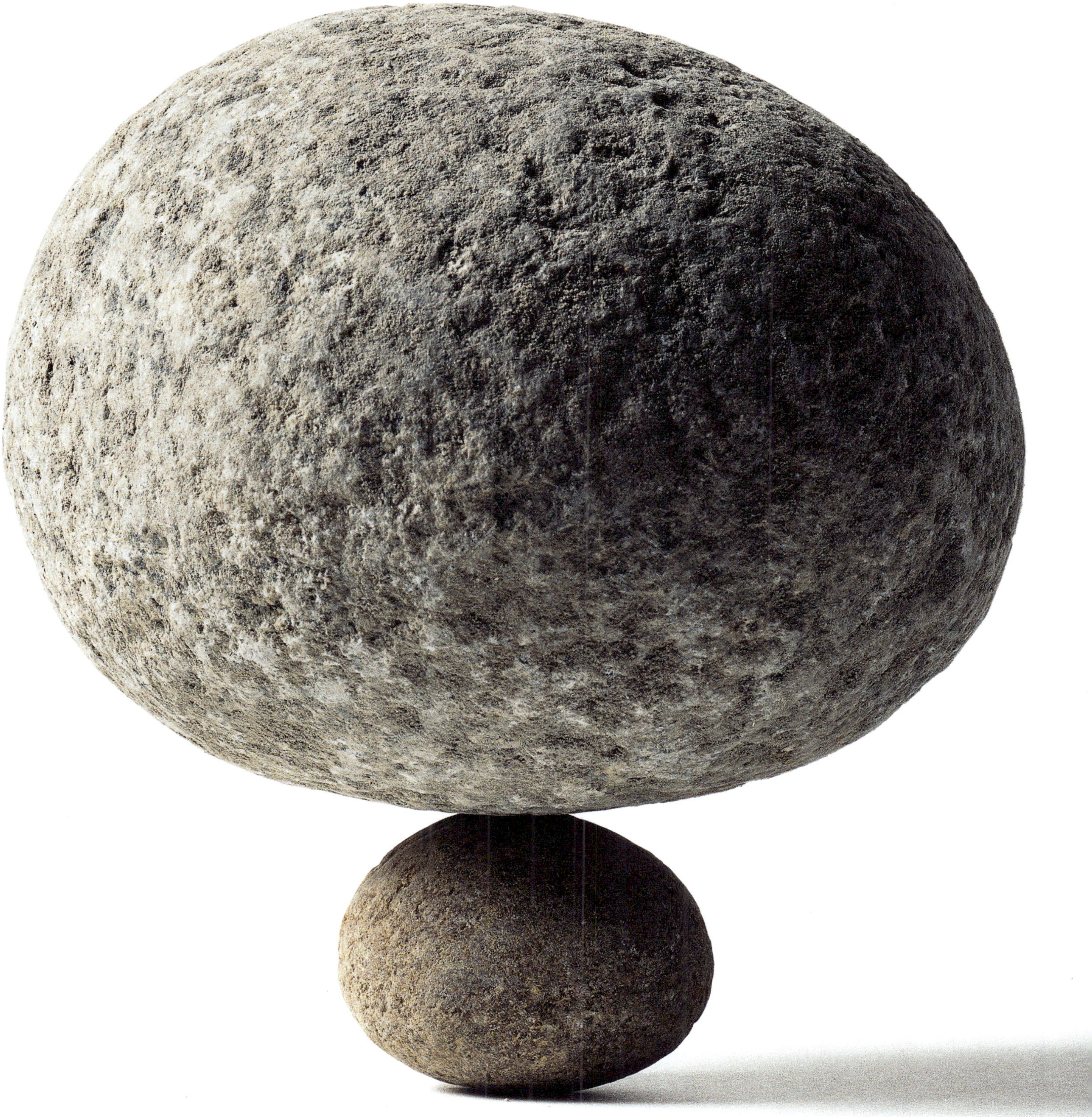

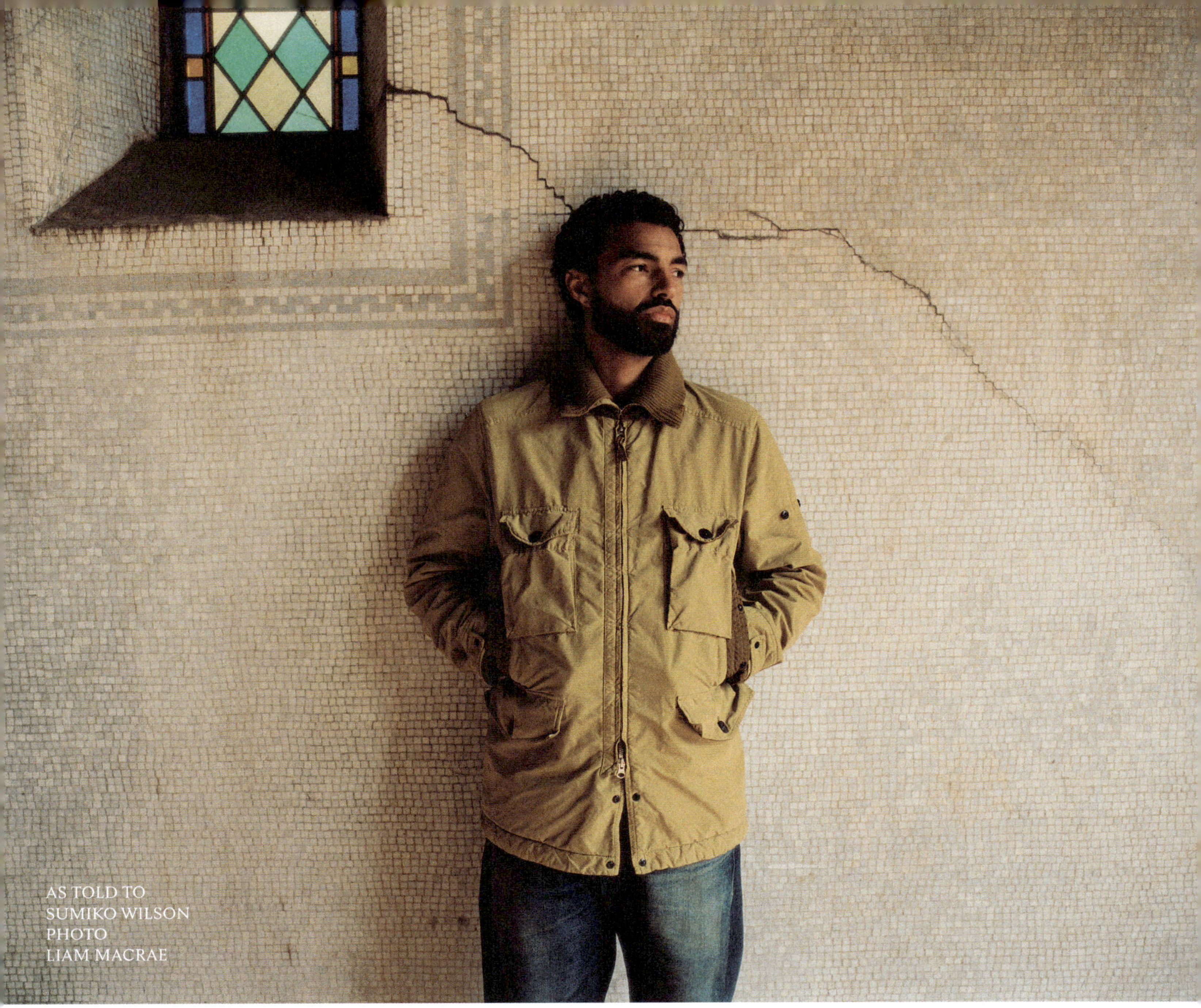

AS TOLD TO
SUMIKO WILSON
PHOTO
LIAM MACRAE

STARTER FOR TEN
Skater Sage Elsesser's essentials.

The Giver, Lois Lowry: I read this book in elementary school and had a spiritual experience—one that would change me forever. It walked me into my imagination in a way that still feels almost inexplicable. Seeing the words come alive in my mind was exhilarating.

Ester: My sister Kanya and I made a last-minute decision to try this restaurant before we headed back to New York from Sydney, Australia. One of the greatest decisions ever. The universe saw fit that we were seated without a reservation. The duck dumplings stole the show.

Sentimental Value, Joachim Trier: A beautiful, beautiful film that feels like watching your heart beat in your hands. As my brother [the rapper] Cavalier says, "My heart only breaks to keep it open."

White Label Yerba Mate Soda: A local favorite in NYC for a calming boost of energy—perfectly sweet.

"On Love," Kahlil Gibran: A poem from a book that was introduced to me by my dear mother. I return to it often, as it grounds me in the universal connective tissue that is love.

Cease: A great clothing brand: Great product. Great quality. Great colors. Made by friends. Made in the USA.

Tender Buttons, Broadcast: When I discovered this band, I discovered a part of me that had been hidden away. Trish Keenan speaks to my heart in ways that I will cherish for the rest of my life.

El Yucateco Hot Sauce: A perfect pepper sauce. Equal parts flavor, equal parts heat.

Pedag insoles: A friend recommended these insoles for arch support. I bought two pairs: one with a high arch and one with a medium arch. I've put them in almost every shoe I've worn since I got them. Great investment, great product.

Fueguia 1833: I was introduced to their fragrances in 2021 and I've been obsessed ever since. It's all in the details with Fueguia. I'm wearing "La Luna" today.

—
—

II

Features

AT WORK

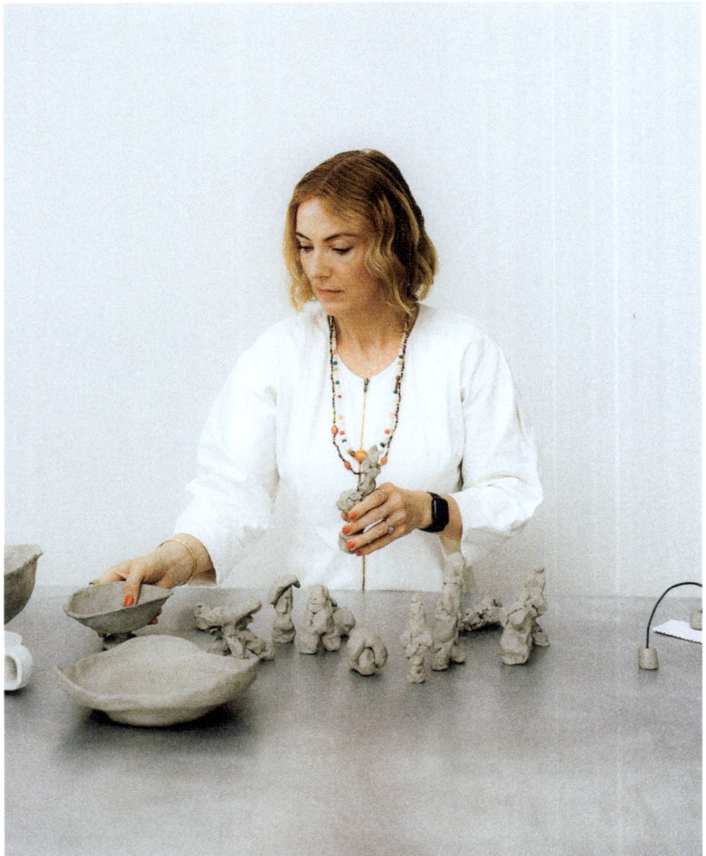

FAYE

Words
ALI MORRIS
Photos
NATHAN WOLF GRACE

WITH:

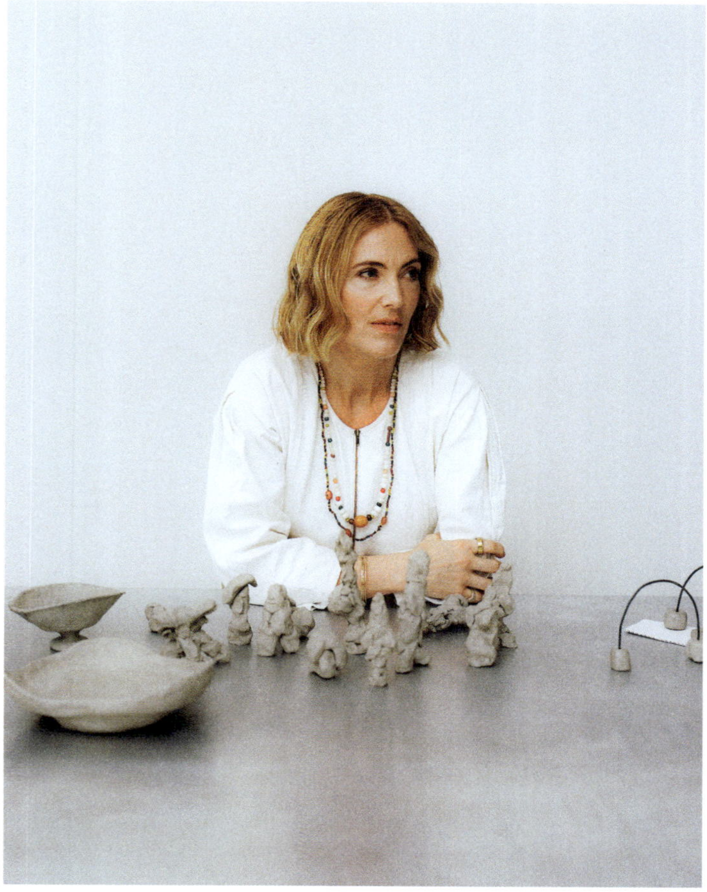

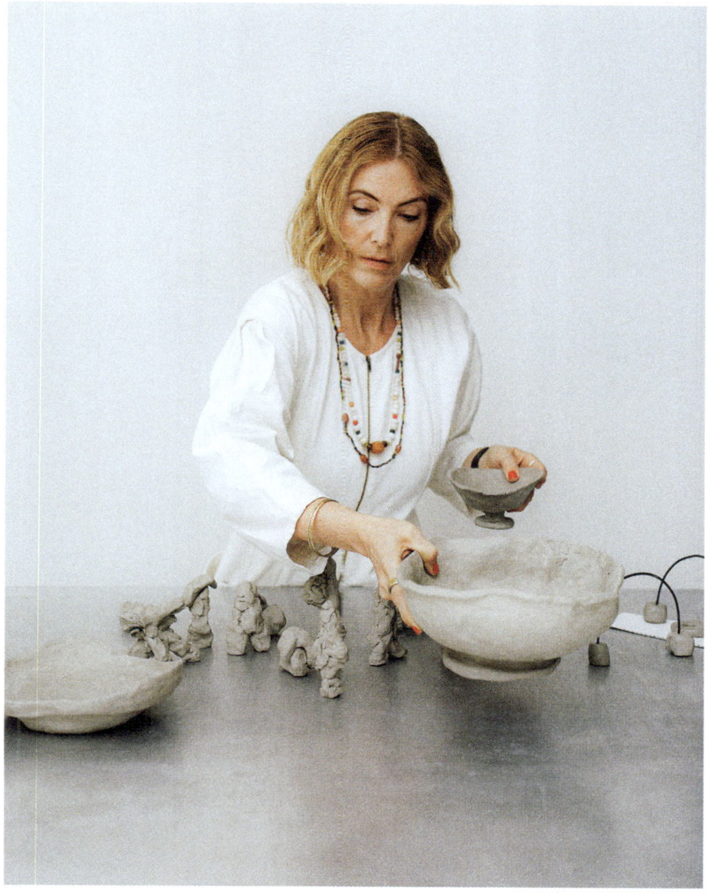

TOOGOOD

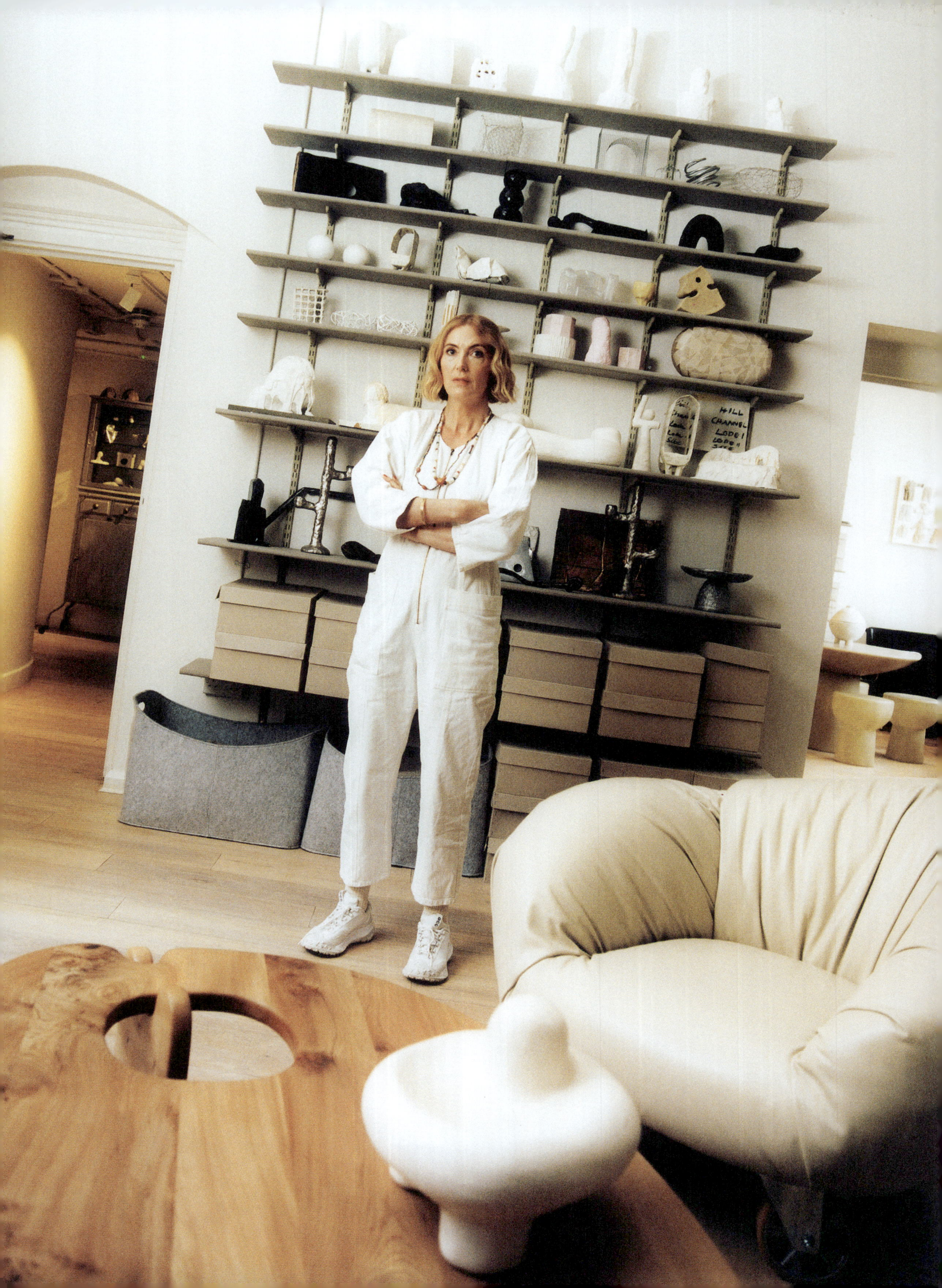
HILL
CHANNEL
LODE 1

OPPOSITE:
Faye Toogood in her new studio in London's Borough neighborhood—
a space that marks a new chapter for her practice. Previously, the studio was based in a three-story Victorian house in Shoreditch before moving to a workspace in Camden.

T

here are only a few subtle signs that announce you have arrived at the new studio of British designer Faye Toogood. Stepping into a courtyard through wrought iron gates in Borough, south London, there is a brick wall half-painted in "Drab" by Farrow & Ball—a somber greenish brown hue that the studio often uses. A series of cube-shaped ceramic stools—Cobble, from 2023—with rounded edges in glossy neutrals is arranged around a worktable scattered with tools; a deer skull rests on an occasional table beside the entrance. A curious door handle—a cast bronze fox skull from Toogood's Sticks and Stones and Broken Bones collection created for Izé in 2010—welcomes you inside. Each detail hints at the tactile, slightly surreal and talismanic design language that Toogood has become known for.

Inside, the seven-person team is busy inspecting a prototype lamp with a paper shade. The studio is made up of just two main rooms painted in pale neutrals: an office and open-plan kitchen, and a flexible studio space for meetings, experiments and making. A large communal table sits in the center of the studio area while shelves are lined with models, maquettes and material samples. Toogood's own seats and lamps create informal meeting corners around the room. Hanging from the ceiling is a giant textile *koinobori*—a carp-shaped wind sock—that the designer found at an antiques market in Japan and carried home in a suitcase.

It's a space, however, that is still in a state of becoming following the studio's recent move from Camden in north London. "We've gone from 35 to seven people in the last six months," says Toogood. "It has been quite full-on: moving, closing down a business, and also making a collection of furniture."

The move is part of an intentional shift in the studio's direction. Founded in 2008, the Toogood studio has grown into one of the best-known names in contemporary design, spanning collectible furniture, interiors, fashion and collaborations with major international brands. But in March 2026, Toogood announced the closure of the fashion label she founded in 2013 with her sister, Erica, after realizing that the demands of running a large business had overtaken the act of designing itself.

"I felt like I was just running a business, and I wasn't focused on creativity and imagination and making anymore," she explains. "I needed to get back to making."

The search for a new studio, she says, was difficult. Toogood drew a rough radius around Waterloo station, which she commutes in and out of from her home in the South Downs, where she lives with

Hair & Makeup: Mari Kuno

her husband, the Modern House founder Matt Gibberd, and their three children. She spent a day walking the streets looking for "To Let" signs. "Looking for studios is basically looking for a home for your creativity," she says. "It's a home for your soul, in a way."

Eventually, she came across a former Victorian school building on Union Street adjoining the arts venue Jerwood Space. It had generous light, high ceilings and a courtyard garden. "It said 'let agreed,' but something made me call," she recalls. "And actually, the day before, it had fallen through. A photographer was going to take it—a twist of fate!"

Here, in this Dickensian corner of London, Toogood and her newly condensed team are focusing on sculpture and furniture—a combination she feels is more accepted now than when she first began working as a designer. Having trained in fine art before becoming a stylist at Condé Nast's seminal interior design magazine, *The World of Interiors*, Toogood had arrived through a distinctly unconventional route.

Earlier in her career, she often spoke about feeling like an outsider within a profession dominated by industrial design and rigid categorization. "Everybody had to define what they were, who they were, personally and in a work environment," she says. "It felt wrong. It felt counterintuitive. It felt counter to being a human being."

"I've always been interested in blurring the boundaries between art and design," Toogood continues. "Maybe now the world is okay about me painting and sculpting and making furniture. I'm just going to do what I want to do and stop worrying how it fits or where it goes." Recent presentations at galleries such as the Future Perfect and Tiwa Select have reflected that shift, combining hand-painted furniture, lighting and sculptural works that move freely between collectible design and fine art.

That sense of not quite fitting in persists, however. "Do I still feel a misfit? Probably," she says. "I think inherently I always will."

Being the public face of her brand is another role she has learned to inhabit over time. Contemporary designers are increasingly expected to operate as personalities as much as practitioners, and magazine covers and photo shoots are now part of the job. "I call myself a shy show-off," she says, laughing. "I'm able to get up on stage as a shy show-off and do my performance bit when needed, but I have to retreat."

Many of the themes Toogood once resisted addressing directly, as they were regarded as "taboo"—femininity, motherhood, emotion—have become increasingly central to how she understands her work. In her *Womanifesto* exhibition, staged following her appointment as Maison & Objet's Designer of the Year 2025, she reflected on the pressures of working as a woman in design and the compromises involved in balancing creativity with motherhood.

"In the beginning, I really didn't want to be defined by my gender," she says. "I just wanted to work alongside the male industrial designers at the time." It was precisely those differences that would come to define her work, however: her unconventional background, instinctive approach to materials and rejection of hard-edged industrial aesthetics.

"I feel like I've broken down a door, and that now there are others that can have the freedom that I perhaps didn't have," Toogood says. She also speaks candidly about the pressures of returning to work after having children. "Expecting your creativity and your career to be continuous is quite an unrealistic expectation, and often not talked about," she says. "After my first, I ran back to work. Within 10 to 12 weeks, I was back at work full-time, and that was a mistake for my mental health. For two years, I was really not well, but I had to keep going."

Looking around the studio, it's apparent how much of Toogood's work echoes the human body. Chairs slump, swell and fold; surfaces feel tactile and protective. Pieces such as Roly Poly, Puffy, Gummy and Butter all share soft curves and fleshy silhouettes in subdued pastels and skin tones.

"I work a lot around the human body, but I don't think I totally realized that before," she explains. "Design for me is an act of nurturing care. I genuinely care how someone feels when they sit in one of my chairs. It's not just how it looks aesthetically. It's the feeling that it generates."

OPPOSITE:
The London studio, which Toogood and her team moved into this summer, is filled with her artworks and furniture designs. Pictured are the Soft Slump armchair, the Roly Poly chair and the Palette table, alongside a *koinobori*—a traditional Japanese carp streamer found at an antiques market in Japan.

"Expecting your creativity to be

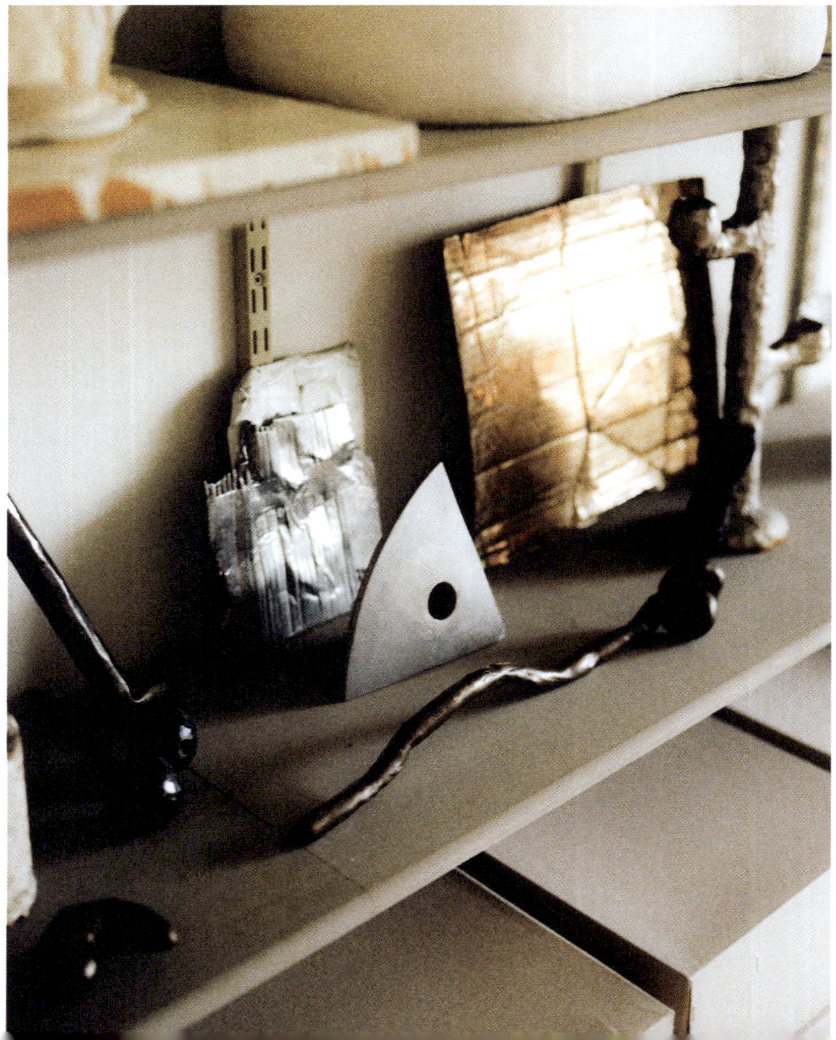

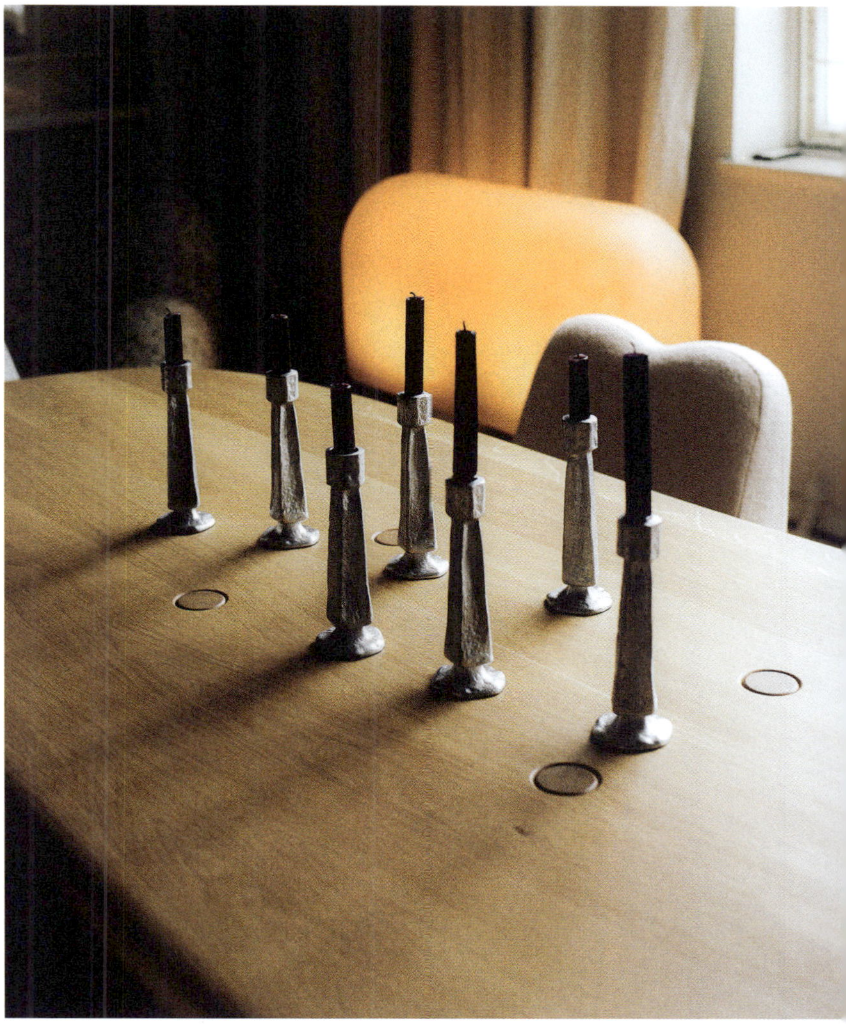

continuous is quite an unrealistic expectation."

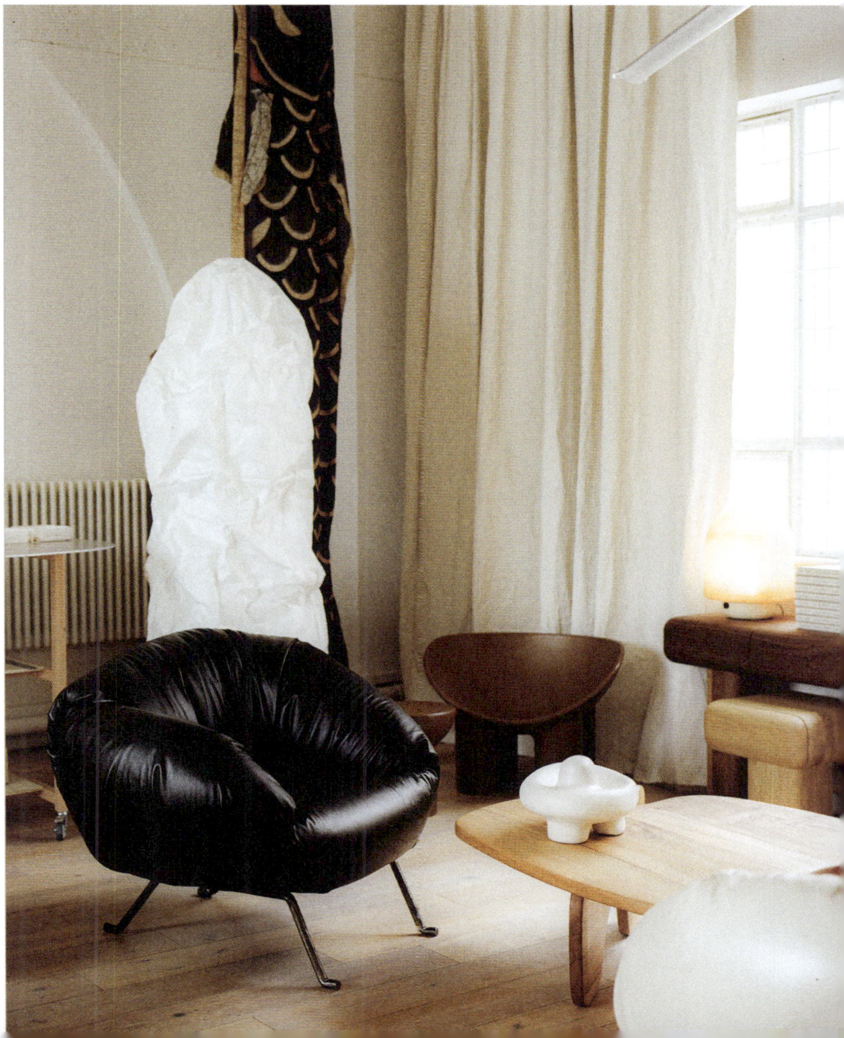

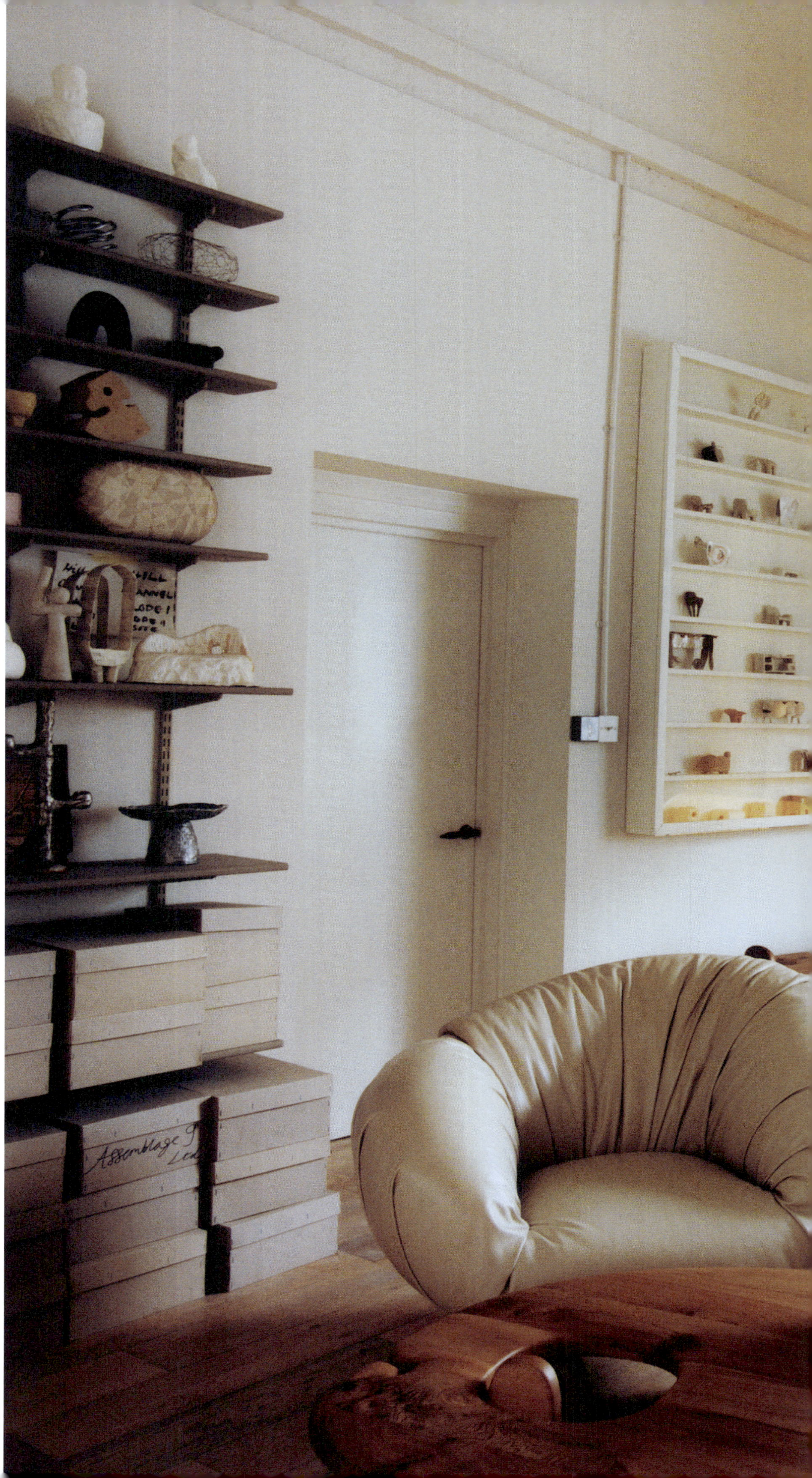

OPPOSITE:
Furniture sits at the heart of Faye Toogood's practice. In the foreground, the Soft Slump armchair takes its cue from the drawstring closure of a duffel bag. Bone dining chairs surround a Bone dining table, while above a Gummy armchair, a cabinet houses Toogood's archive of maquettes.

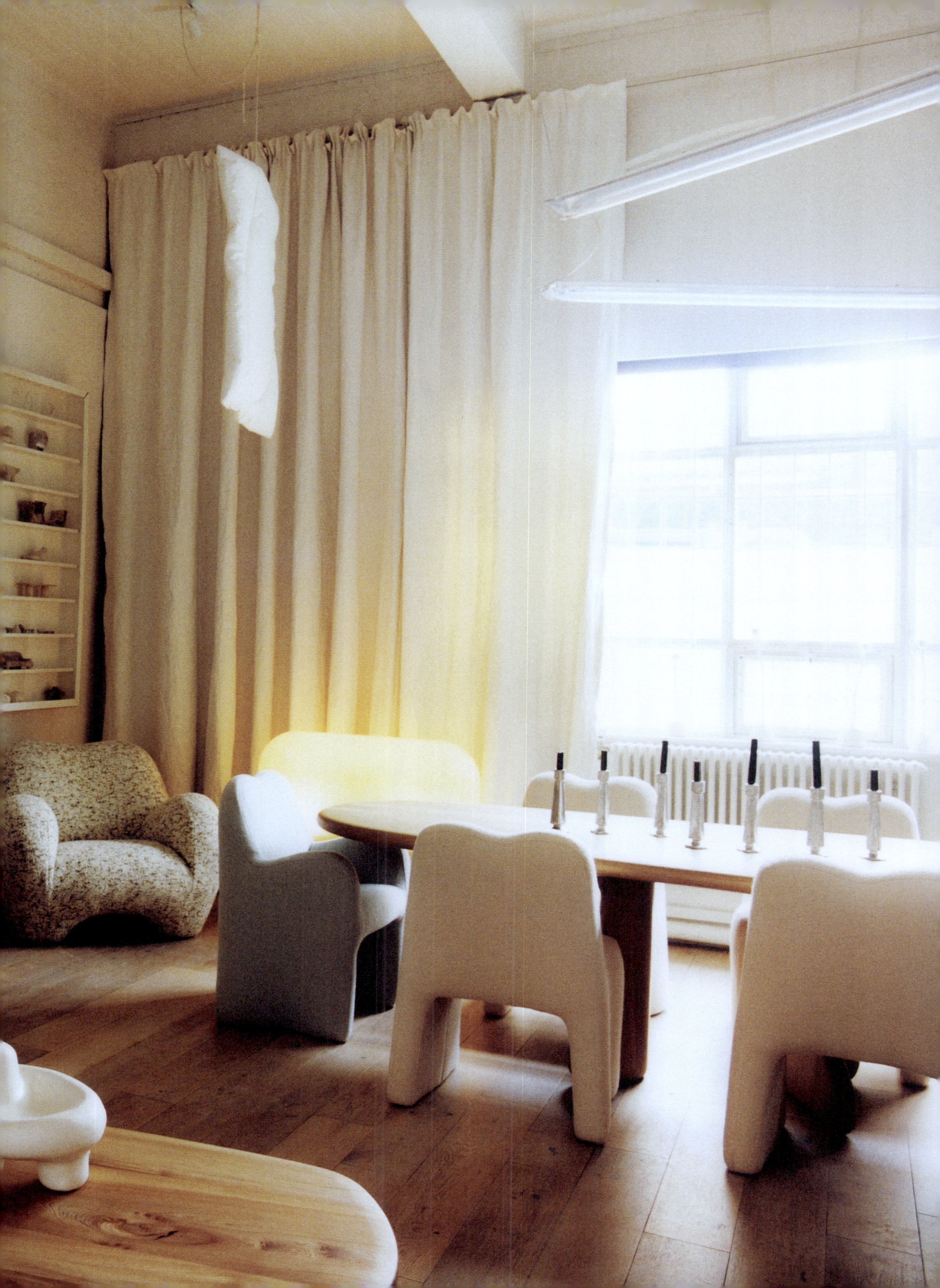

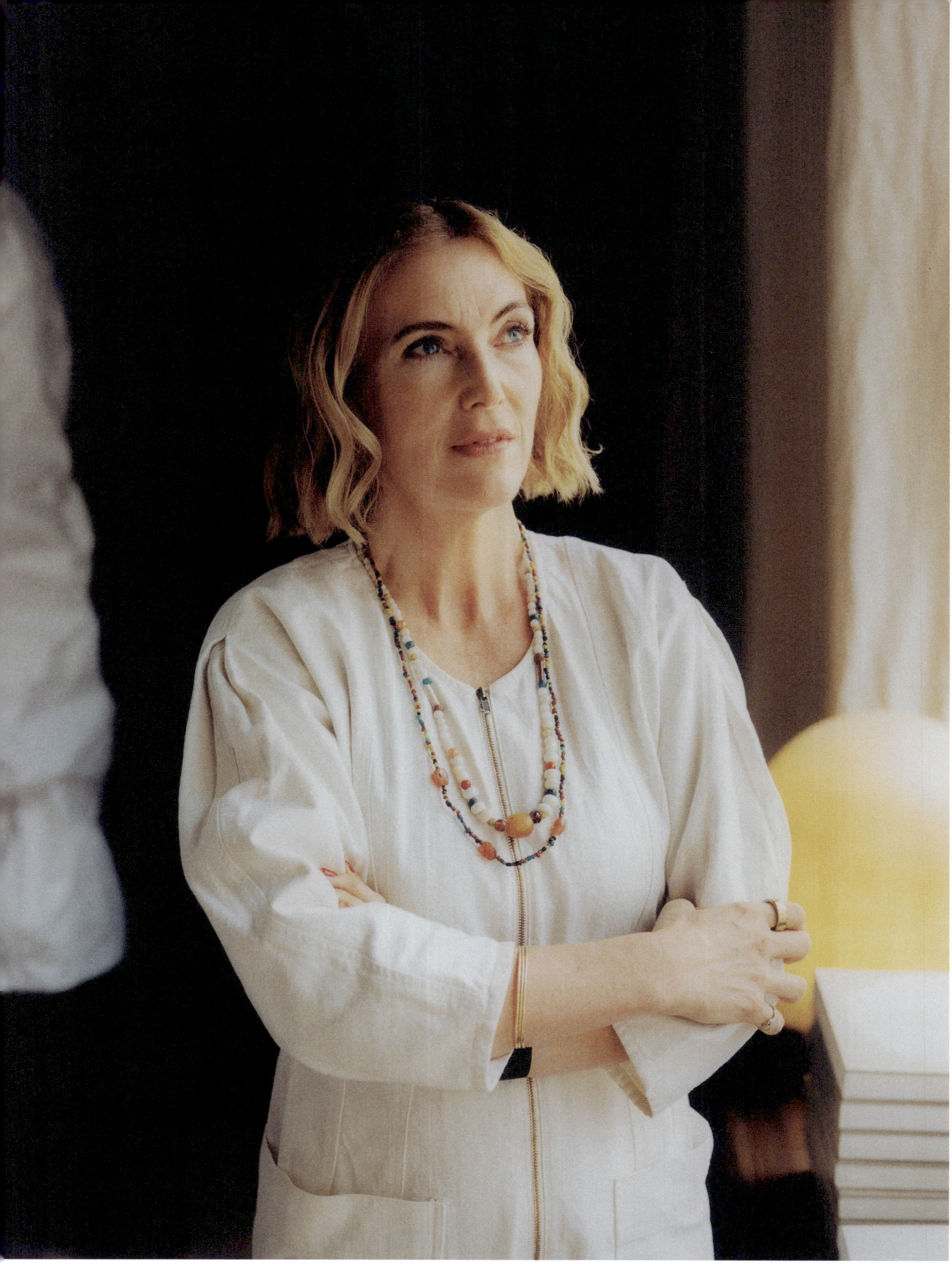

“I’m just going to do what I want to do and stop

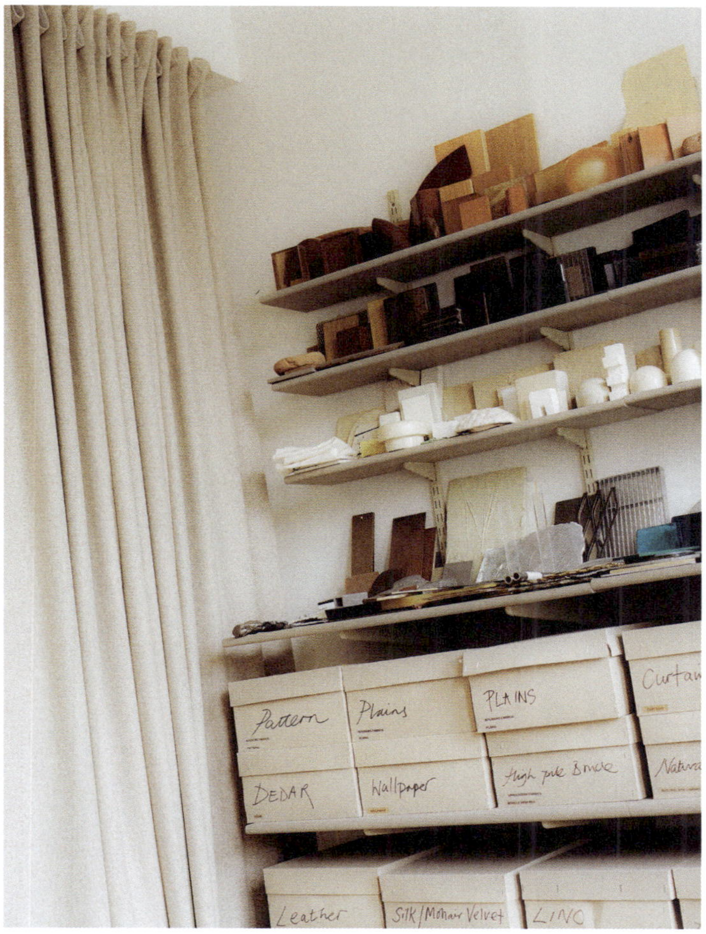

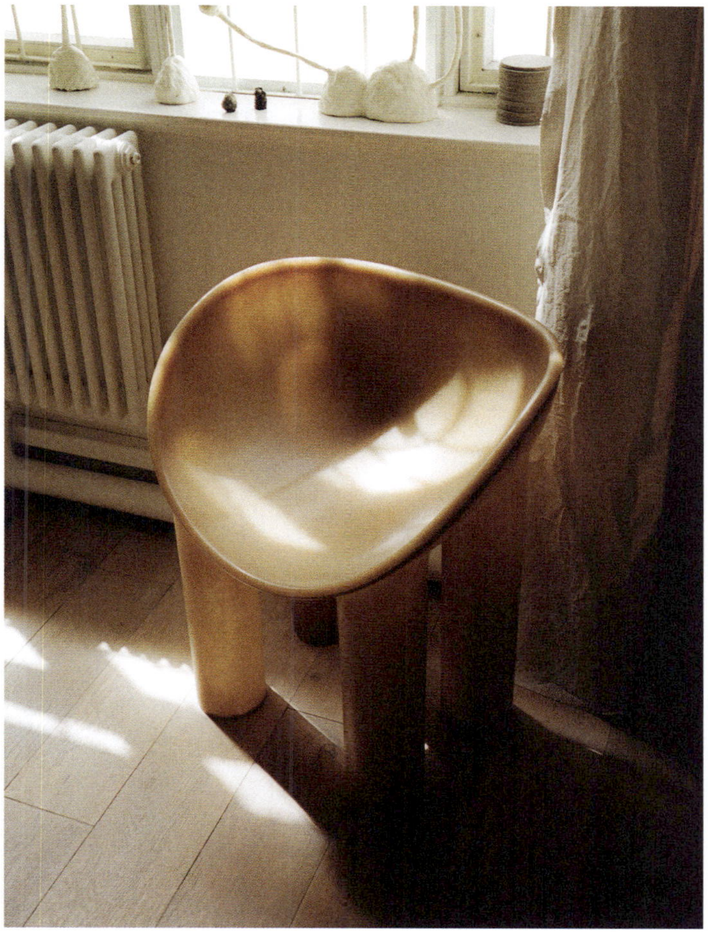

ABOVE (RIGHT):
Launched in 2014, the Roly Poly chair was inspired by Toogood's experience of pregnancy and motherhood, and went on to establish her international reputation. It is now held in the permanent collections of the Philadelphia Museum of Art and the National Gallery of Victoria in Melbourne.

That shift toward emotion, tactility and meaning has continued to shape her recent work. In Milan this year, Toogood launched a new sofa, Crease, with Meritalia; a line of ceramics, Kiln, with the Japanese brand Noritake; and Material Anthology, an immersive installation for Tacchini, exploring texture and materiality.

These brand collaborations are a vital component of her practice and are what enable her to retain a presence at large design weeks, like Milan, which have become increasingly inaccessible for independent practitioners. "Years ago, I used to be able to load up a van and show something in Milan," she says. "Now it's simply not feasible financially, and that's a shame. It's something we're really missing—we need a curator and someone with a budget to bring back all that emerging talent, to show furniture—because there is a serious lack of furniture now!"

Back in London, Toogood opens her studio two or three times a year for the city's various design and craft weeks, and finds herself increasingly drawn toward work that exists beyond the collectible design world. She hints at future projects involving glass, ceramics and a forthcoming high street collaboration, but is particularly excited by the idea of her work being more accessible.

"I would love to do something more public-facing—public seating, sculpture, maybe a playground," she says. "I still produce furniture that is expensive, and not everyone can access it. So how can I create something that touches people in a more everyday way?"

When we step outside into the courtyard, Toogood shares her plans to fill it with greenery and seating—she's working on an outdoor furniture collection for next year. For now, there is a palpable sense of reinvigoration and renewal in the air—of stripping things back in order to move forward again. "Previously, I would have measured success on data, numbers, graphs and things, but I've been through all that," she reflects. "That's just not the barometer I want to work with. Now, it's a very simple barometer of joy."

worrying how it fits or where it goes."

ESSAY:
GAMING THE SYSTEM

On the stratospheric rise of prediction betting.

Words
Asher Ross

In 1988, three economists were having a beer in Iowa City and grousing to each other about the unreliability of election polling. Jesse Jackson had just scored a landslide victory in the Michigan Democratic caucuses, an outcome polls and pundits had utterly failed to predict.[1] The three economists wanted a better mechanism, and they had an idea: What if markets could predict voter behavior better than polls? If, as the economic theory went, the price of a stock reflects all existing information about its value, couldn't a betting market do the same for elections? Polling can miss and analysts have their biases, but a market might compel participants to set aside their preferences in favor of what they really knew.

The result was the Iowa Electronic Markets, an early digital exchange that allowed users to place small wagers on election outcomes. It was a success. From 1988 through 2004, the IEM outperformed traditional polls roughly three-quarters of the time. By the early 2000s, the idea had been widely co-opted: Many large corporations set up in-house exchanges to surface collective wisdom, finding that employees were more honest about deadline feasibility when betting cash anonymously than when reporting to a VP. Wall Street firms began offering financial products that would pay off if an investor could accurately predict macroeconomic reports on hiring, inflation or retail sales. Around the same time, Defense Advanced Research Projects Agency (DARPA), the Pentagon's research wing, began developing a market that would let CIA analysts, academics and vetted outsiders bet on geopolitical contingencies such as coups and conflict. Two senators caught wind of the plan and condemned it as a "federal betting parlor on atrocities and terrorism," leading to the program's cancellation. Umbrage won the day then, but it didn't last.

Since the 2024 election, prediction markets—exchanges that allow investors to buy contracts on the outcome of a future event—have ballooned to vast proportions, and have embraced every imaginable contingency. Industry leaders Polymarket and Kalshi now process tens of billions of dollars in bets from hundreds of thousands of users every month, propelling themselves to a joint valuation of more than $30 billion. Anyone with a smartphone (and in some locations a VPN) can bet on virtually any outcome, including but not limited to the exact chart position of a Justin Bieber single, the daily high temperature in Paris, the arrival on Earth of aliens or a messiah, Eurovision, an invasion of Taiwan, Taylor Swift's choice of bridesmaid, and whether Donald Trump will utter the exact word "discombobulator" in the coming week.[2]

The founders of these platforms say the trend is still in its infancy. Tarek Mansour, the CEO of Kalshi, has stated that the "long term vision is to financialize everything, and create a tradable asset out of any difference in opinion." He believes that prediction markets will soon become a $1 trillion asset class, and could eventually be larger than stock markets themselves. Like Polymarket founder Shayne Coplan, Mansour emphasizes that prediction markets provide value in an Internet- and AI-powered information environment where it is difficult to differentiate hyperabundant noise from reality. "Prediction markets are an antidote...," Mansour has said. "They do a very good job of distilling information and surfacing truth to people." Coplan famously called Polymarket a "global truth machine" after it accurately forecast Trump's 2024 election win.

"Why just like a post, or comment on a news story, when you can bet and potentially profit off what happens next?"

This idea, that prediction markets can aggregate dispersed information that helps human beings anticipate the future, is taken directly from the Iowa Electronic Markets. Whether it remains true in the current application—whether these apps are clarifying a world crippled by bad information, or simply turning it into a casino—is open to debate. In either case, one thing is already abundantly clear: Prediction markets have proved an irresistible target for insider trading and outright fraud.

In April, the Justice Department indicted a soldier in the US Army Special Forces for using classified information about the impending capture of Venezuelan President Nicolás Maduro to reap more than $400,000 in profits on Polymarket.

The case is only the most notorious in a pervasive trend, with one study finding that more than half of all long-shot bets about military actions on Polymarket have paid off. (Long-shot bets, by definition, should only pay off in a minority of cases.) French authorities are currently investigating whether bettors made thousands of dollars by tampering with weather sensors at Charles de Gaulle Airport in order to rig temperature readings.

The exchanges have begun rolling out increased measures against insider trading, but Coplan has at times embraced the trend. "I think that people going and having an edge to the market is a good thing," he told CBS news. "And, you know, people will adapt." Whether the public sees it that way is a different question. An Ipsos poll found that 61% of Americans see prediction markets as "closer to gambling," while 8% said that they were "closer to investing." A separate study found that just 3% of accounts on Polymarket reliably beat the odds, leading the authors to conclude that "Prediction market accuracy thus reflects the wisdom of an informed minority, not the wisdom of crowds."

A picture is forming of how these markets work. A large group of "noise" traders—users betting on instinct, preference or merely a coin flip—create a financial incentive for a small group of sophisticated—or inside—traders to make more informed bets, thus exposing their insights to the public and improving information signals. For those who have the capital and savvy to use them, prediction markets may indeed provide unique information about the outcome of future events. For the majority, though, it can seem like a surrender to that noise.

In many ways, prediction markets are nothing new. Gambling is, of course, as old as money itself, but scholars usually trace the roots of prediction markets to 16th-century Italy, where local banking houses organized the logistics of odds and spreads for substantial bets on the *papabili*, sometimes made on behalf of the cardinals gathered in conclave to elect the next pope.[3] The practice thrived until Pope Gregory XIV banned it in 1591, under threat of excommunication. In early 18th-century London, gentlemen's clubs and venues like Jonathan's Coffee-House (a precursor to the London Stock Exchange) became hubs where the elite could place bets on parliamentary scandals and changes in prime minister, with odds reported in Fleet Street newspapers. As one historian quipped, "The only sure test of English opinions was the state of the odds." From roughly 1868 to 1940, the United States had a large prediction market for presidential elections that operated openly near the New York Stock Exchange, with volume sometimes exceeding that of traditional stock trading during election years. It closed as a result of anti-gambling measures and the rise of scientific polling.

It's clear that the idea has come and gone through history, surging in popularity, and then often facing backlash. But what does seem new in the era of Polymarket is who is involved. Polymarket and its peers have democratized access, letting anyone with a smartphone and a hunch wager on what comes next. In one sense this is a natural progression of the Internet itself, which has allowed most of the world's population to see what is happening, everywhere, in real time: to watch the powerful; to track wars and elections by the minute; to understand, with enough patience, how almost any system works. And once you can see everything, the question is what to *do* with what you're seeing: Why just like a post, or comment on a news story, when you can bet and potentially profit off what happens next?

We live more than ever in a passive register. The pandemic taught a generation to observe rather than participate; the so-called "Gen Z stare" sometimes seems less an affect than the resting face of a citizen of the infinite scroll. The world arranges itself in front of us on our phones—markets decide what is built, algorithms decide what is seen, the democratic instinct seems to slacken a little each year—and we mostly just watch.

A bet is not, it is worth saying, a vote. A vote is a matter of principle and preference, a voice rising to say how the world should be. But it's possible that when we begin to forget our ability to shape the world to come, we find that the next best thing is to bet, and watch.

(1) Jesse Jackson was a civil rights activist and two-time Democratic presidential candidate. He finished second in the 1988 primary to Michael Dukakis, who later lost the presidential election to George H. W. Bush.

(2) There is a long history of attempts to predict the Second Coming. In 1844, the followers of Baptist preacher William Miller gave away their possessions and awaited Christ's return. The day in question—October 22—has come to be known as the Great Disappointment.

(3) *Papabili*—literally "pope-ables"—are cardinals considered likely candidates for election. There is a well-known saying in the Catholic Church: "He who enters the conclave as pope leaves it as a cardinal."

ONCE YOU CAN SEE EVERYTHING, THE QUESTION IS WHAT TO DO WITH WHAT YOU'RE SEEING.

THE FLOW STATE

Mind. Body. Clothes: The total absorption of creative play.

Photos
ALEJANDRO ARRIAS & DAVID BRAVO
Styling
MANU MENDI

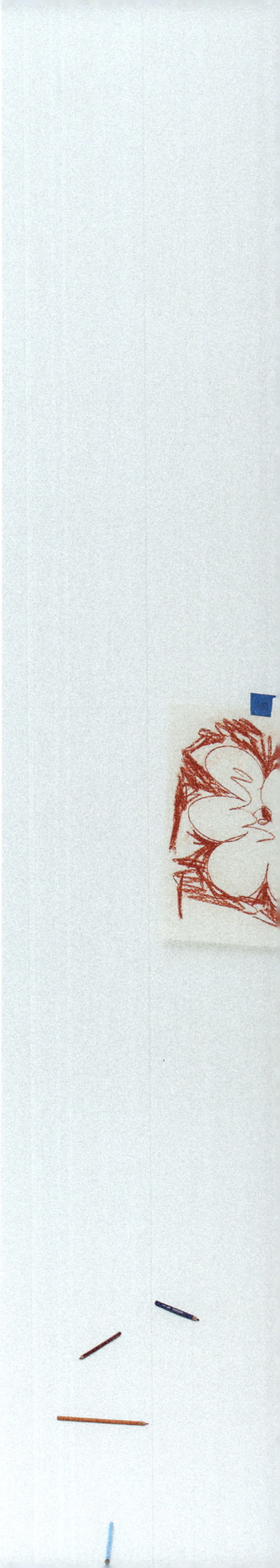

(opposite) Rui wears a shirt and shorts by HABEY CLUB, socks by CALZEDONIA and shoes by CAMPER.
Anna wears a shirt and shoes by HABEY CLUB and trousers by ERNESTO NARANJO.

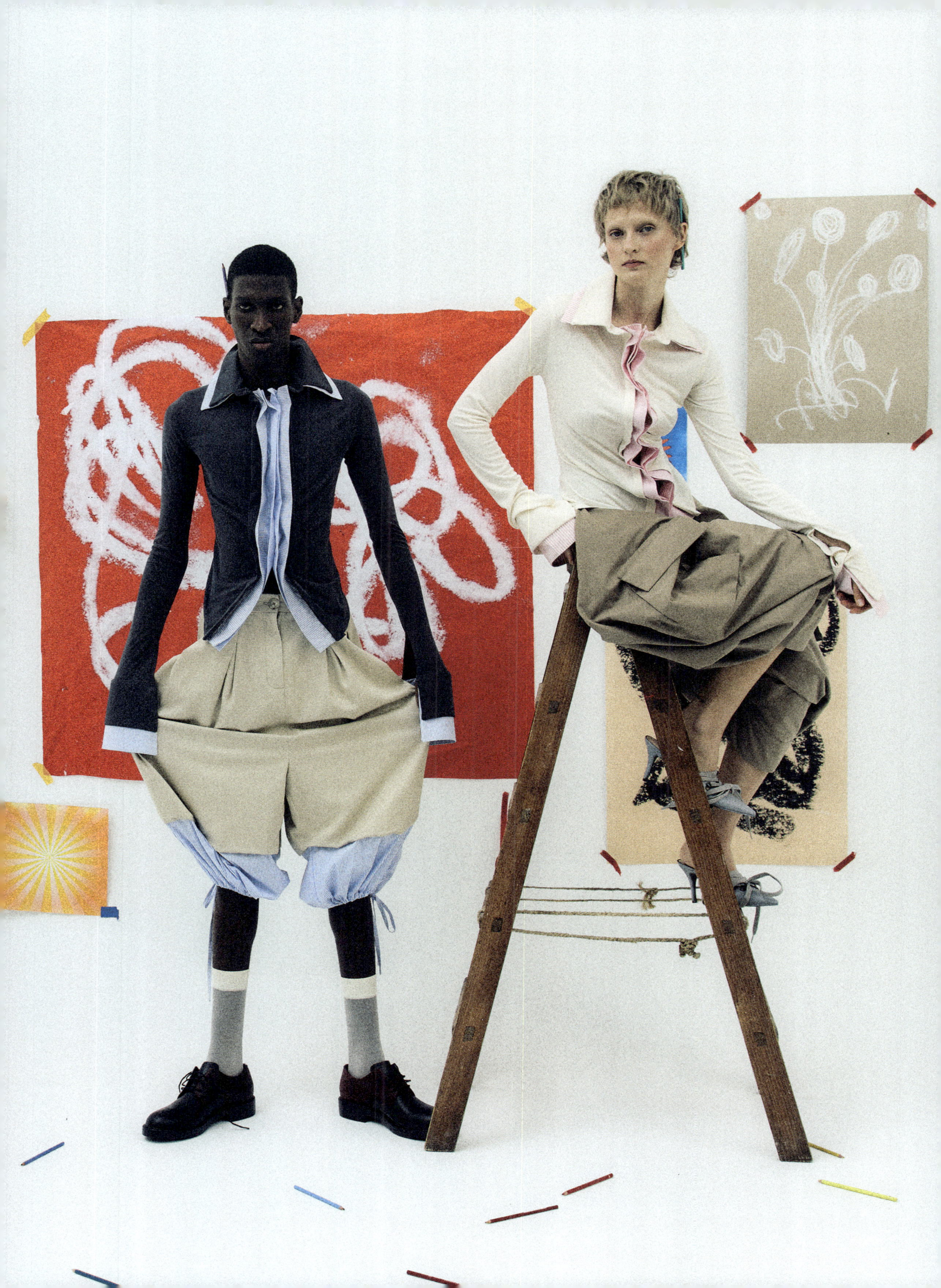

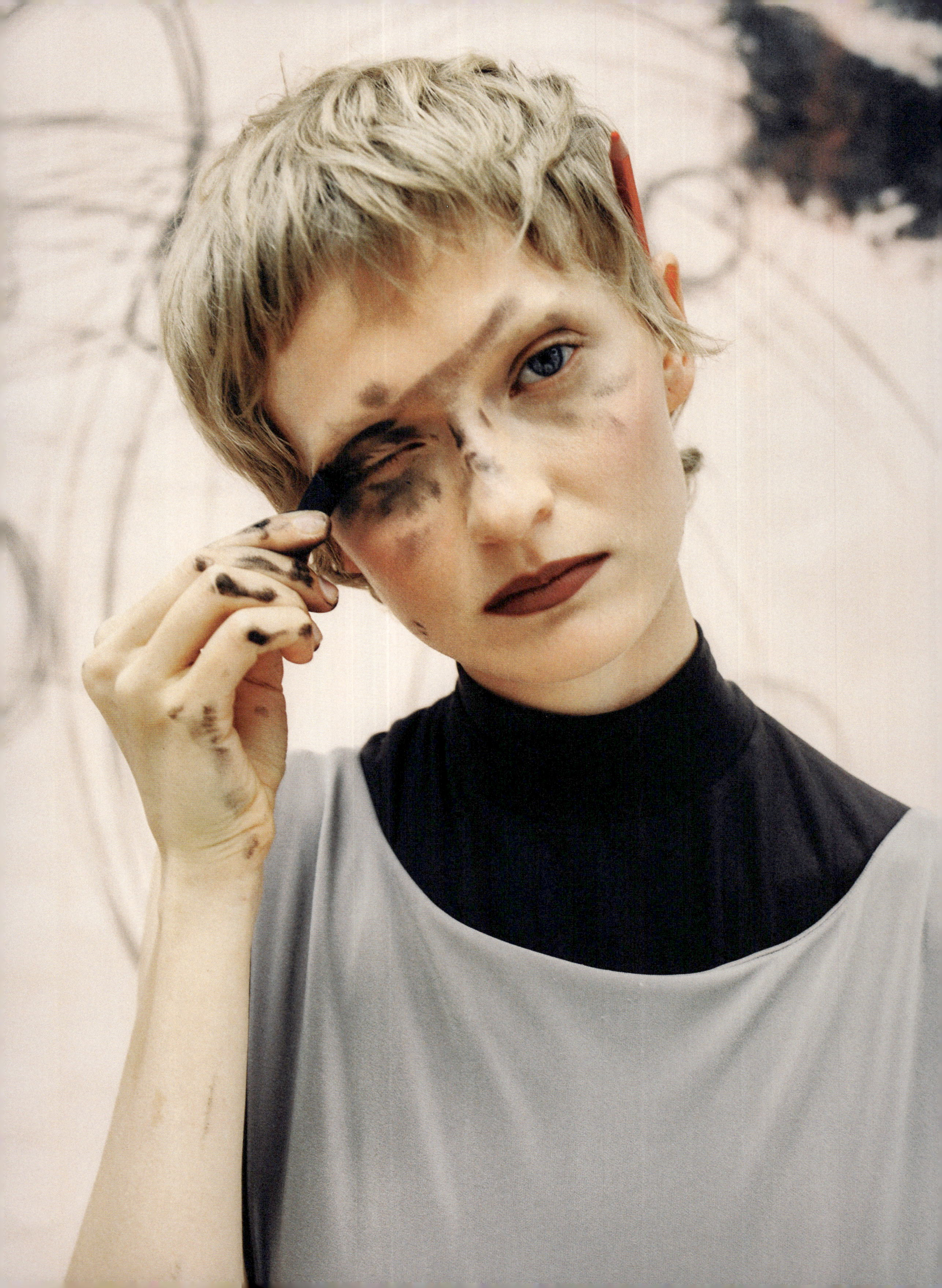

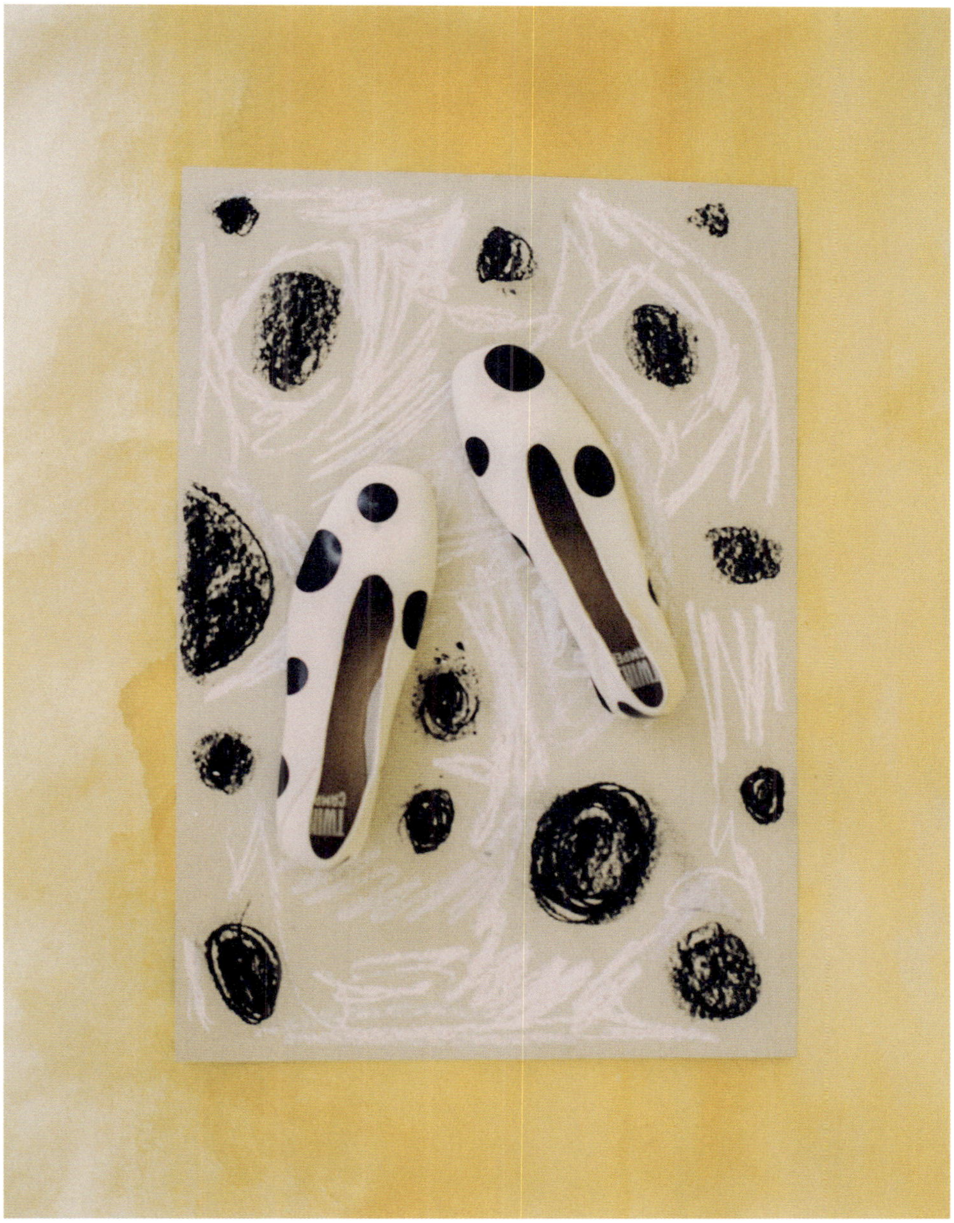

(above) Shoes by CAMPER.
(opposite) Anna wears a dress by MANÉ MANÉ.

Art Direction & Set Design: Jhonson Camilo. Producer: Laura Meijueiro.

(below) Rui wears a suit by BIBENCIA, a shirt by BRUNO LANGARICA BLANCO, socks by CALZEDONIA and shoes by FERRAGAMO.
(opposite) Anna wears a top and skirt by DOBLAS and earrings by MAISON MESA.

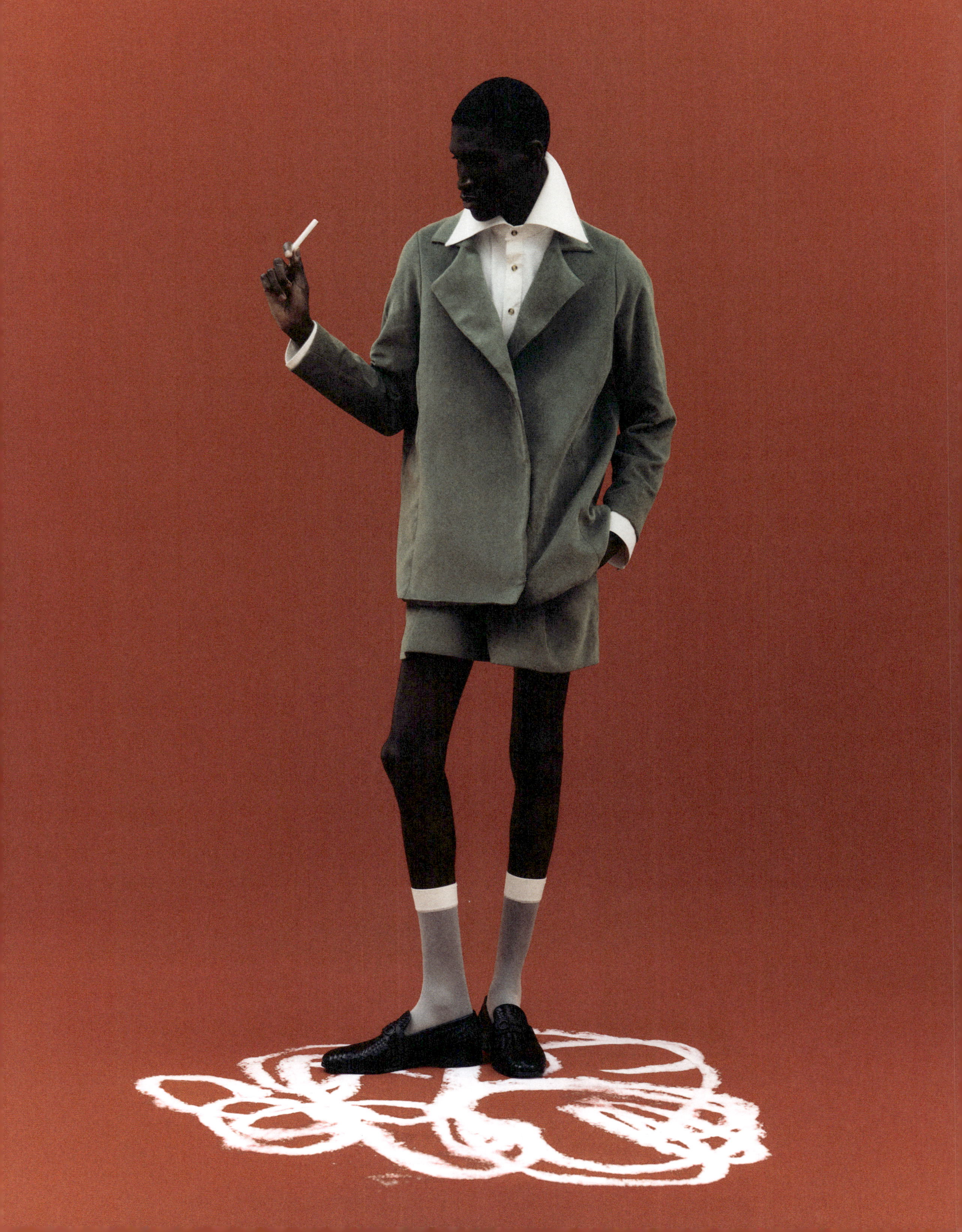

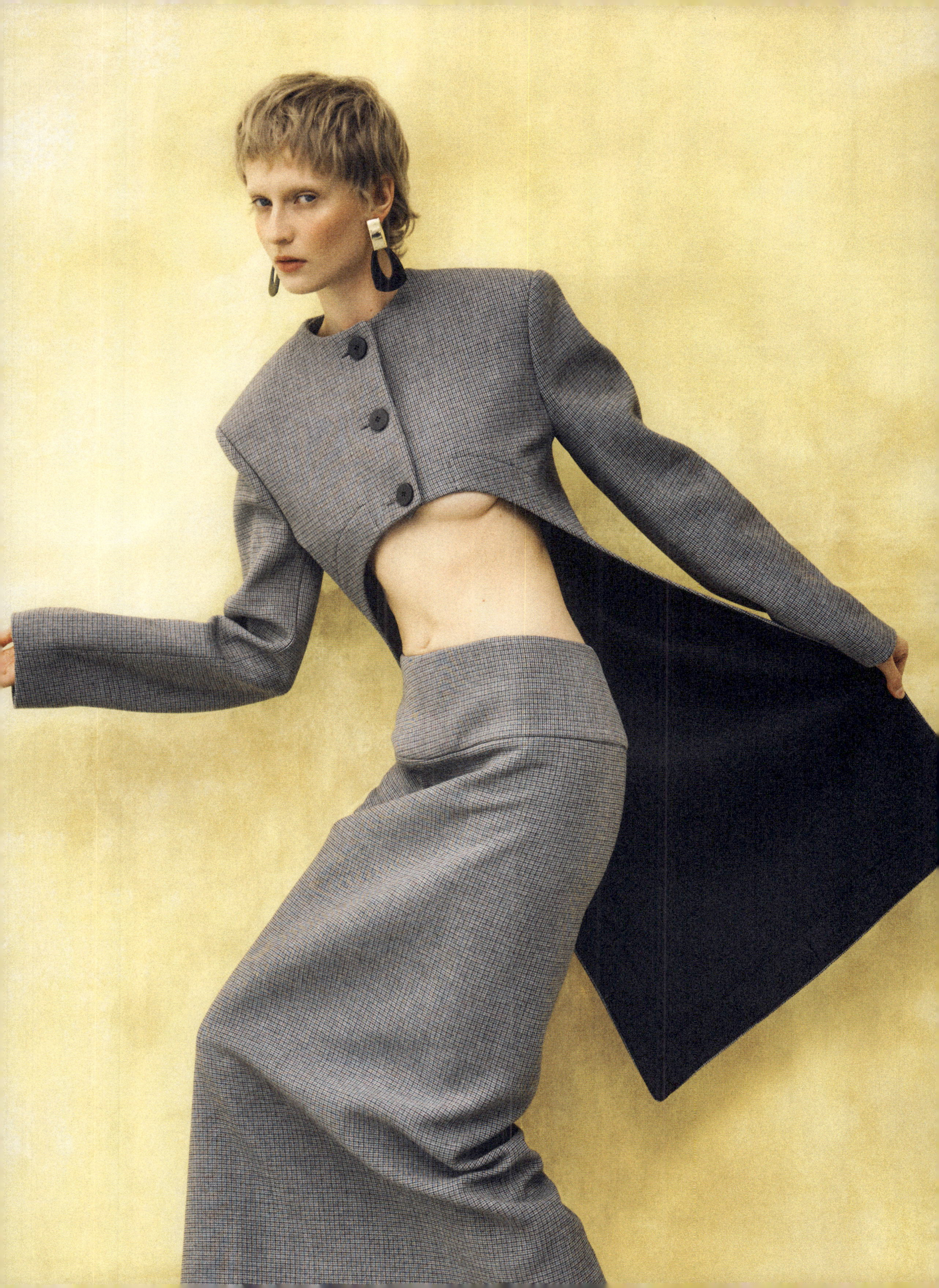

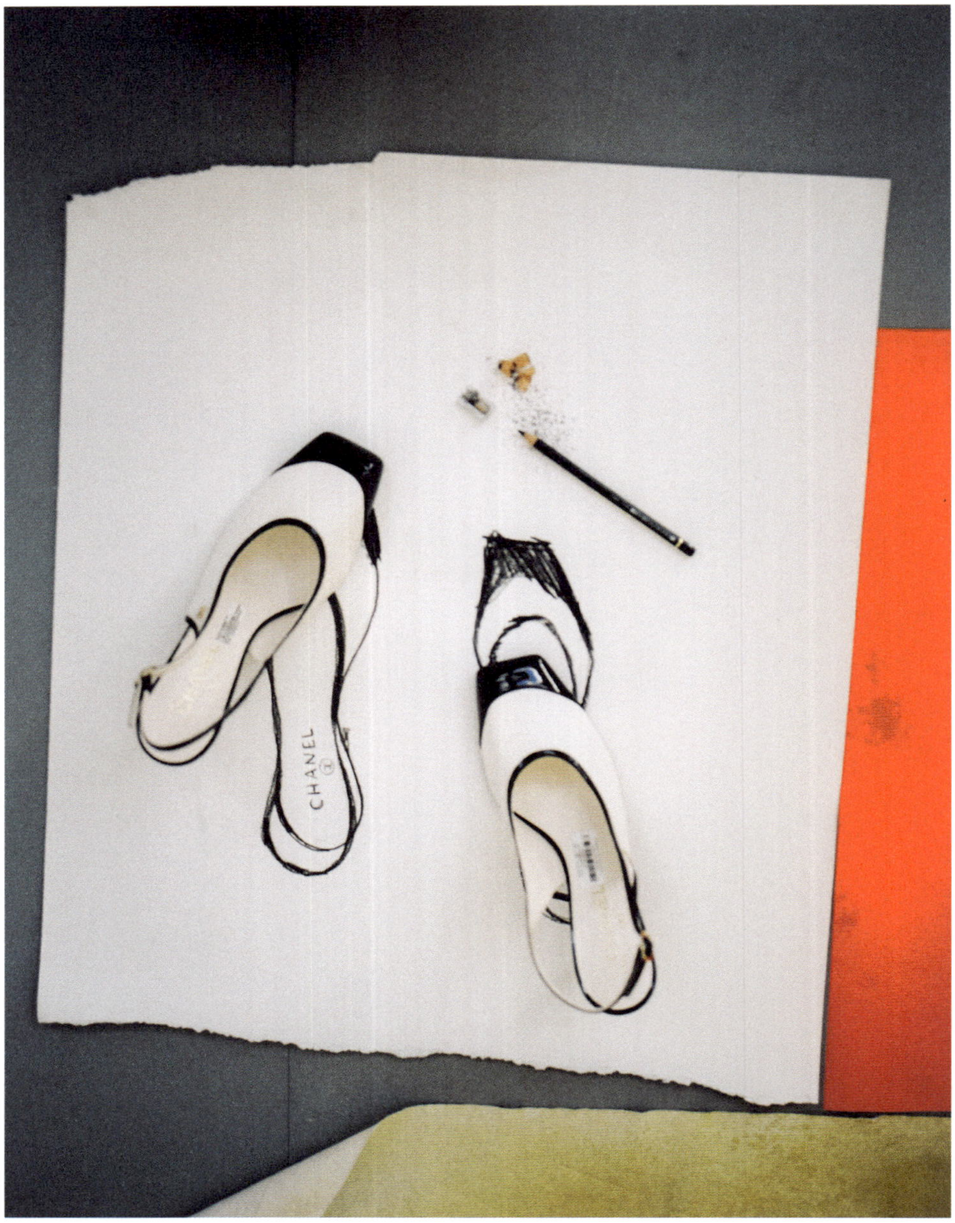

(above) Shoes by CHANEL.
(opposite) Rui wears a shirt and ties by LIMO, shorts by BRUNO LANGARICA BLANCO, socks by CALZEDONIA and shoes by FERRAGAMO.

Hair & Makeup: Victor Maresco. Models: Rui Huila at Uno Models and Anna Pavlova at Two Management.

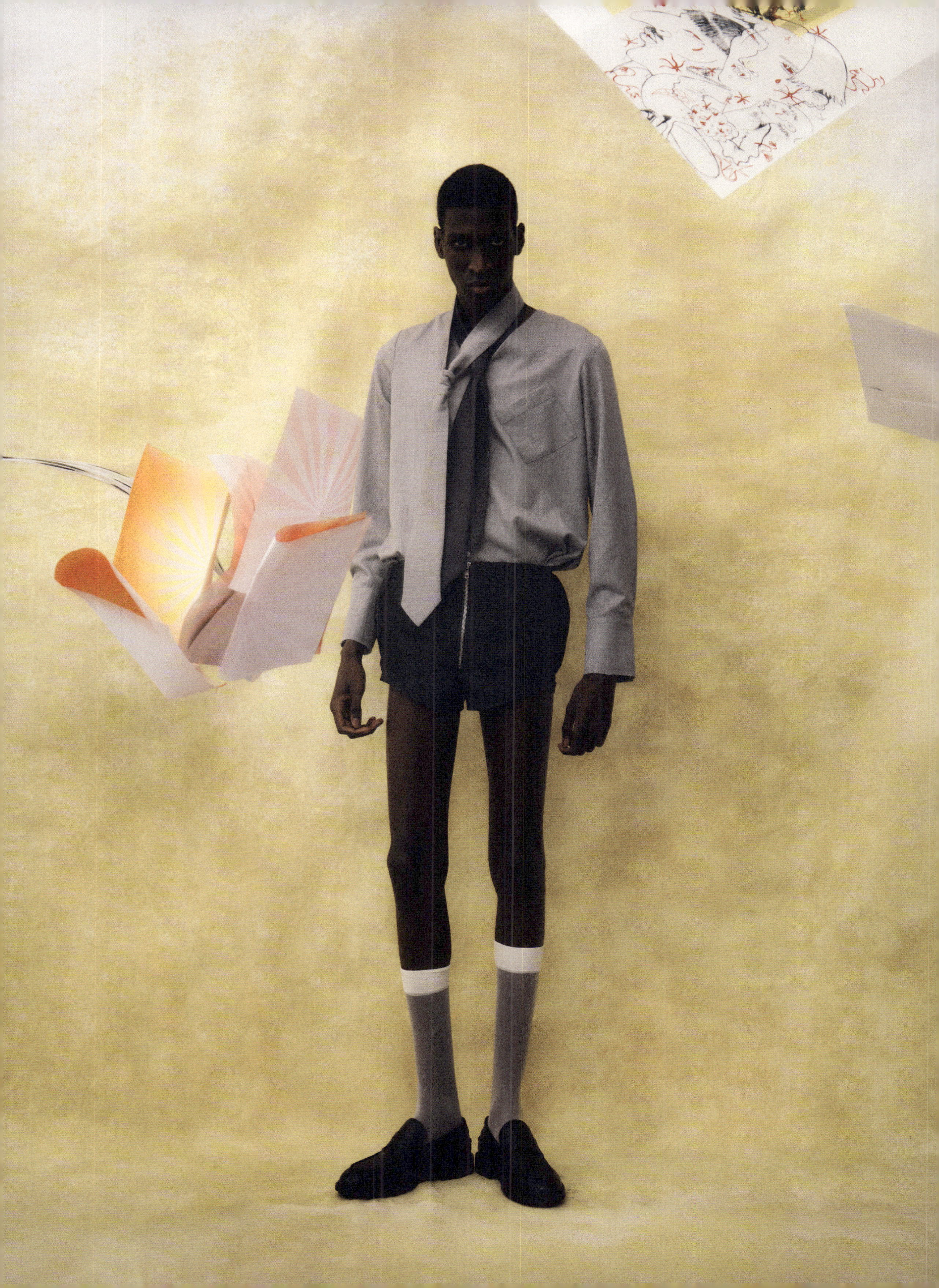

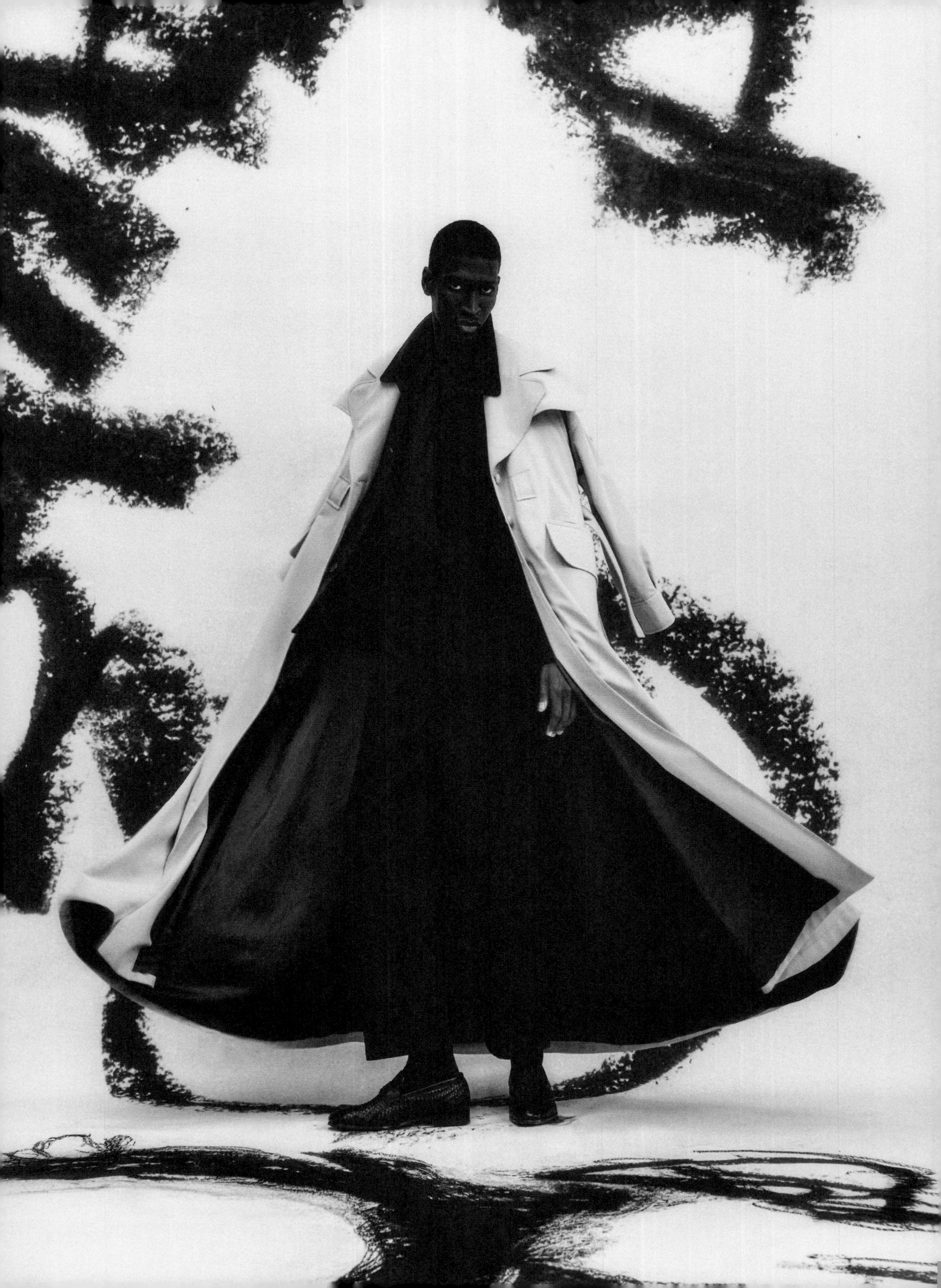

(opposite) Rui wears a coat by MAISON MESA, a jacket by SANDRO, a shirt by ANTIK BATIK, trousers by CARLOTA BARRERA and shoes by FERRAGAMO.
(below) Anna wears an outfit by CHANEL.

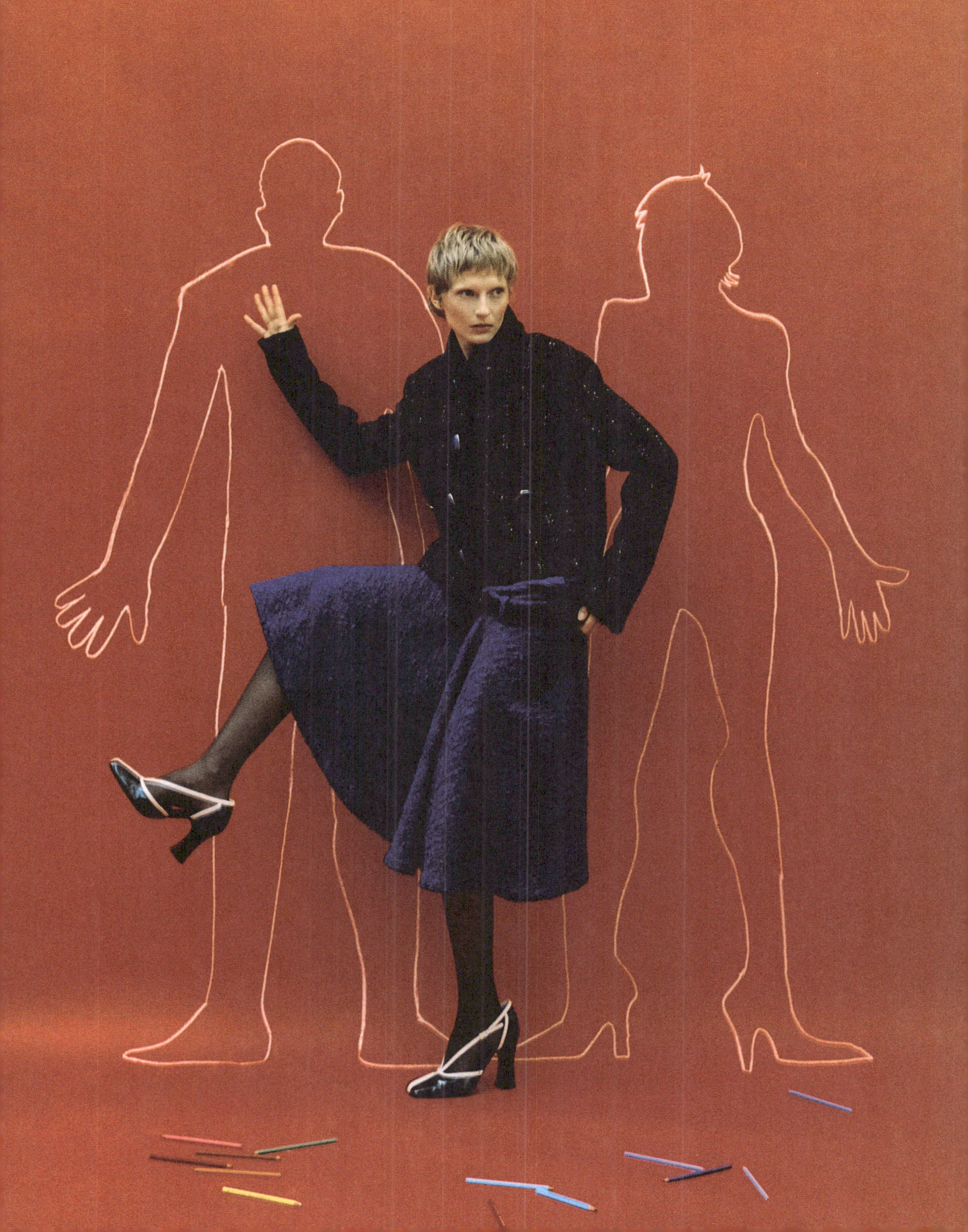

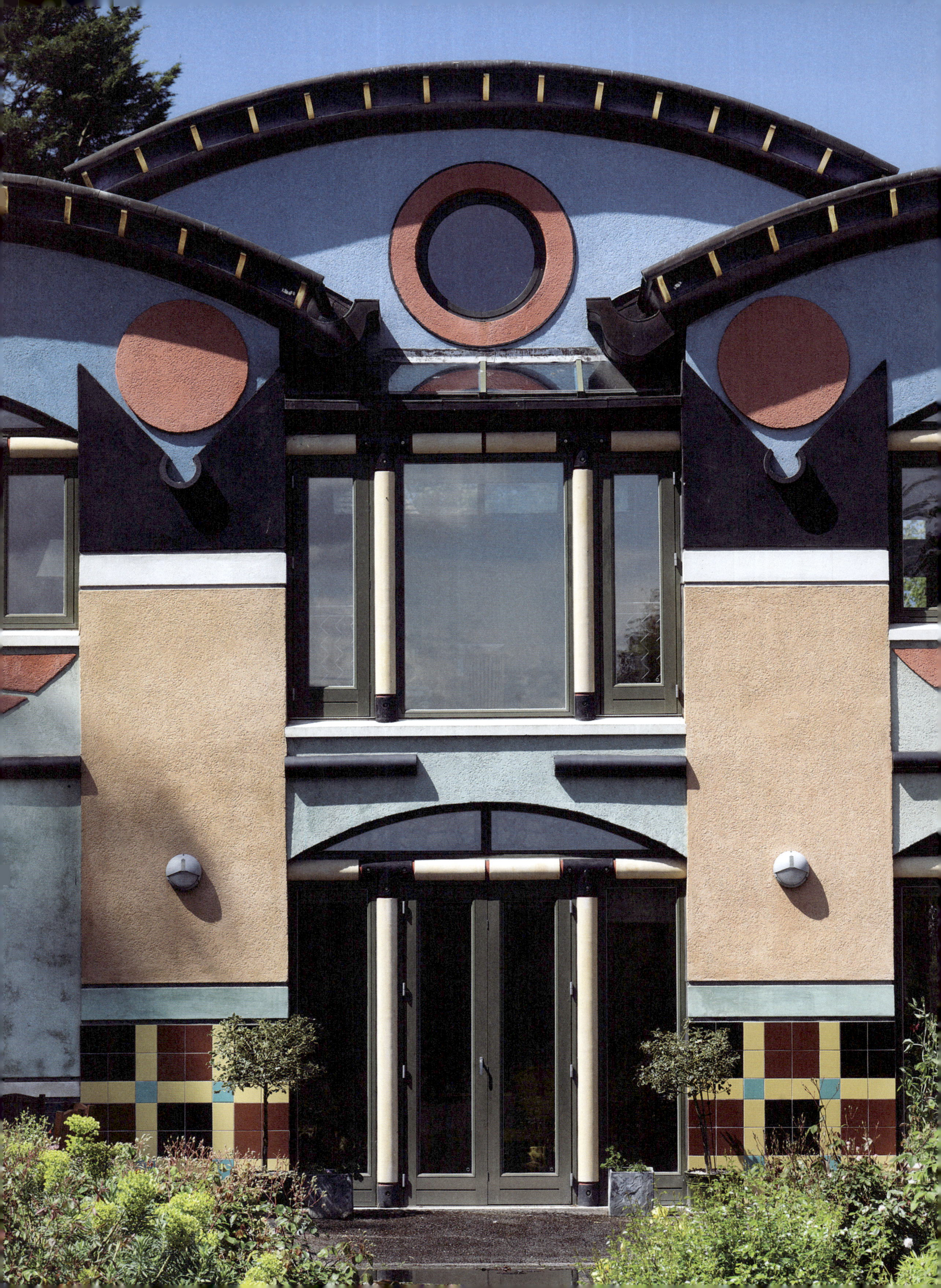

HOME TOUR: SPHINX HILL
John Outram's postmodern Egyptianate fantasy.

Words
Emma Moore

Walking the Thames Path near the English village of Moulsford, there's a moment when the pastoral harmony of riverside meadows and well-mannered Victorian and Edwardian villas is broken. Suddenly, from behind the trees, appears a roofline of three sky-blue colliding arcs. Ocher pilasters rise between walls of willow green, terra-cotta discs hovering at their summits. The whole building sits long and low, its symmetrical facade facing the rising sun and the River Thames, which here in Oxfordshire goes by another name: the Isis. It may derive from the river's Roman name, Tamesis, rather than the Egyptian goddess of magic and motherhood, but it's nevertheless fitting as the watery border to Sphinx Hill, a masterful piece of Egyptology-infused postmodernist architecture.

Sphinx Hill was commissioned in 1994 by Christopher McCall, a barrister, and his late wife, Henrietta, an Egyptologist, and was completed in 1999. Henrietta was interested in Egyptian revival—the recurring impulse, from Napoleon's campaigns onward, to insert the imagery of the ancient Nile into everything from architecture to earrings. When they sold the property four years ago, Christopher recalled how it had all started, having joked that, if they were to really take Henrietta's interest seriously, they needed to commission a house. The jest became a dream project, and then an architectural icon. Twenty-five years after it was built, it became the youngest building in England to receive listed status, legally protecting it from future changes that might diminish its architectural interest.

For its design, the McCalls turned to John Outram, an architect who had spent his career cheerfully ignoring every consensus about what buildings should look like. Having started his eponymous practice in 1974, he spent the subsequent decades challenging the reductionist approach that modernism had brought to industrial and municipal infrastructure, loading his buildings instead with arching vaults, temple-like pediments, extravagantly proportioned columns concealing services, invented materials (his experiments in concrete have established entirely new building techniques) and colorful embellishments grounded in mythological motifs.

The culmination of these ideas manifested in his 1988 design for the Isle of Dogs Pumping Station, which drew from the monumental architecture of ancient Mesopotamia for its flourishes. Around the same time, Outram also completed his first major residential project, the New House for Hans Rausing, the Swedish industrialist and inheritor of the Tetra Pak fortune. Photographs of this now Grade I–listed house in Wadhurst Park, East Sussex—described by an architecture critic as "probably the best house built since the war"—and the pumping station were what led the McCalls to Outram.

To understand how the exotic Sphinx Hill can land deep in the lush pastures of the English countryside, you need to understand Outram. Born in 1934, raised in colonial India and trained in London, he belongs to no particular school of architecture—or rather, he embodies many. He's part pragmatic planner, part architectural fantasist, and his approach is perfectly chronicled in the Capriccio-like pictures he has commissioned for projects—realized or conceptual—from painter Carl Laubin.

Outram is at once a writer, philosopher, historian and architect. He references Le Corbusier and Louis Kahn but subscribes to the "Less is a bore" philosophy of American architect Robert Venturi, the postmodern riposte to the modernist "less is more" mantra of Mies van der Rohe. Indeed, he is regularly described as Britain's foremost postmodernist, though it is a label he has been known to shun.

Photo: James O Davies / Historic England

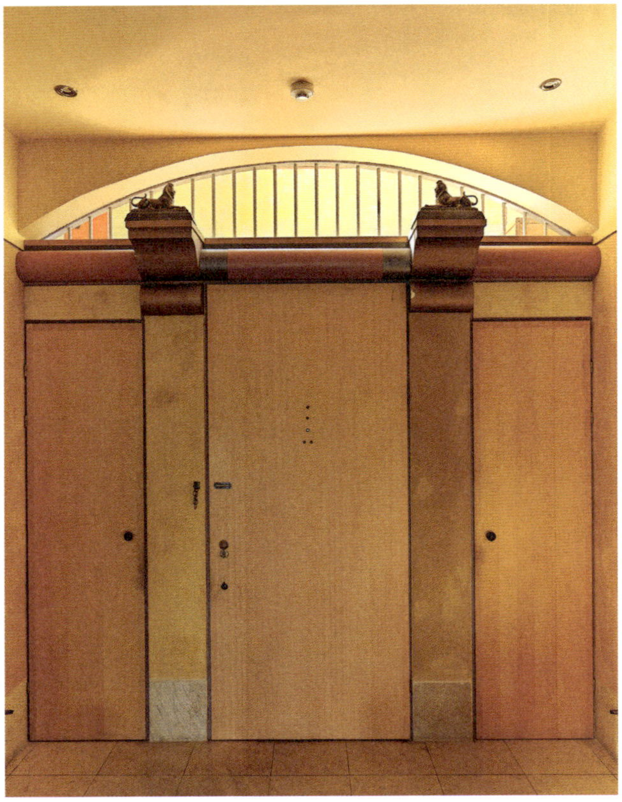

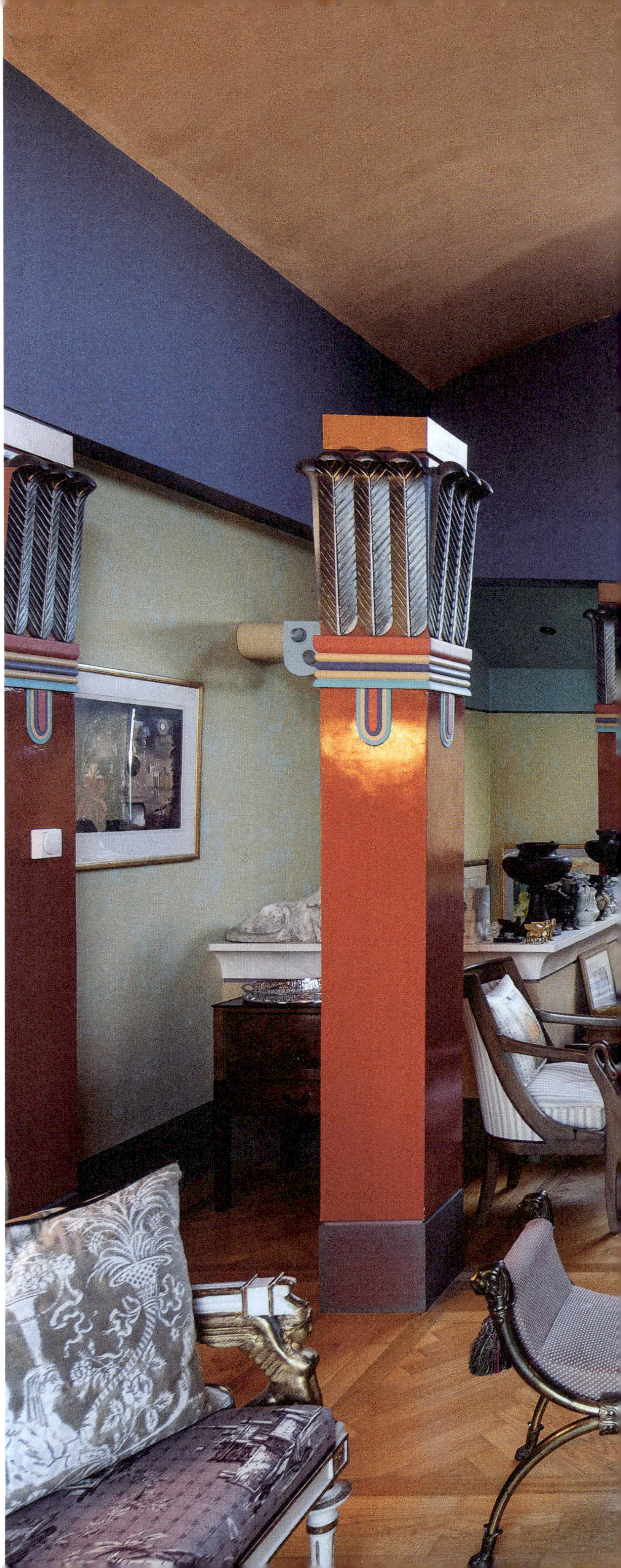

(opposite)
The living room of Sphinx Hill is set on the piano nobile—literally, the "noble floor"—following the Renaissance tradition of placing the grandest rooms on the second floor. It is one of many ways Outram folds thousands of years of architectural history into the house.

Right Photo: Phil Sayer / C20 Society. Left Photo: James O Davies / Historic England

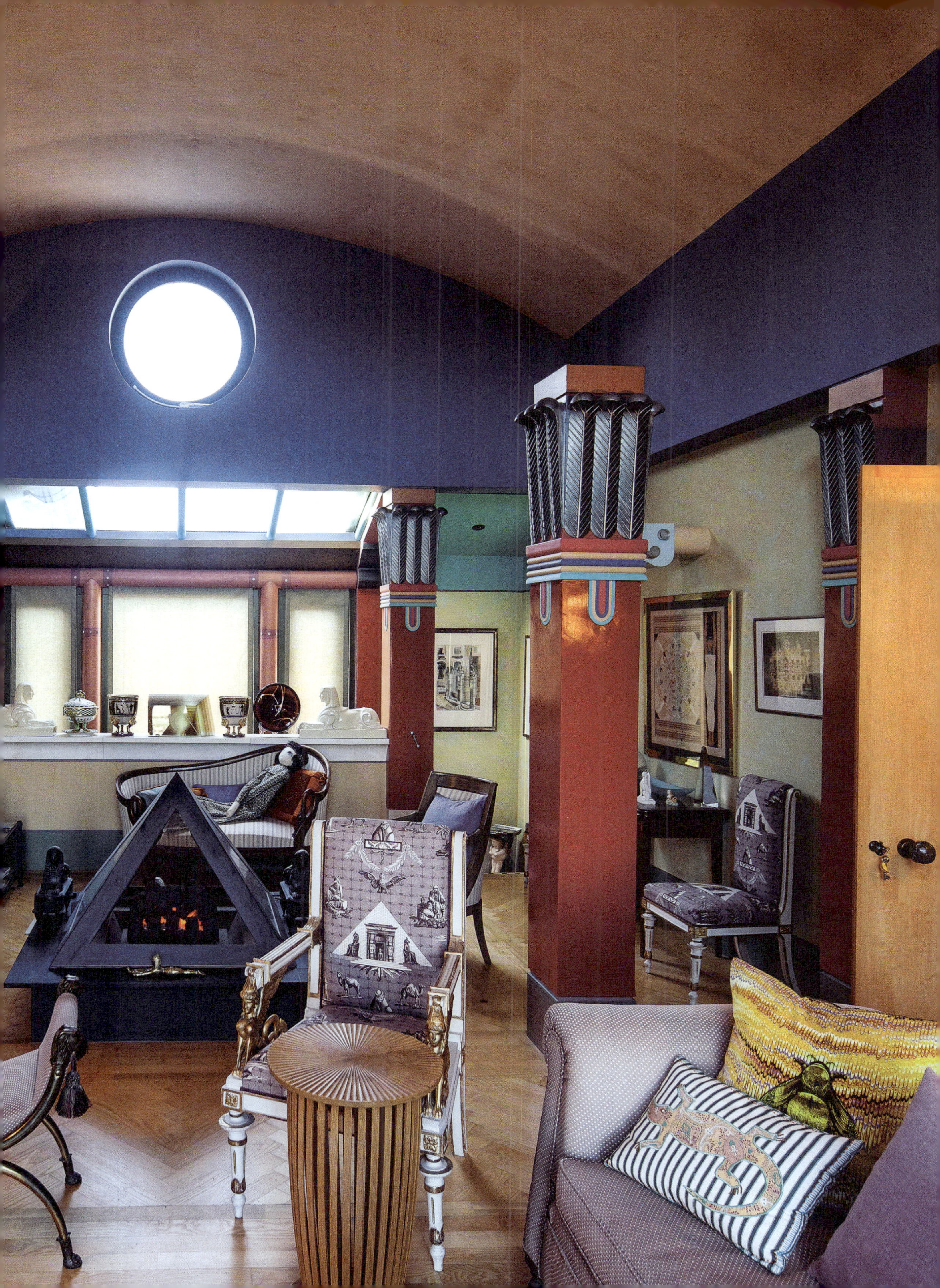

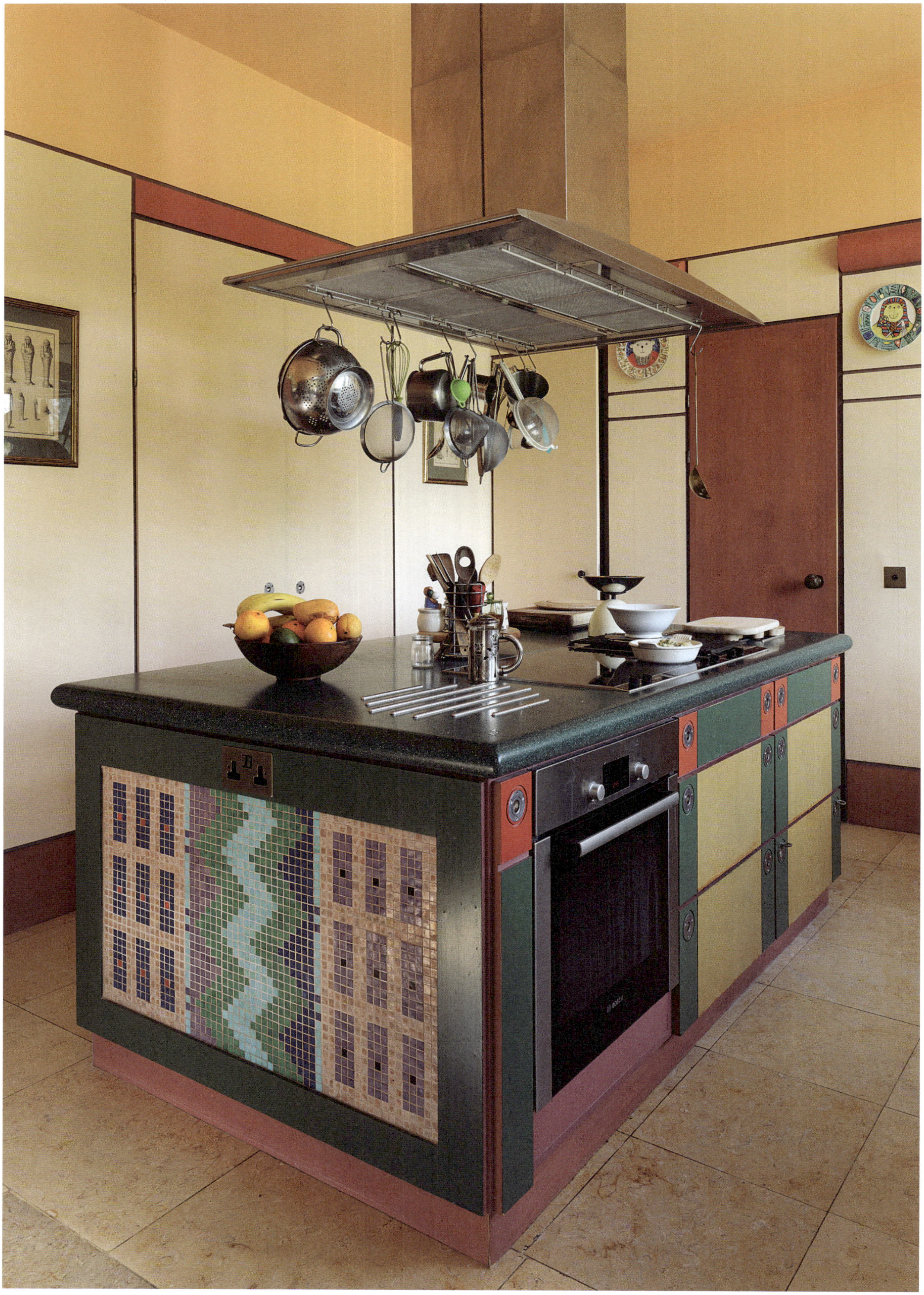

Photo: James O Davies / Historic England

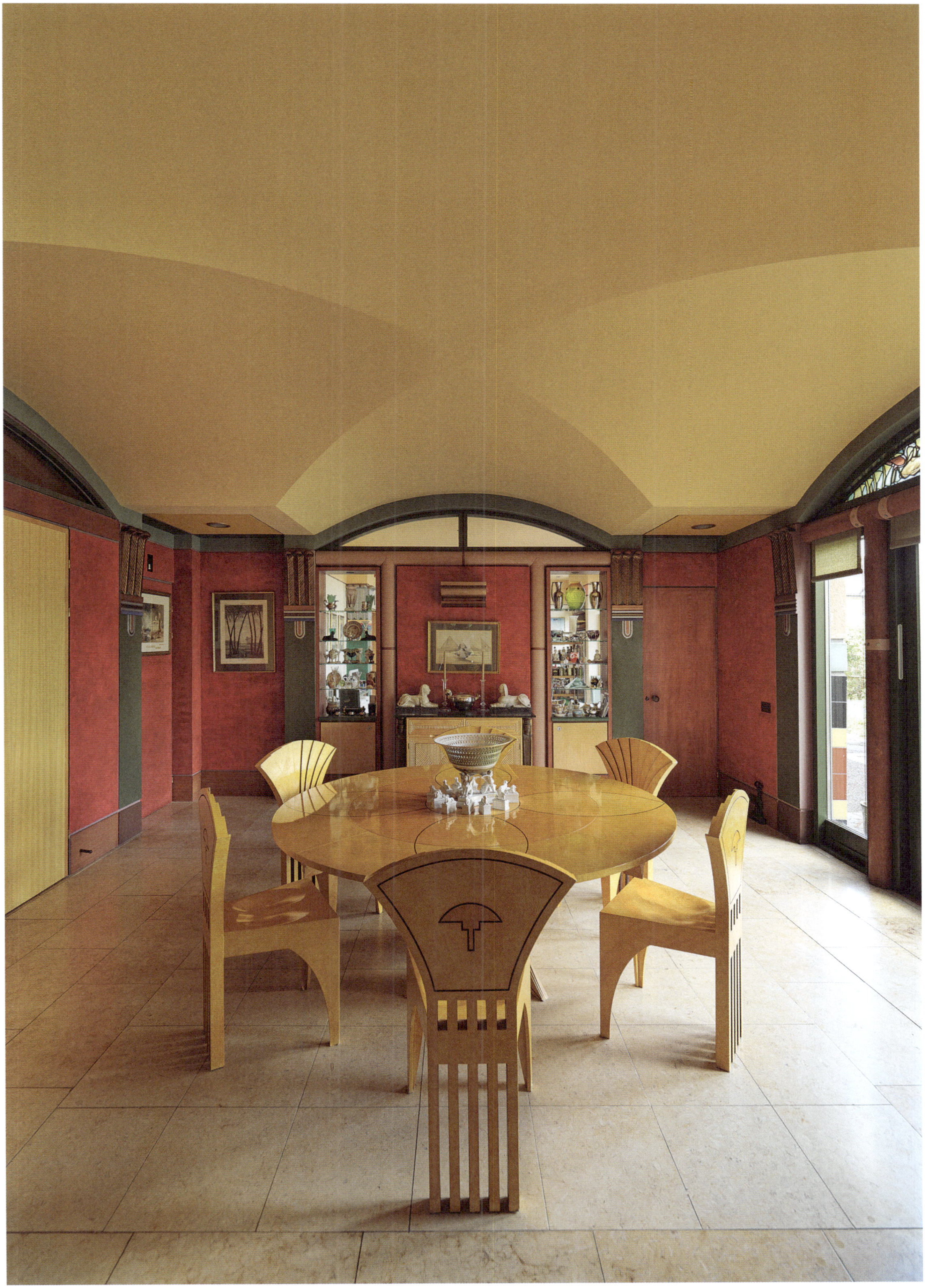

Photo: James O Davies / Historic England

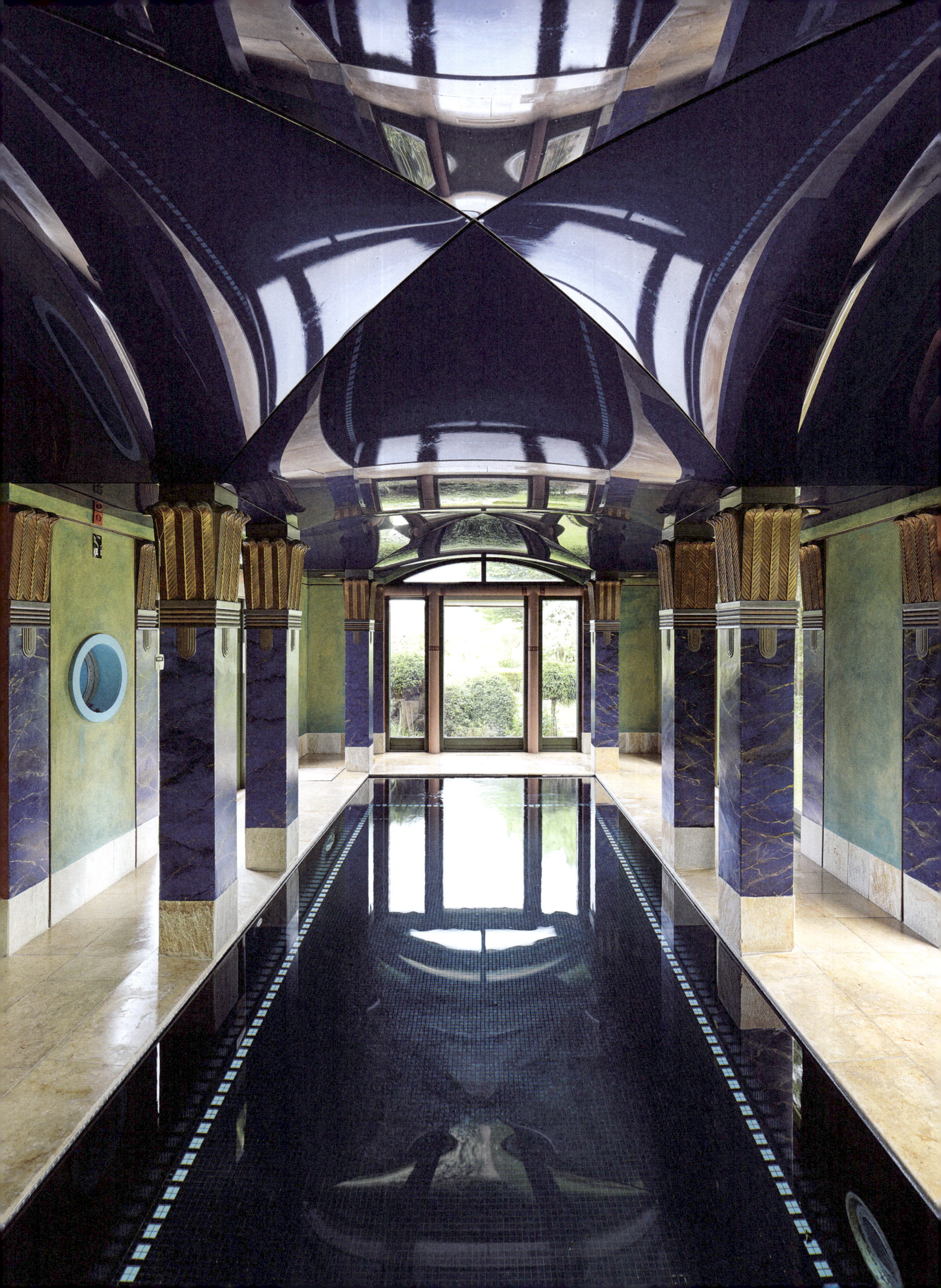

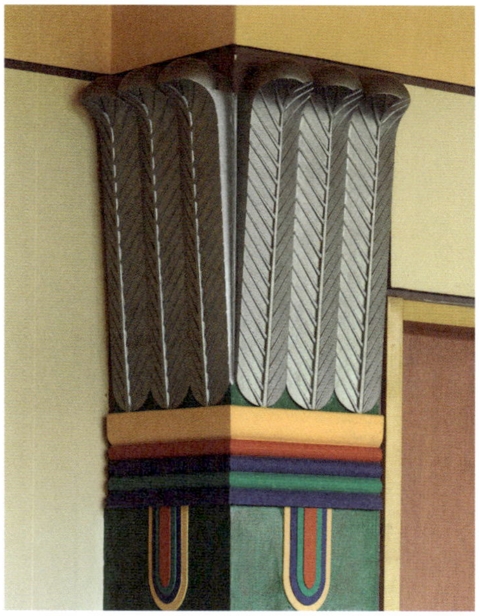

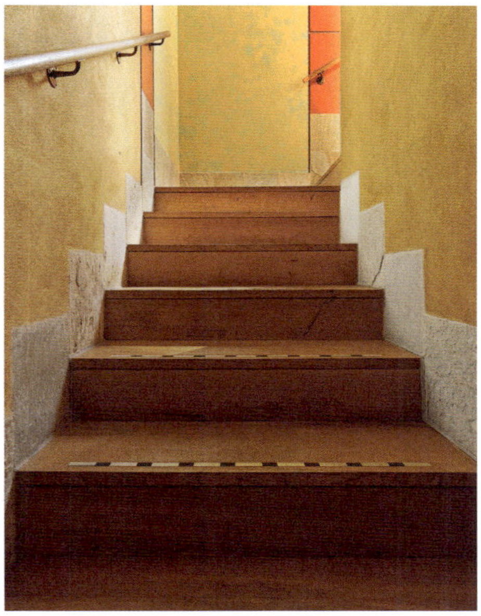

(left)
The swimming pool at Sphinx Hill occupies a separate wing. Henrietta swam here every morning "in water as black as outer space," as Outram once described it. *Above*, the roof serves as a second-floor terrace connected to the primary bedroom.

Photos: James O Davies / Historic England

"His joyful, transgressive, sincere strain of architecture has persistently defied categorisation," writes Geraint Franklin in his 2022 book, *John Outram*. "If a label [to define him] cannot be done without then one might opt for post-modernism, formulated by Charles Jencks as 'a double coded language—one part modern and one part something else.'" But really, Outram's practice is something quite singular: an architecture grounded in the conviction that buildings should *mean* something. His influences are omnivorous and ancient: Egyptian, Vedic, Mesopotamian, classical, surreal—all filtered through a mind that is also perfectly at home discussing the philosophy of Heidegger. The result is an architecture that is simultaneously learned and playful, reverent and irreverent, serious about being ridiculous. The American postmodernist Michael Graves once warned that "you have to keep your eye on Outram, he never knows when to stop."

The McCalls proved ideal clients for Outram. Henrietta's expertise gave the project its palette of references; Christopher's open mind gave it permission to be as theatrical as Outram wanted. The brief was intentionally open; the couple preferred to see where the architect's ideas would take them, rather than impose fixed requirements from the start.

The classical narrative runs through every element of the design: following Palladian symmetry and proportion and echoing the Egyptian hypostyle—the densely columned temples of ancient Egypt—through a repeating structural grid that informs the organization of rooms, the floors, wall panels and the tartan-patterned tiling at the base of the pilasters. Ancient Egyptian inflections scatter across the facade; the barrel-vaulted roofline is inspired by the funerary complex of Djoser in Saqqara. Centered in the middle vault is a round window representing the Eye of Horus and above each arched window float winged solar discs, the ancient Egyptian symbol of divine protection. The terra-cotta circles that top the columns represent *akhet*, the hieroglyph for the sun rising over the horizon. Such is Outram's attention to detail that the bespoke bronze doorknobs feature scarab beetle reliefs.

The house is a true Gesamtkunstwerk—a total work of art—with its story woven through all the interior fittings. The kitchen is dominated by a large island featuring colorful cabinetry in green, ocher and red. The living room sits beneath a barrel-vaulted ceiling painted oxblood red, with polychromatic bands and silver palm capitals on its freestanding columns—a flourish that repeats throughout the house. At the room's center stands a black open-sided pyramid: the fireplace, whose smoke is drawn beneath the floor to a hidden flue, in homage to the visionary neoclassical architect John Soane's invisible stoves at the Bank of England. The standout feature is the pool, beloved of Henrietta, which occupies its own wing. Inky, by virtue of its black tiles and flanked by blue and gold columns, it sits under a glossy midnight-blue vaulted ceiling that reflects the water below. Christopher came to regard the color scheme as the house's greatest gift, calling it "enormously rewarding."

"You have to keep your eye on Outram, he never knows when to stop."

"In the design of Sphinx Hill, Outram wove aspects of Egyptian culture into his own mythological code," writes Franklin. "The result is a more creative but oblique response to architectural history. I suspect the McCalls enjoyed explaining the hidden references to visitors in much the same way as we can imagine John Soane doing so at his house."

Outside, in the formal garden, the references continue. A central rill, representing the Nile, cascades from an infinity fountain through three rectangular pools with watchful sphinxes before opening into a banked delta at the river's edge, and two further stone sphinx guards. Yew hedges divide the garden into a grid that echoes the rhythms of the house's facade, and a retaining wall of Staffordshire blue engineering bricks mitigates the flood risk from the river.

The campaign to list Sphinx Hill was led by the Twentieth Century Society, an organization working to save 20th-century British architecture. The director, Catherine Croft, described it as "the most extraordinarily complex and ideas-packed house... bursting with polychromatic Egyptianate motifs." The decision was announced on the eve of Outram's 90th birthday and he was reportedly gratified. Egyptologists from the British Museum had once made the journey to Moulsford to see it, he recalled, and concluded that the house had done more for Egyptology than many an exhibition. Whether he believed this to be high praise or a scandal is not clear.

The McCalls sold Sphinx Hill in 2022 after living there for more than 20 years. Christopher remembers leaving with a heavy heart, describing it as paradise, willingly surrendered to someone who might enjoy it as a work of art to live in. The house may have now passed to new private owners but its listed status has ensured it will continue to intrigue walkers on the Thames Path for decades to come.

BALMING TIGER:
An hour with the alternative K-pop group.

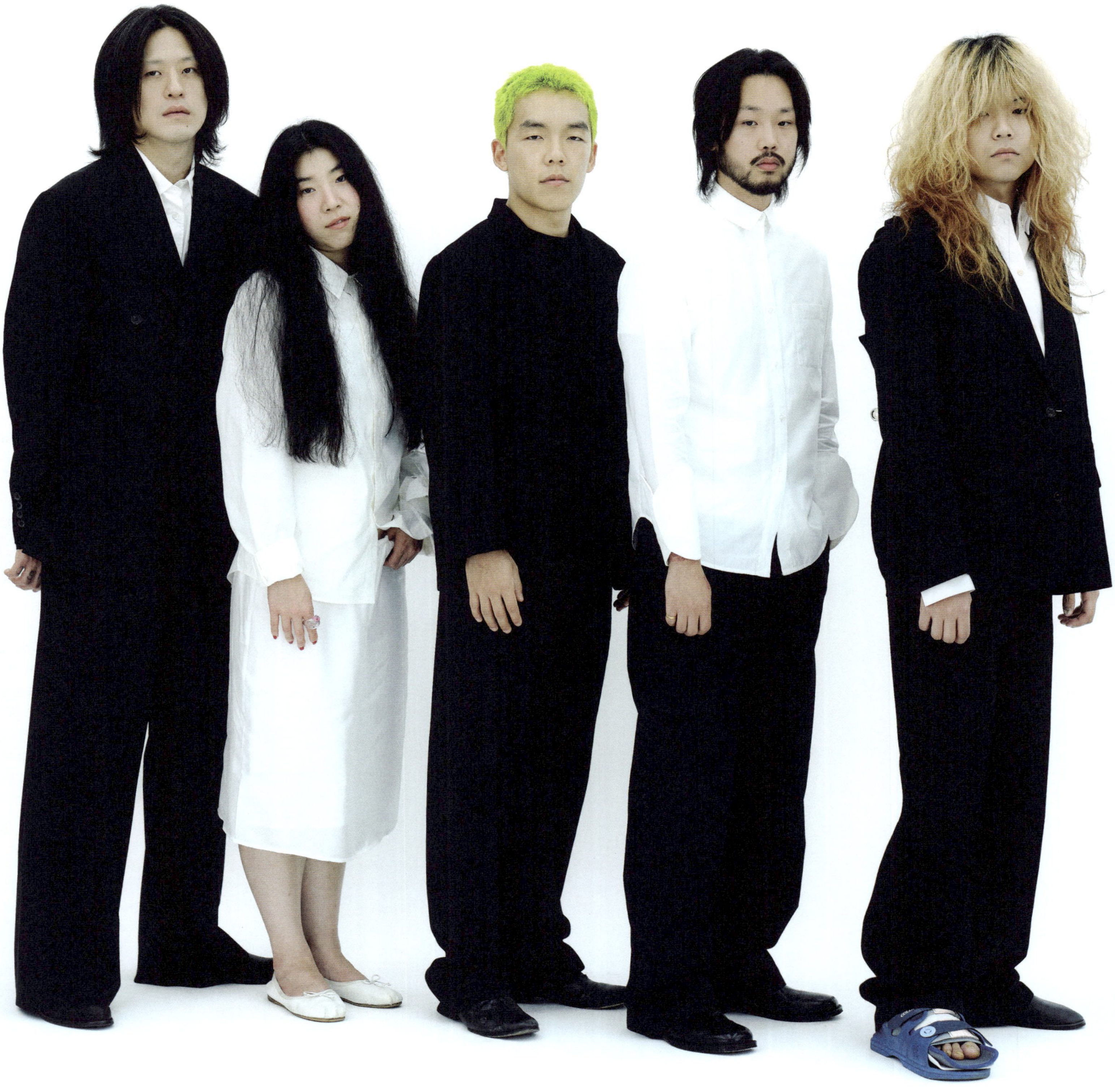

My Zoom interview with Balming Tiger is chaotic. Five of the eleven members are on the call, each in a different location in Seoul. Omega Sapien is at a salon, dyeing his hair green for a music video. Leesuho is munching on a snack with a soda. Unsinkable is strumming a guitar, on mute. bj wnjn is lying in bed in sweatpants. Mudd the Student sits calmly, his long wavy hair dyed like a lion's mane. There are multiple conversations all happening at once as we wait for the other members, some of whom never show up.

When the interview starts, however, the group is focused and attentive. A self-described "alternative K-pop group" from South Korea, Balming Tiger is composed of two women and nine men. They've been described by critics and fans as pioneering, experimental, an artist collective beyond music and, last but not least, "a group of hairstyles that elderly Koreans would definitely hate," a running joke among fans online. In their two studio albums and a debut mixtape, released in 2018, they sing about alienation, absurdist humor, friendship and love, pigeons and frogs.

"We want Balming Tiger to be its own genre," says Omega Sapien, a rapper and singer-songwriter, holding up the phone as his hair, now fluorescent green, is being rinsed out in the sink.

Ironically, Balming Tiger's alternative identity depends on its proximity to South Korea's best-known cultural export. K-pop, literally Korean popular music, is itself less of a distinctive genre than a cultural phenomenon. Within South Korea, it can refer to a wide variety of styles including ballads, EDM and hip-hop. Abroad, K-pop most often means idols: entertainers whose music and image are strictly produced by massive entertainment conglomerates, such as mega-groups like BTS and Blackpink, or soloists such as Somi and G-Dragon. However you define it, K-pop is a glittering symbol of Korean soft power. The stratospheric success of different Korean musicians in the past decade—especially BTS on the US charts—has catapulted K-pop into a household name everywhere.

"Honestly, we don't really think about what genre we are, other than during interviews," says Leesuho, one of Balming Tiger's producers and video directors.

True as that may be, the label they have chosen—alternative K-pop—is a strategic choice, devised by the group's founder and creative director, San Yawn. With K-pop's international popularity, Balming Tiger has smartly positioned themselves as adjacent to something familiar to the global audience—giving themselves a wide playground to try anything and everything.

"It's always more fun when the possibilities are open," San Yawn later explains over email. "Whatever we are now won't be 'the final version' of us. We have no idea what we'll be in the future, but we want to continue to express the little joys of the world in our own language."

It's true that the structure of Balming Tiger is wildly different from a conventional K-pop idol act. Idols are usually conceptually defined by an agency, with clear roles differentiating members, for example "lead vocalist" or "lead dancer." Idol wannabes train, sometimes for years, to audition for a role. Once the group is formed, the performers are the faces of a much larger and more intricate corporate structure.

There were no trainees in Balming Tiger. And no auditions—think more "Wanna join?" conversations at waffle houses and barbecue joints. Nor are all of Balming Tiger's members performers—their 11 members include producers, photographers, music video directors, A&R managers and DJs. Some faces are more familiar, like those who sing, rap and dance in the music videos (usually Omega Sapien, bj wnjn, Mudd the Student and Sogumm, with cameos by others), but behind the scenes, everything is more collaborative and collective.

Balming Tiger can be seen as less a band with a signature sound than a creative universe, a rainforest of different species colliding and coexisting with each other. From their critically acclaimed debut mixtape, *Homie304*, to their first studio album in 2023, *January Never Dies*, to the 2026

Words
Haeryun Kang
Photos
Nikolai Ahn

Stylist: Hwayoung Kim. Hair & Makeup: Mahito Ohtani.

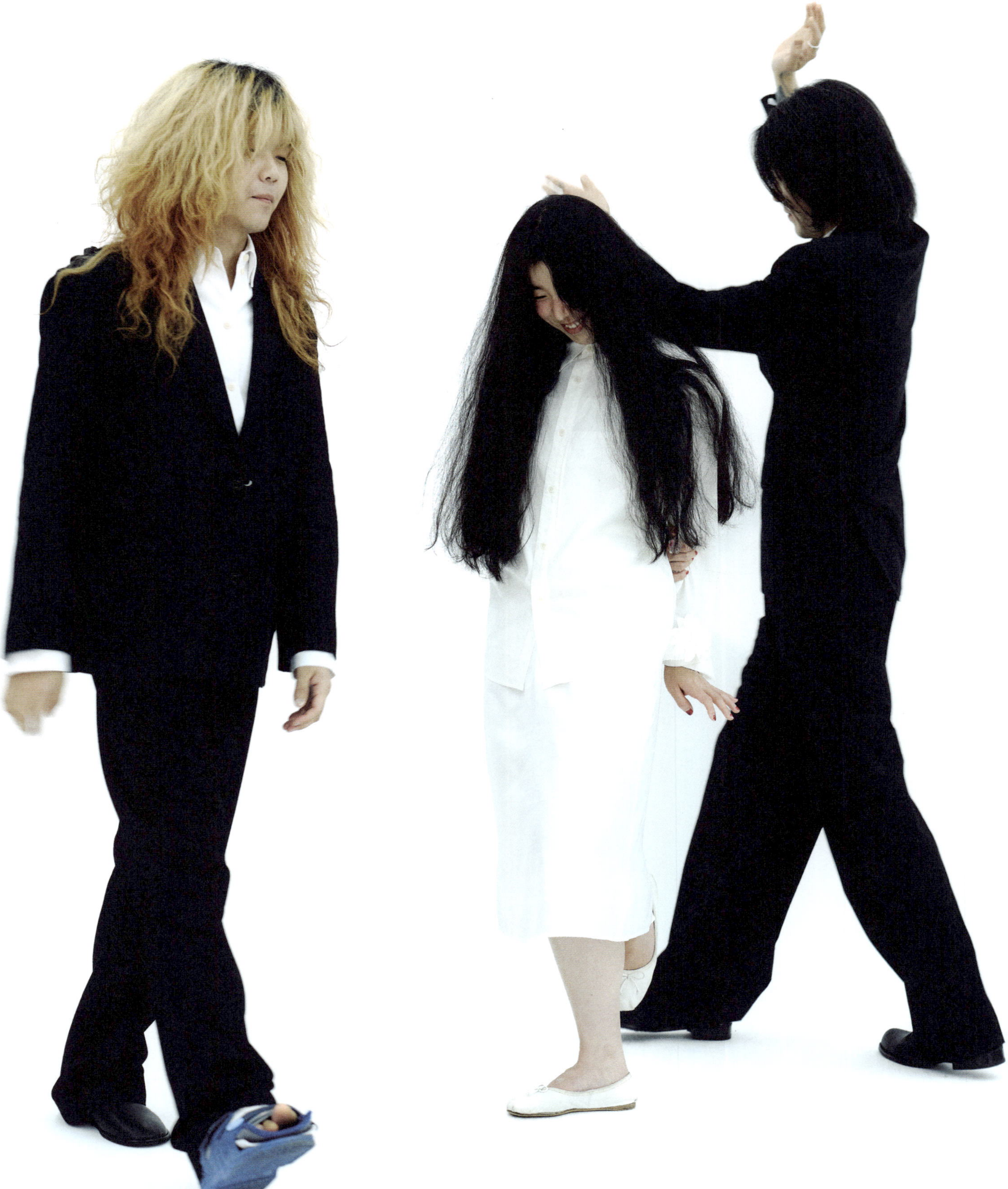

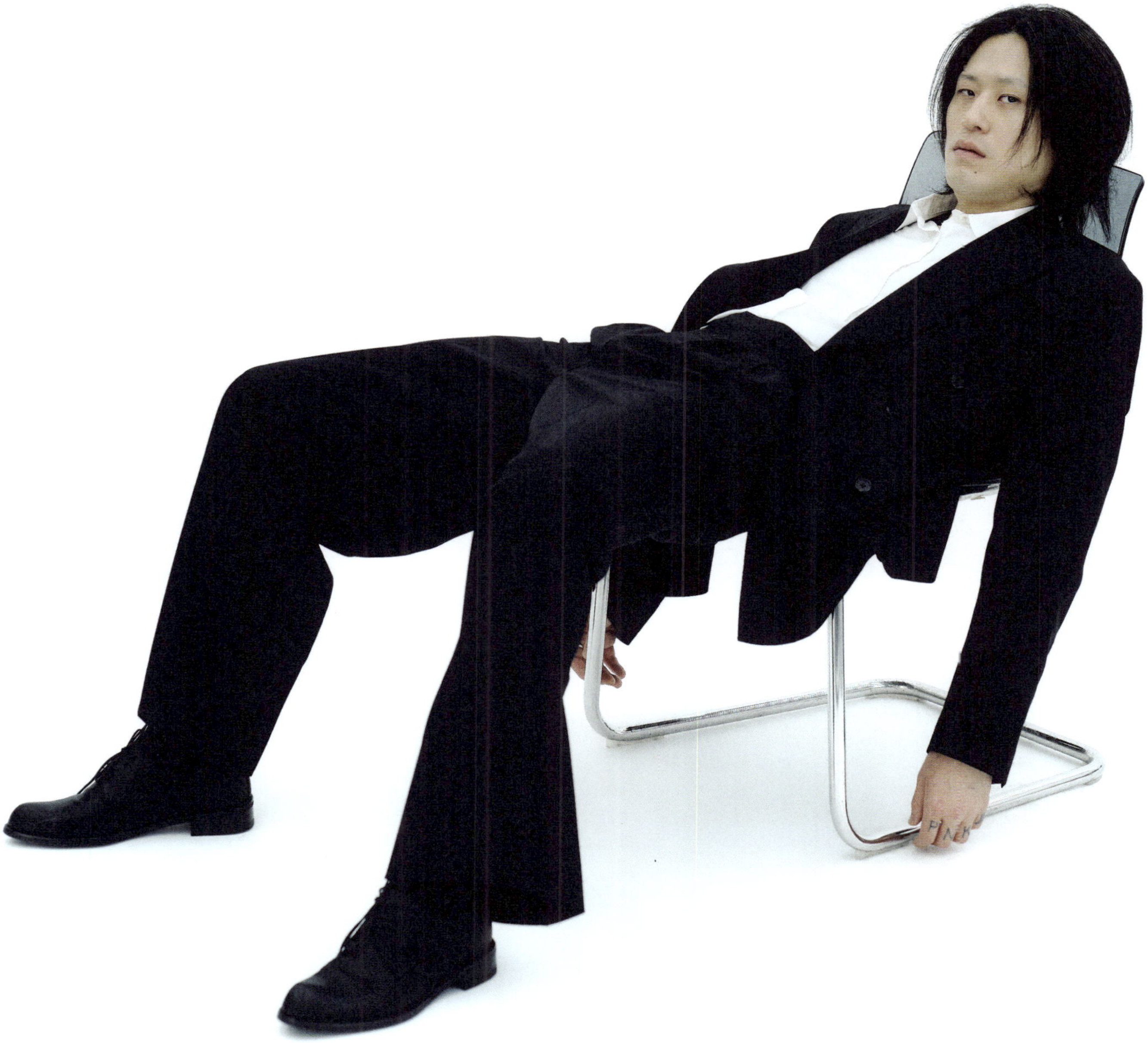

album, *Gongbu*, Balming Tiger's music defies classification—as does their creative direction. Their videos embrace Hong Kong noir ("SOS"), a '90s boy band parody ("Big Butt"), and the industrial-era alleyways of the Euljiro neighborhood in Seoul ("Sexy Nukim," featuring BTS member RM). Their sounds traverse old Korean pop, EDM, psychedelic rock and—of course—hip-hop, many of the members' first love and forays into music.

The origins of Balming Tiger can be traced to Itaewon, one of the most culturally diverse neighborhoods in Seoul. It's a place where the city's only mosque towers over a hill, next to mom-and-pop stores and cockroach-filled villas, the US military base and ritzy alleyways that are home to the Samsung family and BTS members.

"Balming Tiger is basically a meeting of people that are full of holes," San Yawn once said on the Korean talk show *Moneygraphy*. These "holes"—loneliness, for instance, and the desire to fill them through music and art—were what brought together this cacophonous collective through a random series of events starting in 2017, when San Yawn began looking for a crew.

They met at Trans 201, a house on the second floor of a run-down villa on Transgender Hill, as the area is popularly called. The members started connecting in various ways: through friends of friends, an Instagram message, a chance listening to a future member's SoundCloud account. "Trans 201 was Omega Sapien and bj wnjn's house," recalls Mudd the Student. "The space was very damp and full of dark energy."

"After a heavy rain, the ceiling in my room was bulging with water, like a giant pimple," Omega Sapien adds. "We had horrible mold problems. bj wnjn and I split the rent, which was like 600,000 won [approximately $400], and I didn't even have that money, so my older sister helped pay half of my 300,000. It really was an awful time."

"Not for me," says bj wnjn, a vocalist, singer-songwriter and producer. "That space is one of the most memorable moments of my youth. Even with the cockroaches and all that noise from the clubs outside, there was a joy particular to that time."

Memories like this are specific to Balming Tiger, to Seoul, and permeate their art in ways that can't be manufactured. The evolving members remain consistently curious about their own experiences and the world around them. There have been some member changes over the years, including the exit of Byung Un, a beloved front man in the early years. But the joy—and the DNA—from that early, formative period is still alive, holding everyone together 10 years later. "There's a childlike attitude that we never lost as a group," Sogumm, a singer-songwriter and vocalist, says in an email. "A simplicity that feels honest."

Often, Balming Tiger's childlike experiments feel much deeper than mere fun and play, resonating like a sharp resistance against the norms imposed by others. Sometimes this critique feels particularly Korean—like in the 2023 music video of "Kamehameha," where exhausted office workers are forced to drink with their superiors at a *hoesik*, an after-work company gathering notorious for heavy alcohol consumption. And at other times it feels fantastically delocalized, like in "UP!" where a cashier at a mega supermarket climbs up the mountain of objects he must clear, reaching for the sky.

"It's different for me," says Omega Sapien, who grew up in Korea, China, Japan and the US. "I'm not trying to be rebellious. But I do like provoking a sense of discomfort in others. I like creating differences of opinion through what we do."

"I'm less interested in making others uncomfortable than in creating a sense of wonder," says Mudd the Student, who is from Busan, down south. "I love art that makes me feel things for the first time. I suppose that can sometimes make people uncomfortable."

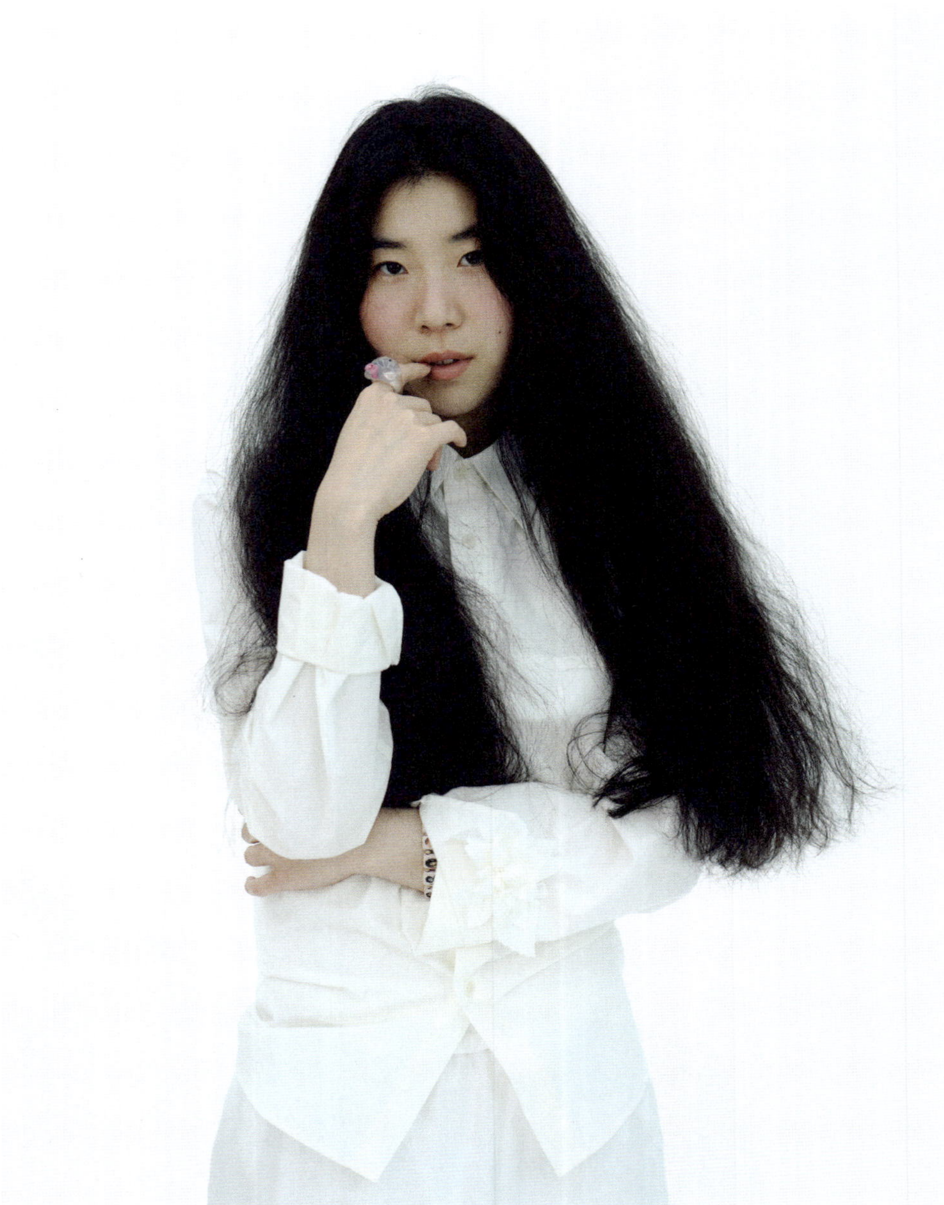

(above)
Sogumm wears a shirt by AMOMENTO and a skirt by MEMORY.NYC.

(opposite)
Omega Sapien (left) wears a jacket by POST ARCHIVE FACTION, the stylist's own T-shirt, trousers by COMMISSION and shoes by ATHOCE. Leesuho (right) wears a shirt by JACQUEMUS, trousers by COS and shoes by POST ARCHIVE FACTION.

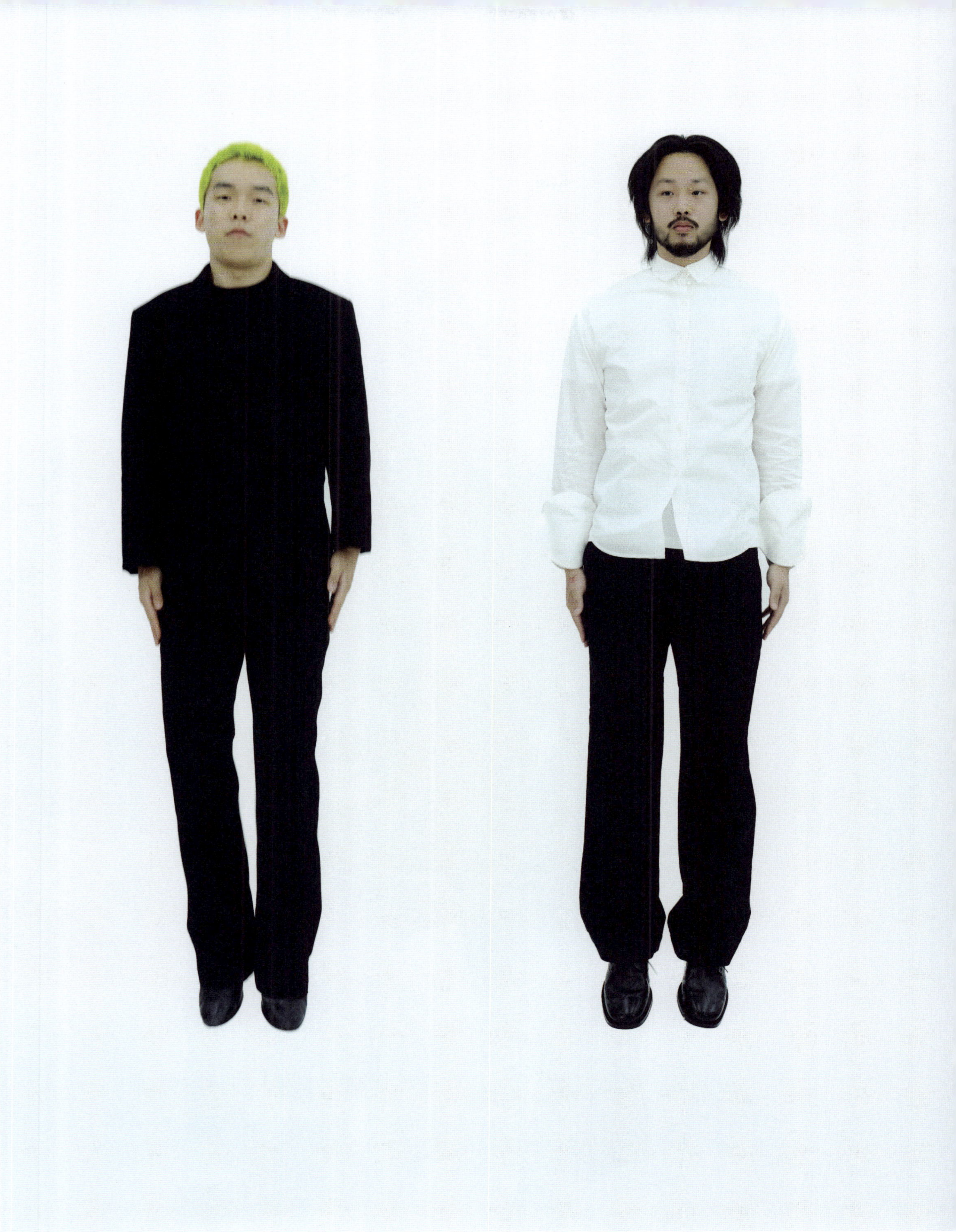

"We have our own thing: We're Balming Tiger,
young people living in South Korea, exploring our identities.
Doing this is what's Korean, what's true to ourselves."

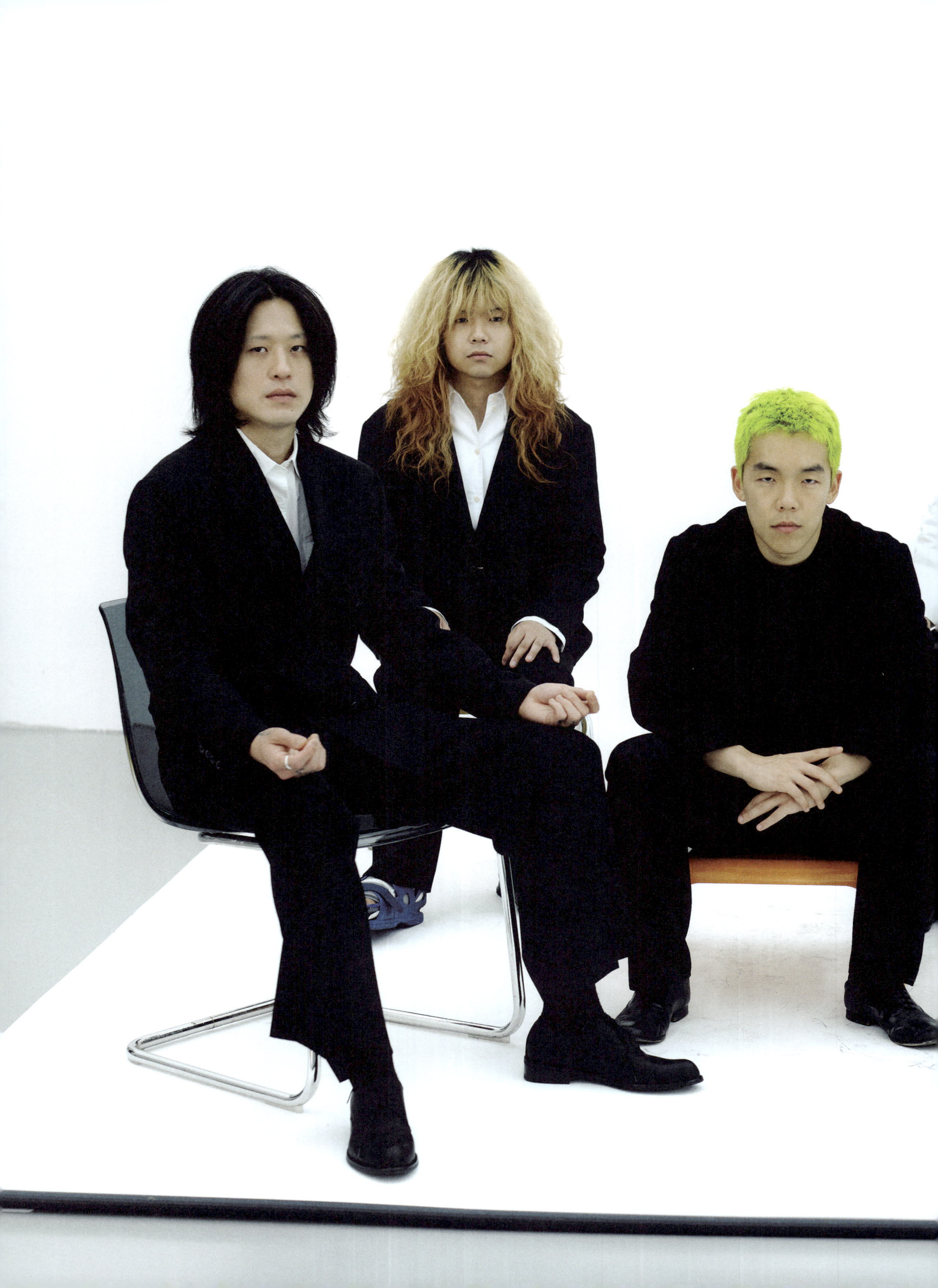

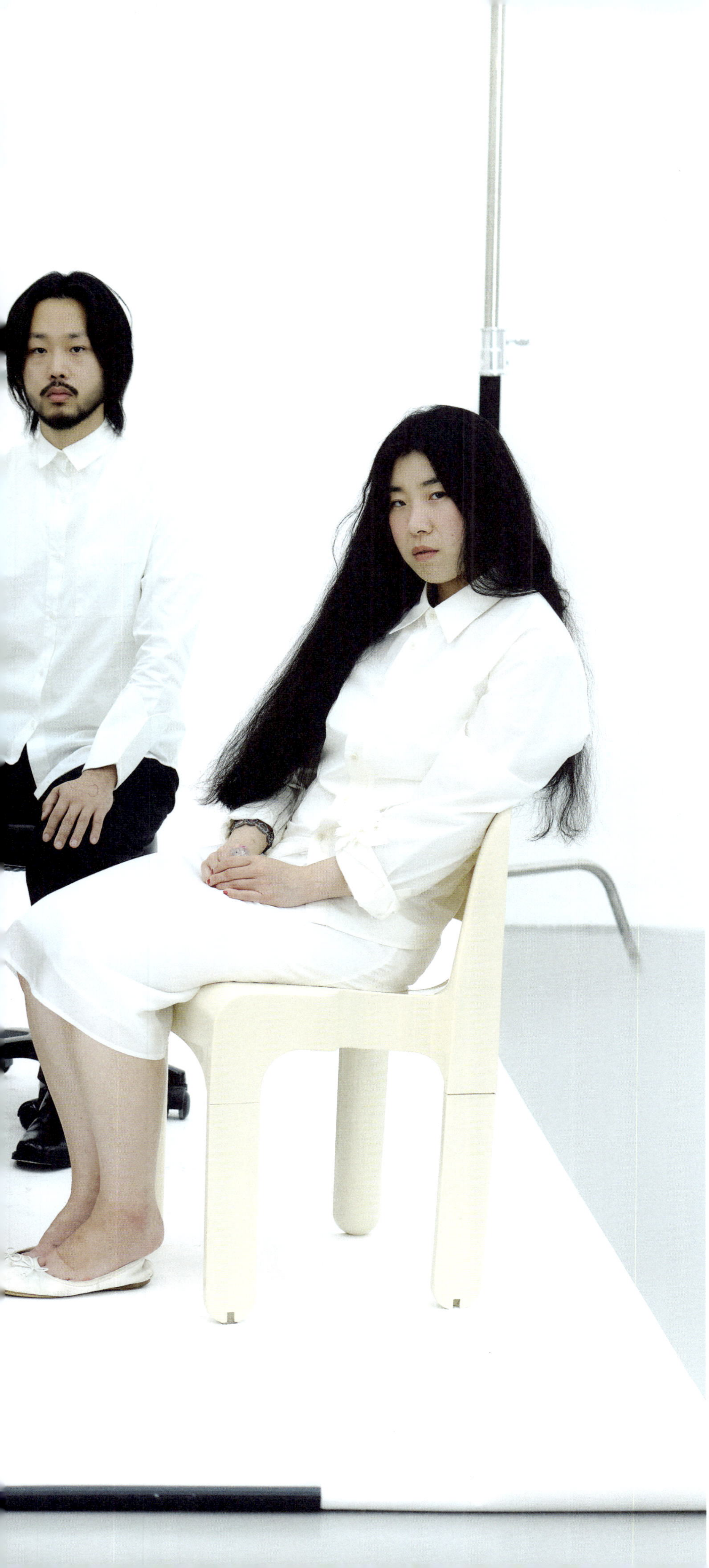

Despite their almost tongue-in-cheek label as alternative K-pop, Balming Tiger is grateful to the K-pop industry for opening doors for other Korean musicians. The group has performed at major music festivals like SXSW in the US, Primavera Sound in Spain and Fuji Rock Festival in Japan. They've collaborated with a dazzling spectrum of artists, including ATARASHII GAKKO!, a Japanese girl group; contemporary Korean artist Lee Bul; Thai filmmaker Apichatpong Weerasethakul; and of course, RM from BTS, whose featured music video "Sexy Nukim" is Balming Tiger's most viewed at 20 million.

"People often think of idols as these puppets, who only do what they're told," says Omega Sapien. "But creative languages within the idol industry are changing too. I really love groups like CORTIS. I think their work is raw and fantastic."

"I'm really interested in girl groups," says Unsinkable, a producer and DJ. "These days we see groups that are more like crews, with more creative independence from their company. I sometimes wonder if new idol acts are inspired by what we do."

In *Gongbu*, Balming Tiger explores themes of Korean and Asian identity. The single "Home" is absurdist and nostalgic, evoking Korean folk music while mixing synthesizers, rap and ritualistic chants. The music video is black and white, reminiscent of a Park Chan-wook film or a Lee Gap-chul photo. It's inspired by the architecture of Kim Chung-up and the traditional marriage ritual *hamjinabi*.

"What does it mean to be Korean? To be Asian? When we were younger, we looked up to American hip-hop," says Omega Sapien. "I wanted to be like J. Cole. But now I see that that's his thing. We have our own thing: We're Balming Tiger, young people living in South Korea, exploring our identities. Doing this is what's Korean, what's true to ourselves."

(opposite)
Left to Right: bj wnjn wears the stylist's own jacket and shirt, trousers by MAISON MARGIELA and shoes by YUJI. Mudd the Student wears a jacket and shirt by YUJI and trousers by PRADA. Omega Sapien wears a jacket by POST ARCHIVE FACTION, the stylist's own T-shirt, trousers by COMMISSION and shoes by ATHOCE. Leesuho wears a shirt by JACQUEMUS, trousers by COS and shoes by POST ARCHIVE FACTION. Sogumm wears a shirt by AMOMENTO, a skirt by MEMORY.NYC and shoes by MIU MIU.

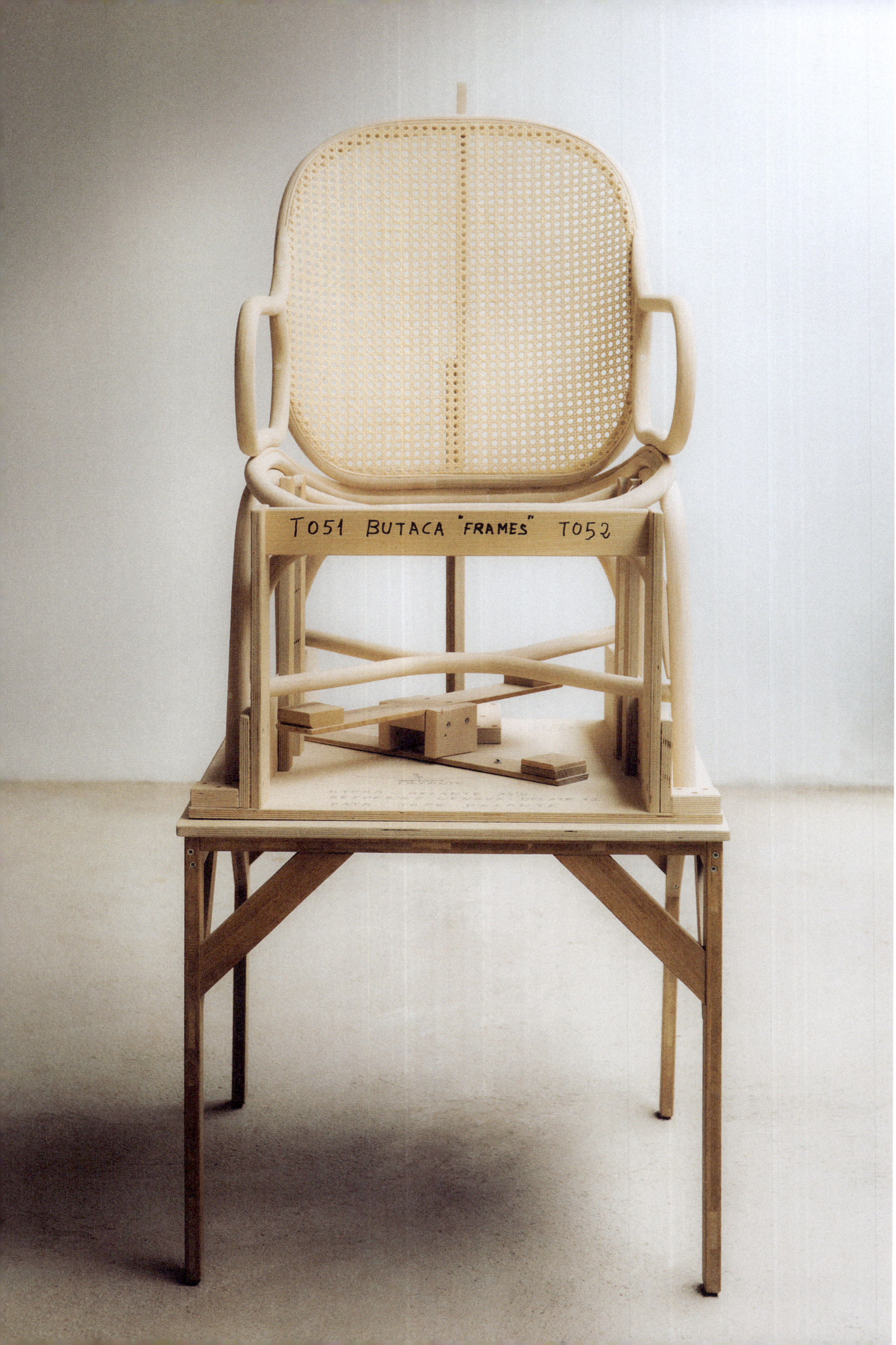
T051 BUTACA "FRAMES" T052

INTERPLAY: Inside the Spanish furniture company preserving the art of rattan.

Words
Agnish Ray
Photos
Silvia Conde Oliván

"There's a before and an after," says Paco Melió, comparing a freshly sanded stick of rattan, smooth and pale brown, with a raw, unworked equivalent. The seasoned craftsman is in the furniture factory where he's worked for over 50 years, and where his mother worked before him, making the wicker baskets once widely used in this rural corner of southeast Spain. Now 67, Melió is delaying retirement as long as he can: The factory feels too much like home.

The factory in question belongs to Expormim—a familiar name here in Moixent, a town an hour's drive inland from the coastal city of Valencia. Founded in 1960, the company started out by using wicker to produce baskets, trays, bread bins, wine holders, room dividers and decorative items. In the 1970s, they switched to rattan, a vine-like palm species native to tropical climates. Its firm, resistant quality lends itself to sturdier structures required for furniture design, which is now the company's mainstay.

"Originally, rattan was used with the skin," says Melió, explaining how Expormim has refined its approach to working with the material over time. "Now, all the rattan in this factory is calibrated and peeled." He shows where the long sticks of the peeled bark are stacked upright by the hundreds; the bunches are organized according to diameter, as well as their natural hue, which determines what color they can be painted.

Expormim thrived through the 1980s and '90s, expanding its technical and industrial capacities and producing straightforward, good-quality household furniture with wide appeal. At the turn of the century, however, cheap imports and e-commerce challenged the company's business model. Expormim had to decide between targeting the middle- and high-end markets, and design collaborations have helped them pivot toward the latter. The Fontal chair, designed by Oscar Tusquets in 2012, for instance, celebrates rattan's flexibility through components molded into curved, continuous shapes and woven seamlessly together; small details in the finish elevate the chair into something refined and elegant.

Today, external designers make up around 90% of Expormim's catalog, from the late Miguel Milá—among the first independent designers to create signature pieces for Expormim—to Norm Architects, whose Brae outdoor sofas have a gently curved shape, and Roberto Lazzeroni, who has used sapele wood in the frames of the recently released Meridies sofas. New for 2026, Javier Pastor's Leku collection of tables and chairs was inspired by Basque sculptor Eduardo Chillida.

Celebrated Valencia-based designer Jaime Hayon, who designed the Frames collection in 2014, was drawn by Expormim's expertise in rattan. The five chairs in the collection feature peeled, tinted rattan frames with upholstered seats and backs made of latticed octagonal wicker; a footstool, a room divider and two coffee tables complete the collection. "Rattan feels human and flexible," explains Hayon, who won Spain's national design award in 2021. "It allows fluid, lightweight shapes. It also conveys optimism and approachability—something that rigid materials rarely achieve."

While Hayon's studio is known for explosive color combinations, whimsical shapes and vivid imagery, he channeled Expormim's more muted style with Frames. "It was important to respect their craftsmanship and historic relationship with rattan, which naturally guided the collection toward a more essential and refined expression," he explains. "Although Frames is more restrained than some of my other works, it still reflects my design language: sculptural lines, organic curves, playful proportions."

Expormim was in a unique position to realize Hayon's designs—which he compares to "drawing lines in space; graphic, but warm and approachable"—with the necessary care and attention. The company is the last in Europe still producing rattan furniture by hand, with around 50 craftspeople working in teams dedicated to tasks including cutting, molding, assembly, upholstery and painting. Amidst the immediacy of mass-produced, fast-moving, machine-made goods, Expormim's artisans champion slow, considered making.

There is one notable exception at the factory, however: the 5-axis CNC, a machine that transformed many operations around a decade ago. It punctures holes and carves grooves into the various components—whether in rattan, wood or metal—that make up each piece. Melió's son-in-law, Moisés Miralles, is stationed here. Together, the two craftsmen represent the exchange of skills and knowledge across generations at Expormim.

This intergenerational community of craftspeople forms Expormim's heart and soul, mirroring the company's ownership, which has remained with the same family since its founding. "There are people here who have worked with my grandfather, with my father and with me," reflects Mercedes Laso, the CEO, who is actively nurturing the region's next generation of makers to secure the company's future. "We're collaborating with a vocational training center that teaches upholstery and carpentry, exploring workshops and other ways for students to better understand what it means to work at a company like ours," she explains. "It's a way of encouraging people to see Expormim as a place where they can do their very best work." Only through these learned, patient hands can the company continue to mediate between the industrial and the artisanal—and flourish.

This story was produced in partnership with Expormim. | expormim.com

(below, left)
Designer Jaime Hayon, photographed at his Valencia studio.

(opposite)
Components of the Frames low-back armchair before assembly.

"Rattan feels human and flexible. It conveys optimism and approachability."

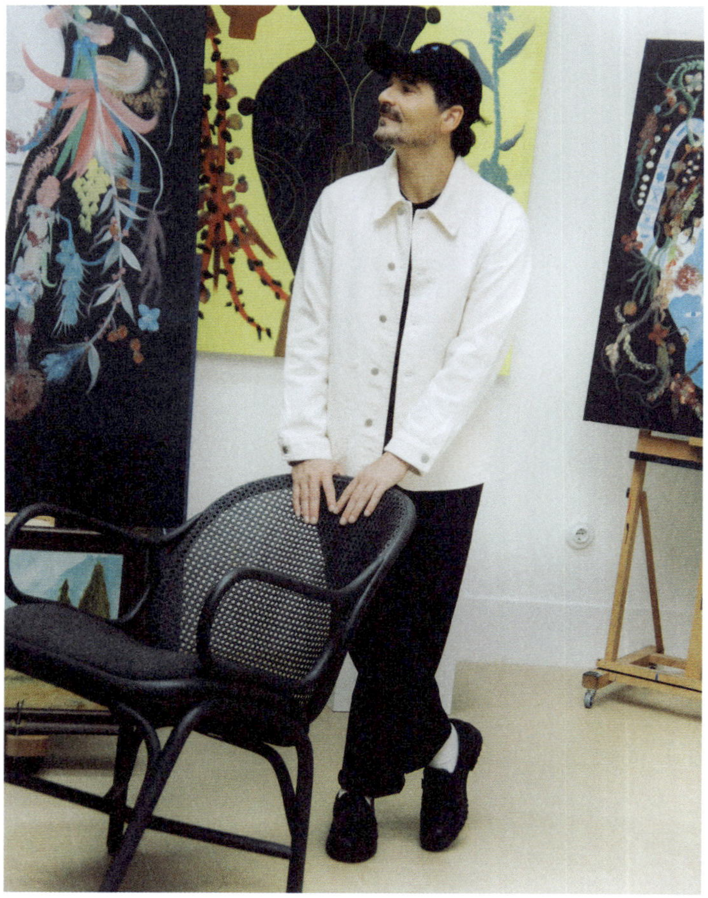

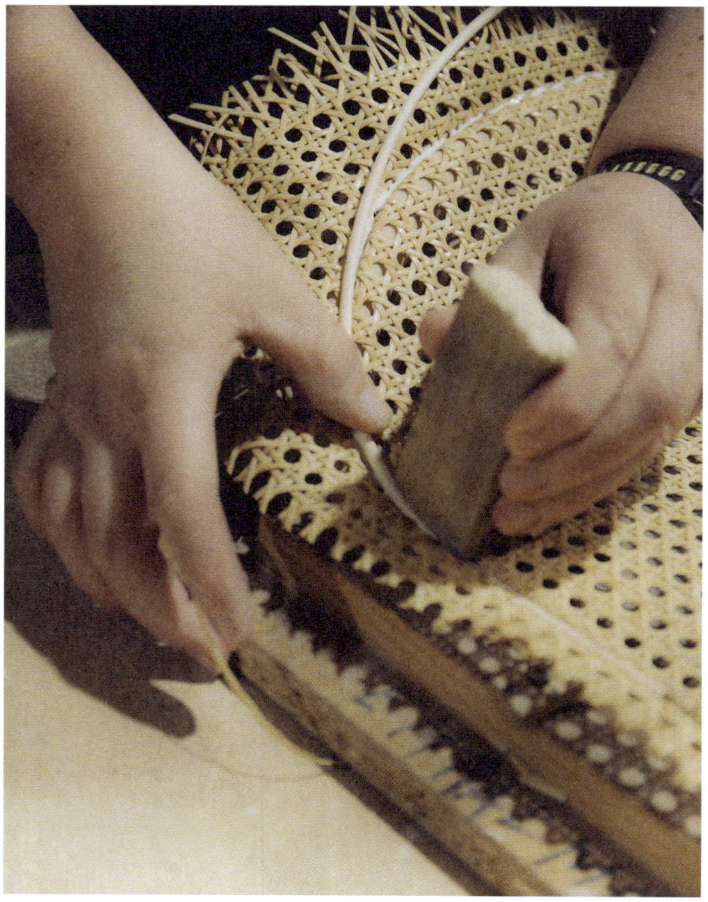

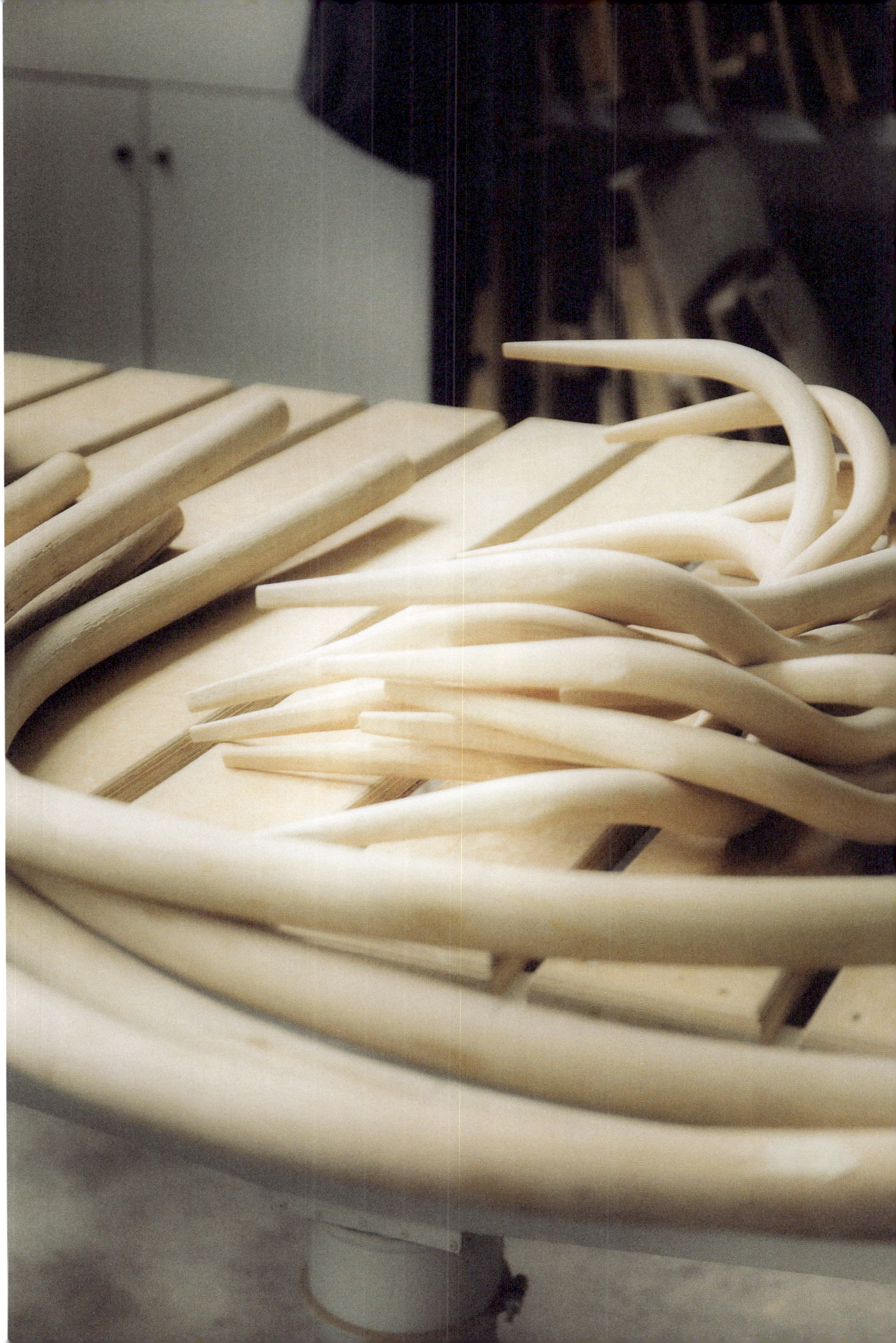

RICE

One staple, five ways to rethink it.

IS

Recipes SANDY HO & Photos AARON BERNSTEIN

NICE

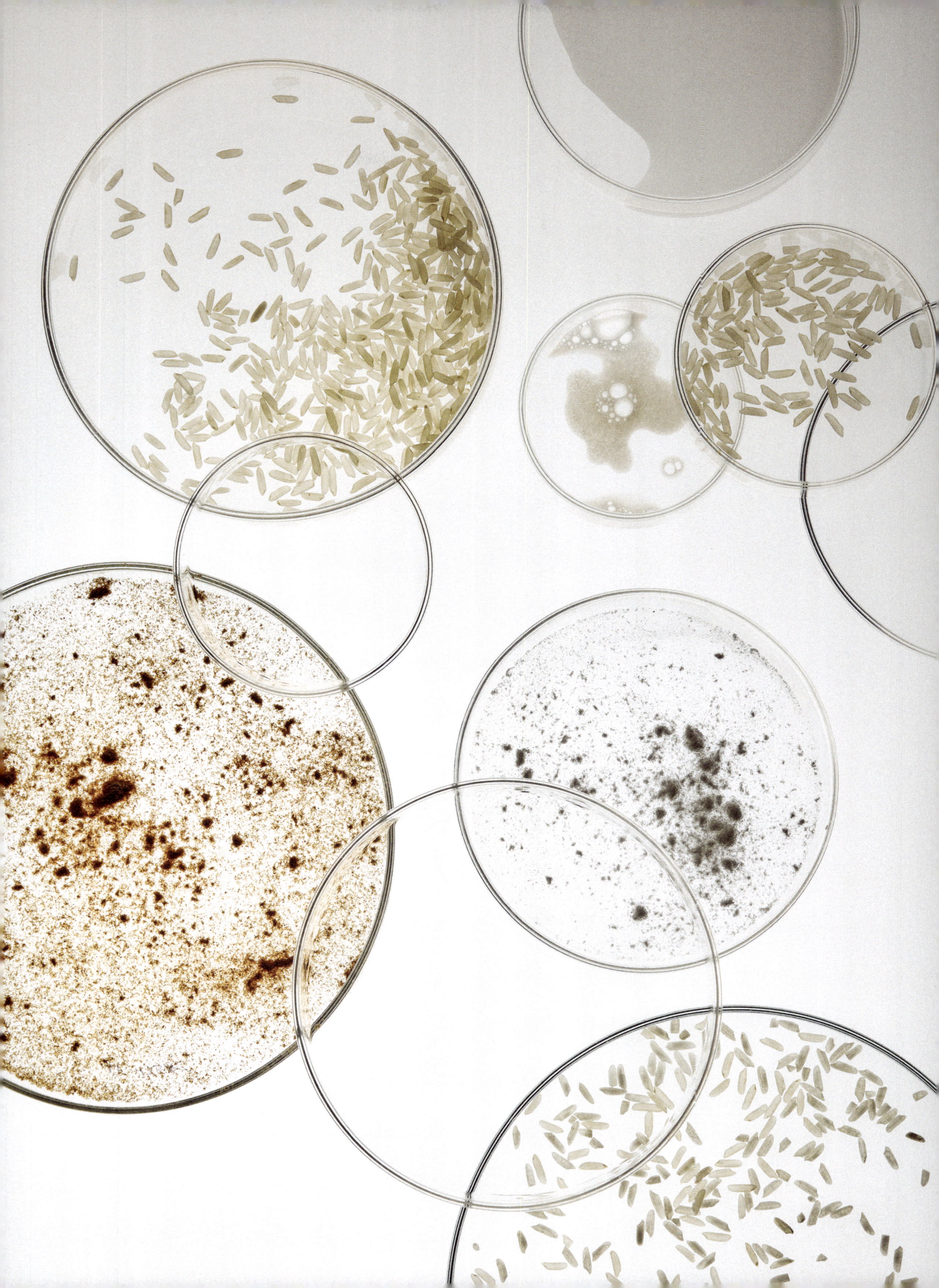

STICKY RICE & MANGO COCKTAIL

MAKES 2

½ cup (100g) jasmine or sushi rice, washed
1 cup (240ml) full-fat coconut milk
1½ ounces (45ml) aged rum or cognac
2 tablespoons (30ml) organic mango purée
2 teaspoons (10ml) fresh lime juice
Pinch of salt
Fresh ripe mango slices dipped in ground toasted sesame seeds, for serving

INSTRUCTIONS

Combine the washed rice with the coconut milk in a small saucepan and bring to a light simmer over medium heat. Remove from heat and steep for 20 minutes. Strain out and discard the rice solids.

To a shaker with ice, add 3 tablespoons (45ml) of the strained coconut milk mixture, the rum, mango purée, lime juice and salt. Shake vigorously until chilled, then strain into rocks glasses over fresh ice cubes (or crushed ice, if preferred). Garnish each with a slice of mango dipped in ground toasted sesame seeds.

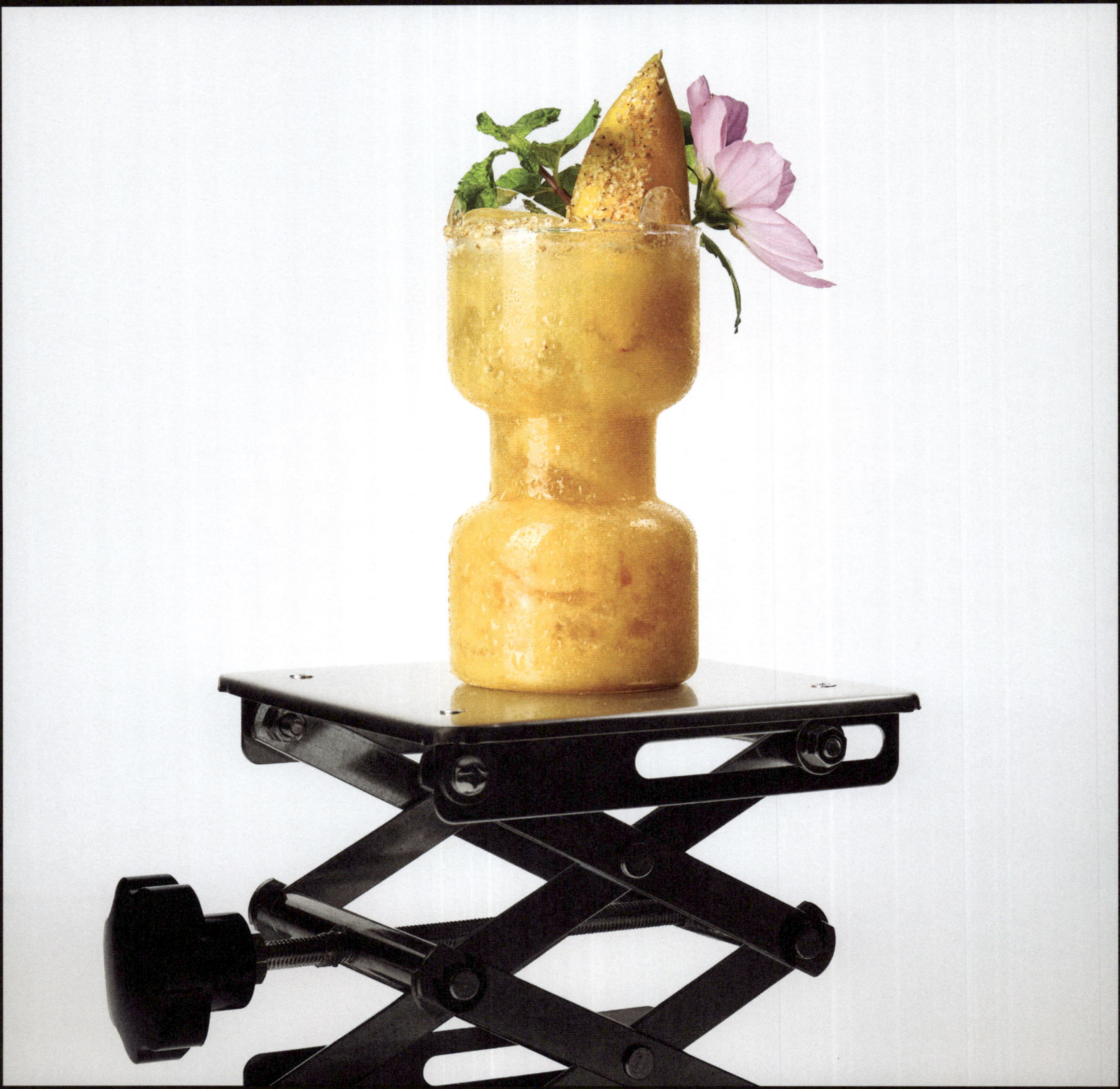

Food Stylist: Judy Kim. Props & Set Design: Tim Ferro.

NAM PLA OYSTERS SERVED WITH RICE MILK GRANITA

SERVES 4

1 cup (190g) long-grain white rice
4 cups (1L) filtered water
3 tablespoons (38g) granulated sugar
½ teaspoon (2g) salt
3 tablespoons (44ml) fish sauce
¼ cup (60ml) fresh lime juice
1 teaspoon (5g) brown sugar
1 garlic clove, finely minced
6 fresh Thai chiles, thinly sliced (use more chiles if you prefer more heat and fewer if not)
1 dozen freshly shucked oysters (sweet oysters like Kumamotos are best)
Fresh cilantro and mint leaves
Toasted rice powder

INSTRUCTIONS

Rinse the rice until the water runs clear. Place the rice and filtered water in a bowl. Let it soak for at least 8 hours or overnight at room temperature.

Add the soaked rice and water to a high-speed blender and blend on high for 3 minutes. Pour the blended mixture through a fine-mesh sieve lined with cheesecloth into a shallow baking dish, then whisk in the granulated sugar and salt to dissolve.

Place the dish on a stable shelf in the freezer. Use a fork to scrape the frozen edges into the center every 30 to 40 minutes. Repeat this for 2 to 4 hours until the mixture is completely frozen into small ice shards.

For the nam pla, in a small bowl, whisk together the fish sauce, lime juice, brown sugar, garlic and chiles until the sugar dissolves. To assemble, place the oysters over crushed ice on a serving platter. Add 1 teaspoon (5ml) of the nam pla to each oyster and, using a small 1-teaspoon scoop, scoop the granita on top of each oyster. Garnish with fresh cilantro, mint and a sprinkling of toasted rice powder. Serve cold and immediately!

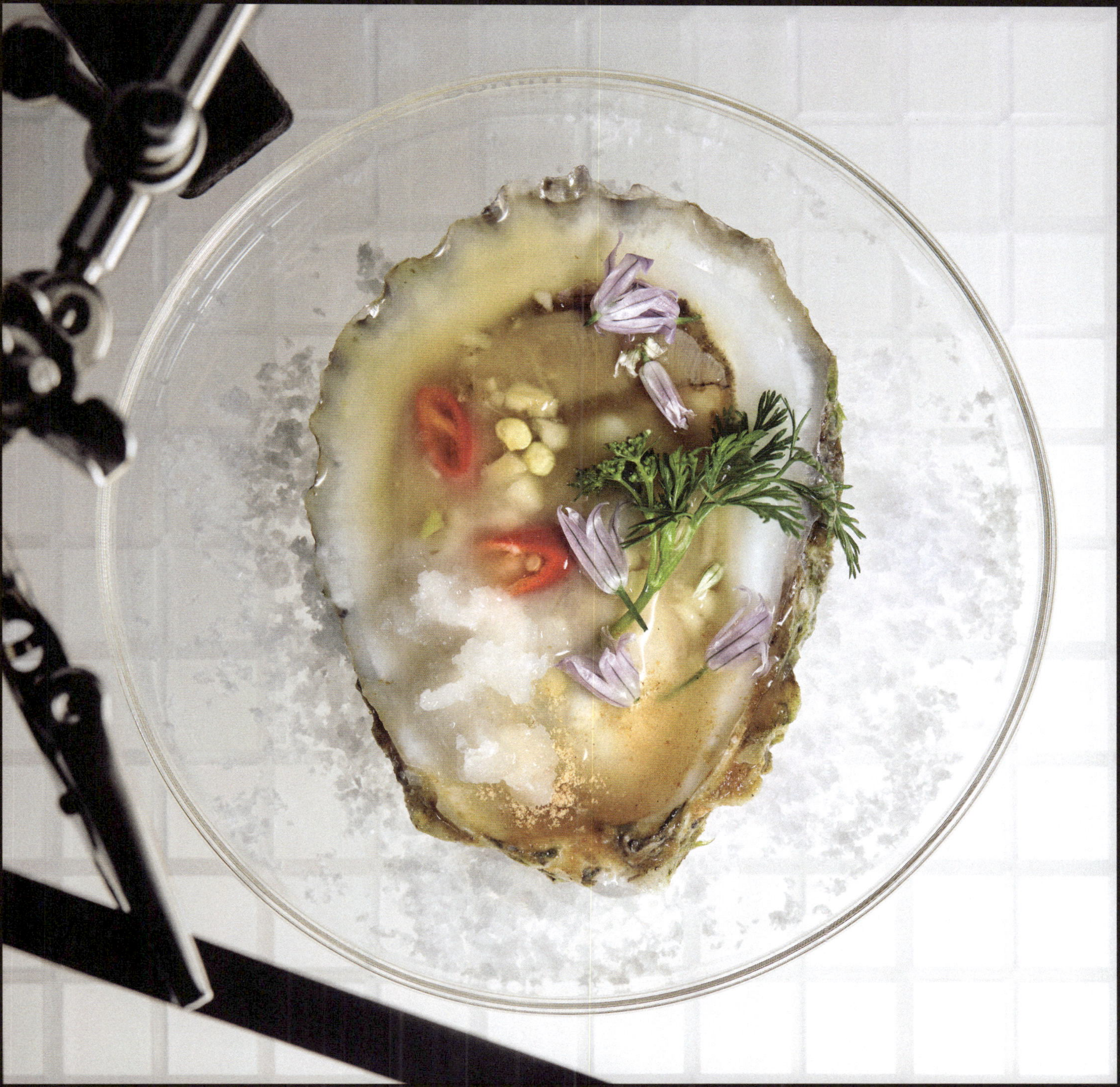

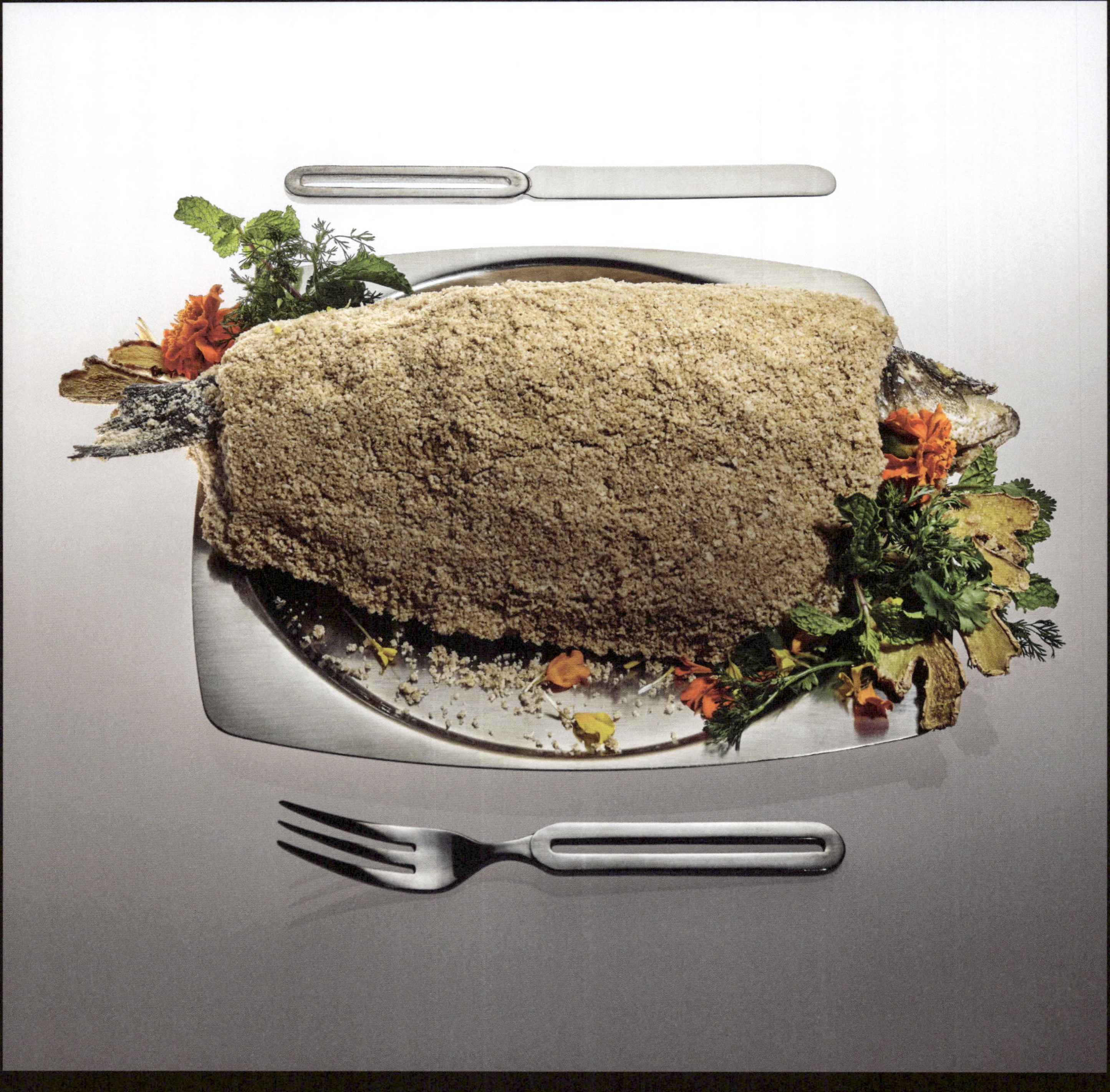

CRISPY RICE SALAD

SERVES 4

—

FOR THE CRISPY RICE:
Neutral oil, for frying
3 cups cold cooked jasmine rice
2 tablespoons (35g) red curry paste (a store-bought one works just as well as homemade)
1 large egg
½ cup shredded unsweetened coconut

FOR THE DRESSING:
1 medium shallot, peeled and thinly sliced
2 makrut lime leaves, hard stems removed and very finely sliced
4 Thai chiles, thinly sliced
3 tablespoons (55ml) fish sauce
1½ tablespoons (22ml) water
¼ cup (60ml) fresh lime juice
1½ tablespoons (20g) brown sugar
½ teaspoon (2g) salt

FOR THE LAMB:
1 tablespoon (15ml) neutral oil
10 ounces (300g) ground lamb (80/20 fat)
2 cloves garlic, finely minced
1 teaspoon (5g) salt
1 teaspoon (2g) paprika
1 teaspoon (2g) cracked black pepper

FOR ASSEMBLY:
1 cup (55g) fresh herbs (Thai basil, cilantro, mint, sawtooth coriander)
¼ cup (40g) crushed roasted peanuts

INSTRUCTIONS

To make the crispy rice: Fill a large, heavy-bottomed pot halfway with neutral oil and heat to 350°F (177°C). In a large mixing bowl, mix together the rice, red curry paste, egg and coconut. Pack and form the mixture into balls the size of a tennis ball. Fry the balls in batches for 3 to 5 minutes until golden and crispy, then carefully remove with a slotted spoon onto a paper towel–lined sheet tray and leave to cool. Crumble the balls into bite-sized pieces once cooled.

To prepare the dressing: In a small mixing bowl, mix together the shallot, lime leaves, chiles, fish sauce, water, lime juice, brown sugar and salt. Set aside.

To make the lamb: In a sauté pan over medium heat, warm the tablespoon of oil until it begins to shimmer. Add the ground lamb and garlic and sauté for 3 minutes, breaking up the lamb as it cooks. Stir in the salt, paprika and black pepper and continue cooking until the lamb is golden brown and cooked through (about 3 to 5 minutes). Keep warm until ready to assemble.

To assemble: In a large mixing bowl, toss together 1½ cups (220g) of the crumbled crispy rice, the dressing and the warm lamb. Fold in the fresh herbs and peanuts. Serve with fresh lettuce cups and cucumber slices.

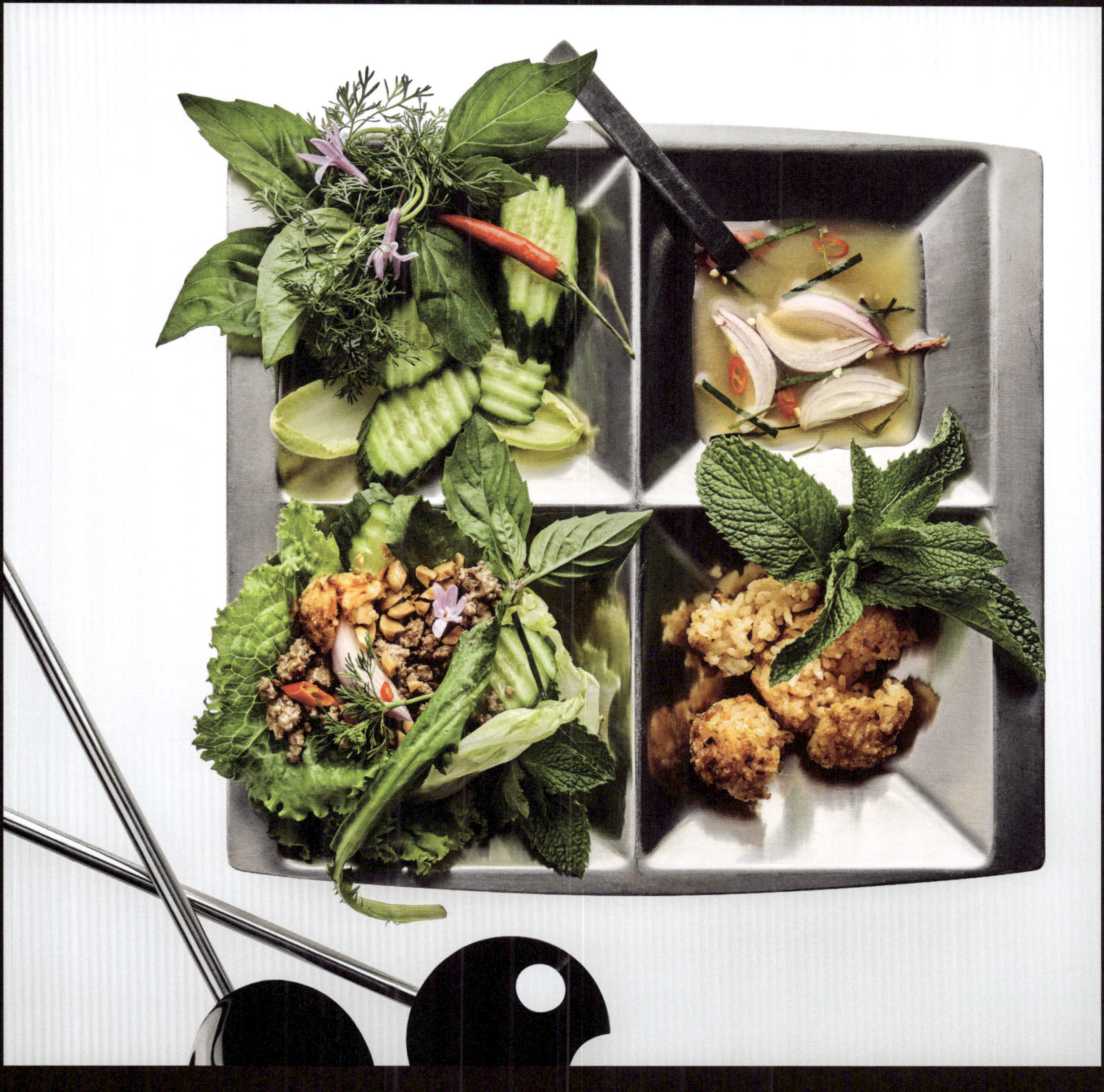

CARDAMOM AND VANILLA RICE CUSTARD BRÛLÉE

SERVES 4

2 large egg yolks
¾ teaspoon (3g) salt
⅓ cup (67g) granulated sugar
½ cup (100g) arborio rice
1 cup (236ml) heavy cream
3 cups (710ml) whole milk
1 teaspoon (2g) ground cardamom
1 vanilla bean, split, with seeds scraped and reserved
1 cup (192g) turbinado or raw sugar

INSTRUCTIONS

In a small bowl, whisk together the egg yolks, salt and granulated sugar. Set aside.

Set a medium-sized saucepan over medium-high heat and add the rice, cream, milk, cardamom, and vanilla pod and seeds. Bring to a boil, stirring constantly. Reduce the heat to low and cover. Continue to cook for 15 minutes while stirring occasionally. Uncover and continue cooking for 15 minutes on low until the rice is tender. Turn off the heat, remove the vanilla pod and stir in the egg yolk mixture, making sure to scrape the sides of the pan to fully incorporate.

Divide the rice custard between 4 ramekins and preheat the broiler to high. Coat the tops of each ramekin with turbinado sugar, enough to cover the surface completely. Place the sugared ramekins on a baking sheet under the broiler for 3 to 5 minutes and watch carefully to prevent burning! Serve hot.

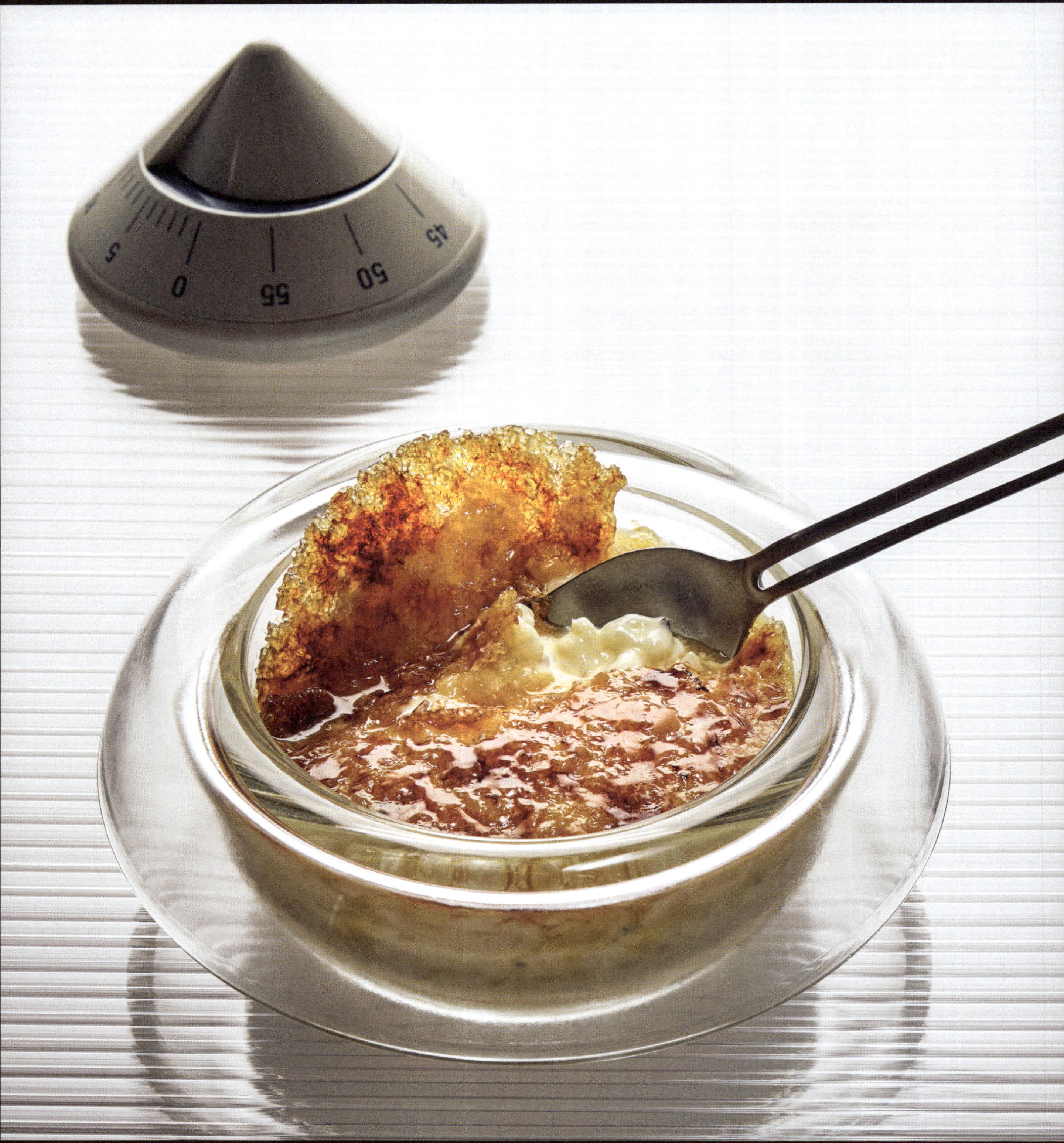

III

Play

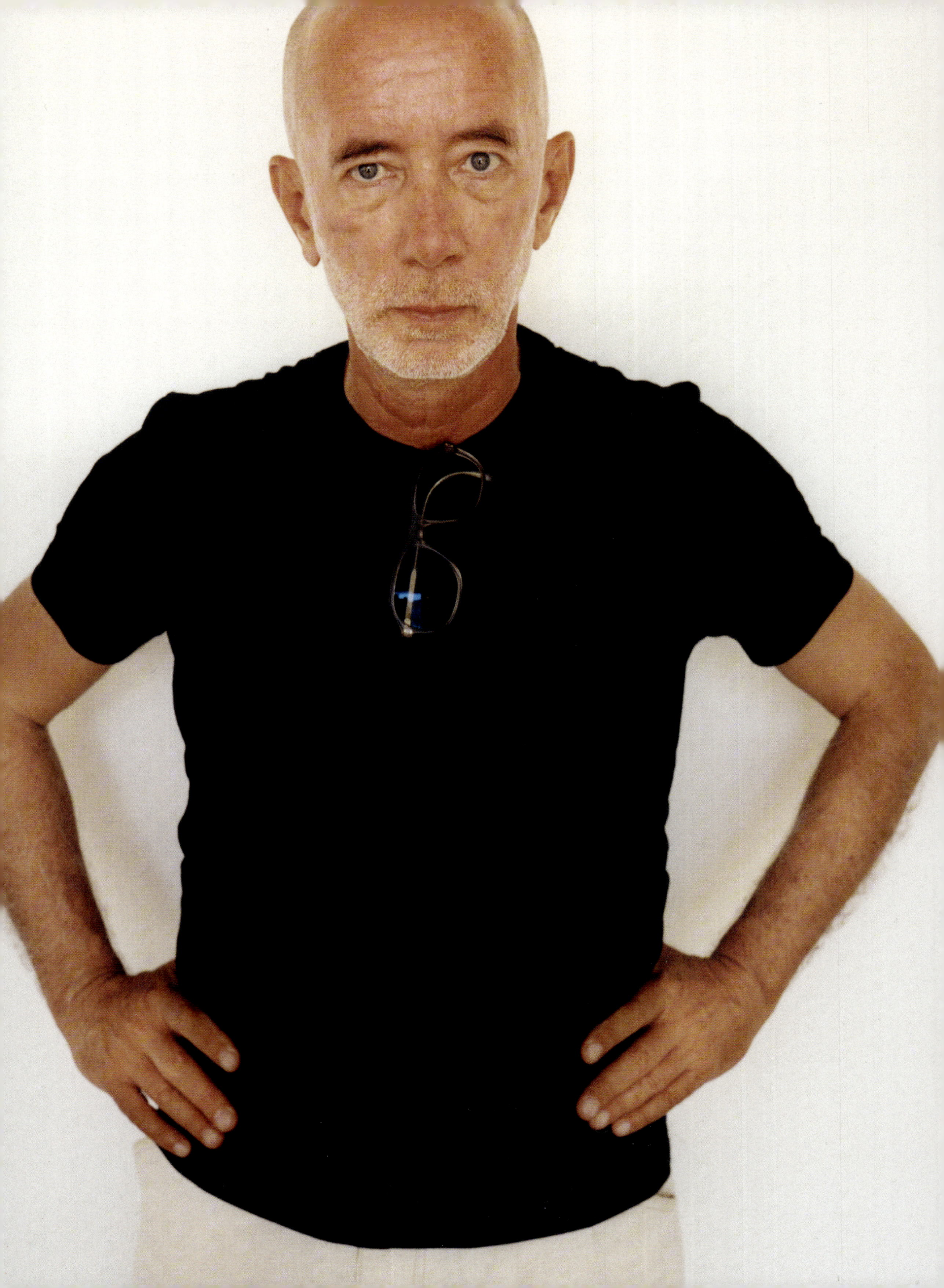

The artist CARSTEN HÖLLER wants to play.

A HELTER-SKELTER

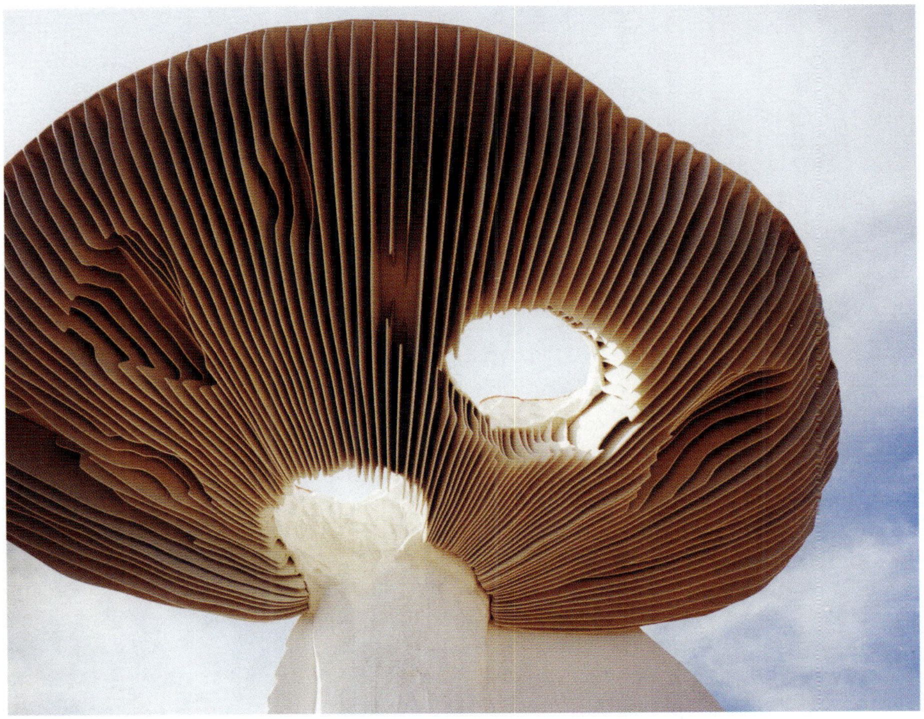

WORLD

Words LAURA RYSMAN Photos EUGENIO INTINI

OPPOSITE:
One of Höller's *Giant Triple Mushrooms* at his home in Tuscany.
The series combines dissected replicas of a fly agaric mushroom spliced with various edible, inedible and poisonous species. For Höller, mushrooms embody uncertainty and ambiguity—organisms that remain deeply mysterious and still largely incomprehensible to science.

"Being an artist is easy—you just need to think of new ways of doing things," says Carsten Höller, as he drinks coffee on the farm he's renovating in Tuscany, the fields of wheat and fruit trees swaying in the breeze.

Höller began his career as a scientist, but once he set his sights on art, his transition was unusually headlong. Cerebral and subversive, he emerged in the 1990s as part of an influential cohort that reimagined art as bodily and interactive experiences, transforming visitors from passive observers into active participants and even making them part of the artwork itself. He soon upended conventions about what belongs in museums, introducing giant slides, amusement park rides, pseudo-experiments, roving beds for museum sleepovers, and other improbable art situations. His aim has always been to prod us into reconsidering our assumptions about the world—to challenge us to think of new ways of doing things, of understanding and imagining things.

Raised in Brussels by German parents, Höller earned a double PhD in entomology and chemical ecology before turning to art. In 1991, while studying insects in College Station, Texas, he spent his weekends visiting installations at art sites like Marfa, where Donald Judd transformed a military base into the setting for his minimalist works on a monumental scale.

"It was a place where it felt as though anything was possible with art—where there were no boundaries," Höller says. "I was becoming frustrated with science and all its false certainties, and I realized there that I wanted to try to make art instead." He explains that we have very little knowledge of ourselves, of consciousness, of all forms of life. "But where science is limited," he says, "art can open new doors of understanding."

Many of Höller's artworks retain a sense of laboratory experiments, designed to derange participants' senses and alter their perceptions. Sliding mirror doors disorient visitors; inversion goggles flip their field of vision; slowed-down carousels—like the hot pink version he installed this winter on the ice rink of the Kulm Hotel in St. Moritz, Switzerland—compel riders to consider their experience of time. He describes them as "fun-producing machines that don't allow you to have fun." They are scientific and yet anti-rational experiments intended to unsettle our frameworks for reality.

He has also installed colossal steel slides too towering and vertiginous for any child, where brave riders hurtle downward before emerging delirious, afraid or discombobulated. Höller's slides have twisted through the Tate Modern in London and pierced the floors at

Producer: Alisa Hirvonen

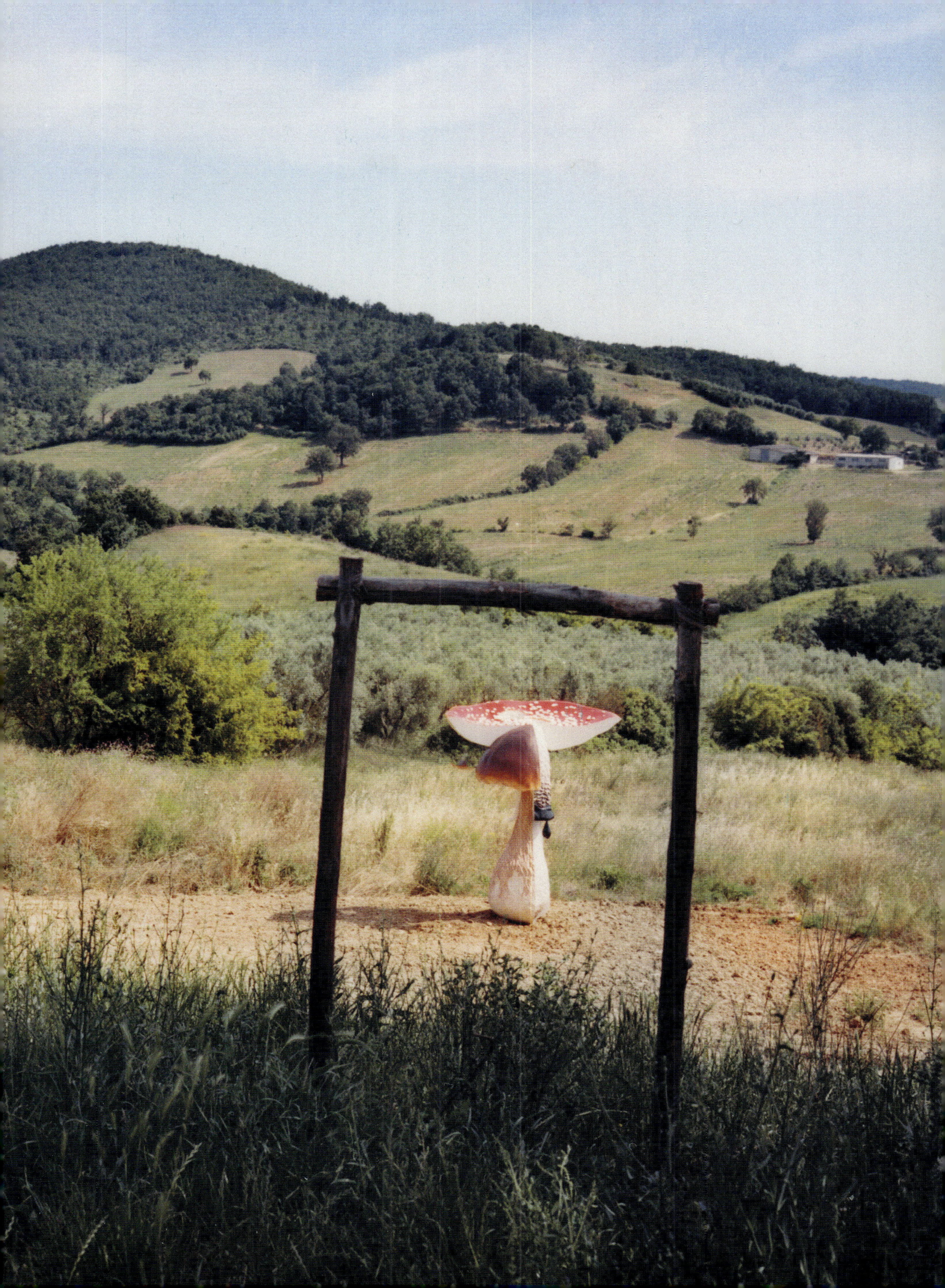

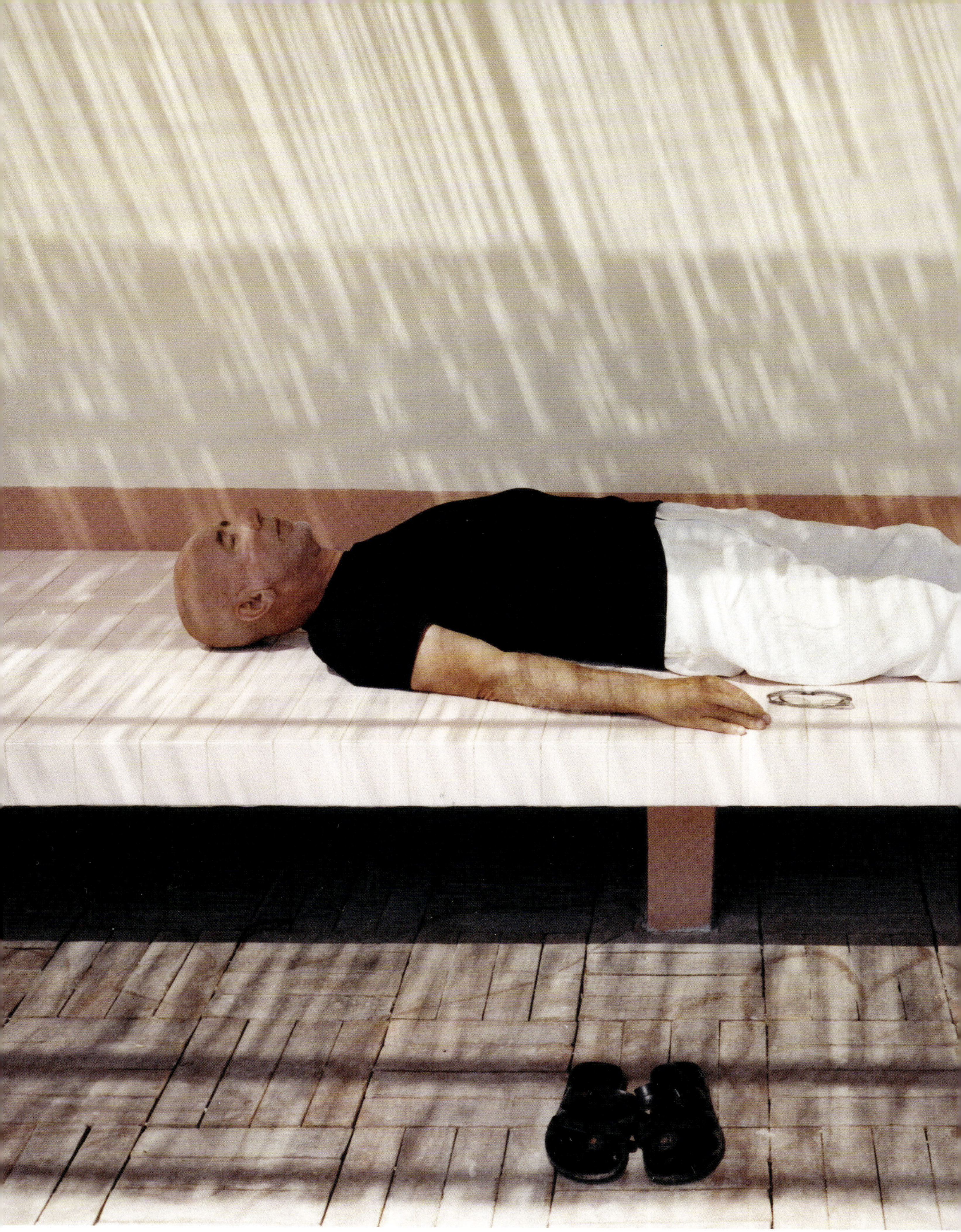

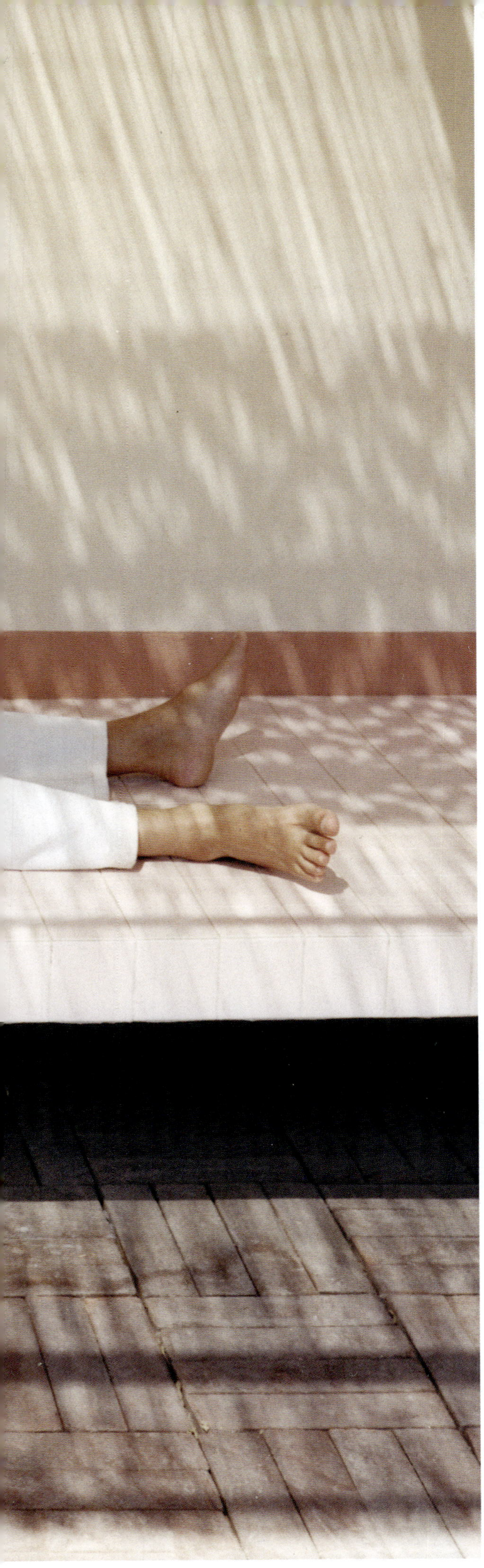

New York's New Museum, and permanently spiral through Frank Gehry's tower at Luma Arles in the south of France. He refers to his creations as "unsaturated art," a term borrowed from the 19th-century logician Gottlob Frege. "The unsaturated artwork is meaningless without subjects fulfilling its function," says the artist. "It's unfinished."

At the Hamburger Bahnhof in Berlin, Höller once installed a dozen live reindeer that fed on psychedelic fly agaric mushrooms, alongside a rotating bed for overnight visitors, who—if they wished—could drink the reindeers' urine to test if they would hallucinate. Such moving beds "sow doubt and confusion," Höller explains, and his recent projects go further still, probing the unconscious of participants. In collaboration with Massachusetts Institute of Technology dream scientist Adam Haar Horowitz, he has developed kinetic beds incorporating visual and sonic stimuli—floating mushroom sculptures, suggestive voices—that influence the dreams of sleepers.

Although defined by his probing outlook rather than a particular aesthetic, Höller is most recognized for the larger-than-you mushrooms he has been producing since early in his career. "Mushrooms," he explains, "are monuments to incomprehensibility," and incarnate how little science can tell us about the world; their psychoactive properties illuminate how faint our grasp remains on the mechanism and content of consciousness.

For the Venice Biennale in 2026, Höller installed a two-story-tall mushroom at the end of the Arsenale gardens. Towering amid grassy hillocks, it's the final work visitors encounter after the profusion of art on view—a characteristic parting shot from the artist, an injunction to broaden our awareness if we hope to uncover anything meaningful about our existence.

"Where science is limited, art can open new doors of understanding."

OPPOSITE:
Höller playing "Pure Thinking," one of 336 pastimes, social experiments and pranks featured in his *Book of Games*. Edited with Hans Ulrich Obrist and Stefanie Hessler, the collection ranges from the philosophical to the delightfully absurd—including a version of patty-cake played with buttocks rather than hands.

FIVE GAMES

Try to apply Höller's deceptively simple, subversive provocations to your own life and you may find that it's quite difficult to devise new ways of making art, or writing, or whatever your pursuit may be. We accept so much of the world as we perceive it, relying on what we've absorbed from the adult and professional world, but Höller insists on questioning all of it—and he's created a book of games to help people begin.

Published by Taschen in 2024, *Book of Games* contains Höller's instructions for hundreds of challenges for which the only requirement is a willingness to try odd and occasionally socially uncomfortable acts. They are games for adults—games of confusion, games that experiment on participants the way that his exhibitions turn audiences into collaborators and sometimes bewildered guinea pigs.

Activities include blindfolded participants identifying one another by feeling each other's faces, conversations limited to saying only the opposite of what is meant, and the collective invasions of public spaces in which groups repeatedly sing the same song until forcibly removed—destabilizing experiences akin to those that have been the hallmarks of Höller's art. Excerpted here are five of his domestic experiments to try.

1. EXPERIMENT ON YOURSELF
Invent an experiment to perform on yourself. You could rub a little saliva onto your right earlobe every morning and, after a year, compare both earlobes to see if anything has changed. Or you could try putting your left leg behind your head every day and observe whether it affects your gait.

2. THE GOLDEN GAZE
Have an intense conversation with someone, but do not look them directly in the eyes. Instead, focus on a point nearby—one of their temples, for example—so that your interlocutor remains unsure whether eye contact is actually being made. Stay focused: the other person will likely begin shifting position in an attempt to meet your gaze.

3. PURE THINKING
Think about how you perceive the world and the framework through which you perceive it. Then step outside that framework and consider what larger framework might contain it. Hold both ideas in your mind at once: the original framework and the one surrounding it. Then, with all of that specificity in mind, try to quiet it entirely, as though turning a volume dial down to its lowest setting. This is pure thinking. It will either inspire new ideas or send you to sleep."

4. THE NO-KILL EATERS
Avoid eating any foods that require killing—not just animals, but also plants, fungi and any multicellular organisms. Eating a head of lettuce means the death of the plant and should be avoided, for example, while fruits and berries are "openly offered for consumption by the plants bearing them," explains Höller. "Their mother survives unharmed." Mushrooms, the fruiting bodies of fungi, may be eaten, leaving the mycelium intact. Milk, unfertilized eggs, and found roadkill may be eaten, as can, according to Höller's suggestions, antlers shed by deer, skins shed by snakes and seashells without inhabitants.

"As sedentary beings, plants live in a different reality, but they exchange complex information with each other both underground and through air and water, partially with other living beings," he writes. "Relegating the lettuce to an inferior status solely because of one's own inability to understand it is a very sad demonstration of the limits of the human mind."

5. DRY DANCING
Find a partner and dance without music. Bonus points for music-less dancing in a public place.

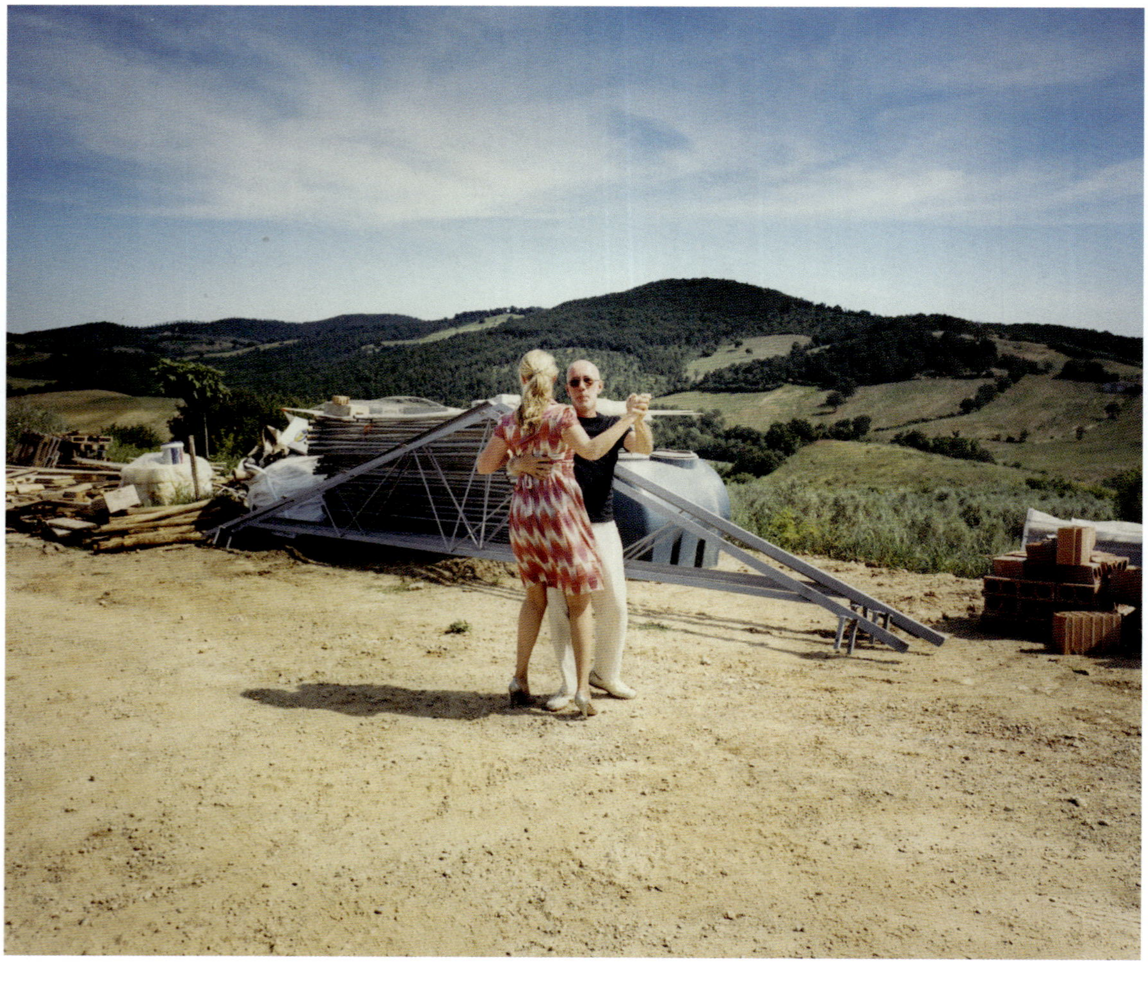

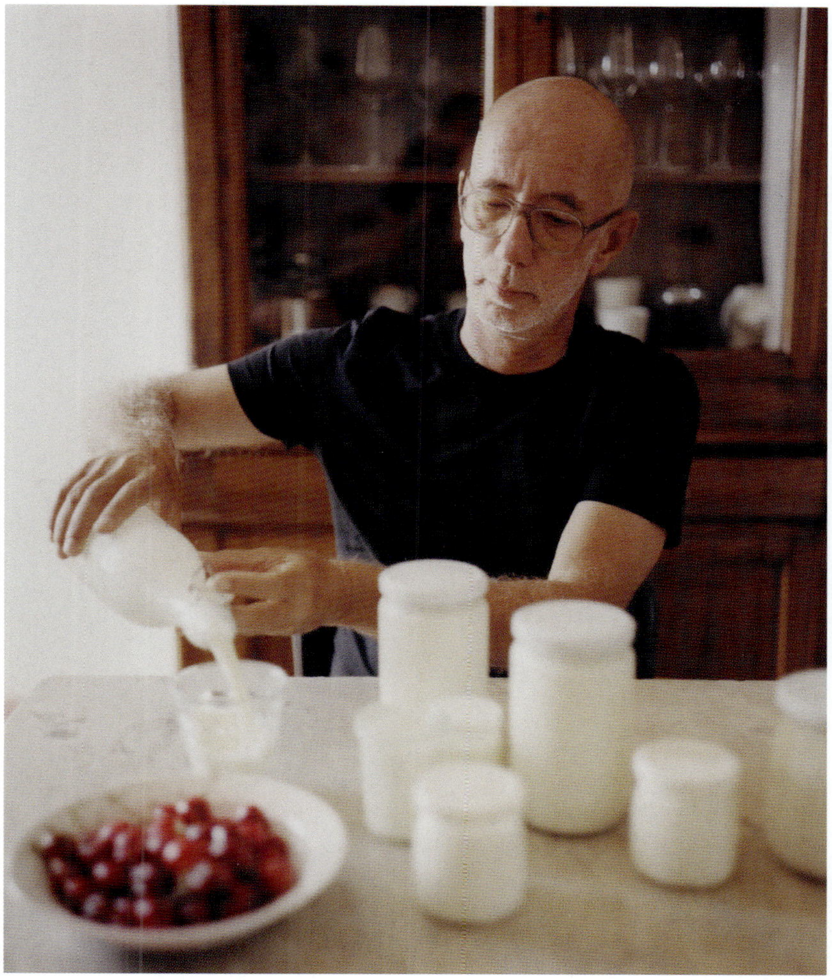

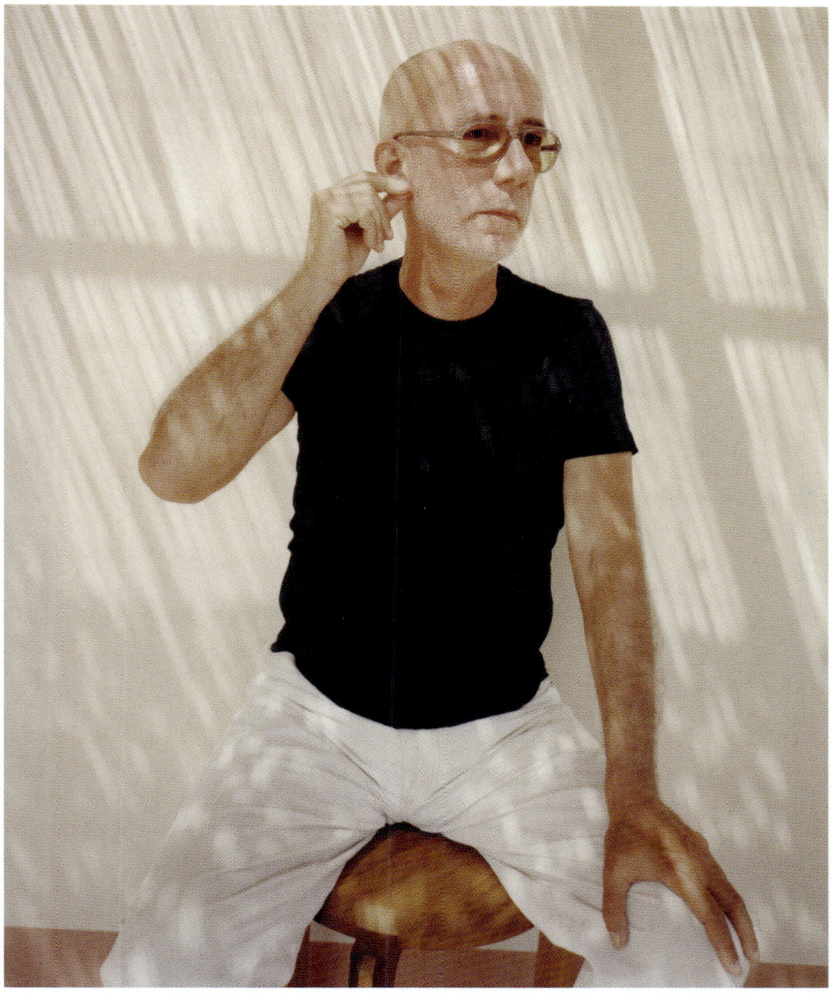

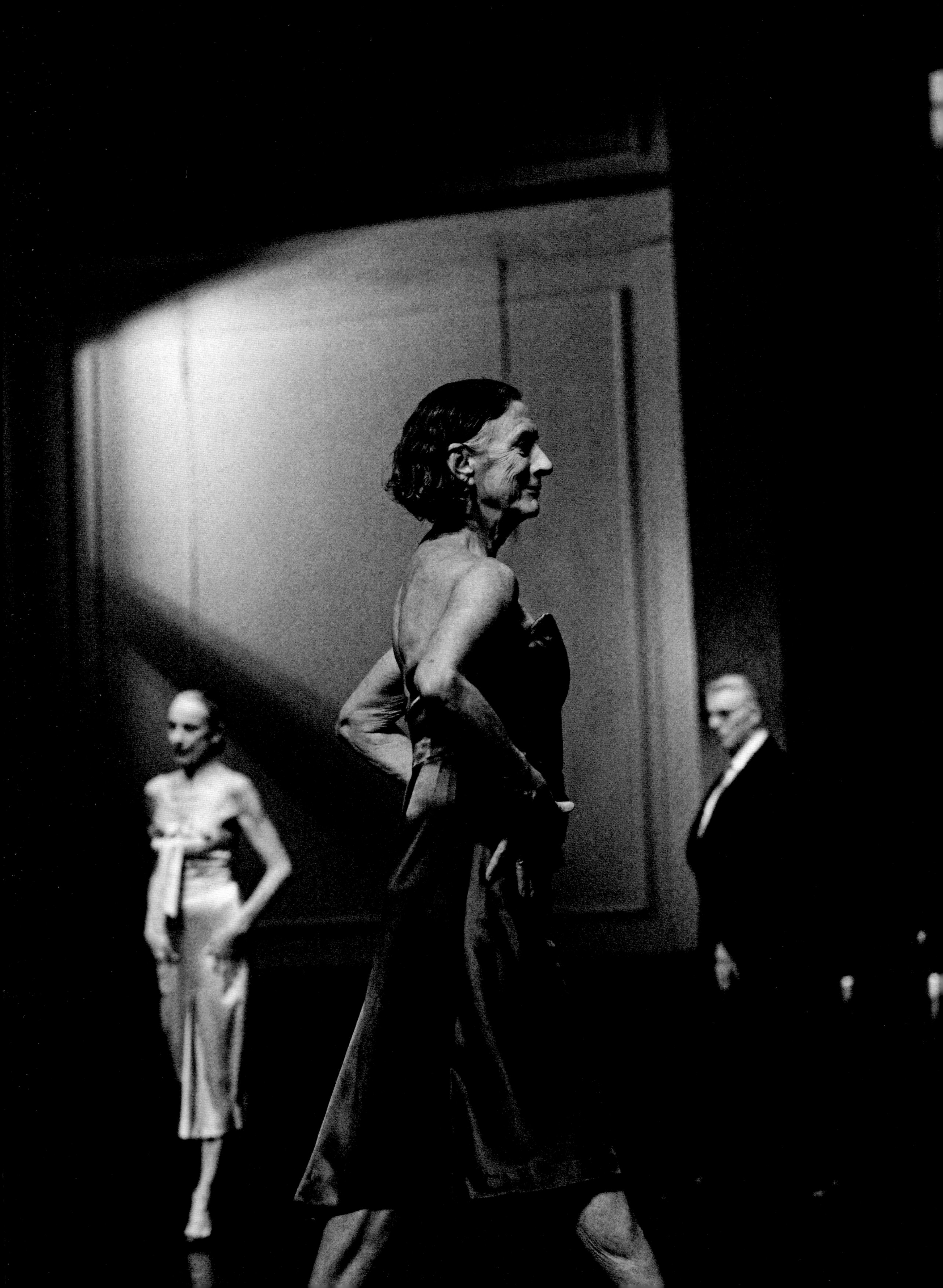

YOUNG HEARTS: Behind the scenes with Pina Bausch's original *Kontakthof* dancers.

Words
Emily May
Photos
Camilla Greenwell

Restaging iconic dance pieces can be a daunting undertaking—at least, it was for Meryl Tankard. "I thought I would get ripped to shreds," the 71-year-old dancer, choreographer and filmmaker says on a video call from Australia.

Tankard is referring to *Kontakthof—Echoes of '78*, her now critically acclaimed 90-minute reimagining of the seminal dance work *Kontakthof*, originally created by the late German expressionist choreographer Pina Bausch for her legendary company Tanztheater Wuppertal. Tankard's project began in 2024 when Bausch's son and director of her foundation, Salomon Bausch, reached out, inspired by his mother's reported musings about what the piece might look like if performed by its much older original cast, of which Tankard had been a member.

Originally, Salomon had conceived of a faithful restaging of the original three-hour work, with younger dancers filling in for those unable to return. It was Tankard who insisted that only the original cast—now in their 70s and 80s—should be onstage. After working out that "there would be nine or ten of us that were healthy enough," she developed the idea of evoking absent colleagues through projections of archival, black-and-white footage filmed by Rolf Borzik during the original production of *Kontakthof*.

Bausch's original *Kontakthof* was a meditation on male-female relationships, on "tenderness and what arises from it," as Bausch once said. Reimagined as *Echoes*, however, the thematic focus shifted toward loss, loneliness and the passage of time. Set within a village hall–like environment, chairs lie scattered and empty as performers assume ballroom holds without partners, attempt to kiss thin air and sway in long lines with linked arms, with many missing links in the chain. Accompanied by a nostalgic, melancholy score of tango, jazz and popular German tracks from the 1930s, these absences reflect that half of the company, including Bausch herself, has now passed away. "But you can see them," says Australian dancer Josephine Ann Endicott, 76, on a call from her home in Germany, "you feel them onstage."

These ghostly presences have become the standout feature of *Echoes*, which has spent three years touring Europe until its final performance in Lugano, Switzerland, in June 2026. The projections allow the performers not only to reunite with former colleagues, but also to synchronize their movements with their younger selves.

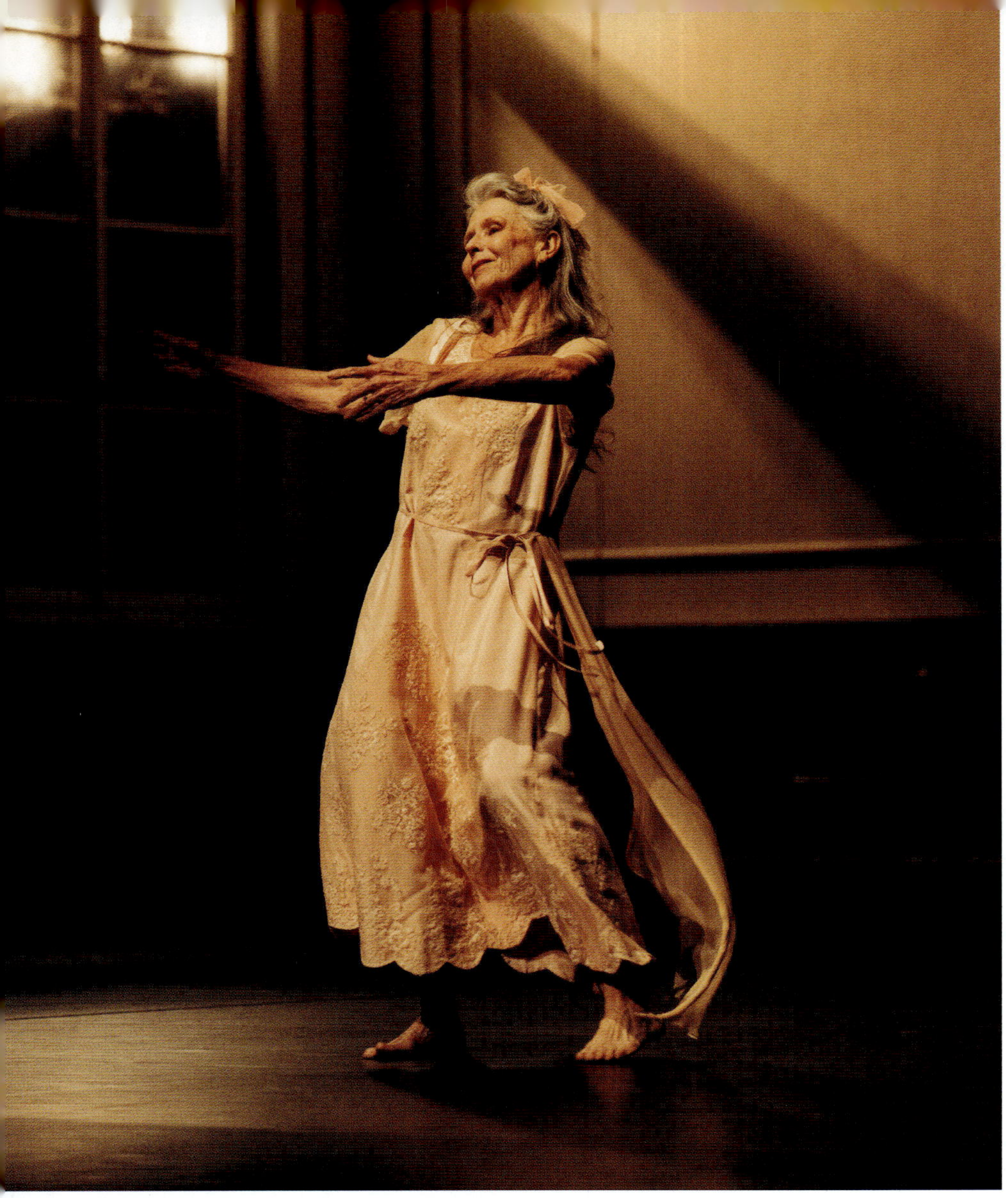

(above)
Josephine Ann Endicott in rehearsals at Sadler's Wells in London for *Kontakthof – Echoes of '78*.

"It's really empowering," says Tankard. "Our bodies are not the same, but in terms of our minds and emotional states, we still feel like those people. Sometimes, if you catch the arm of that 23-year-old, you just sort of breathe together."

Born in 1940, Pina Bausch trained and performed in ballet and modern dance companies in Germany and New York before creating her own work. She was the artistic director of Folkwang Ballet in Essen before taking the helm of Tanztheater Wuppertal, which she led until her death in 2009. There, she became one of the leading exponents of Tanztheater, a style of performance combining choreography with everyday movement, theater, speech and dramatic set design. The goal was not to tell chronological narratives, but to evoke memories and speak to the reality of the human experience. Famously, Bausch drew on her dancers' inner lives to inform her work, saying: "I'm not interested in how people move, but what moves them."

Tankard recalls one such example from her audition for Tanztheater Wuppertal, in which Bausch asked her to cycle through six different ways of looking surprised, at an increasingly rapid pace. "I loved creating characters and being able to be an author," she says.

"Even though on a physical level we're limited, on an expressive level we feel stronger."

(opposite)
An integral part of the staging of *Kontakthof – Echoes of '78* is a projection of archival footage showing the dancers in earlier performances, alongside company members who have died.

For Tankard and Endicott, who both joined Tanztheater Wuppertal in the 1970s, performing in such works was a striking departure from their early experiences in classical ballet. In the first Bausch performance Tankard saw, "People were crying, dancers were reading poems and love letters and wearing chiffon dresses.... It just seemed real, like my life, not like a fairyland with sylphs and princes." The work offered the chance to explore different sides of the self than ballet, where "if you had black hair, you were a witch or a prostitute, and the blonde girls were always princesses," Tankard adds.

Endicott says that Bausch valued spontaneity in performance, recalling the wide range of emotions the original work demanded of her. She maintained that breadth of expression in *Echoes*, shifting from crying to moaning sensually into a microphone and prancing coquettishly across the stage in a childish nightgown and hair ribbon.

She adds that this childlike register is harder to access at her current age, yet she's "still a child at heart somehow." Each night onstage, she never performs the work in exactly the same way. "I like to be spontaneous... and say or do something a tiny bit different. If it's not living in the moment, I don't need to do it."

But while dancers contributed material, Bausch would "never explain why we were doing anything," Tankard says, describing the process as "a mystery." Rehearsals for *Echoes*, however, had to be much more definitive. On the first day, the cast "all expected we'd have all these discussions and talk," says Tankard. But "I had this really tightly edited film, and every scene was timed down to the second. I'd worked everything out in advance, and just said, 'Look, this is it. How are we going to make that work?'"

Tankard saw her fellow cast members "get younger" during the process of creating *Echoes*. While in the first week of rehearsals they struggled to remember things, "in the second, they all came back smarter and faster," she says. "We have to keep challenging ourselves," she says, highlighting how creativity and experimentation become more important with age. "Once things get too comfortable, they just stagnate."

Echoes demonstrates that there are benefits to aging together in the scenes that cut through the prevailing sense of melancholy and celebrate the cast's impressive physical abilities and enduring chemistry. They walk in processional lines—a Bausch signature—cast wry smiles as they form minimalist hand gestures, and surge forward on the diagonal, hiking up their skirts and stomping and leaping with determination. "We have so much warmth for each other... such a feeling of understanding and companionship," says Arthur Rosenfeld, 74, another member of the company. "We don't have anything left to prove. Even though on

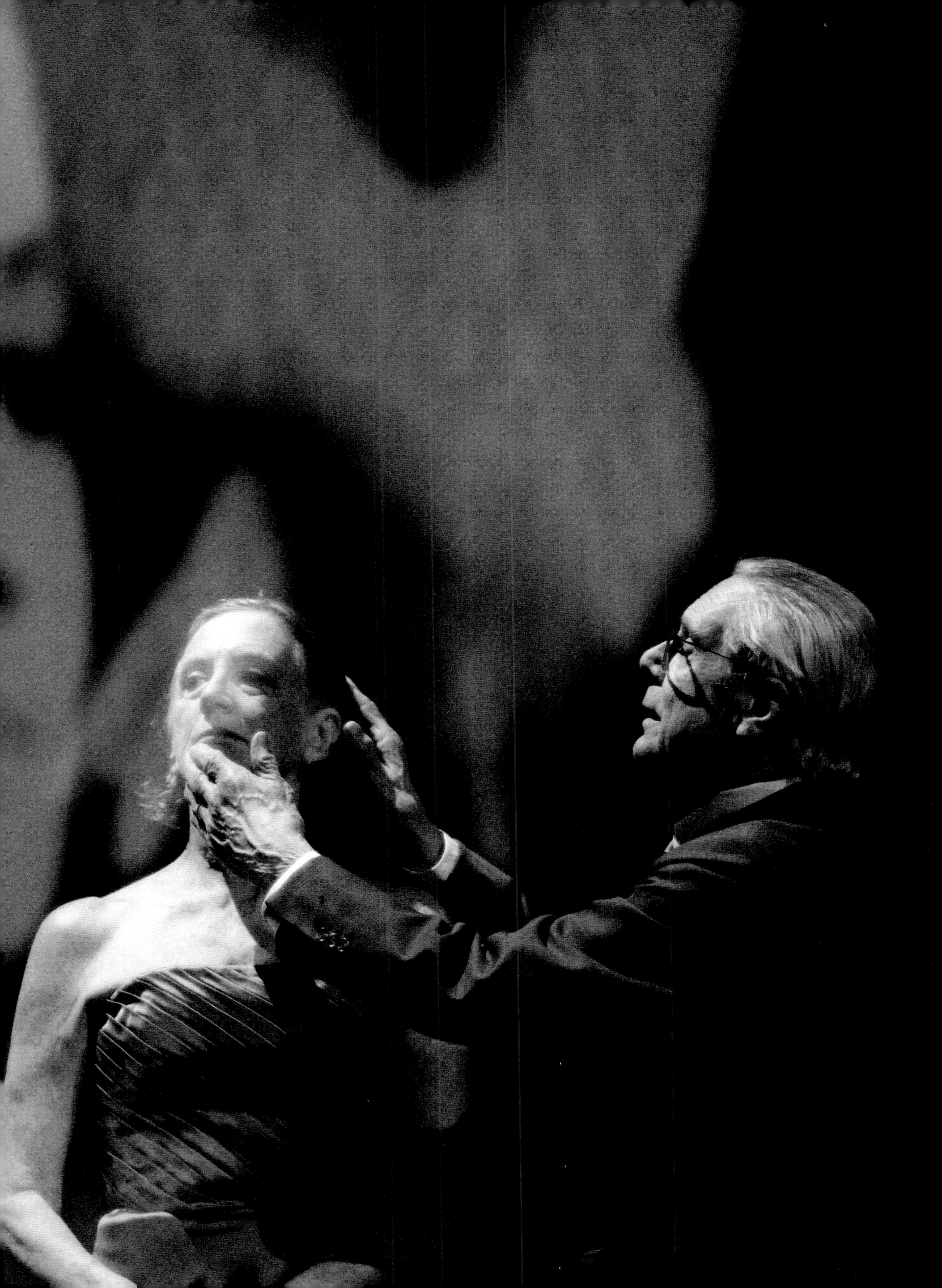

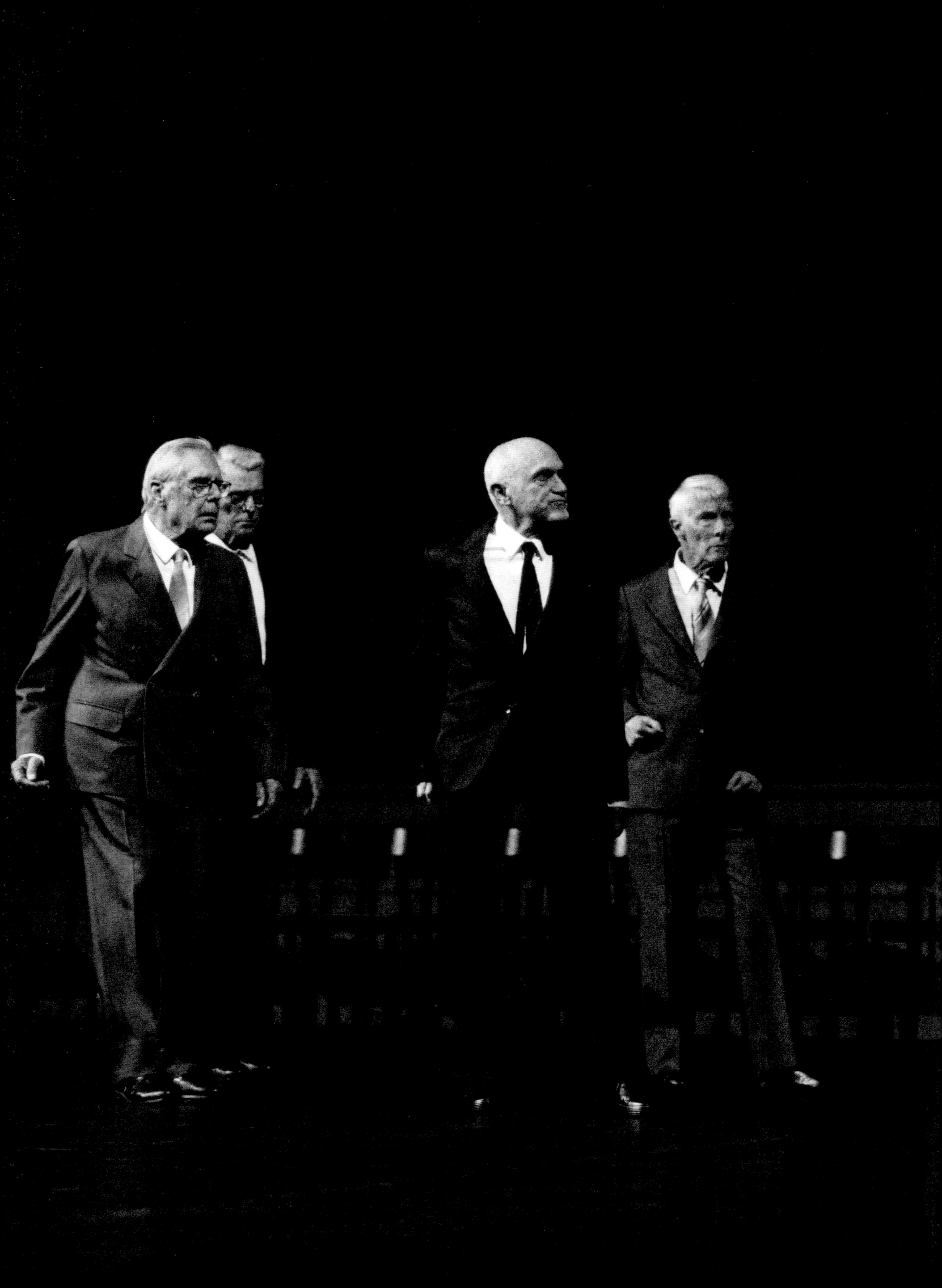

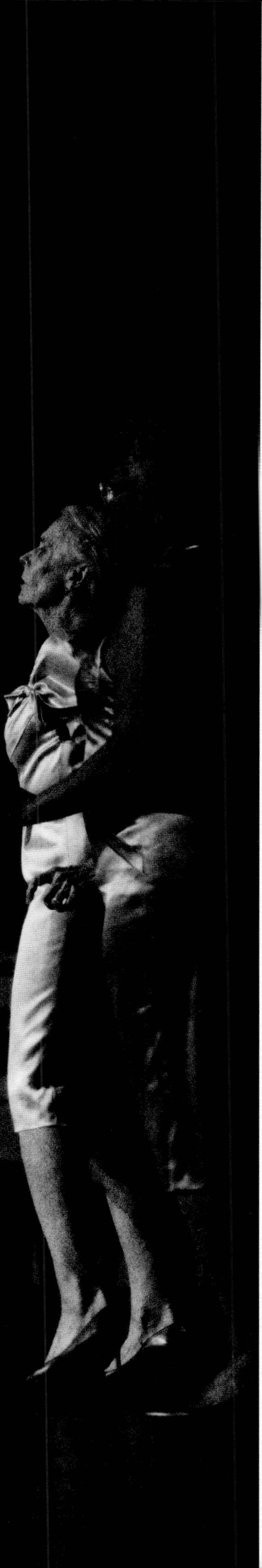

(opposite)
Kontakthof, meaning "a place to make contact, to meet," is set in a dance hall to songs of the 1930s and its choreography parodies courting rituals. Nine of the original dancers returned to their roles for the production.

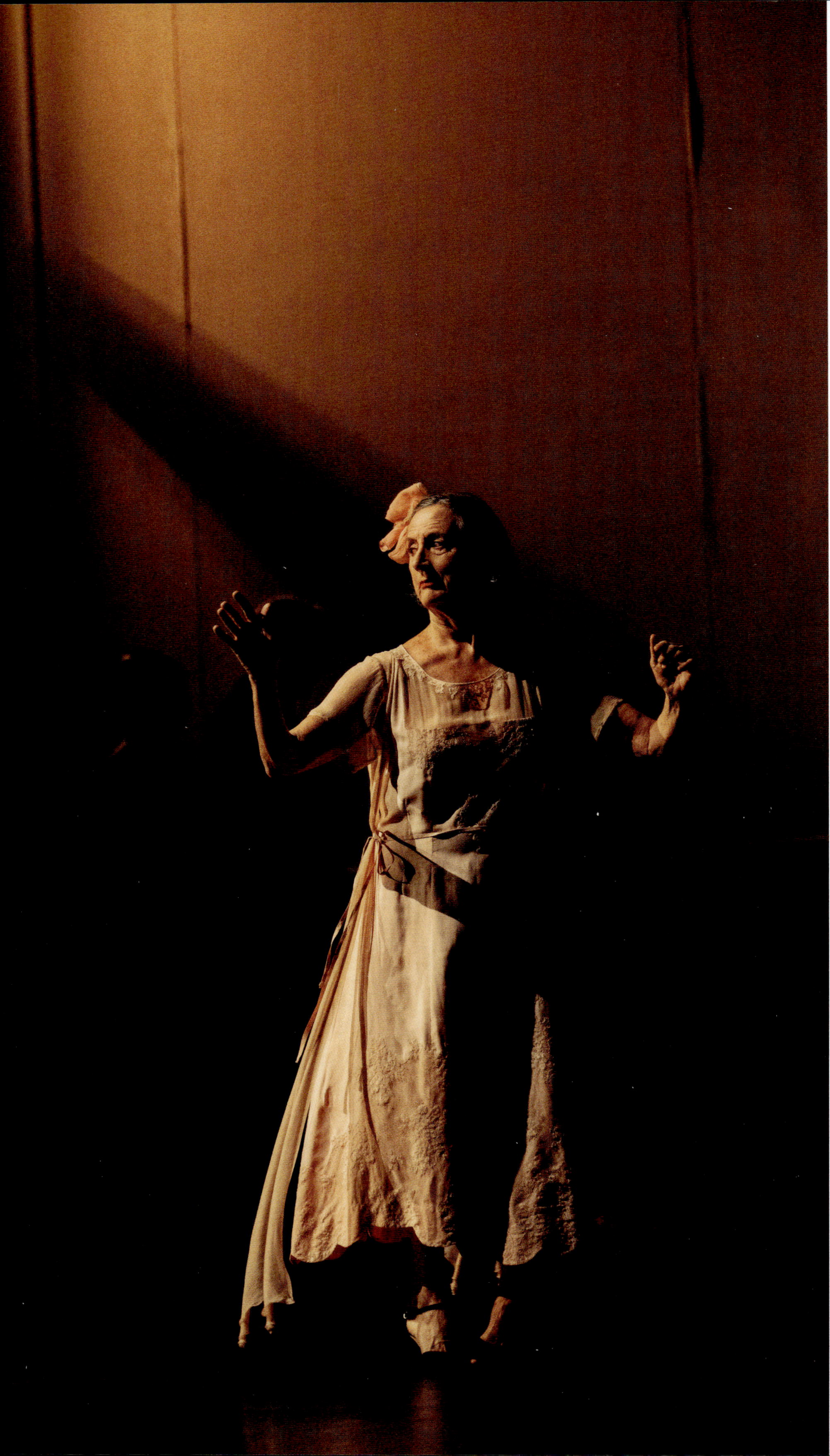

(opposite)
Meryl Tankard, who choreographed *Kontakthof – Echoes of '78*, was one of the production's central performers in its original 1978 staging.

a physical level we're limited, on an expressive level we feel stronger."

This heightened expressive capacity is also felt by Endicott: In one scene in *Echoes*, she sobs at the back of the stage while the rest of the dancers sing the Scottish folk song "My Bonnie Lies Over the Ocean." The moment is informed by all of the losses she has experienced over the years—from Bausch to friends to her mother. "I'm kind of holding back the dogs inside me," she says.

While Endicott describes the moment as difficult, the universality of the emotions it evokes makes it "very beautiful" and, like Bausch's work more broadly, deeply affecting for audiences. Endicott believes that Bausch's raw presentations of humanity are particularly important during the hard times we find ourselves in. "The world is not in a great state," she says, "so it's wonderful to be able to see something like this."

Perhaps surprisingly, *Echoes* has resonated particularly strongly with younger audiences, according to Tankard. Speaking to a group of under-35 theater-makers who saw the performance in Berlin, she asked why they were so drawn to it. "Do you feel sorry for us, that we're nearly dying or something?" she recalls asking. "They said, 'No—you're just so energetic and enthusiastic about life.'"

"Do you feel sorry for us, that we're nearly dying or something?"

That enthusiasm is set to carry Tankard, Endicott and Rosenfeld into future projects. Tankard speaks of leading dance classes in Australia, where there are few options for those over 60; Endicott, who restages many of Bausch's works and has an upcoming project with La Scala Ballet in Milan, admits that she doesn't want to keep working on *Kontakthof* "till I get to the grave," but will continue for as long as people want her to teach it. Meanwhile, Rosenfeld, who performed the London run of *Echoes* with a ruptured Achilles tendon and is "adjusting to what it is to dance when your body doesn't really allow you anymore," also remains open to whatever opportunities arise. "To be on stage is to go home," he says.

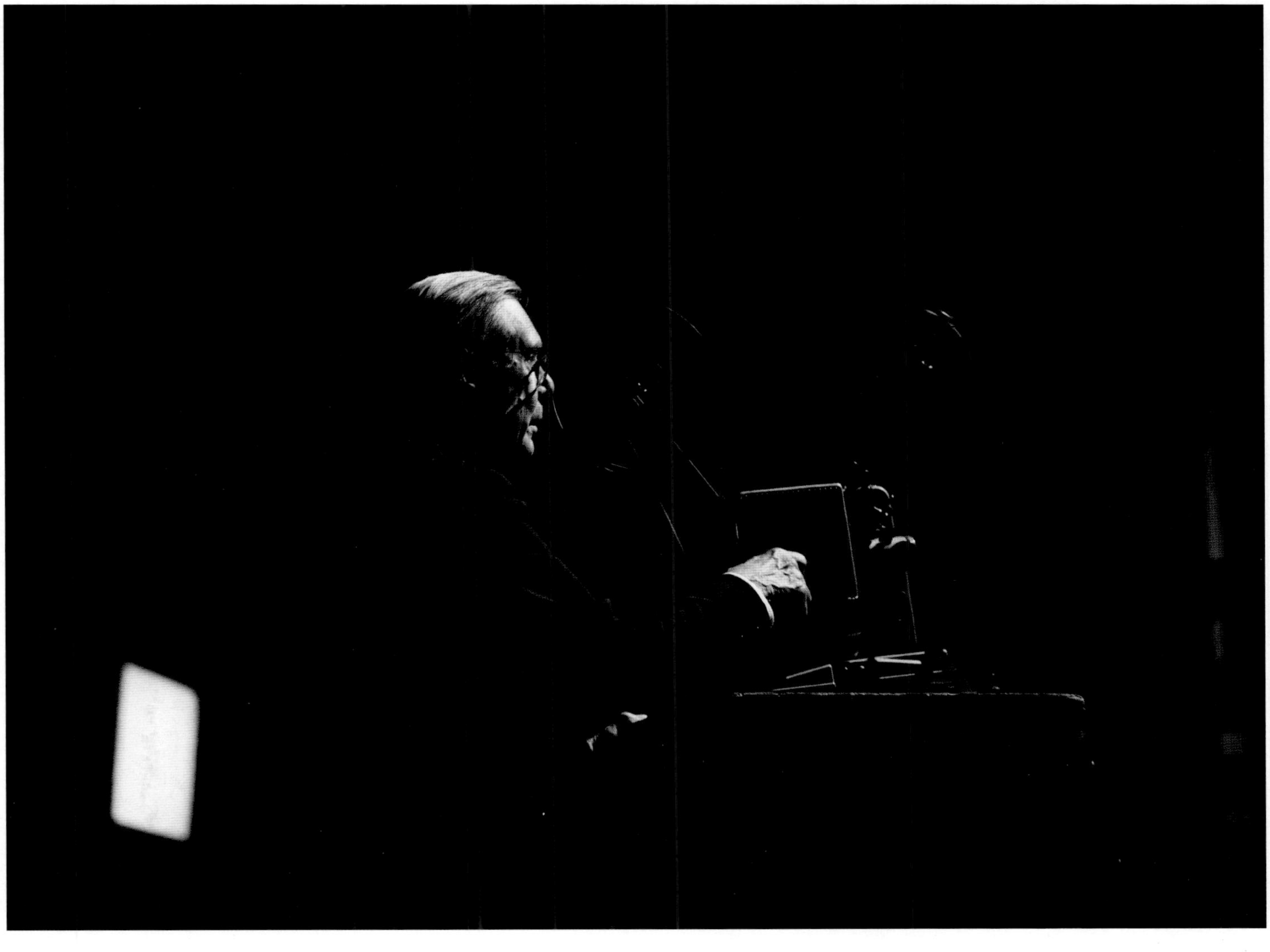

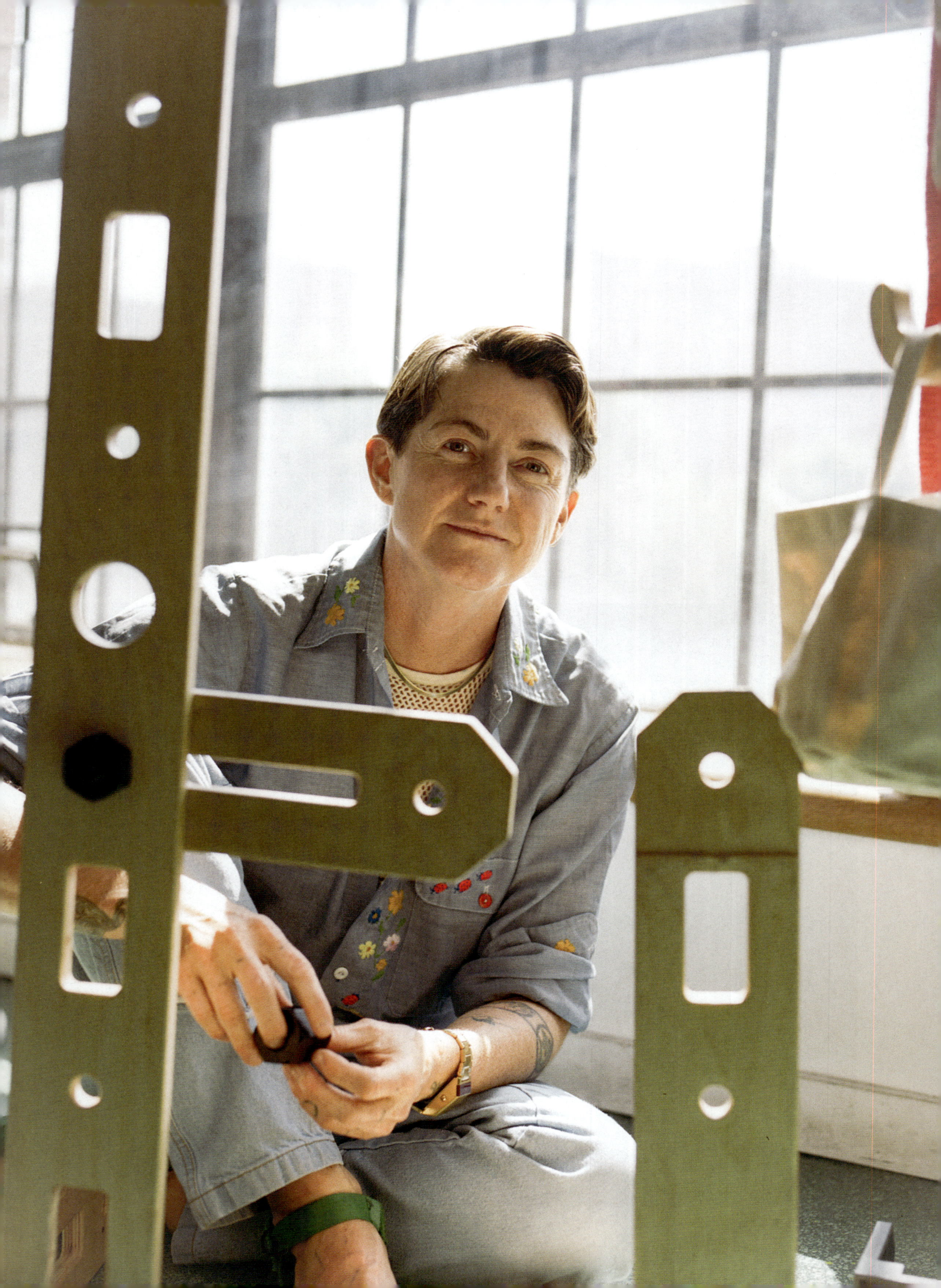

SMÆLL WORLDS

Words
Benjamin Dane
Photos
Raphaël Gaultier

1.
Toy designer CAS HOLMAN on the value of open-ended play.

Cas Holman designs for the moments before a child knows what they are making. The American designer and author is best known for Rigamajig, a large-scale building kit used in schools, museums and public spaces, and has a body of work that treats play as a serious form of inquiry.

Rather than producing toys with fixed outcomes, Holman invites children to test, collaborate, fail, rebuild and invent their own rules. She sees play not as a break from learning but as one of the ways children learn how to move through the world—something she believes adults would do well to rediscover.

BENJAMIN DANE: How did you first become interested in designing for children?

CAS HOLMAN: I usually say that I adventured my way into design, by virtue of not wanting to decide what I wanted to be when I grew up. As a kid, that question always really stressed me out. So I studied sculpture and critical cultural theory, I was a chef, I lived in the Galápagos Islands chasing iguanas as a research assistant, I worked in construction. I took a very playful approach to becoming an adult.

When I was at college, I started making interactive sculptures that I wanted people to play with. That is tricky in an art museum, because people aren't used to touching things. I began wondering why play wasn't considered serious enough for that space.

BD: When did you begin to understand the power of open-ended play?

CH: I had made a piece called Geemo, a flexible building toy with magnetic limbs, and there was a conversation with a mother and daughter that really moved me. The daughter imagined she was on another planet, getting to know the creatures who lived there. The mother said she imagined being

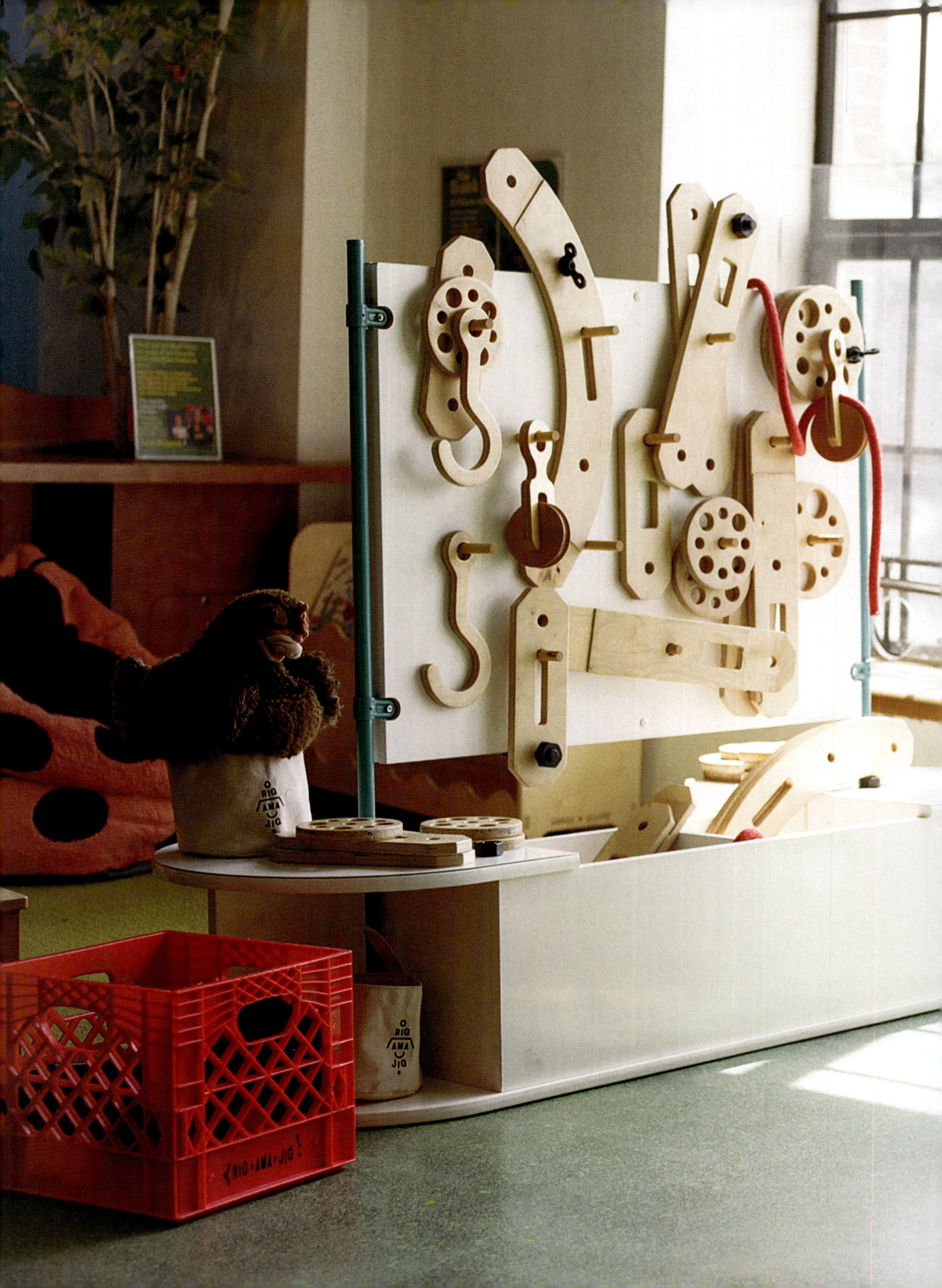
RIG-AMA-JIG

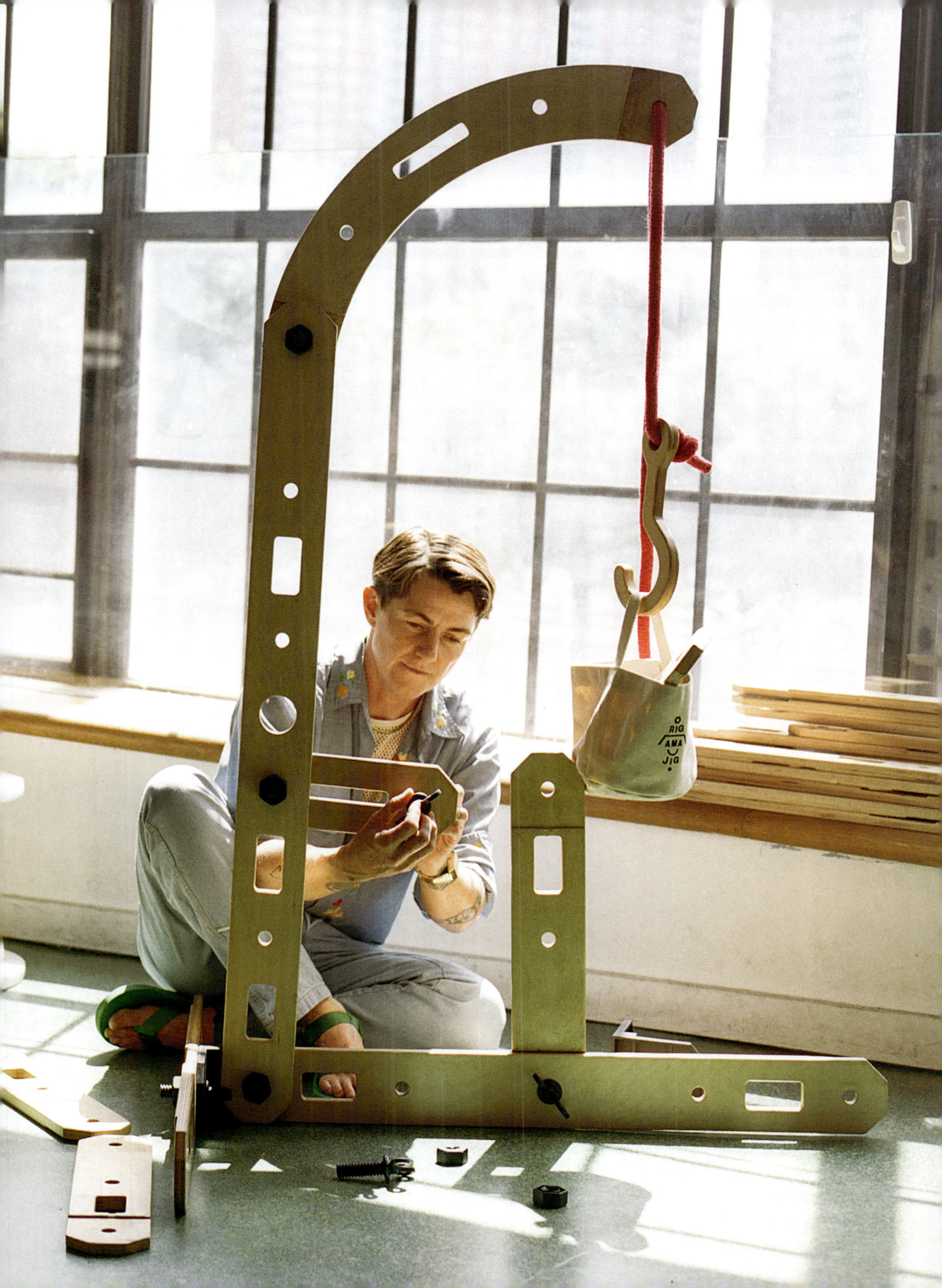
RIG
AMA
JIG

in a cave with stalactites. They were playing together but were inside these completely different imaginations. That was my goal, but seeing it happen was incredible. The mother seemed almost disturbed, as if she were thinking: Do I even know my own child? Of course she did. But how can you know somebody's imagination if you don't look at art, or play?

BD: When designing toys, how do you decide how much guidance to provide?

CH: With Rigamajig, for example, the constraints are built into the design. I call it open-ended, but it's not free play per se. Free play is when a child appropriates something or plays in a way that doesn't require objects. With Rigamajig, the holes line up, the nuts, bolts and brackets work together, and everything is made for children's hands. It's about figuring out the system but also focusing on the creative play. A child might make a dragon or a weird monster, but they could move from that to building a table.

BD: What have you learned about how children approach play?

CH: I've learned that we don't need to control it. We need to support them in exploring and follow what they are curious about. Children's brains are so different from ours. If we try to understand what they are learning only in our own terms, we limit them.

BD: What makes it difficult for children to play freely today?

CH: I don't think it's screens, but a lack of freedom. Children's lives are overly structured. If you give children free time and they have never had free time before, they won't know what to do with it. They have no practice. Screens don't help, because they create habits of attention. But the deeper issue is that children need time to be in touch with their own intrinsic motivation.

BD: What can adults learn from the way children play?

CH: In childhood, play forms us. In adulthood, play affirms who we are. It helps us keep growing. I've been accused of excessive dillydallying, but I think that is the good stuff. For adults, play begins with releasing judgment, reframing success and embracing possibility. Adult play can be small: daydreaming, people-watching, taking a different road, chatting in line at the store instead of looking at your phone.

(previous)
Holman builds with Rigamajig, a large-scale construction kit she designed to encourage hands-on, open-ended play.

(below, left)
Holman at her studio in Brooklyn. In October 2025, she published her first book, *Playful: How Play Shifts Our Thinking, Inspires Connection, and Sparks Creativity*.

"Play affirms who we are. It helps us keep growing."

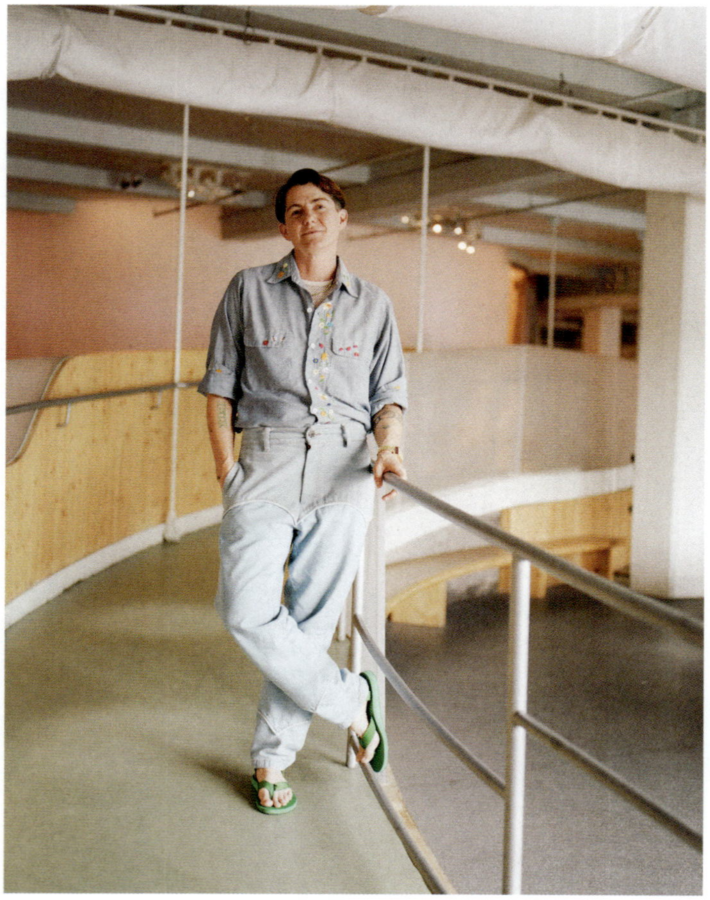

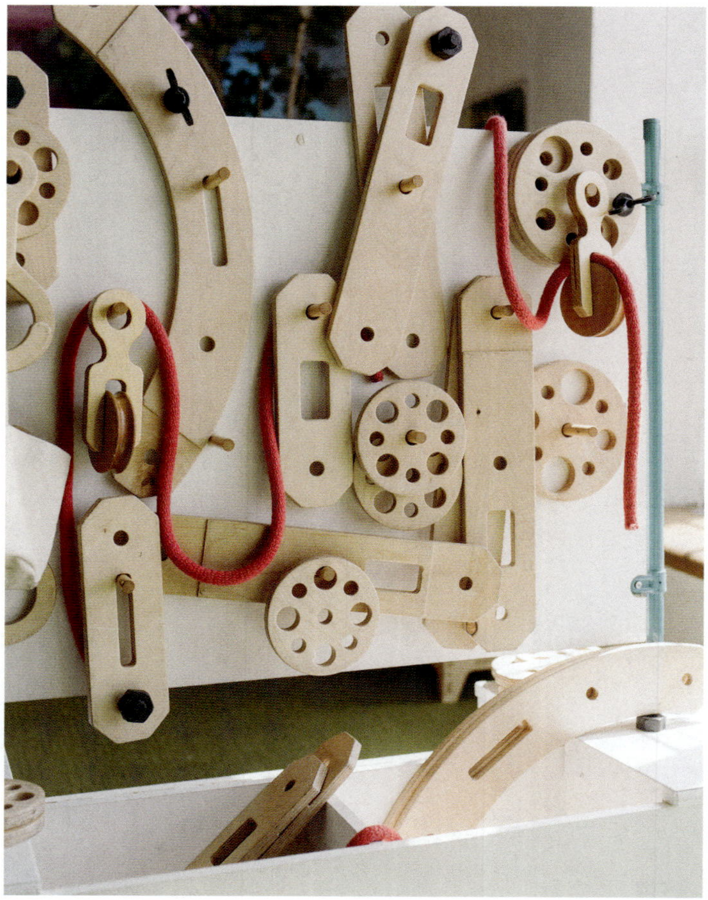

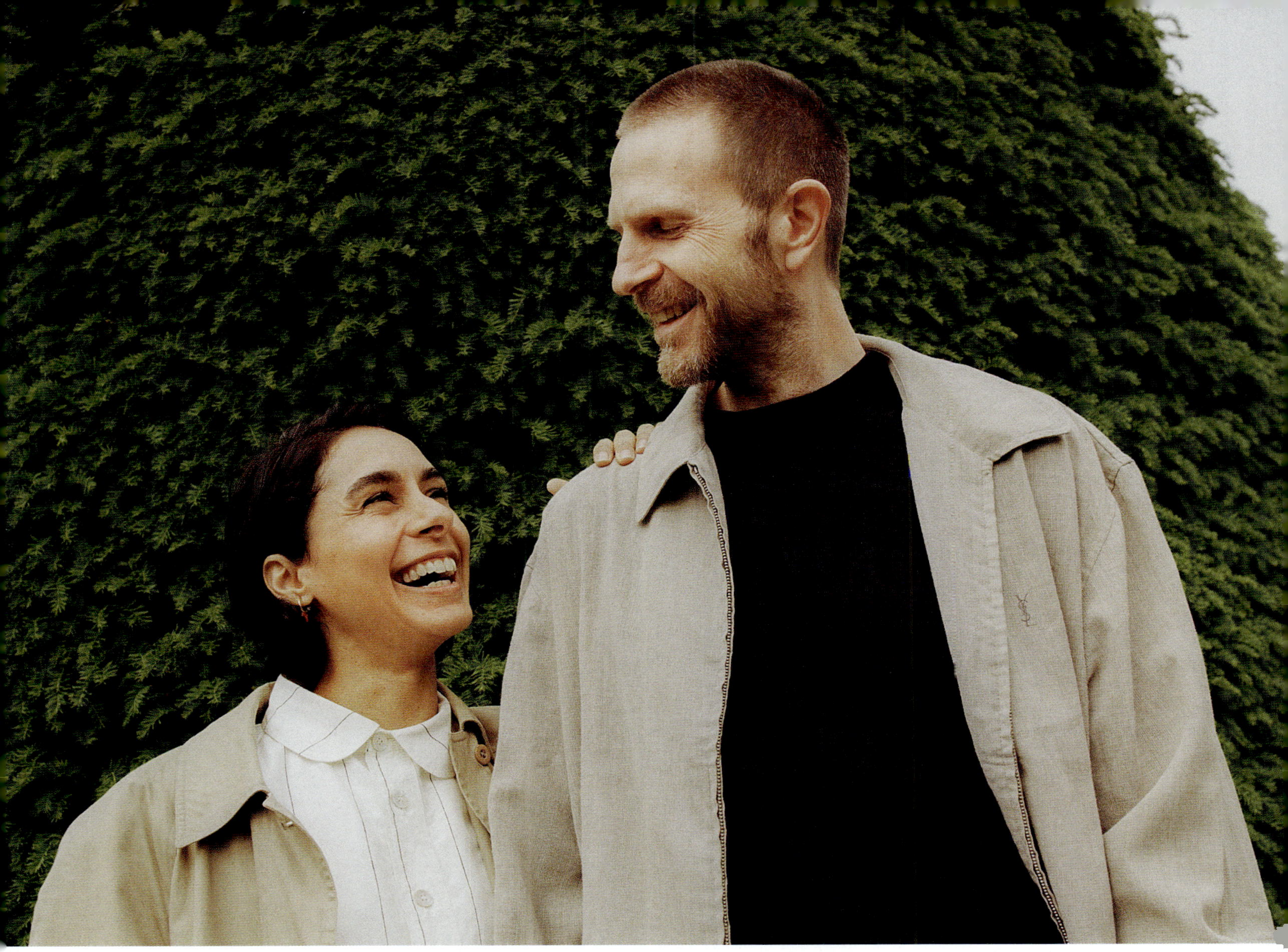

Words Benjamin Dane *Photos* Nathan Wolf Grace

2. PLAYRISE on creating playgrounds for displaced communities.

Playrise began with a question: Where do children play when their communities have been destroyed?

For Alexander Meininger, Ariana Mouyiaris Meininger and their children, playgrounds are part of the rhythm of family life, the place where they can let off steam and explore the world. "If the kids didn't get out into nature or into some kind of play space, they would be stir-crazy. *We* would be stir-crazy," says Ariana. But following Russia's invasion of Ukraine in 2022, a young Ukrainian woman came to live with the couple in London, and Alexander found himself wondering who, if anyone, would rebuild Ukraine's playgrounds.

"Why do my kids have five playgrounds in their one school?" says Alexander, a photographer who studied political science and philosophy at university. "And why do other kids—10,000 kids in a refugee camp in Ethiopia—not even have a single one?"

In 2025, the couple founded Playrise as a charity to create modular playgrounds for children living in displaced or underserved communities. The aim was to build something light, affordable and safe, and which could be shipped easily, assembled without foundations and adapted by the people who install it.

For Ariana, who studied international relations and contemporary design, Playrise is a way to merge her interests—how large political events alter people's lives, and how design shapes the spaces they inhabit. The couple approached the London-based architects OMMX and structural engineers Webb Yates with a brief that was first and foremost practical. The structure had to meet British and EU safety standards, be simple enough to reconfigure and work in radically different environments. In the desert heat of Ethiopia, metal can become dangerously hot; rubber and plastic can melt. Timber, fabric and shade became central to the design, as did slots that allow ropes, drums, climbing holds, hammocks or basketball hoops to be added, and which were designed to stop fingers being trapped inside.

Before Before starting to design, Playrise and OMMX carried out research with organizations working in Ethiopia and Egypt, then visited communities to speak with children and parents. When it became clear that some of the children had never been to school, the team dropped the usual drawing or model-making exercises and created a fabric playground instead, letting the children express what they wanted through play itself.

For Alexander, those workshops confirmed the universality of play. The children wanted to run, jump, climb, hide and gather, much like children anywhere. But every site had its own conditions: questions of supervision, danger, heat, space, daily routines and culture. "I just want to give them a tool," he says. "The communities know best what they want, what they need."

The first Playrise prototype was launched this spring at the Museum of the Home in London. Built of iroko wood, it was, Ariana admits, almost too beautiful, "a very luxurious playground." It has now been packed up to travel to Ethiopia, while the team is researching more scalable materials and manufacturing. They're also fundraising for six sites in Gaza and exploring further test locations in Egypt and the UK.

Underlying the charity's work is a simple conviction: Play is not a luxury; it's a fundamental right that is recognized by the UN's Convention on the Rights of the Child. In displaced communities, where children are often forced into taking on adult responsibilities or marked by trauma, a playground can be a rare respite. It gives them, as Ariana says, "somewhere to recover a sense of normalcy."

Alexander often returns to a phrase he heard from child psychologist Sophia Abdi: Play is the language of the child. If that is true, then the absence of play is not merely the absence of fun, "it is the absence of a way to speak," he says.

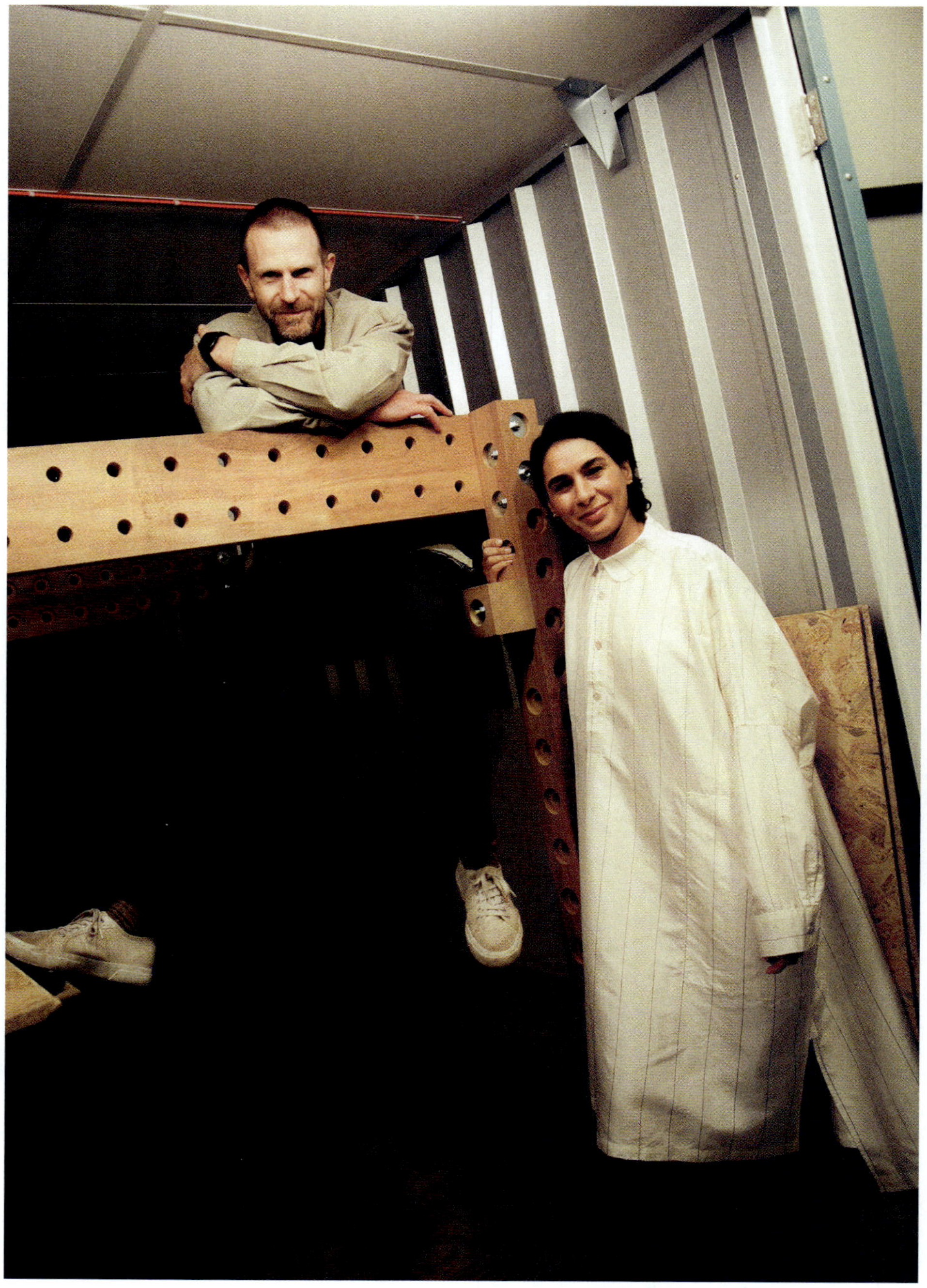

"Why do my kids have five playgrounds in their one school? And why do other kids—10,000 kids in a refugee camp in Ethiopia—not even have a single one?"

(above)
Alexander Meininger and Ariana Mouyiaris Meininger, founders of Playrise.

(opposite)
The first playgrounds were recently exhibited at the Museum of the Home in London and are now on their way to Aysaita Refugee Camp in Ethiopia.

Opposite and Overleaf Photos: Lewis Ronald

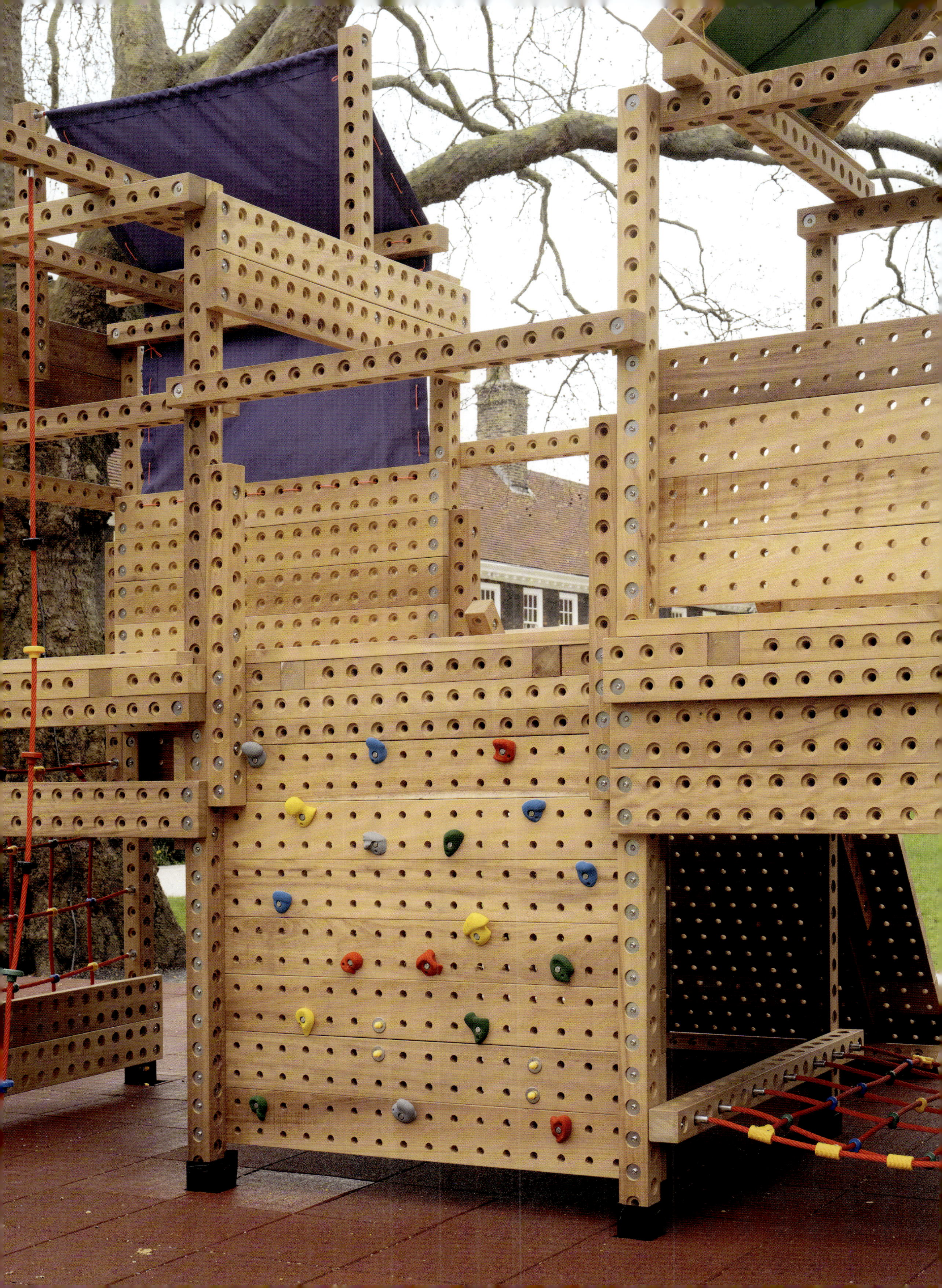

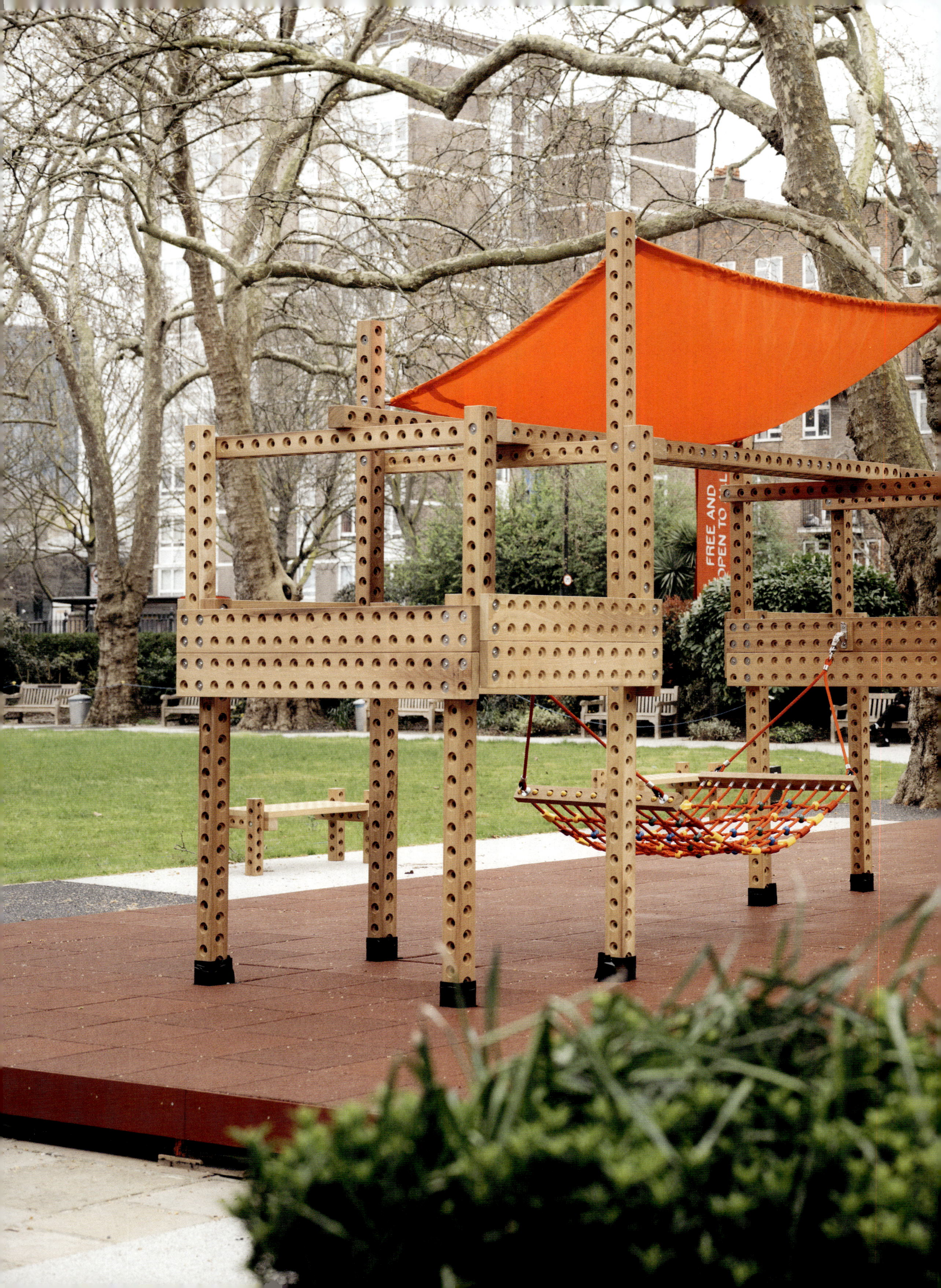
FREE AND
OPEN TO

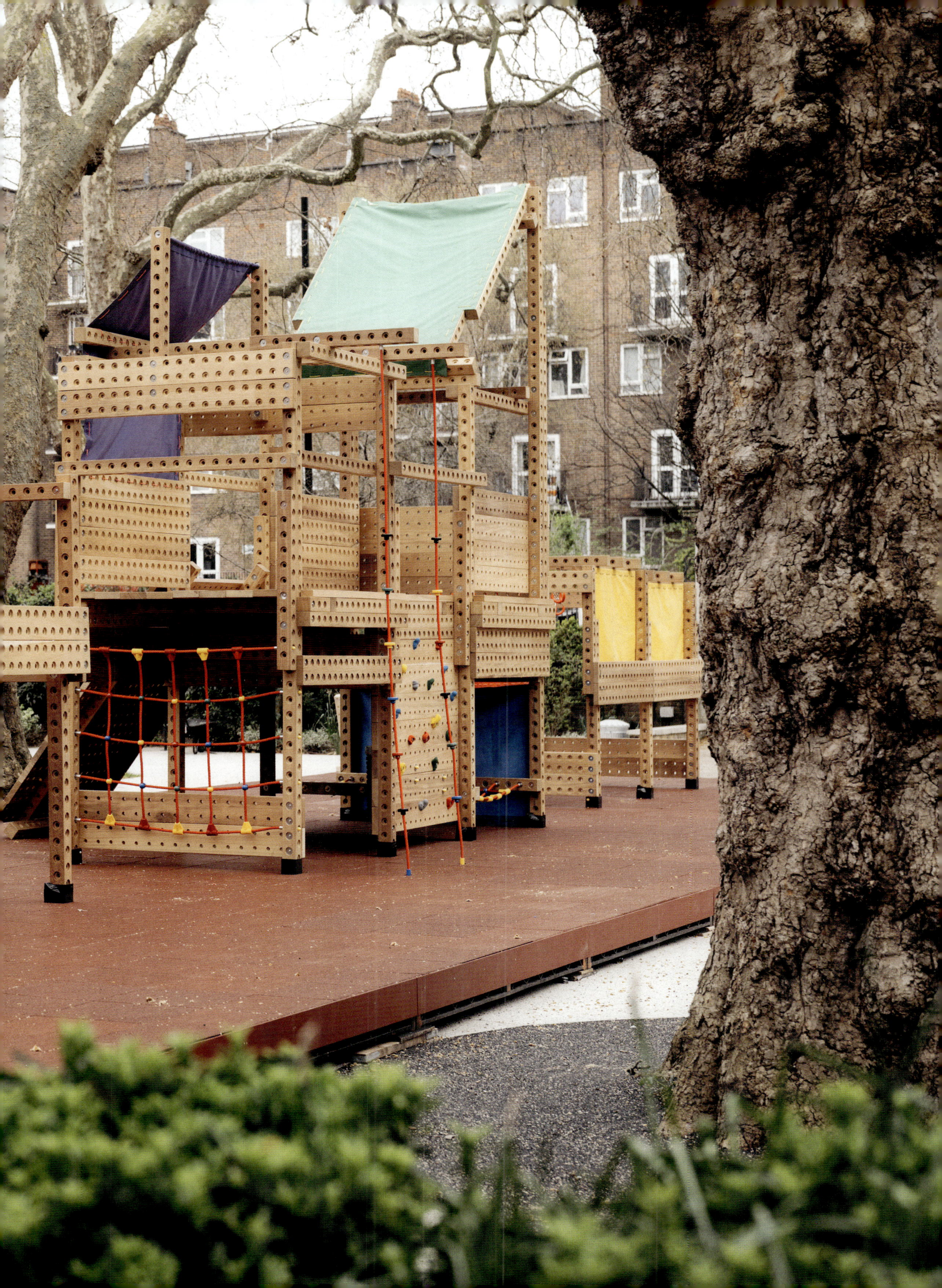

3.
Author BEATRICE ALEMAGNA on balancing the playful and profound.

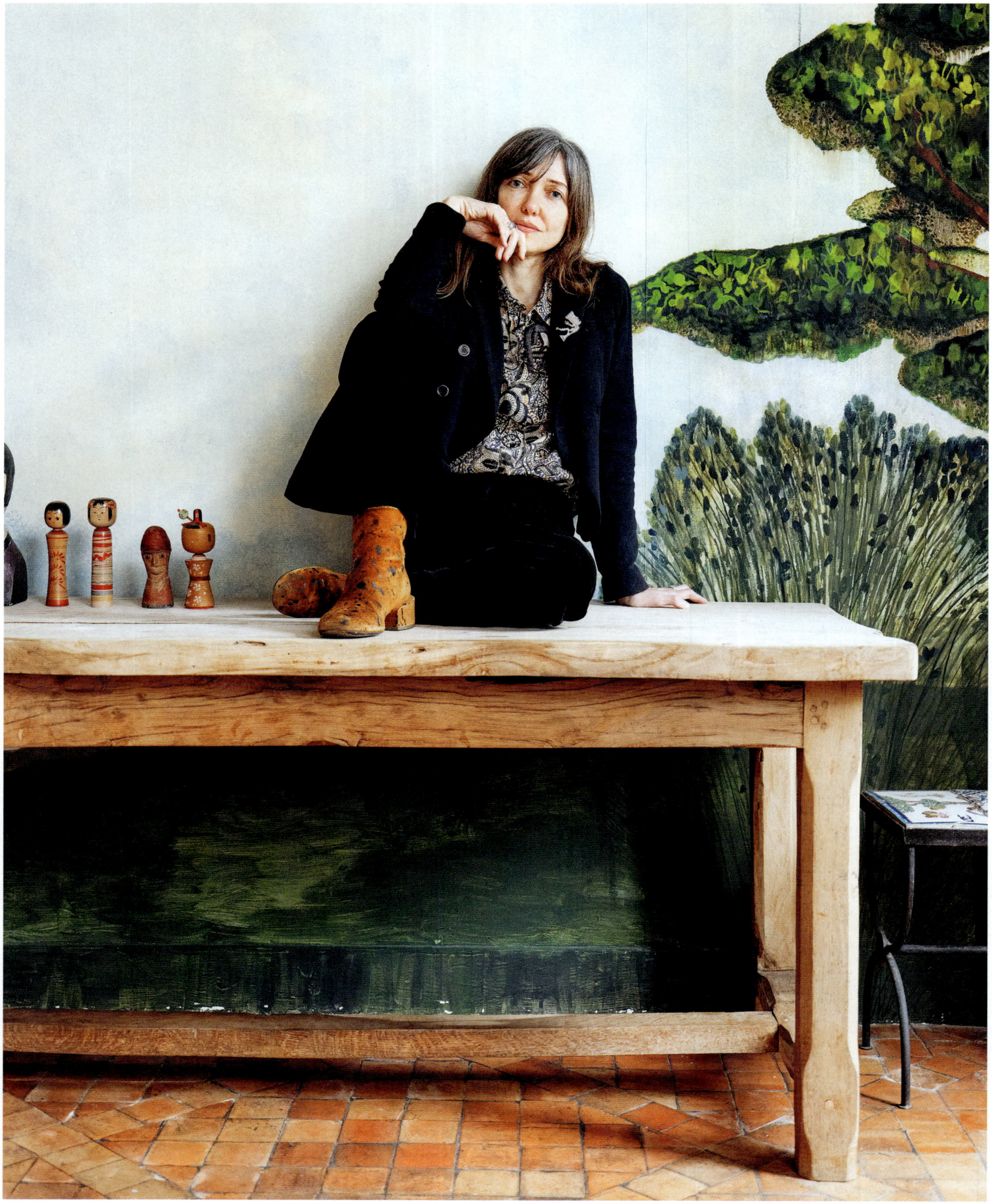

Beatrice Alemagna believes that in every good children's book there's a great story for adults, too. The work of the self-taught Italian-French illustrator and author explores topics that readers, young and old, can relate to—loss in *Pepper & Me*, anger in *Her Muddy Majesty of Muck*, boredom in *On a Magical Do-Nothing Day*, the passage of time in *Things That Go Away*—balancing the playful and the profound in a way that is rare in children's literature.

It's a personal and intuitive approach that draws on the "little girl" inside her. "She connects me to this childlike world," explains Alemagna.

ANNICK WEBER: Why is reading with children so important?

BEATRICE ALEMAGNA: It allows them to live lives they wouldn't otherwise have access to. Books nourish their imagination—their "inner light"—and give it greater intensity. Plus, they help resist emotional dullness, as children develop a wide range of feelings—it's a journey into another universe in the company of words and images.

AW: Why can't a screen replicate the experience of a book?

BA: With a screen, all the images and stories come to you effortlessly, without requiring you to engage with them in the way you do when you read or hear someone's voice, alive with emotion. A book brings you toward life; it cultivates empathy. Sitting in front of a screen only distances you from it.

AW: Who were your own childhood literary heroes?

BA: I loved [Astrid Lindgren's] Pippi Longstocking—seeing this girl, strong and fearless, living with animals and doing whatever she wanted all day long, opened me up to a new world that struck me like lightning. But don't get me wrong, I also watched television. Back then, we had less visual stimulation, so TV felt like a kind of magic box.

AW: Still, you chose books in the end.

BA: When I realized books were made by people, I knew I wanted to become someone who did that, just like how I once wanted to become a horse trainer or hot-air balloon pilot. Books help create vocations. I never studied illustration, but I have made the people and things around me—real and fictional—my teachers.

AW: How do you keep nourishing the "little girl" inside you?

BA: I like to say I put on my antennae. Sometimes they come off, when I'm tired, bored or sad. Then I have to go somewhere where I can connect with her again, where I can look and listen more deeply, and reenter a state of wonder—in nature or while playing with Playmobil with my daughter.

AW: There's wonder, but also melancholy, in your work. Why don't you shy away from "adult" themes?

BA: It's an act of respect toward the child to tell things as they are. I don't want to overprotect or overexplain. A book is also a space for experimenting with difficult situations or emotions, like fear. I don't think that causes any harm, quite the opposite: It prepares them for real-life situations.

AW: What do you mean by not wanting to overexplain?

BA: I trust my readers—I trust that they can create their own space for imagination and understanding, which is why I like to leave some blanks for them to fill in. If you think too much about them and their reactions, you start adjusting things to please them more. And then you lose what I believe in most of all: sincerity.

Words
Annick Weber
Photos
Edouard Jacquinet

"A book brings you toward life; it cultivates empathy. Sitting in front of a screen only distances you from it."

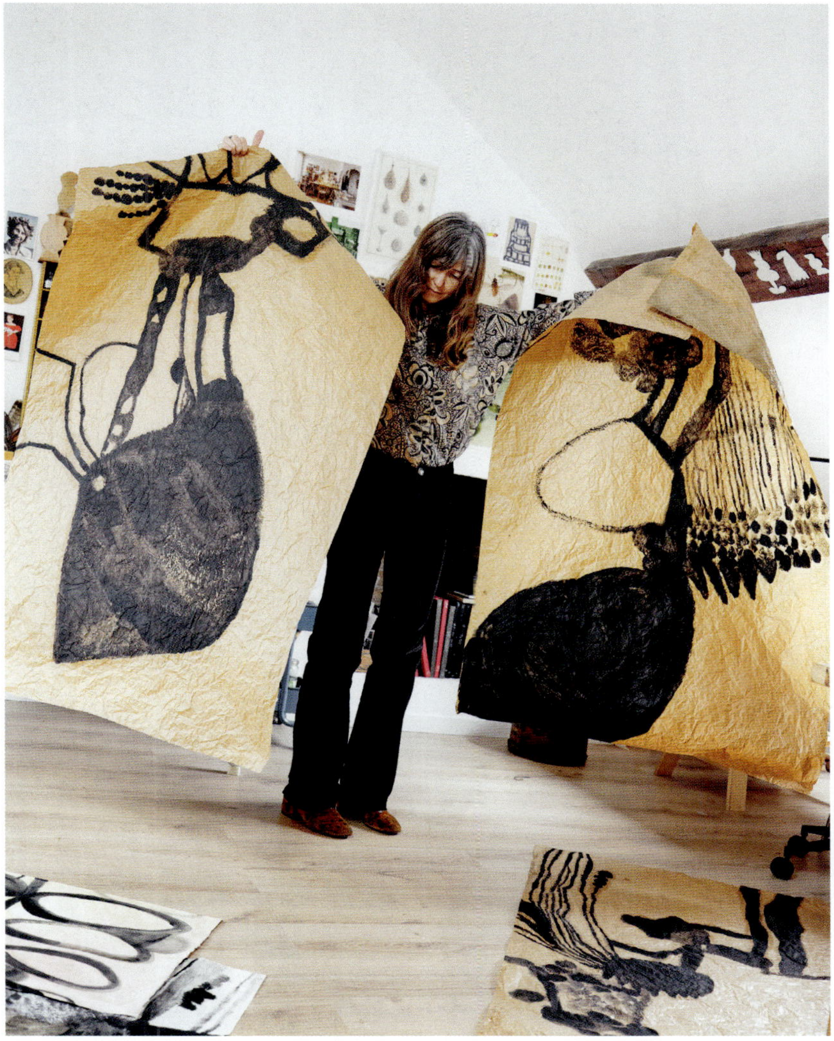

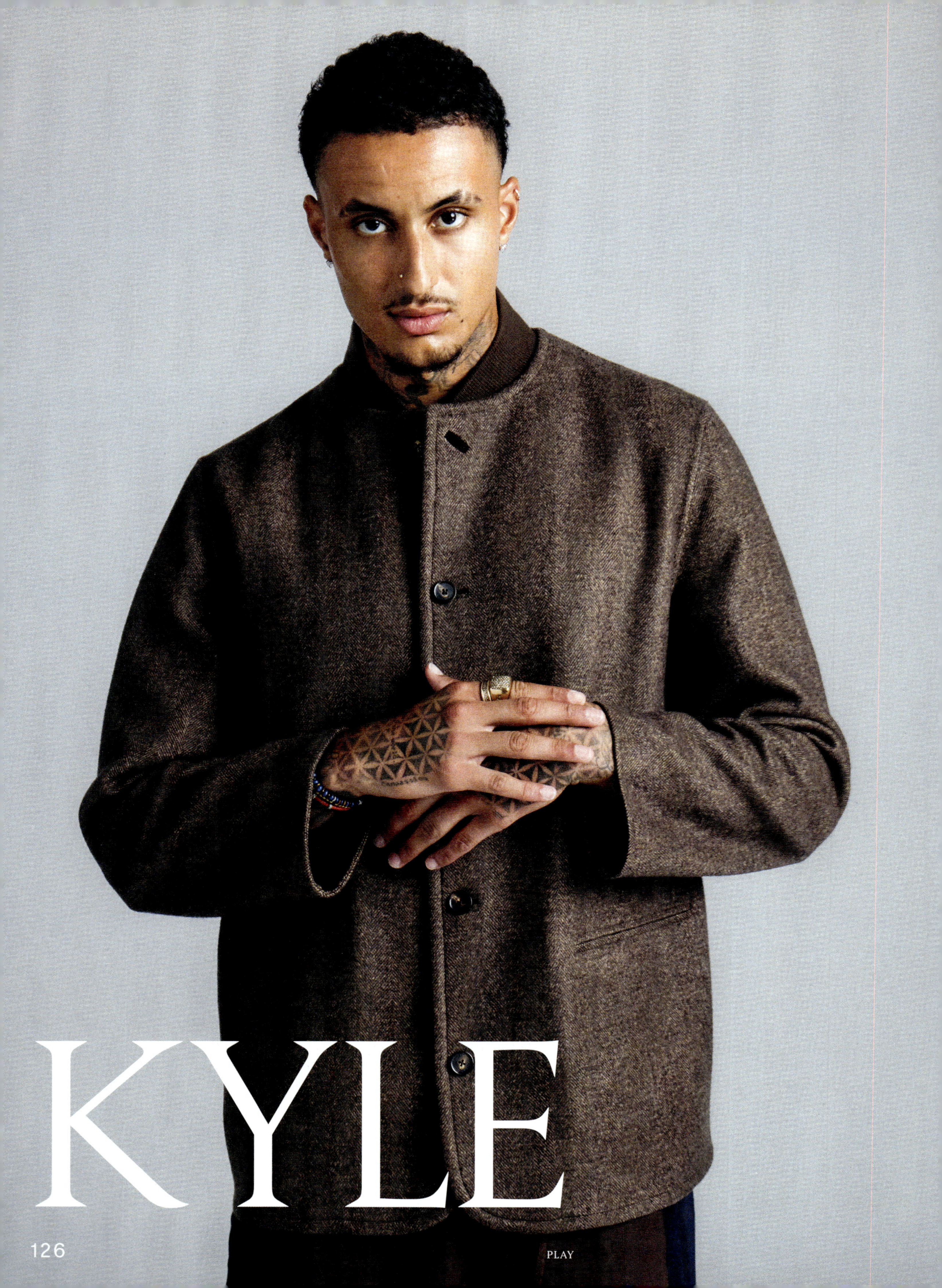

KYLE

Words ROBERT ITO Photos JAMES EMMERMAN

The NBA forward is playing the long game.

KUZMA

(opposite)
Kuzma wears a shirt and trousers by ZEGNA and a bag by BRUNELLO CUCINELLI.

(previous)
He wears a jacket by LORO PIANA.

Kyle Kuzma is enjoying himself. He's about to catch a flight for the south of France, where he'll be attending the Cannes Film Festival, and is midway through the long, complex and, for him, extremely pleasurable process, of picking out what to wear. "If I'm going somewhere in three days, I may already be in my closet, just trying on clothes, seeing what I want to wear, thinking about what type of events I'm going to," he says over a video call from his home in Miami. He's planning ahead for the films, parties and red carpet events.

If a lot of this sounds like fun, Kuzma thinks so too. "Everything is play—unless, you know, it's your profession," he says. This is the challenge because Kuzma's job is, after all, a form of play. He is in his 10th year in the NBA. A first-round draft pick in 2017, he's currently a power forward for the Milwaukee Bucks; in 2020 he won the NBA national championship with the Los Angeles Lakers in only his third year in the league.

With such success, however, comes an existential question about the difference between work and play: If work is, by definition, something you do for money, and you get lots of money for it (Kuzma currently earns around $20 million a season), isn't that work, rather than play? And if play is something you would do even if you weren't getting paid for it, is it still play if you can no longer do it for fun? Because Kuzma sure can't. There are no pickup games at the Y for him, no shootarounds with pals at the local gym. "I'm 30 years old now," he says. "Any extra basketball, other than during the season, that's just a lot of wear and tear on your body. You've got to be a little more strategic with how you go about it."

Kuzma was born and raised in Flint, Michigan, a town known to most people outside the city for its precipitous economic collapse that began in the 1980s (see Michael Moore's *Roger & Me*, the 1989 documentary about the impact of the General Motors factory closing), and more recently for its lead-poisoned water. "When you're a kid, you don't think about all those things," he says. Raised by a single mom who worked two jobs to make ends meet, Kuzma moved around a lot, living in a variety of neighborhoods and homes. But basketball was a constant. "My mother put a basketball in my hands when I was very, very young," he says. "We always used to play in the living room with a Fisher-Price rim. We'd move the furniture out the way and put down tape for the free-throw line."

A basketball standout at the University of Utah, Kuzma went from seeing the sport as something played for fun to understanding it as a serious, high-pressure job, performed under the brightest spotlights. "It's still fun, but it's fun in a different way," he says. When he moved to the NBA, he brought his love of the game with him. But he also brought his love of clothes, something he had been cultivating since his earliest days, going to church as a kid. "You couldn't go to church with sweats on," he says. "You had to put on *clothes*": turtlenecks, half zips, slacks, collared shirts and so on. It was all good practice for what was to come.

Since his time with the Lakers, Kuzma has become a celebrated, and at times controversial, star of the pregame tunnel walk. In less-enlightened days, this was simply the route players took to get from the team bus to the stadium's locker rooms; in more recent years, it has become a sartorial playground—a place where players

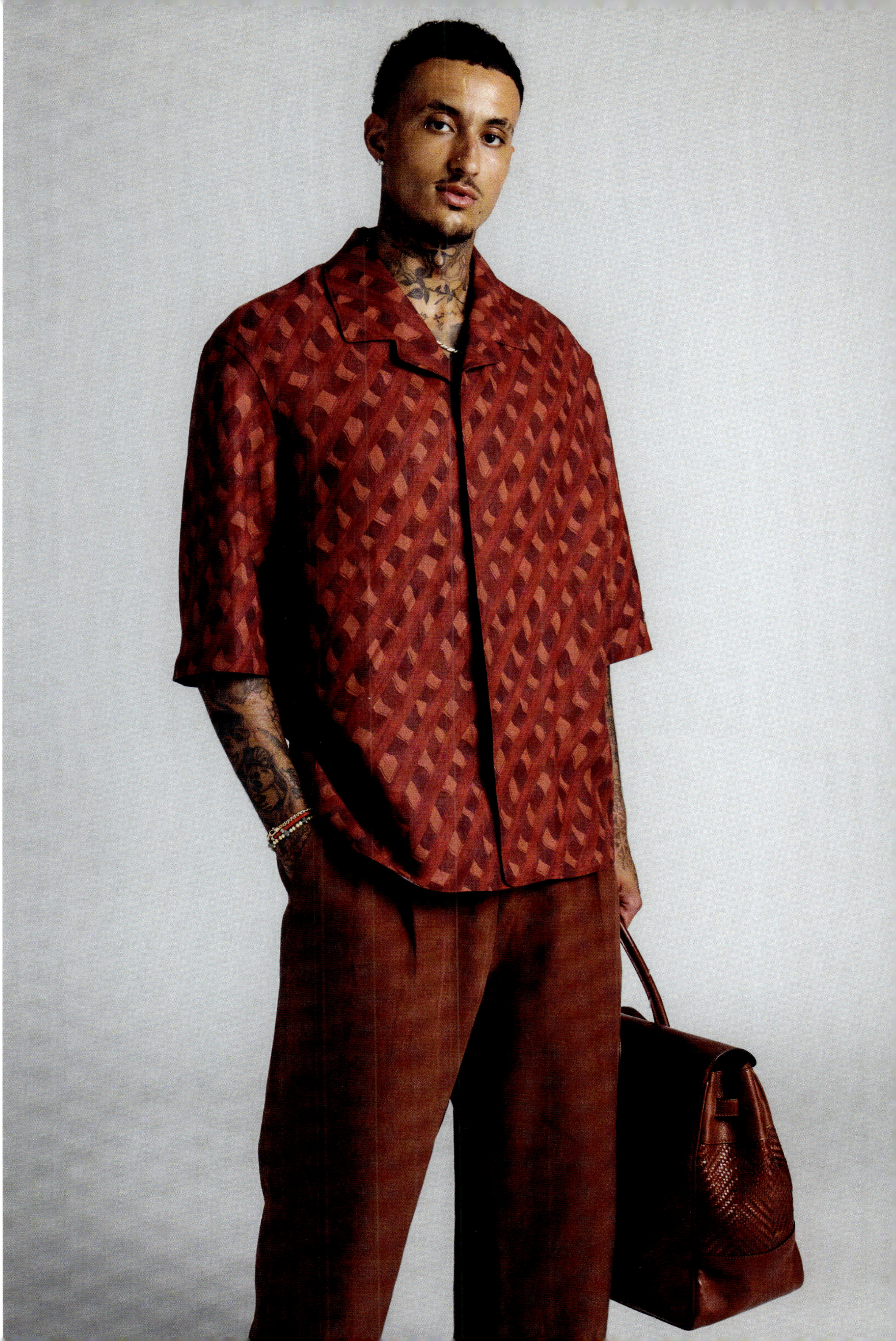

Grooming: Madeline Rouge

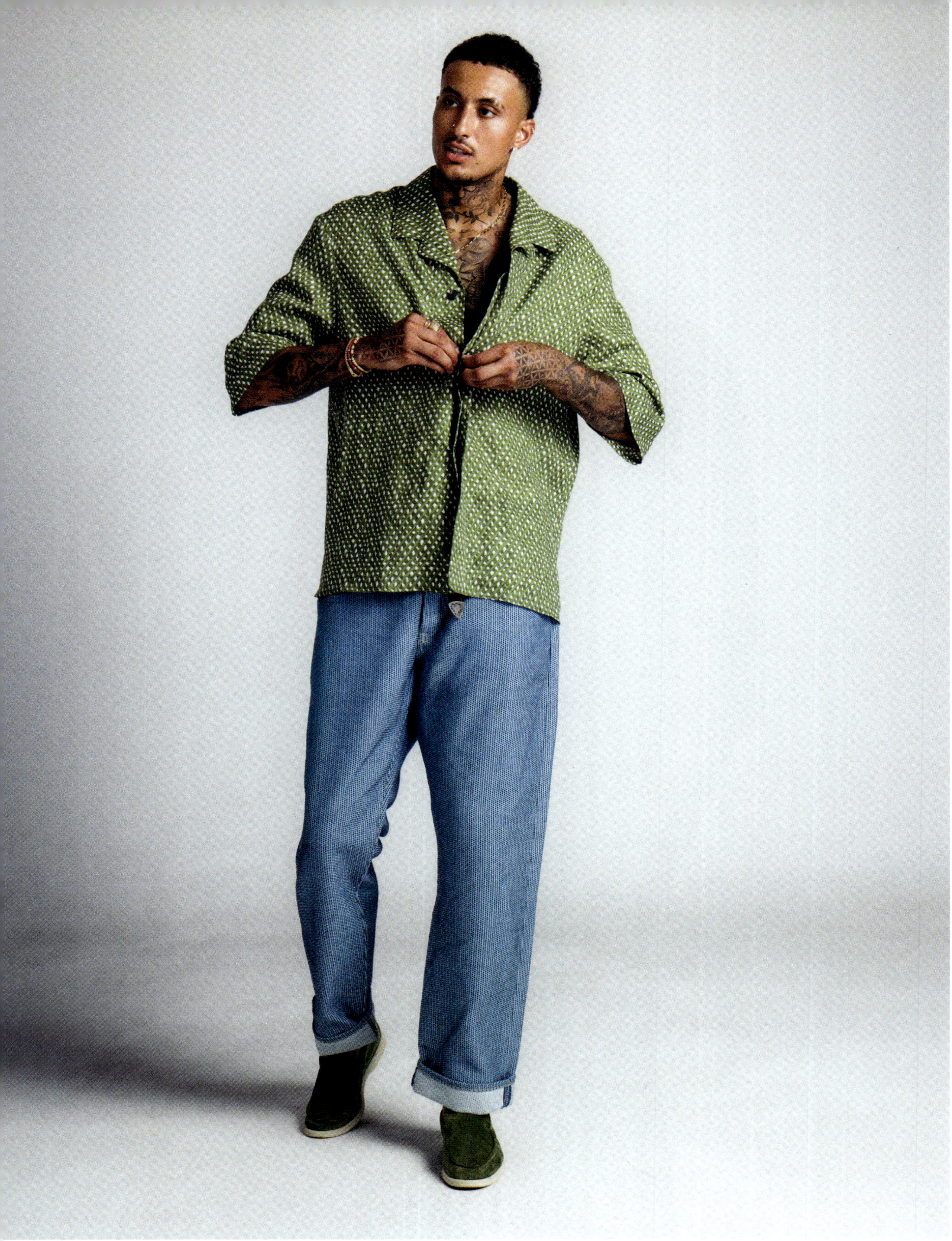

(above)
Kuzma wears a shirt by ZEGNA, trousers by KAPITAL and shoes by LORO PIANA.
(opposite)
He wears a shirt and sunglasses by ZEGNA.

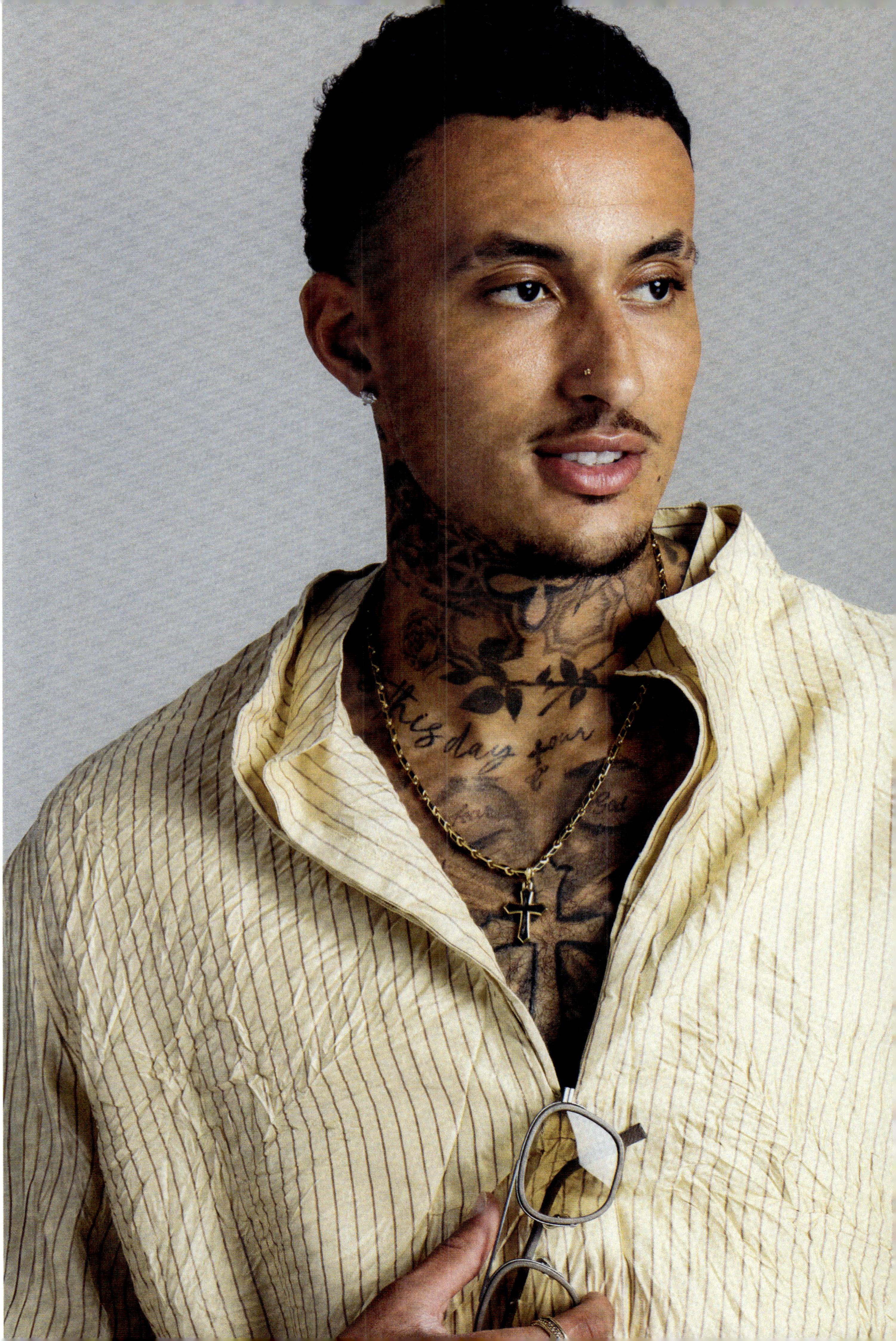

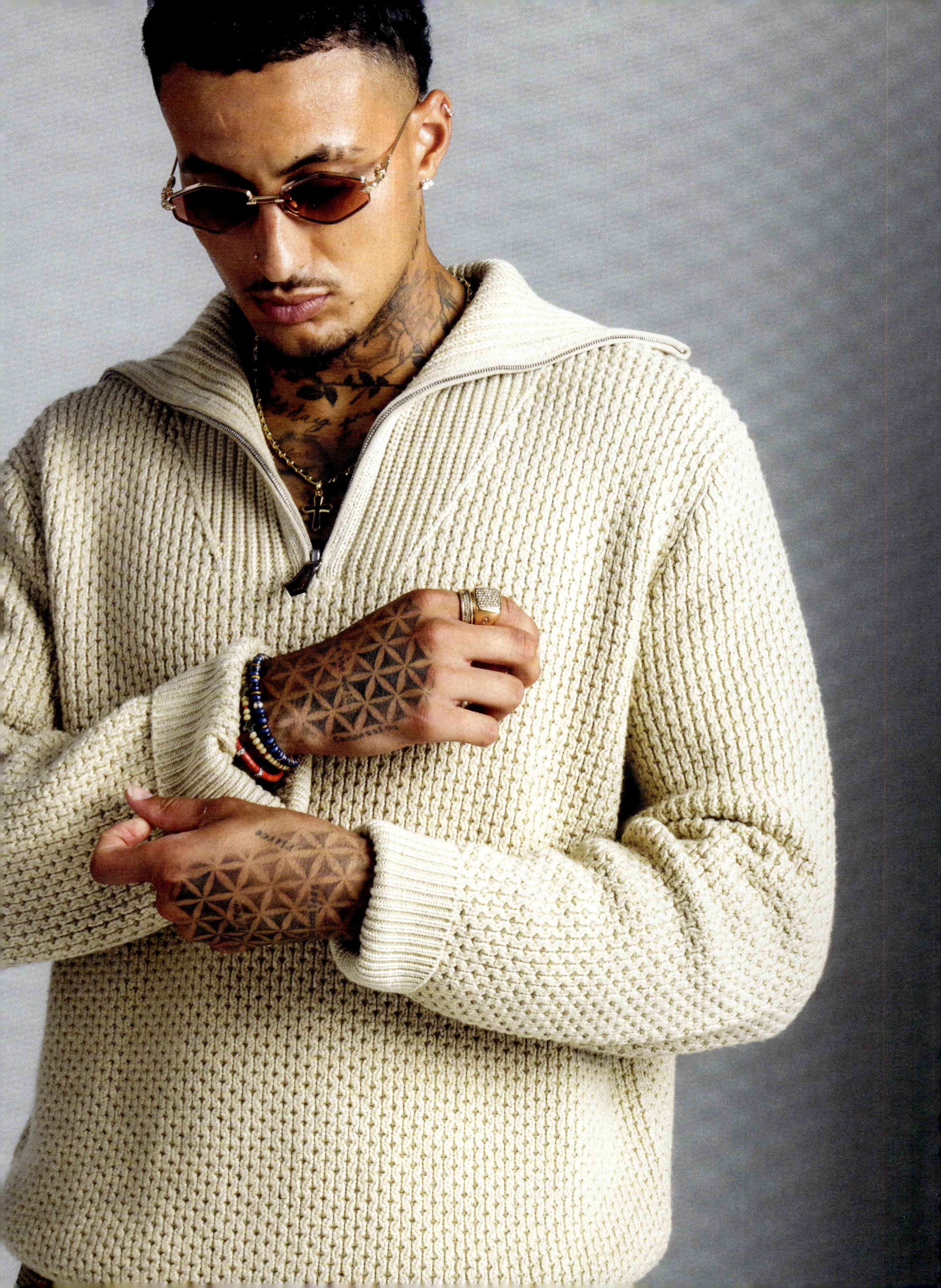

peacock past banks of photographers in a spectacle that attracts million-dollar brand sponsorships. These otherwise drab stadium corridors became Kuzma's runway, where he sported everything from leather button-down shirts and lavish fur coats to an oversized, bright pink Raf Simons sweater that was later immortalized as a gameday giveaway bobblehead and in the pages of *Vanity Fair*. His outfits were lauded in *GQ*, *Vogue* and *The New York Times*—so much so that he ended up on the actual runway during New York Fashion Week in 2022.

Notably, Kuzma doesn't work with a stylist, unlike many of his peers in the NBA. But he has grown tired of the demands of the tunnel walks, citing the fashion churn that comes with them. "You have to show people a new outfit every single game," he says. "That's just not economically smart. I still dress up really well. I still wear clothes. But I wear them a lot more times."

Kuzma has interests beyond fashion, in any case. In between setting style trends and playing basketball, he has become something of an art collector. Art is a good investment, something his NBA salary has allowed him to indulge in, he says, but it also inspires him. "Just imagine you were in prison," he says. "You're in a cell with just concrete walls. If all around you is blank walls, how can you think creatively? You can't."

This year, Kuzma will begin his 10th season in the NBA, a notable achievement in a league where the average career lasts less than five. He's already won an NBA championship ring, and could retire happily—but Kuzma's not going anywhere. "I love the game too much to not play," he says. He might consider leaving if, say, he had some sort of catastrophic injury that prevented him from playing (the look on his face makes it clear how much the thought of this pains him), but otherwise, no. "I just love being around the game. In this league, you can't play this long without loving it."

It's not that playing at the top of his sport isn't demanding: "It's a dog-eat-dog world. It's survival of the fittest," he says. "But I think that just correlates to life as well. There's a lot of pressure. Is basketball a child's game? Yes, it is. Do we play in a child's game? No. It's a man's game."

Still, Kuzma keeps the memory of those old days alive, when basketball was just a child's game, back when he and his mom were shooting hoops with that Fisher-Price basket in their home in Flint. Even now, he brings that mind-set with him to the rigors of NBA practices and the league's grueling 82-game seasons. "You have to," he says. "I feel like everything in life is just a mind game. So you have to go, 'We've gotta have fun, guys, we've gotta play the game that we've always loved.'"

"Stress and anxiety is all a part of life, it's all a part of the game," he continues. "But sometimes you have to remember where you came from, and that it is just a game."

(below)
He wears a jacket and trousers by LORO PIANA with shoes by ZEGNA.

(opposite)
Kuzma wears a sweater by LORO PIANA and sunglasses by CHROME HEARTS.

"Everything in life is just a mind game."

Kuzma's collection currently includes work by Lauren Halsey, who recently created a massive, sphinx-filled sculpture park in South Central Los Angeles that honors local African American female activists. "I think she's the most important artist of this generation," Kuzma says. "Her vantage point of life growing up in the inner city of LA is a perspective that you could only get if you're from there." He's also a fan of Derrick Adams and Tony Lewis, two artists whose work deals with issues of race and identity within the Black community. One of the perks of being a collector, Kuzma explains, is getting to meet the artists themselves. "Tony was actually the first person to put me on to scotch and certain whiskeys," he says. "Now that's all I drink."

Of course, life isn't *all* play. In 2019, Kuzma and his mother, Karri, created the Kyle Kuzma Family Foundation, a nonprofit dedicated to helping single mothers and their children. The organization's activities range from large-scale events (an annual celebrity golf tournament in Florida that has already raised around $2 million for single moms), to smaller but equally important efforts (helping a mom who was close to getting evicted pay her rent). "My mother was a single mother for most of her life, and we were underprivileged as well, so it's all about giving back," Kuzma says.

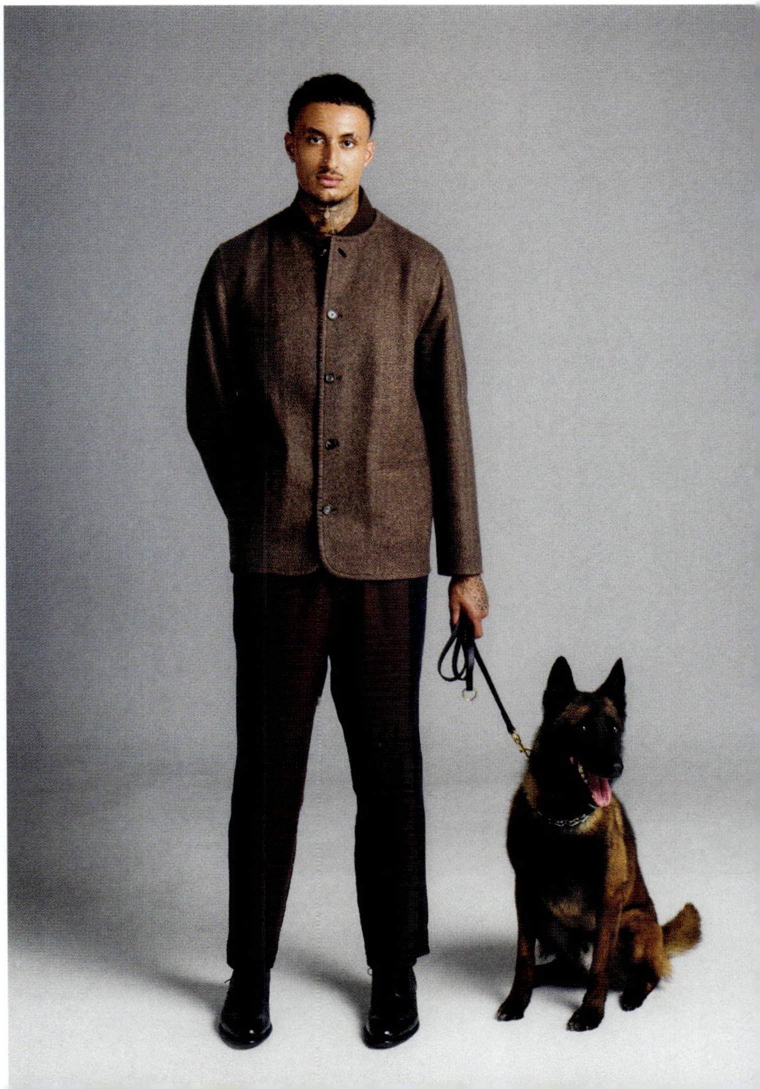

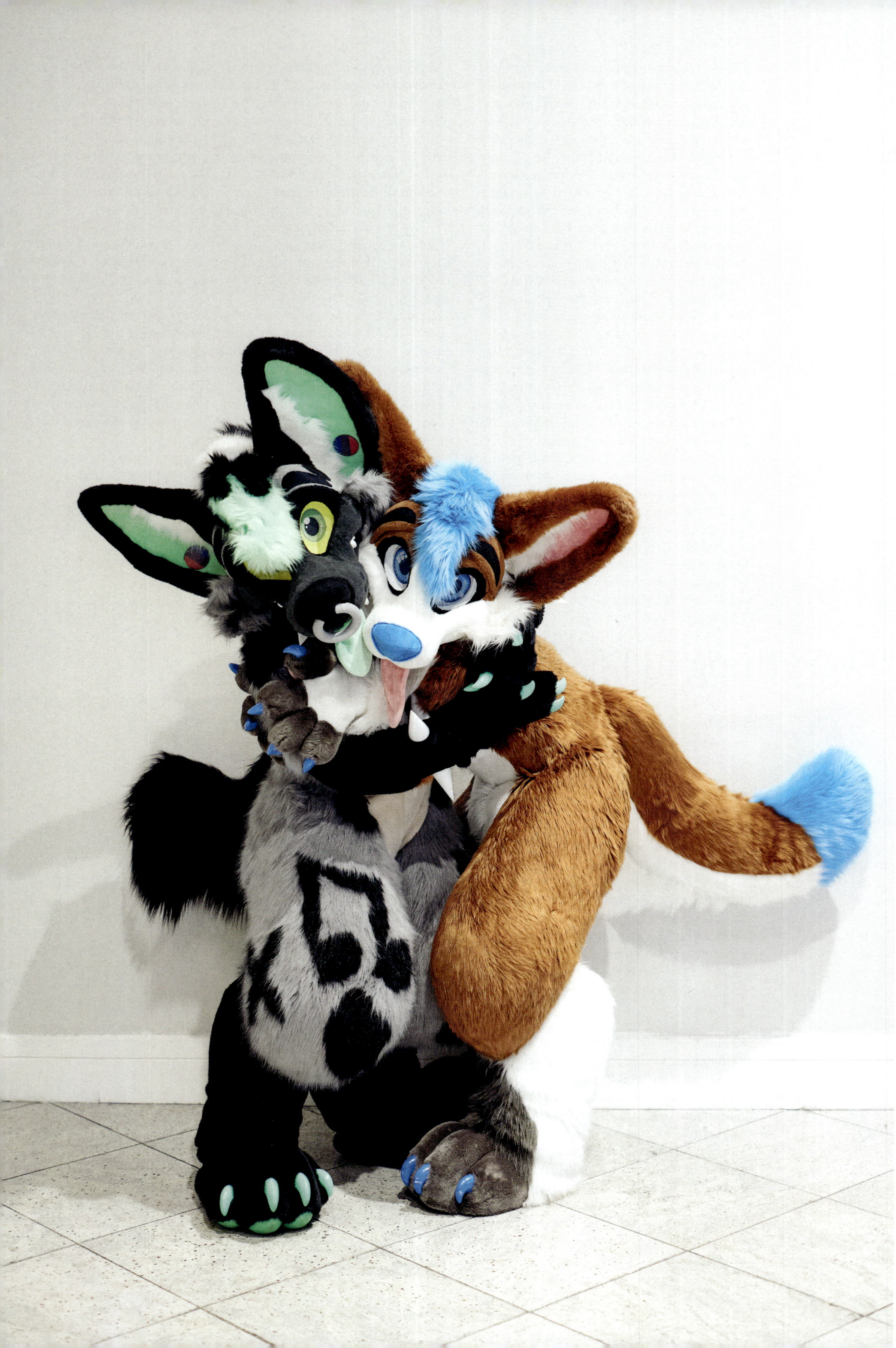

SUIT YOURSELF:
An access pass to Furry Weekend Atlanta.

Words
Kyla Marshell
Photos
Ben Rollins

“At the end of the day, for most people, it’s just a hobby.” Glancing around the Hilton, the Marriott, as well as three other hotels; a nearby parking lot, converted into an exhibition space; and, really, all of downtown Atlanta during Furry Weekend Atlanta, one would be hard-pressed to view the fervor and commitment of the more than 17,000 registered attendees as just a “hobby.” Yet these words, spoken by a furry called Hypofox, are perhaps a way of diffusing and deflecting undue attention on a much misunderstood and maligned passion. This four-day event is one of the few chances for the furry fandom to be in community with people who already understand it.

Not anime, not cosplay per se—and not, as many seem to think, a purely kink-driven interest—the furry fandom arose in the early 1980s when the first con, or “confurence” (puns abound for the fandom), was held as an offshoot of Comic Con. Since then, cons have sprung up all over the world, with 20,000 attendees expected at the largest, Anthrocon, in Pittsburgh in July 2026.

To be a furry, generally, means to have a love of anthropomorphism—human characteristics assigned to animals, often in the form of art, video games and other types of visual media. Most furries create alter egos, or fursonas, instilled with traitsthey can more easily inhabit behind the safety of a mask or avatar, whether online or in person.

For some, these fursonas are straightforward and aligned with animal traits—the strength of a ram or the power of a Siberian white tiger—or designed to incorporate a favorite color. But there is often a backstory to many furries’ reason for being, one that extends beyond a love for animals, and that often stems from the isolation they felt growing up.

According to the International Anthropomorphic Research Project—a multidisciplinary team of scientists from universities around the world that’s better known as “Furscience,” and that conducts academic studies on furries—over 75% of furries are under the age of 25, and more than half identify as gay, bisexual, asexual or pansexual. Nearly two-thirds report being bullied during adolescence. The harm caused by ostracization, othering and unhealthy family dynamics is often still fresh for this young demographic, and is something that binds them together.

“I honestly have been socially excluded since pre-K,” says Timothy Montgomery, a 19-year-old furry from New Jersey. Not all furries wear fursuits or animal-coded outfits, and instead of an animal fursona, Timothy Montgomery is styled as a World War II veteran character, in camo fatigues and a beret, and has a British accent. “And once I left high school, I was on my own. This group took me in. I developed this wonderful relationship between me and the furries.”

“I was very shy and very much isolated in high school,” says 29-year-old Milo Kiyoshi, who is also from New Jersey. His fursuit—gray fur with green ears, hair and

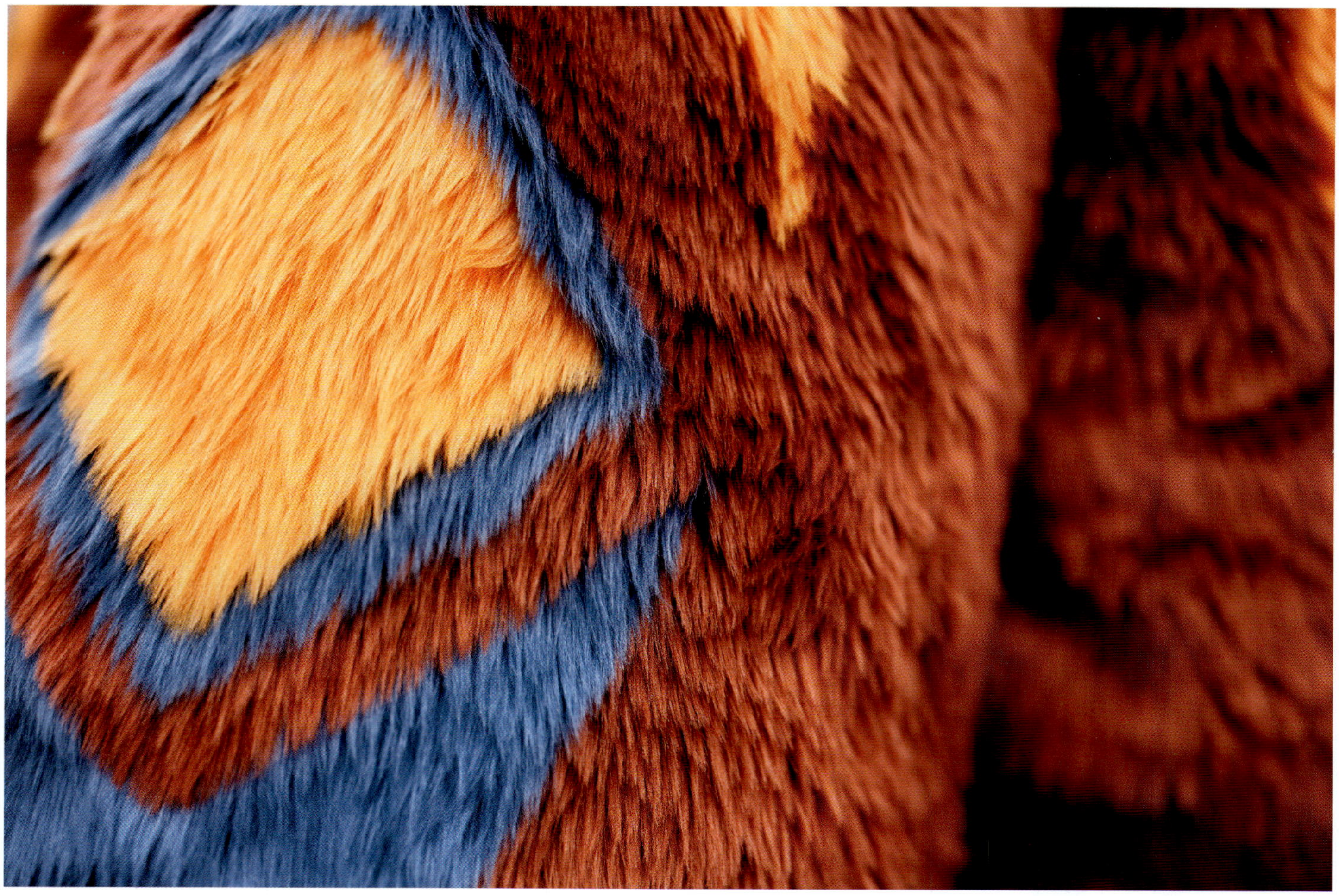

claws, with music notes patterned onto the legs—was inspired by a hyena from *The Lion King*. He was first exposed to furries via the media coverage that propagated harmful misconceptions. But joining the community, he not only became an LGBTQ+ ally, something he'd once opposed, but he found friends online and in person whom he could relate to. "I'm very introverted, so it's very hard for me to reach out and talk to people. But with the suit on, I feel more outgoing."

There's a concept in the fandom called "the ideal self"—the idea that your fursona embodies who you'd be if you could heighten all your best qualities, particularly the ones you struggle to show in your regular life. According to Hypofox, who also serves as FWA's audiovisual manager, it's not part of every furry's fursona; but feeling empowered to connect with strangers while disguised is something attendees repeat over and over.

"He is my everyday personality turned up to 11," says Shackle Ram, who's been a furry since 2001. Shackle, who has huge, curled horns and a green jersey, is an alternate fursona, which is a common phenomenon—having multiple fursonas with different looks and traits that evolve as their creators do. "He is everything that I would like to be able to be at my nine-to-five job or around my family." Competitiveness and arrogance are two qualities his fursona allows him to showcase and experience.

(above)
Despite how little most people know about them, furries are a sizeable community. Exact numbers are difficult to determine, but estimates suggest there are between one and three million worldwide.

"We've got people that work for the government. We've got people that are working at Wendy's."

(opposite)
Wolves are the most popular animal for a fursona, followed by dragons—often referred to as "scalies"—and then foxes.

Fur cons are also a conduit to connect over many of the things furries love. At FWA, one hotel hosts an entire video arcade; there is also a dance competition, a vendor hall selling everything from premade clip-on tails to stickers to herbal tea, and, in a nearby lot, a car show, where furries have brought their flashiest vehicles to show off. And they do all these things—dance, talk, meet new people—while in varying degrees of elaborate fursuiting: neon colors, helmets with LED screens spelling out messages, platform hooves elevating their wearers to the heavens.

These suits are almost exclusively custom-made: different gradations of faux fur to create animal stripes; foam sculpted into detachable heads. Some suits lean deep into playfulness with giant earrings, sunglasses or other accessories. Vision and voices are tempered—furries expect to bump into each other while suited (and also learn to give grace because of it)—and temperatures inside can reach 120°F. Prices for suits can run into the thousands of dollars.

The creativity involved in making the fursuits is what intrigued Eclipse, 22, who's in town from Long Island, New York. "I'm not gonna lie to you—my time started watching a bunch of furry cringe compilations on YouTube," she says. "Initially, I was laughing at it. And then the more I watched them, I was like, 'They low-key creative.' So I started looking into it. And eventually I

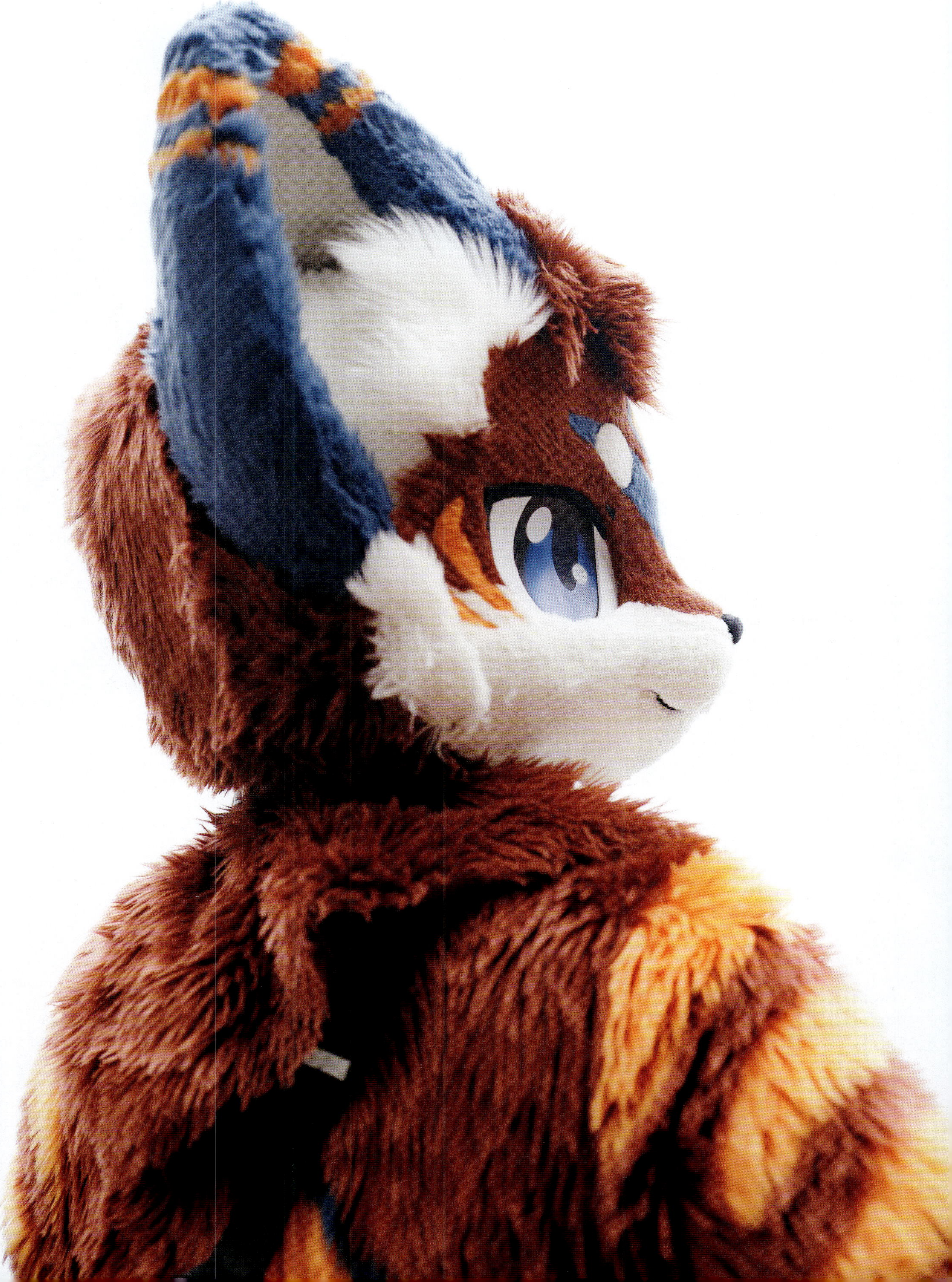

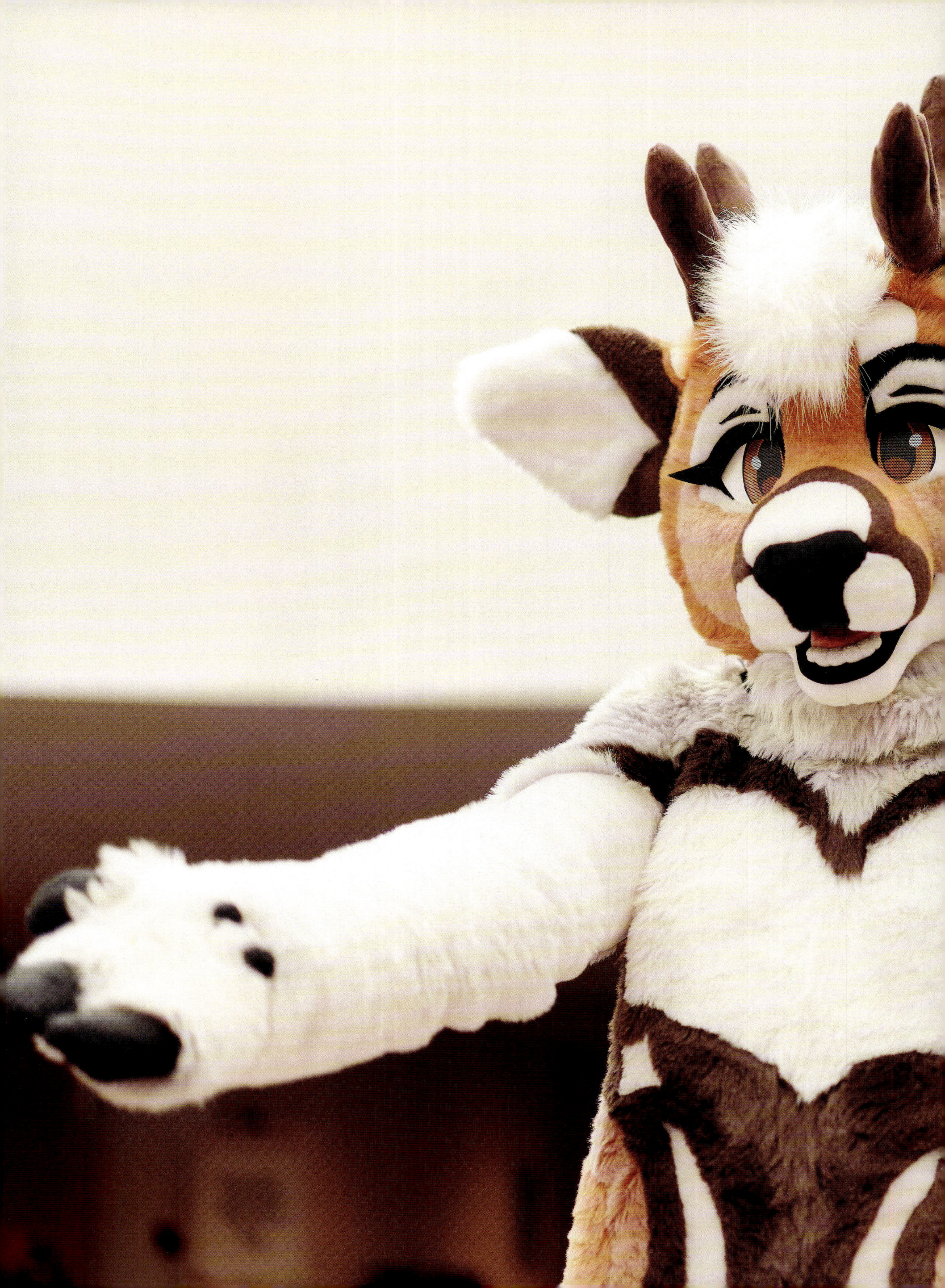

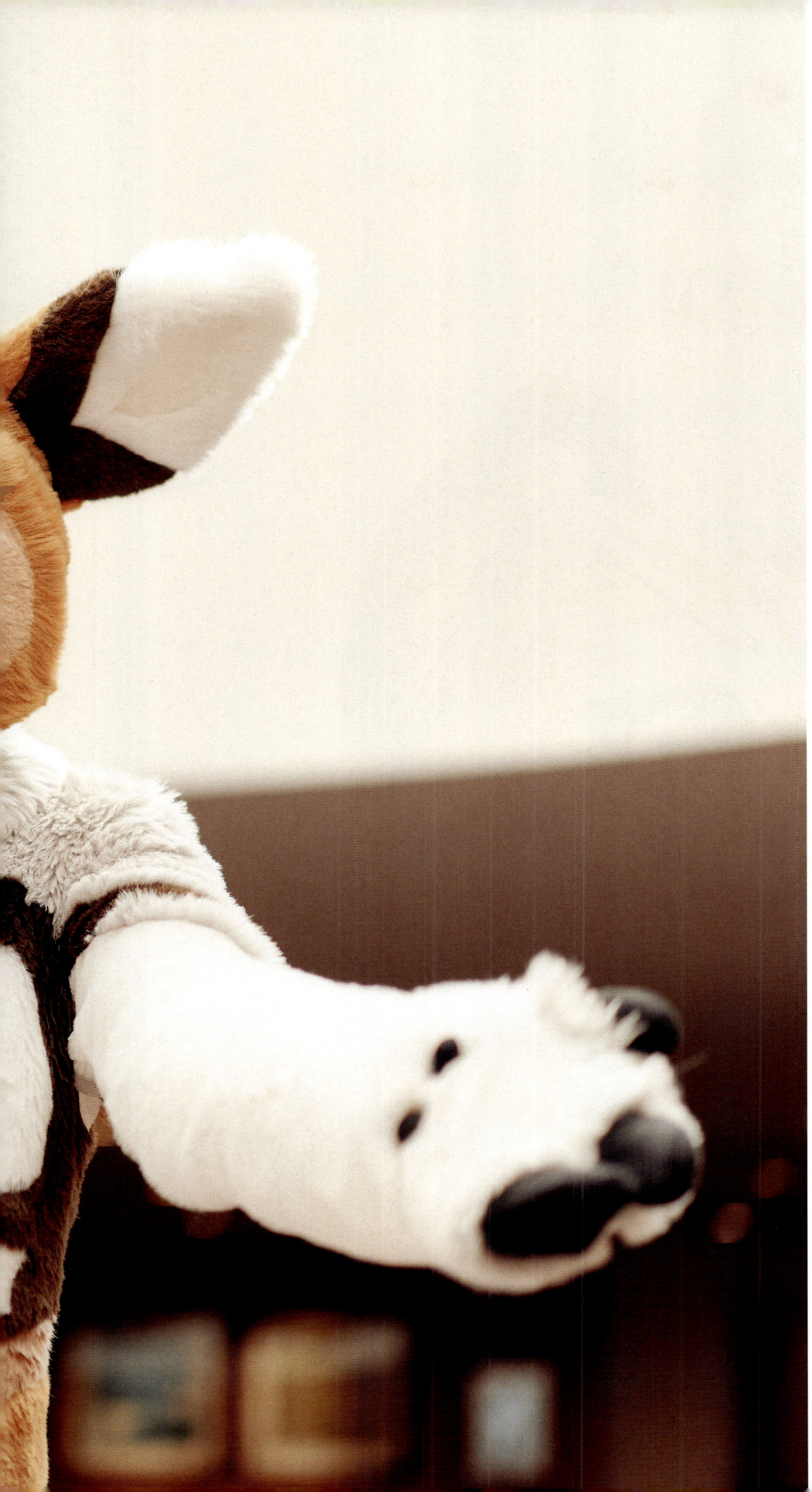

(opposite)
Held each year in late March or early April, Furry Weekend Atlanta has grown into one of the world's largest furry conventions, attracting more than 17,000 attendees.

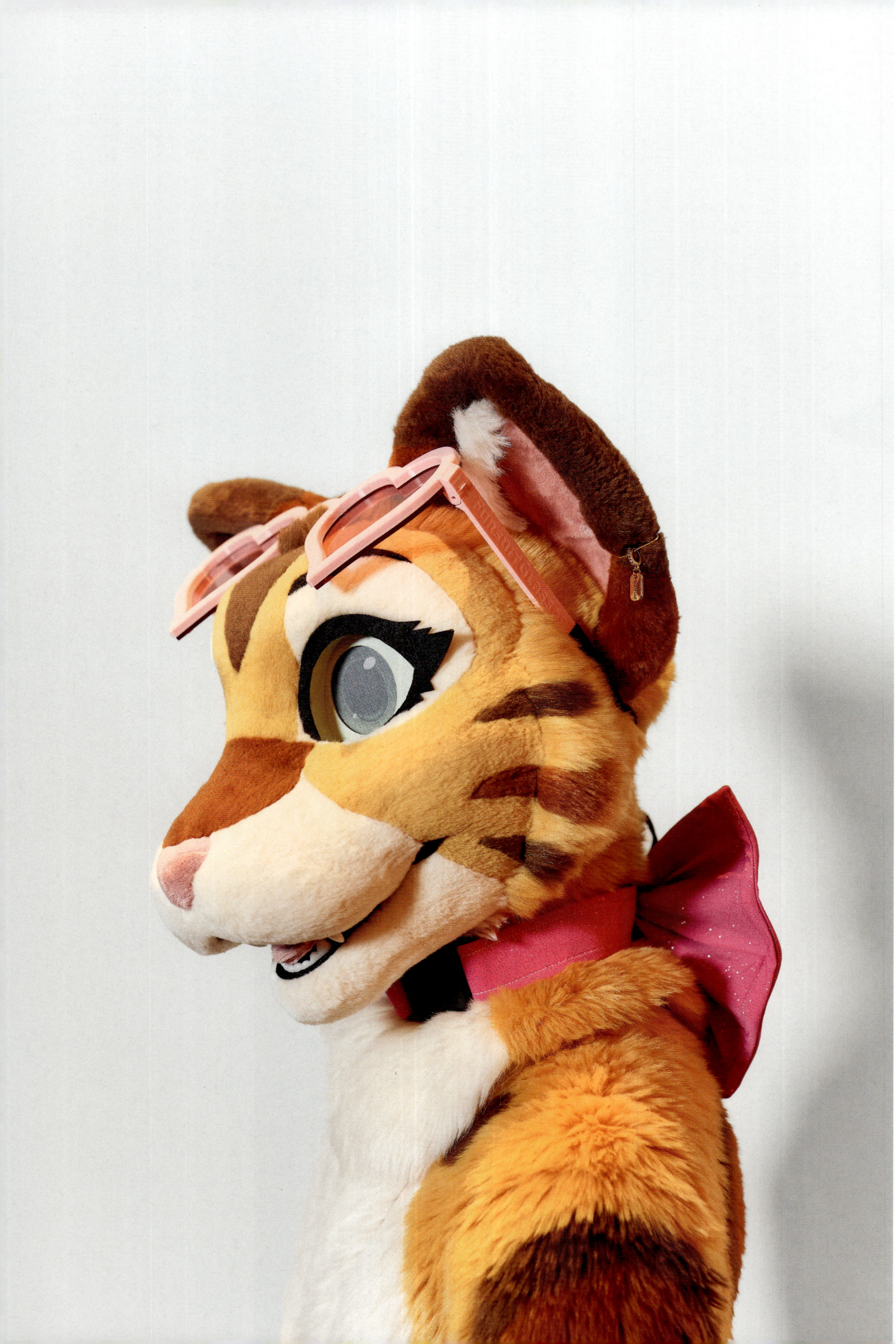

ended up making a bunch of furry friends and now I go to conventions."

Gia, 25, is a part-time fursuiter based in Maryland who makes custom suits on commission. She is at FWA as Gaga, her alt-fursona who's a cat, created in part to show off her feminine side. "I've made over 20 suits at this point. And it's brought me great income. It makes it so I can afford to go to cons and afford little extra luxuries here and there." She explains that some suits take up to six months to complete, and that she only accepts a commission if she really feels she can bring the customer's fursona to life.

There's a stereotype that furries mostly work in tech—who else could afford all these accoutrements? As a community that exists online as much as it does in person, there's certainly a tech-savvy inclination among them. But a number of furries explain that cons are an opportunity to meet people from across class and educational backgrounds whom they would not find themselves in community with otherwise.

"We've got pilots, we've got cybersecurity, we've got people that work for the government. We've got people that are working at Wendy's," says Gia. "I mean, all of those people don't normally interact on a daily basis, and now they're all in the same room, with one thing in common."

It's part of why fur cons appeal to Eclipse, Timothy Montgomery and Senpai Pirate, who are hanging out in the Hilton lobby on day two of the con with three other young Black furries. They explain that cons offer more than a typical club setting.

"When you go to a club, you only expect them to do club [stuff]," says Eclipse. "With furry conventions, there's other things you can do. There's gatherings of people, talking about our experiences. We talking about how we got through it. We talking mental health and wellness. It's different than a club."

"He is everything that I would like to be able to be at my nine-to-five job."

"A whole bunch of backgrounds all leading to one community," adds Senpai Pirate.

Having variously connected online, at Midwest FurFest and earlier that day, they bonded over their love for music, a central part of fur cons. Furry Weekend Atlanta has three raves per night; trance and EDM spill out of every crevice of the hotels, vendor halls and parking lot the group had taken over. Insanitylaxity, 19, from Long Beach, California, is playing his own music from a speaker he is perched on.

Sitting in the Hilton lobby, only Senpai Pirate alludes to connecting with this particular group of furries because of race; cons, and the fandom overall, are predominantly white. In 2025, an energetic furry from New Orleans named Fendi, 31, who describes their hot pink dog fursona as "a mascot of themself" started a party at FWA called Pink Social Club to make the space more welcoming to Black furries. "We created a nightclub, like a simulation of what it's like to be BIPOC. It's for you and me to come and hear the music we listen to, to feel like we at the cookout," they say. "It's open to everyone. Our allies love it. They've been waiting for [something] like that. They're tired of EDM!"

Fendi says that they and their Pink Social Club partner, Jaylaflame—both furry rappers—were fully supported by FWA to create this space because it's aligned with a core value of the con, and the fandom overall: inclusion.

"One of the founding principles of the community is being yourself—being able to truly express yourself and not have to worry about anyone judging you or looking at you weird," says Hypofox. And within the fandom, despite the emphasis on uniqueness, the hope is that everyone will be treated equally.

"It's like a Mardi Gras, you know?" says Timothy Montgomery. "A time in which kings are the same as just regular people. It doesn't matter how big you are. We're still flesh and blood regardless."

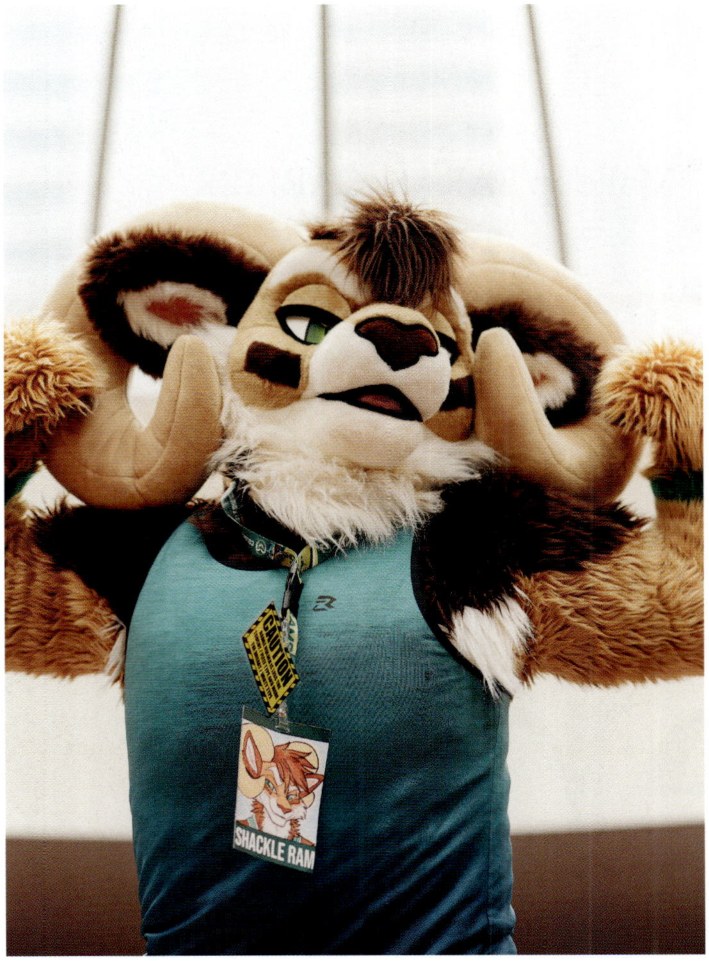

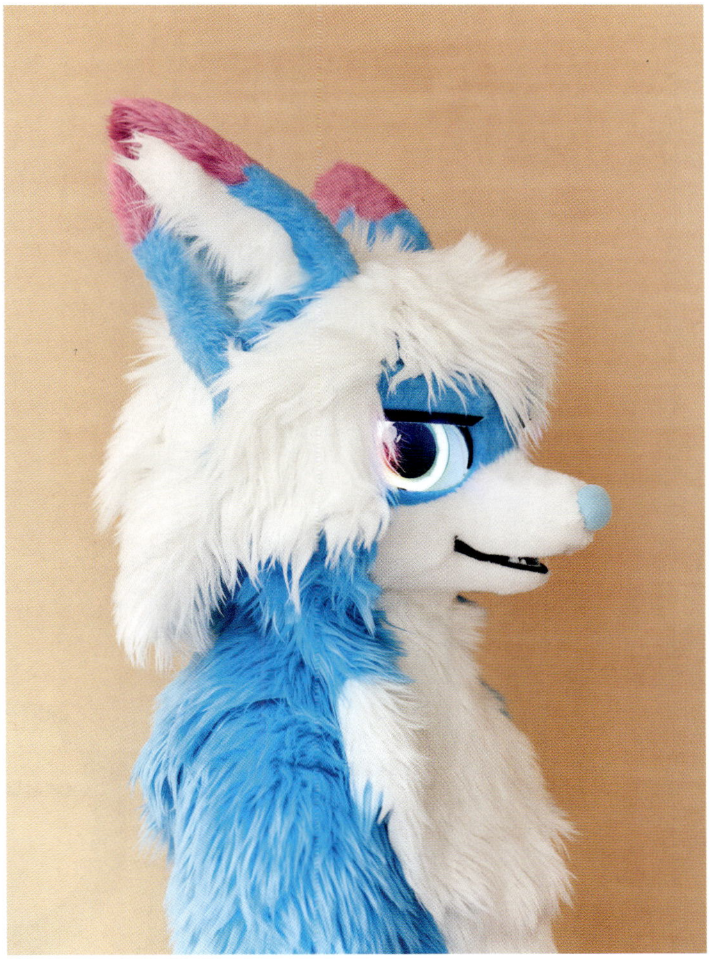

Press

A visual guide to giving a massage.

Photos YUHAO CHANG Makeup SARAH CARLIER

Here

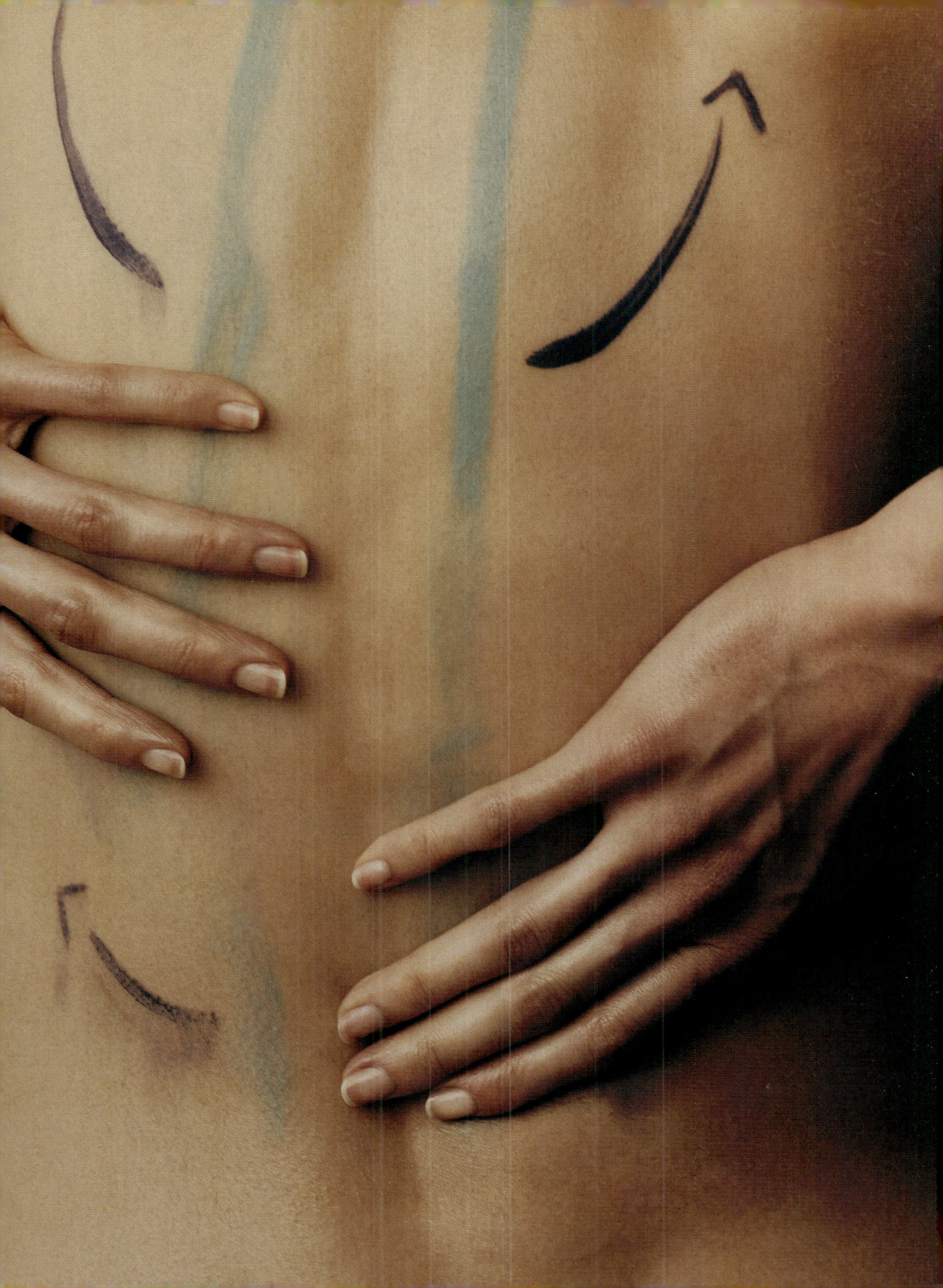

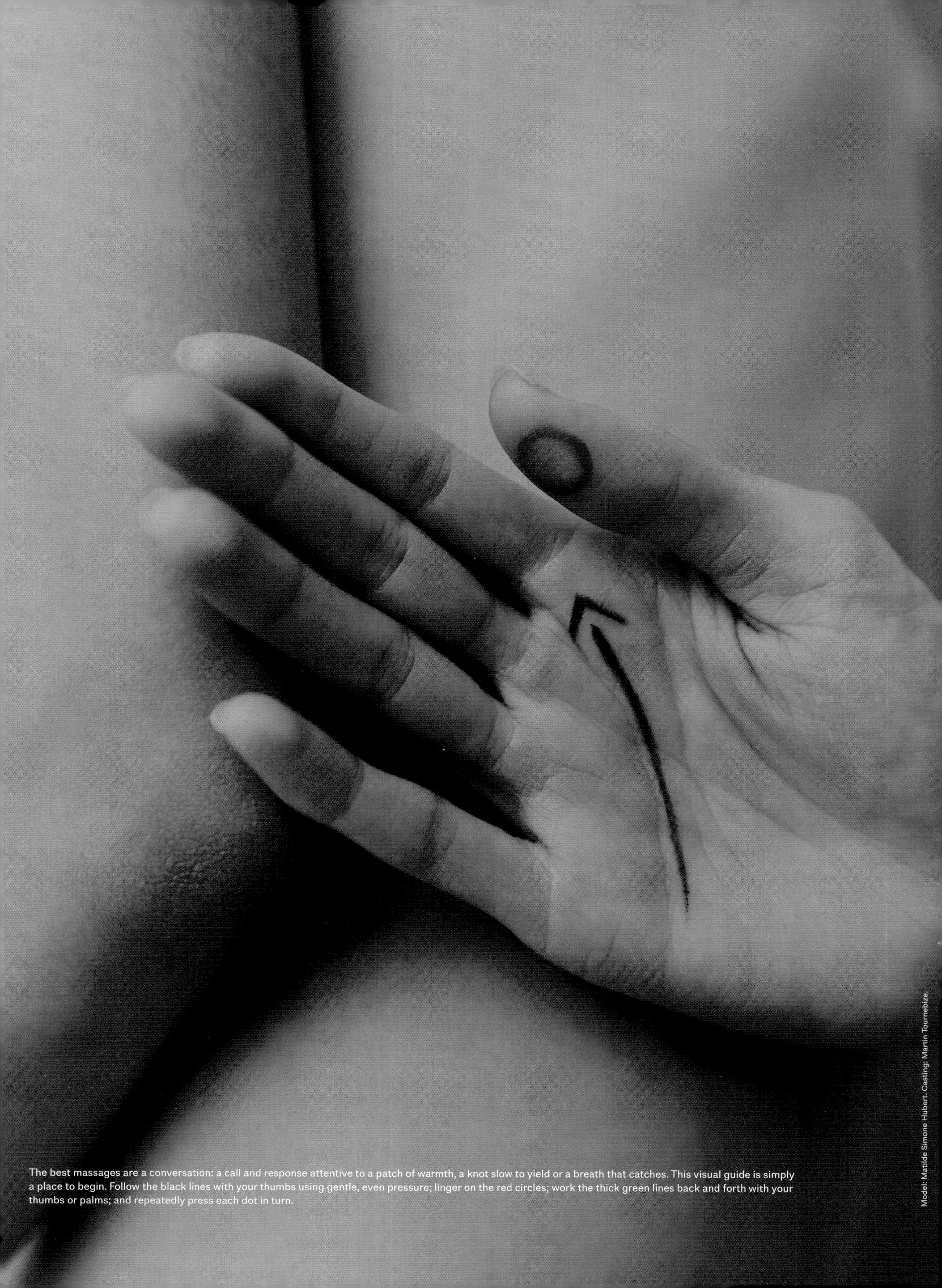

The best massages are a conversation: a call and response attentive to a patch of warmth, a knot slow to yield or a breath that catches. This visual guide is simply a place to begin. Follow the black lines with your thumbs using gentle, even pressure; linger on the red circles; work the thick green lines back and forth with your thumbs or palms; and repeatedly press each dot in turn.

Model: Matilde Simone Hubert. Casting: Martin Tournebize.

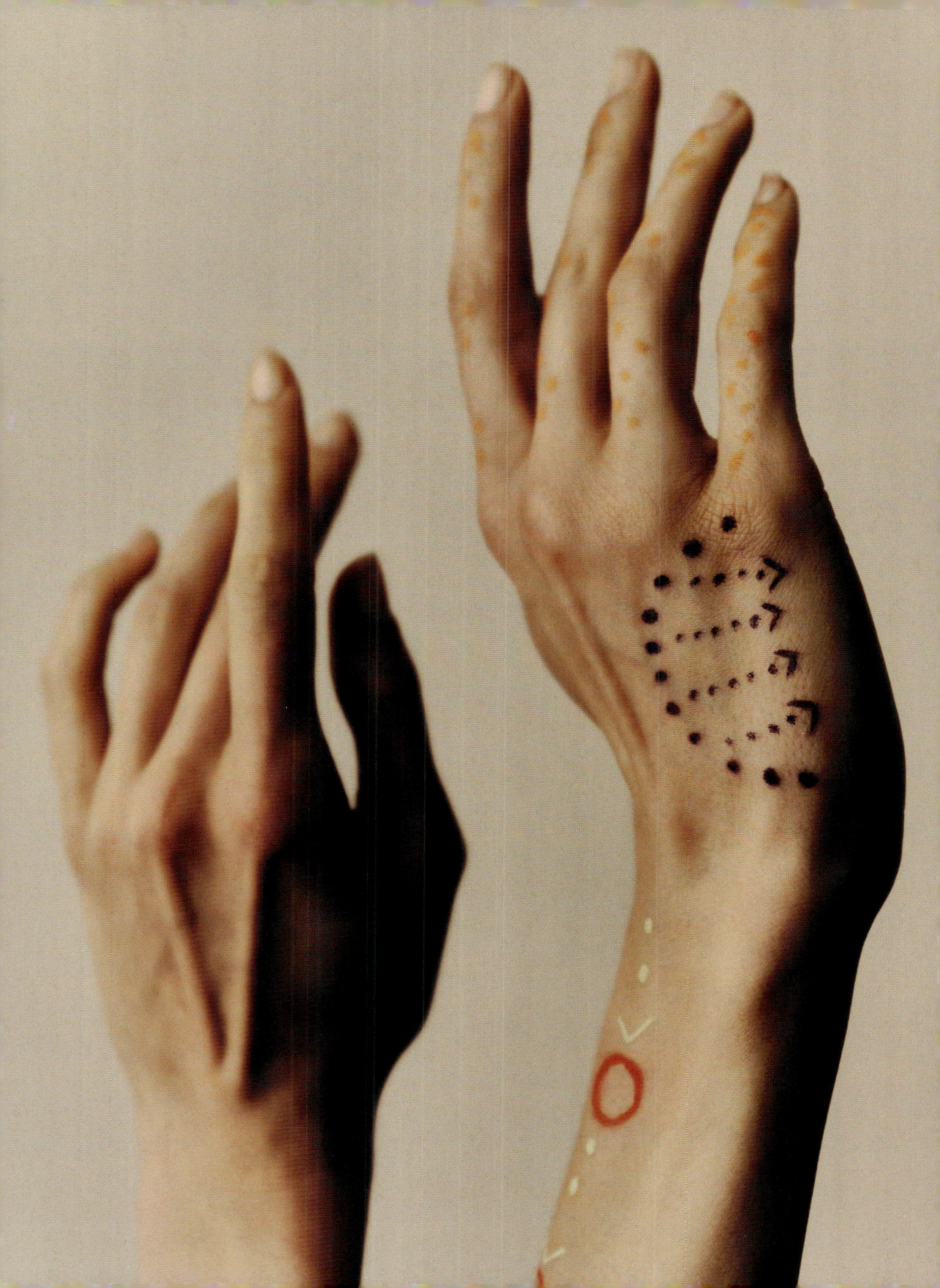

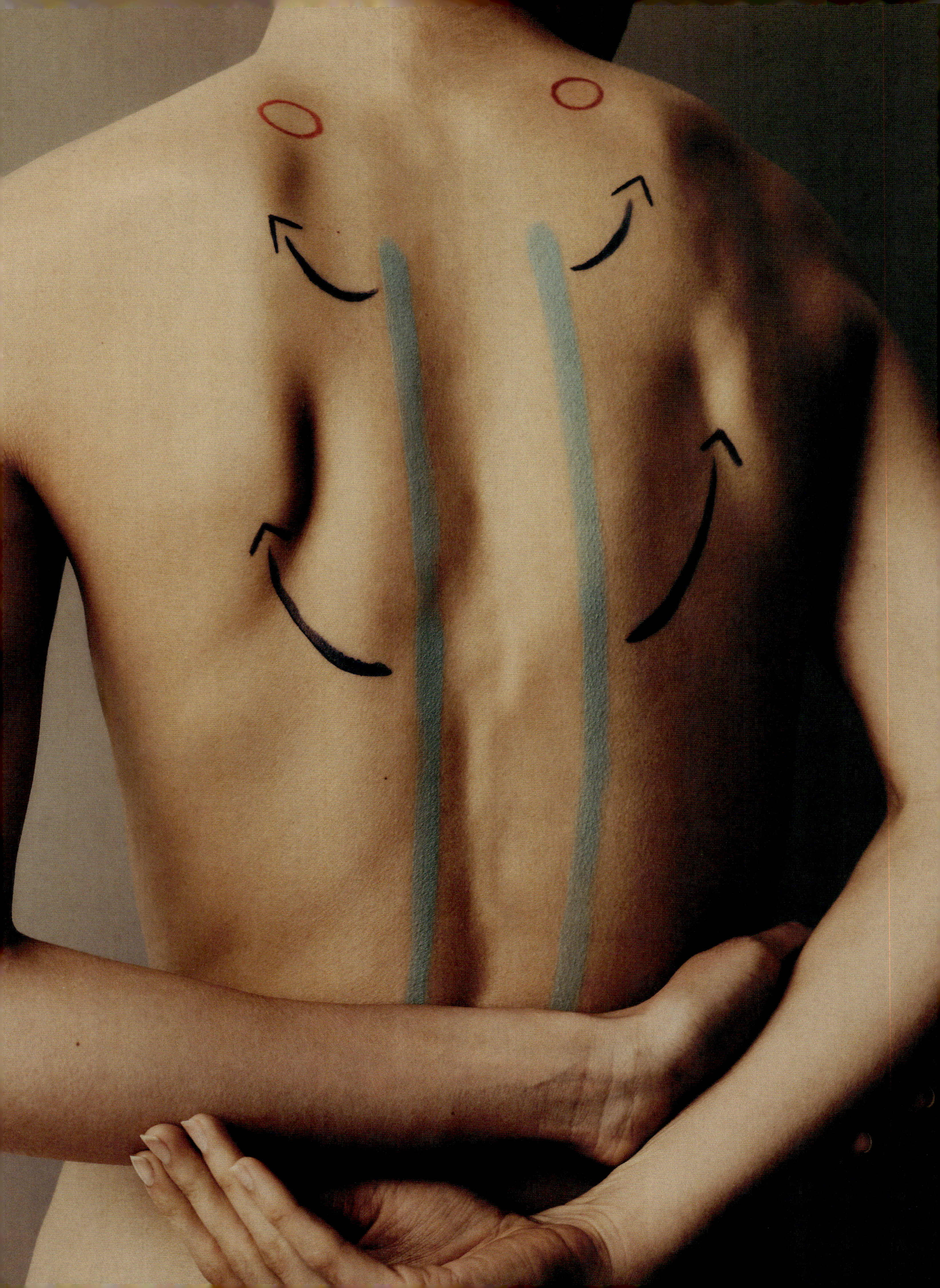

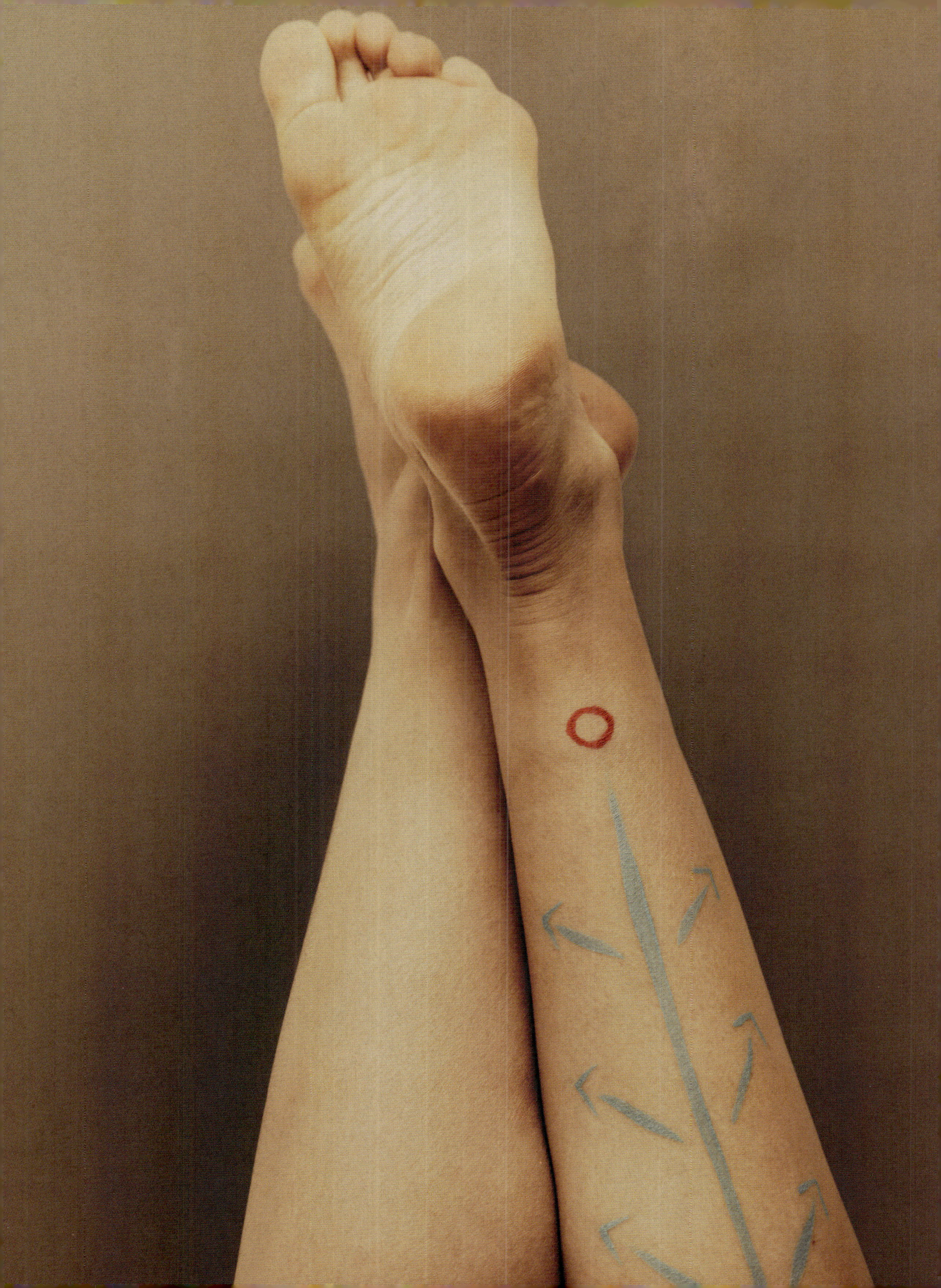

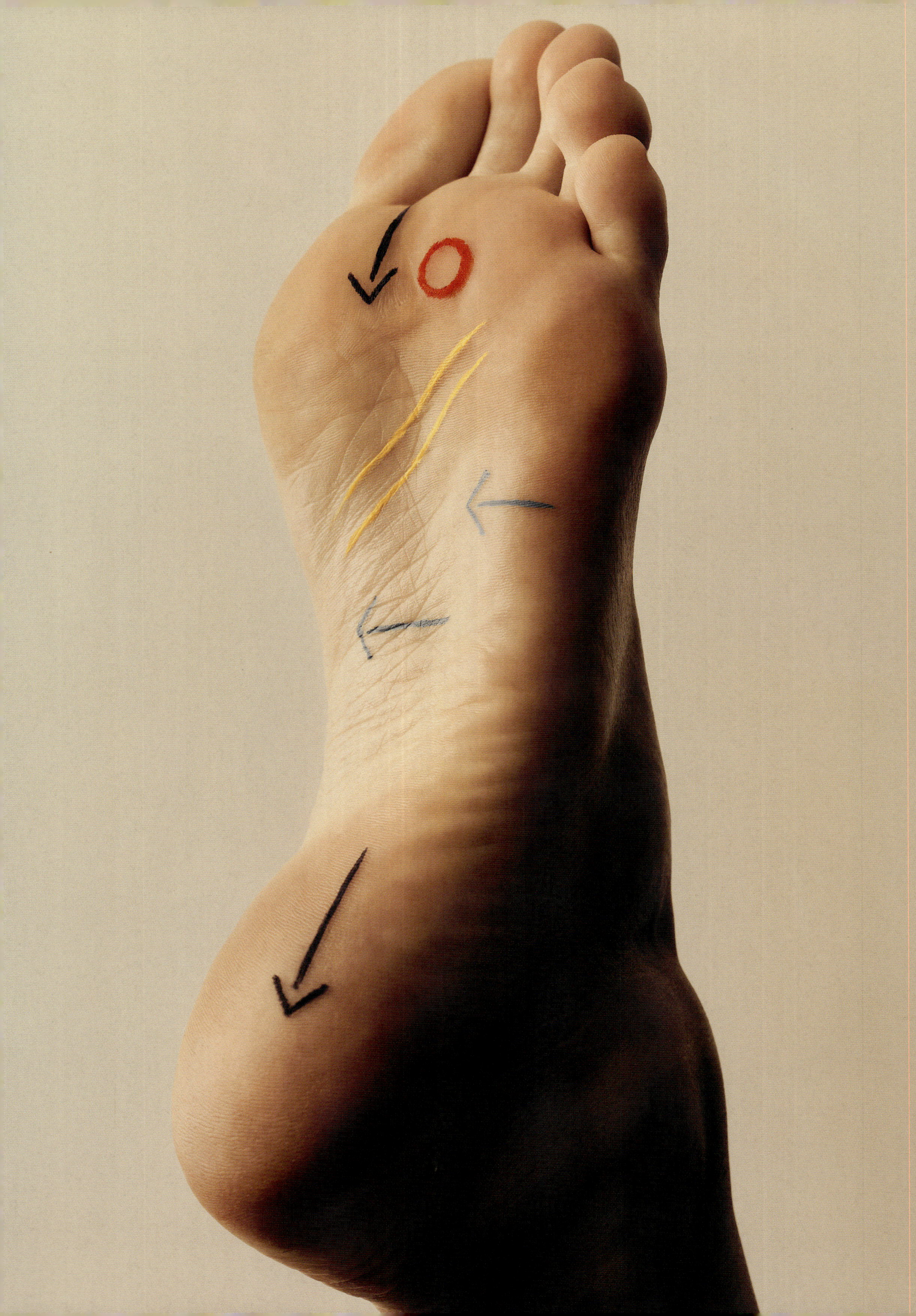

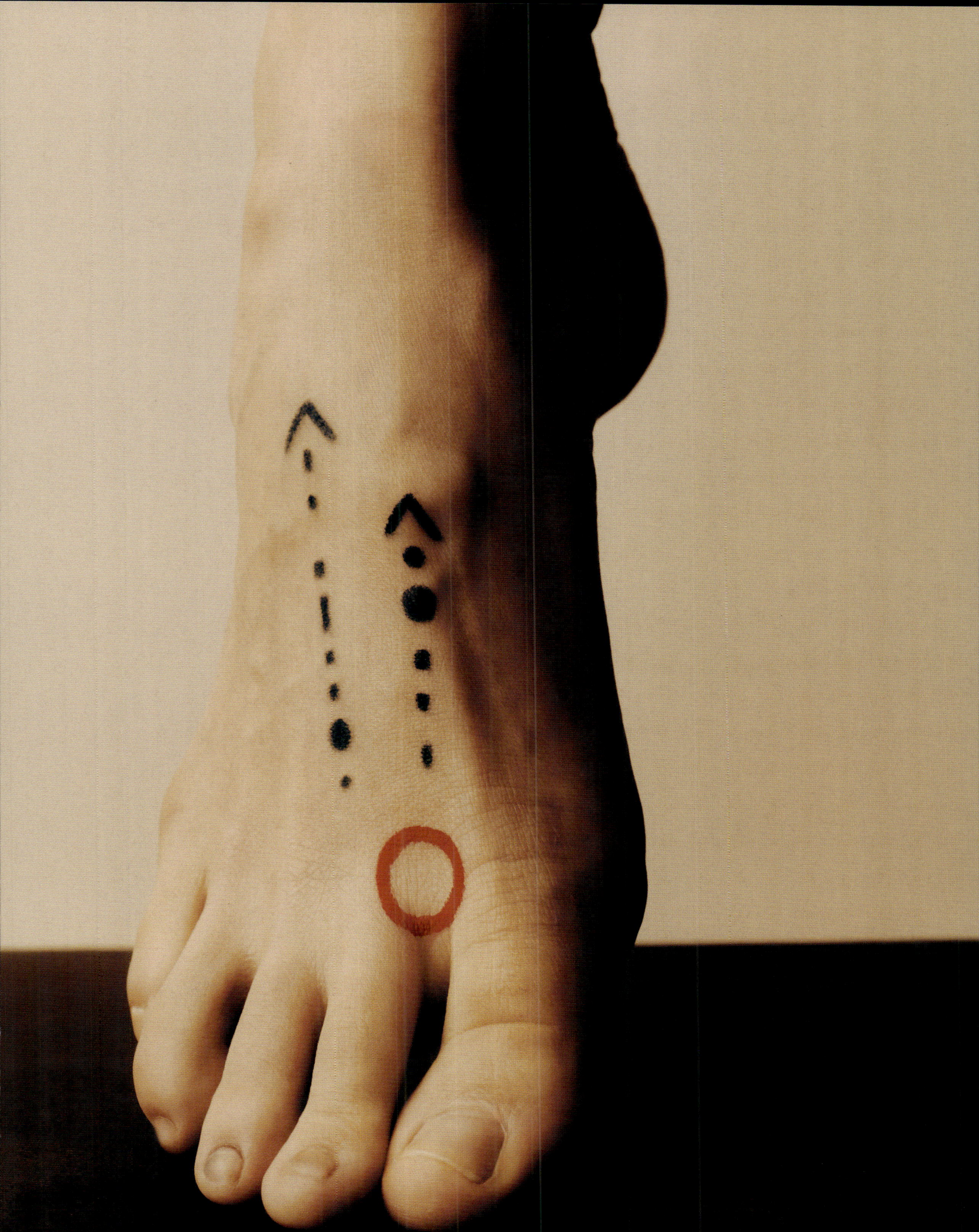

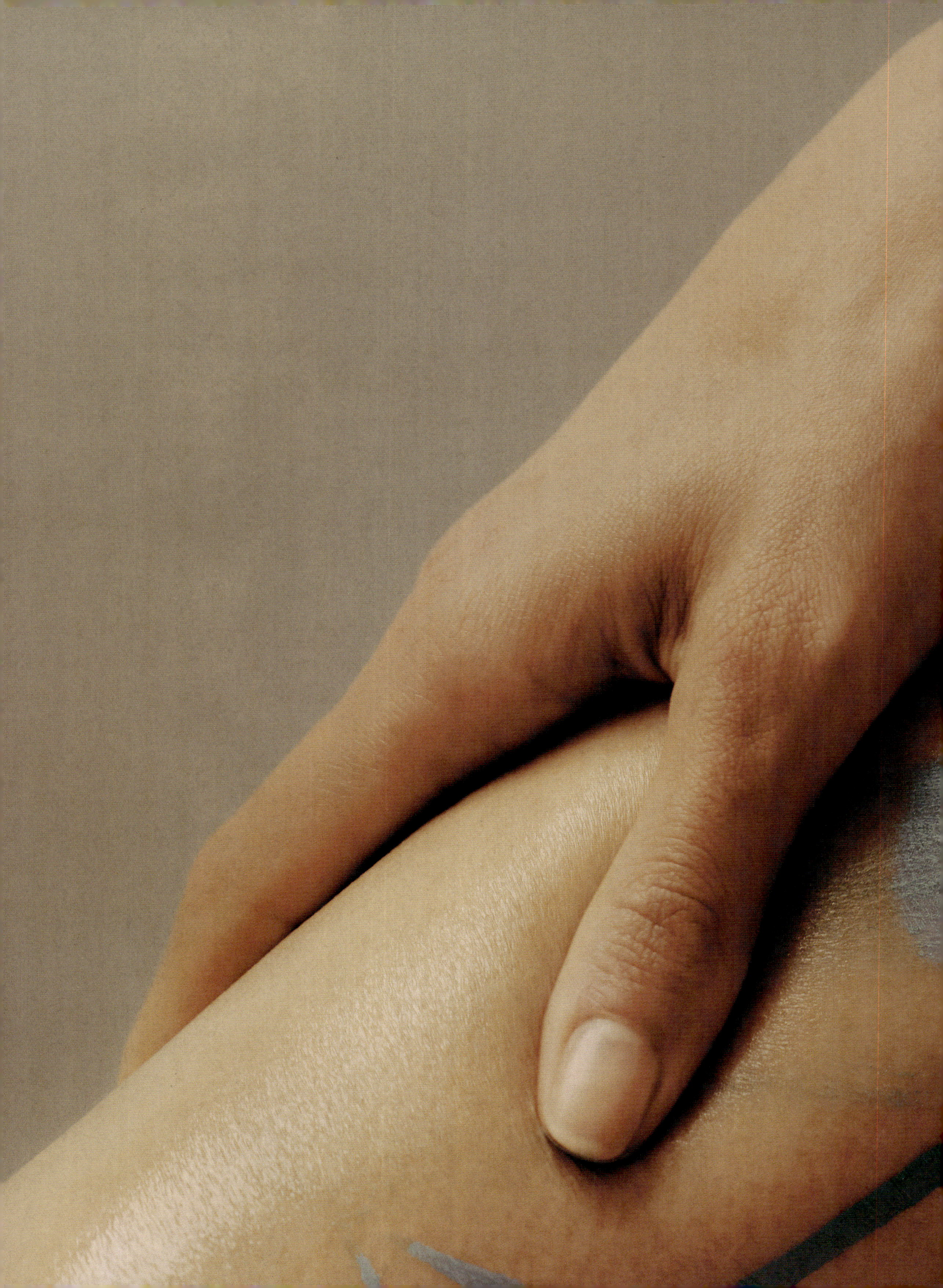

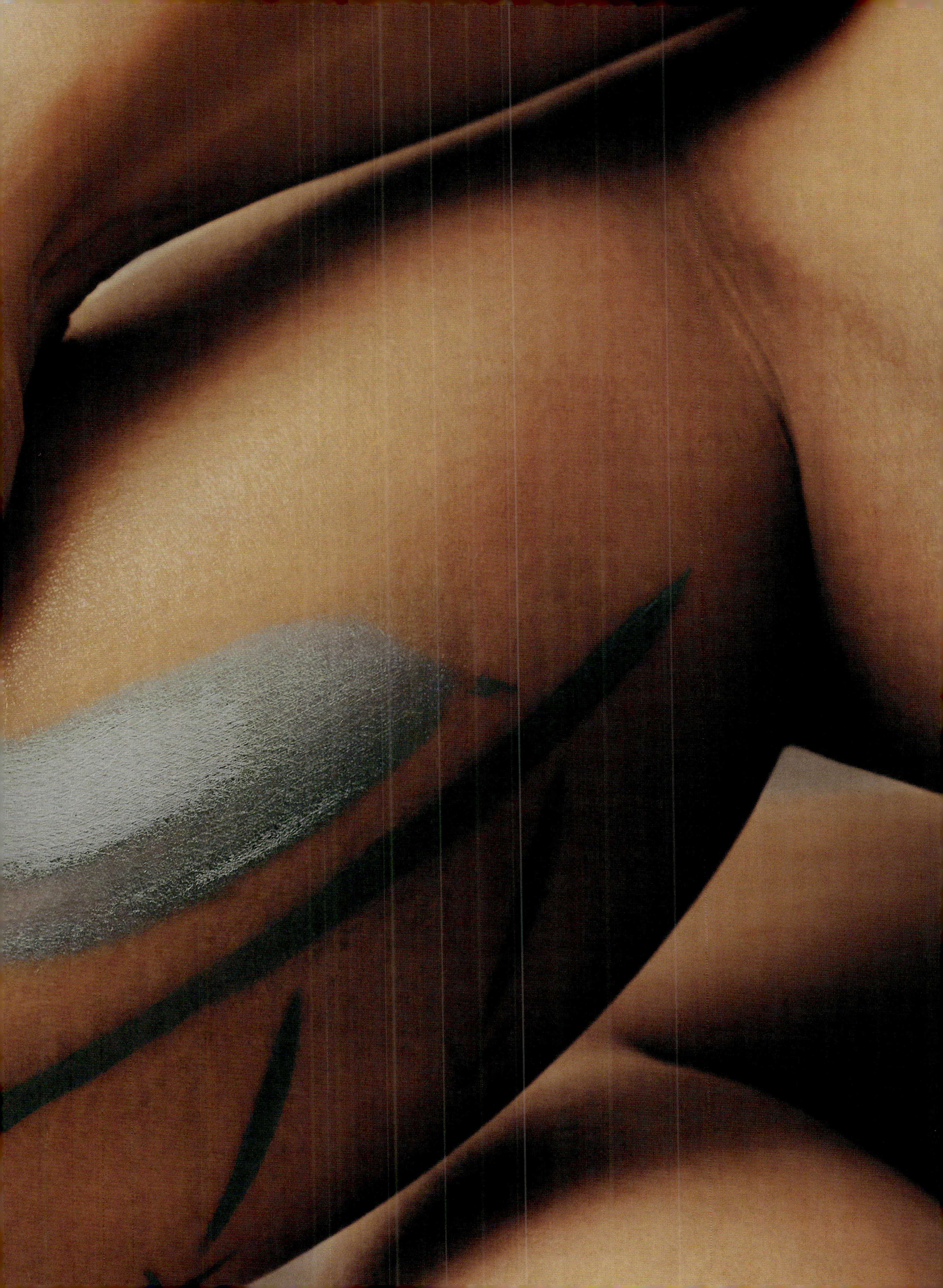

TAKING PLAY SERIOUSLY
A conversation with the National Institute for Play.

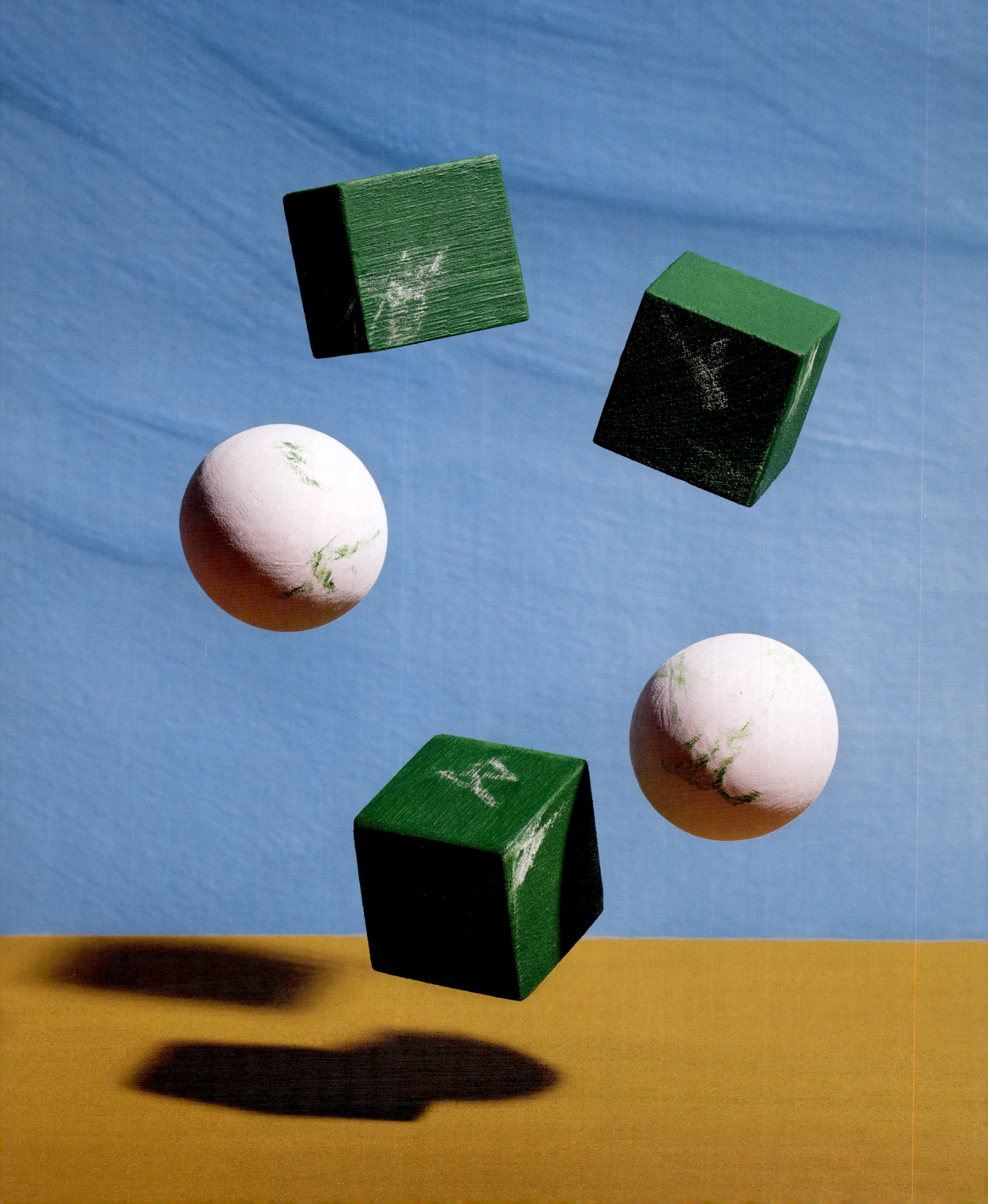

Words
Ellen Peirson-Hagger
Photos
Aaron Tilley

In 1966, psychiatrist Dr. Stuart Brown was appointed by the governor of Texas to investigate a mass shooting at the state university—at the time the deadliest in American history. Brown realized there could be a connection between the gunman's actions and his oppressive childhood, which had been dominated by his controlling father. He would go on to spend the following decades showing that the need for play is biologically hardwired into the brain stem—the part of the nervous system that governs our essential functions like breathing and heart rate.

"When we're deprived of play, it can be similar to being deprived of sleep and nutrition and connection—the things that fundamentally make us human," explains Mia Sundstrom, Dr. Brown's granddaughter and the CEO of the National Institute for Play—a nonprofit organization Brown established in 1994 to champion play as a public health necessity. "I grew up through play," she says, "and have firsthand seen the benefits of it."

Appointed to her role earlier this year, her mission at the institute is to show "how people can incorporate play into their lives to promote cognitive, social, emotional and physical health."

ELLEN PEIRSON-HAGGER: Why is play important?

MIA SUNDSTROM: Here's the paradox—and it's why it's so difficult to convince people that play matters: One of the core definitions of play is that it's purposeless, that it's not done for any specific outcome. Yet there's a ton of purpose in the outcomes we get. We have taught ourselves that play is the opposite of work, but actually play is productive, play is learning; it is not a waste of time.

EPH: What are the benefits of play?

MS: When we are in a state of play, it boosts the production of brain-derived neurotrophic factor, which is the neuroplasticity protein that helps to create new neural connections and strengthen existing pathways. Play also calms down our amygdala—our emotional processing center—meaning it takes us out of a stress response, which is great for emotional regulation. And in the case of social play, our mirror neurons—which light up when we observe the motor activity of someone else—allow us to develop the basic foundation of attunement, which is the first seedling of connection with another human being, and which in time leads to trust, to community, to belonging. So on a neurobiological level, play promotes our cognitive health, our emotional resilience and our social competence.

Physical play is obviously good for us: Exercise is healthy, whether we enjoy it or not. But we're a lot more likely to sustain it when it's something we enjoy, so we might as well try and find a form of physical exercise that feels like play.

(opposite)
ROUGH-AND-TUMBLE PLAY
Rough-and-tumble play is a key form of risky play, encompassing wrestling, chasing, play fighting and other high-energy physical interactions. These activities help develop cooperation, social awareness and an understanding of boundaries and fairness.

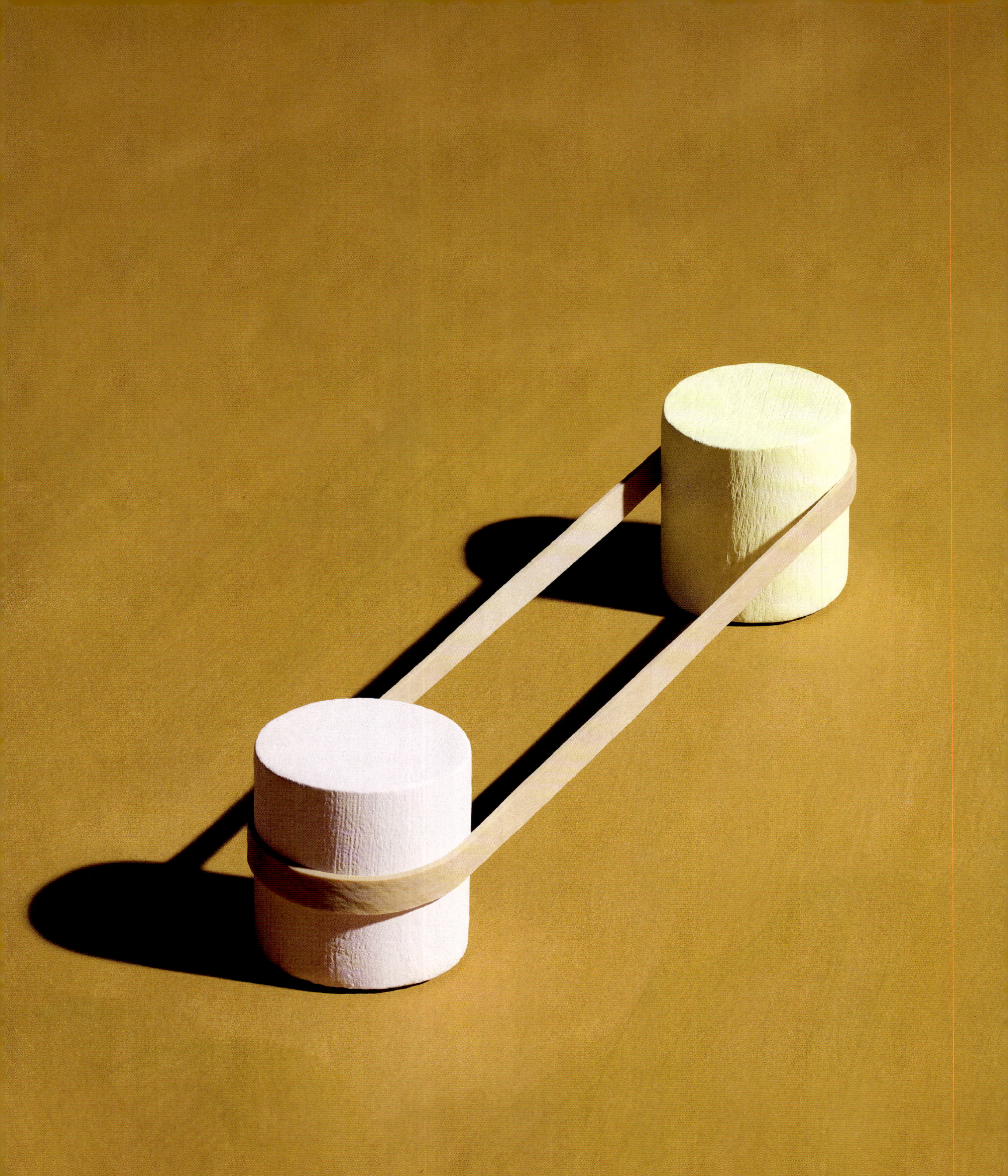

ATTUNEMENT
Attunement forms the basis of all other kinds of play. When we play together, our brains begin to synchronize, creating a shared emotional and neurological rhythm that supports emotional regulation, empathy and social connection.

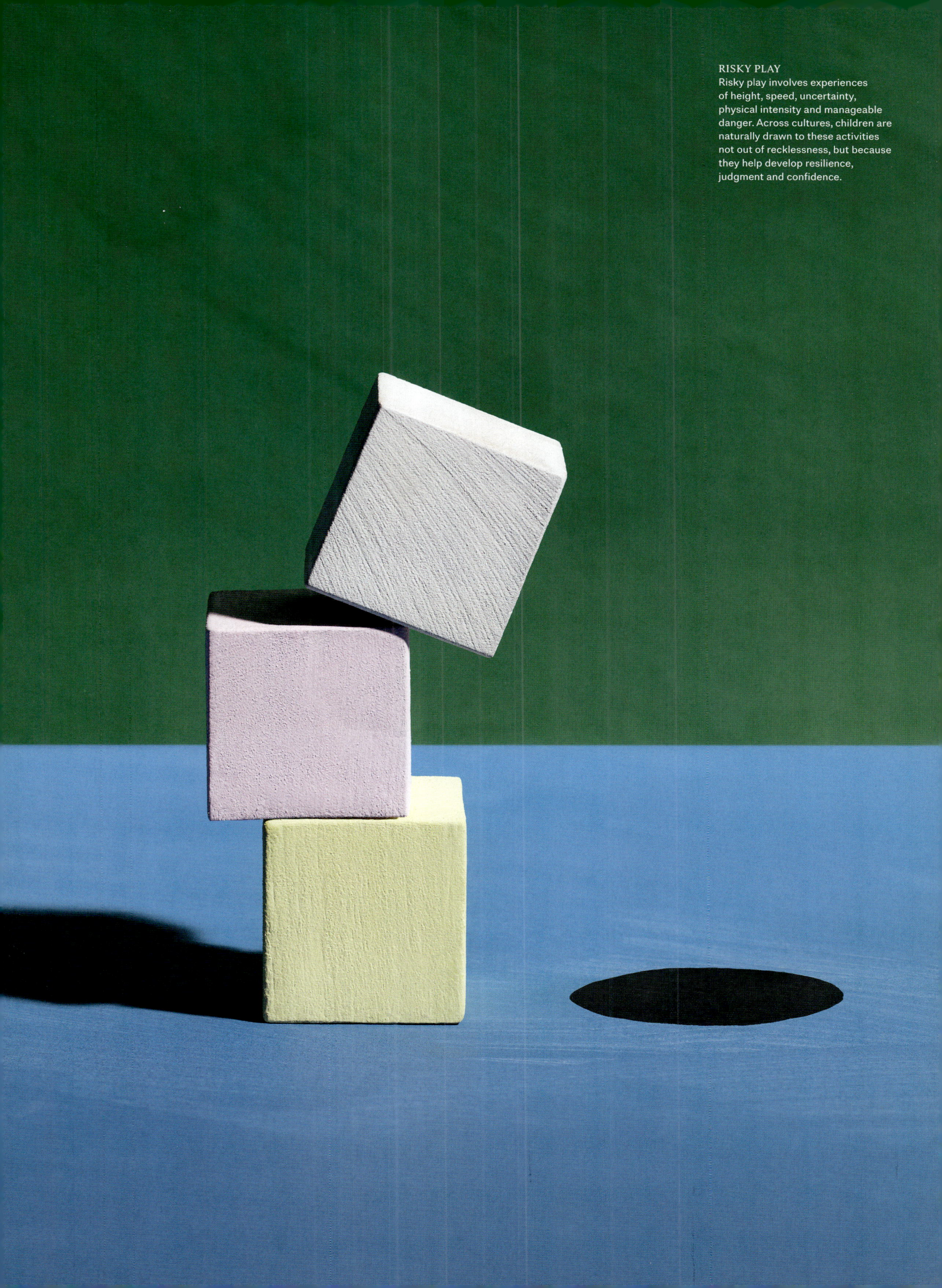

RISKY PLAY
Risky play involves experiences of height, speed, uncertainty, physical intensity and manageable danger. Across cultures, children are naturally drawn to these activities not out of recklessness, but because they help develop resilience, judgment and confidence.

EPH: If we don't play, are those things lost?

MS: When we're play-deprived, there can be really severe consequences. It can lead to cognitive rigidity, which is when you can't think outside the box and solve problems creatively. We have seen that a lack of play can lead to susceptibility for anxiety and depression, and toward addictive behaviors, because we try to find those things that we need from play in other forms—alcohol, drugs, social media, sugar—all these things that offer short-term relief rather than long-term benefit.

And then there's social incompetence: As my grandpa's research showed, when we don't play it's hard to build tolerance and empathy for each other because we miss that fundamental level of attunement. This leads to diminished well-being.

EPH: How does our need for play change as we become adults?

MS: There's a misconception that it has to change like crazy, that what you do as a kid is not what you should do as an adult. But we don't ever lose the desire to play, we're just socialized to stop playing in certain ways. For example, as you go through grade school, the playgrounds change—there is no longer the opportunity to go down a slide at recess—and then all of a sudden you forget that you love to do that, and you might never do it again.

I don't think adults should stop swinging, or playing at parks, or jumping on a trampoline in the backyard. We often think that we outgrow these things, but we really shouldn't. Lego is a breaker of this rule: Lego adult sets are selling so well right now because of their connection to nostalgia and childhood. And what's great about moving from childhood to adulthood is that the possibilities to play open up significantly: Instead of exploring your backyard with a stick and turning your cardboard box into a rocket ship, you have access to a car and a plane.

EPH: Is play different to different people?

MS: Everyone is born with a deep natural predilection for play, but that looks different for each of us. There are people who love to make things—art, music, building, tinkering with objects. There are people who love to dream or get lost in a book or movie and create imaginary worlds in their mind. There are people who love to compete, who play through mastering. There are people who love to organize—collecting new things, arranging social gatherings, even cleaning out a junk drawer. These are all different play styles, and one of the greatest gifts you can give a child is to notice what those natural tendencies are and help nourish them.

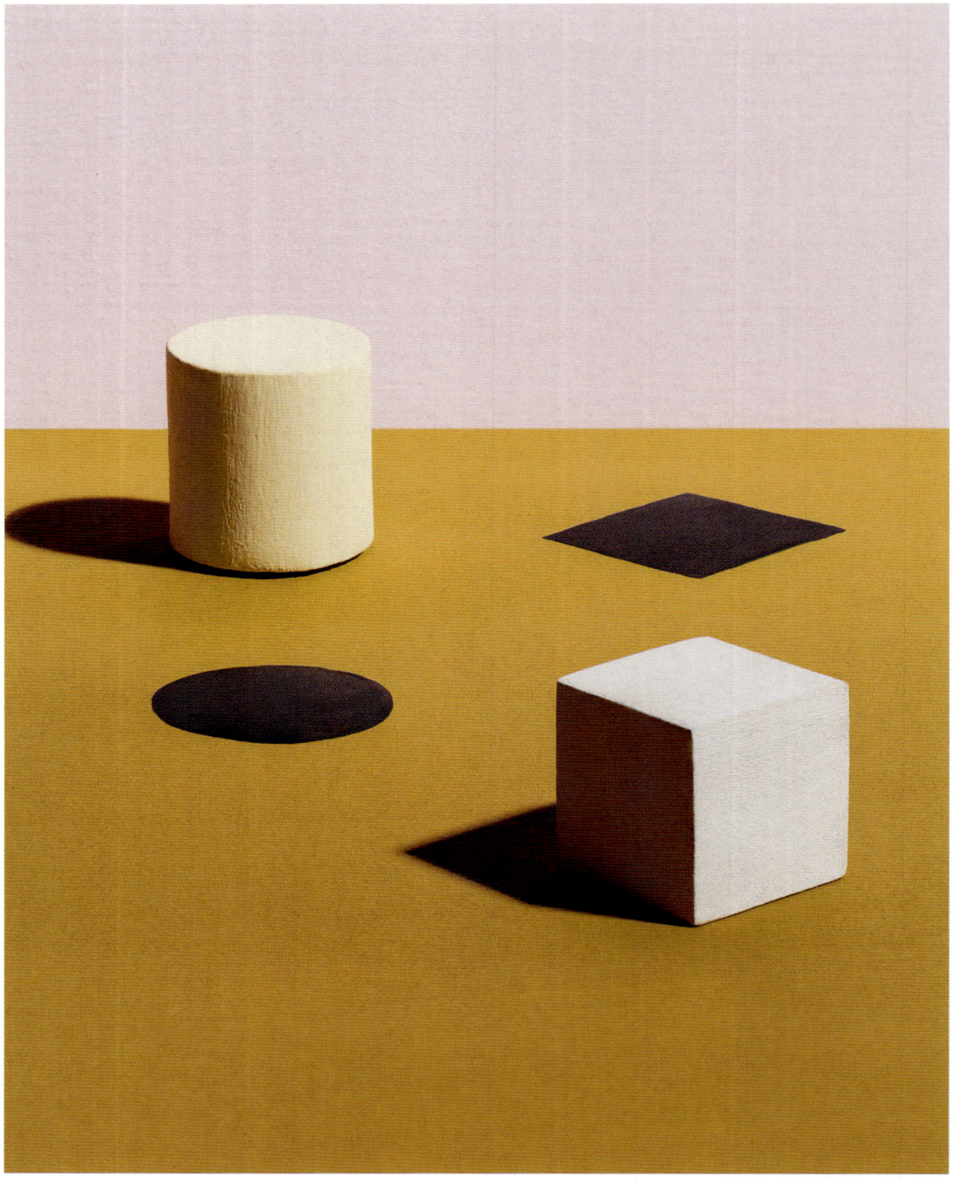

(above)
EXPLORATORY PLAY
Exploratory play is driven by curiosity: the urge to seek out, discover and experience the unfamiliar. It is one of the earliest and most fundamental forms of play, emerging in infancy as we begin to make sense of the world. At the beginning of life, play and exploration are almost inseparable.

EPH: Do you think we need to take a broader view of what play is or can be?

MS: Yes! Most of the time, when I ask people "What is play to you?" they say "a board game" or "my kid's sport." We have confined play to this really narrow scope, when actually play is any activity that brings us into the play state, which is an altered state of being, almost dreamlike, that takes us out of the usual experience of time and space and evokes positive emotions like joy and awe. It is intrinsically motivated, not coerced, so it's done for its own sake, and it's self-reinforcing, so the benefits of a play state last beyond the time we're playing.

Any activity that meets that criteria can be play—that could mean coding for someone who loves to code, or cooking for someone who loves to cook. Heck, that could even be cleaning if you put on a great song and you turn your broom into a microphone.

EPH: Why is society so resistant to play?

MS: Well, the psychologist and play

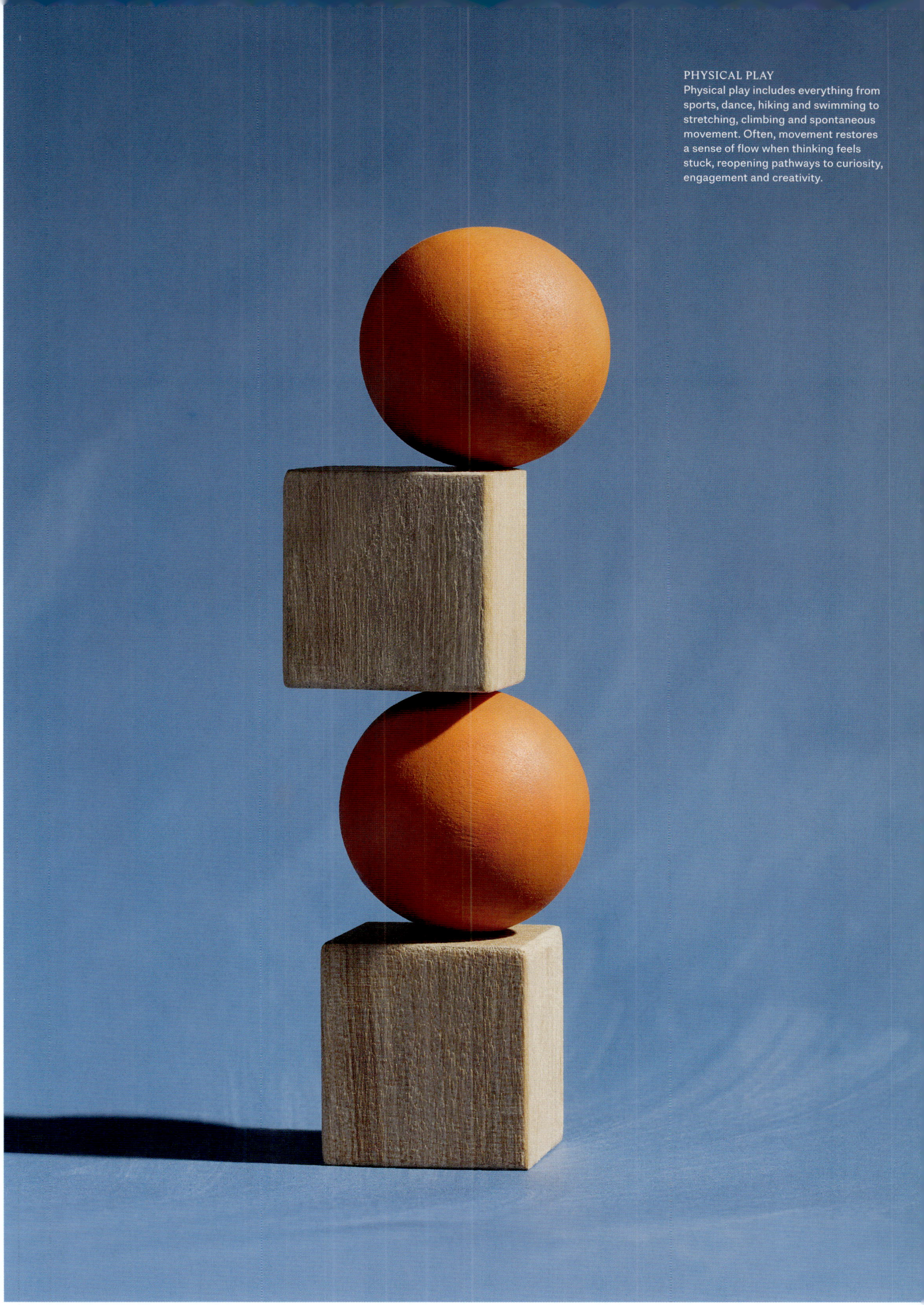

PHYSICAL PLAY

Physical play includes everything from sports, dance, hiking and swimming to stretching, climbing and spontaneous movement. Often, movement restores a sense of flow when thinking feels stuck, reopening pathways to curiosity, engagement and creativity.

SOCIAL PLAY

Social play is how humans rehearse relationships. From casual banter and shared meals to team sports and collaborative experiences, it is one of the primary ways we learn to connect, communicate and develop a sense of belonging.

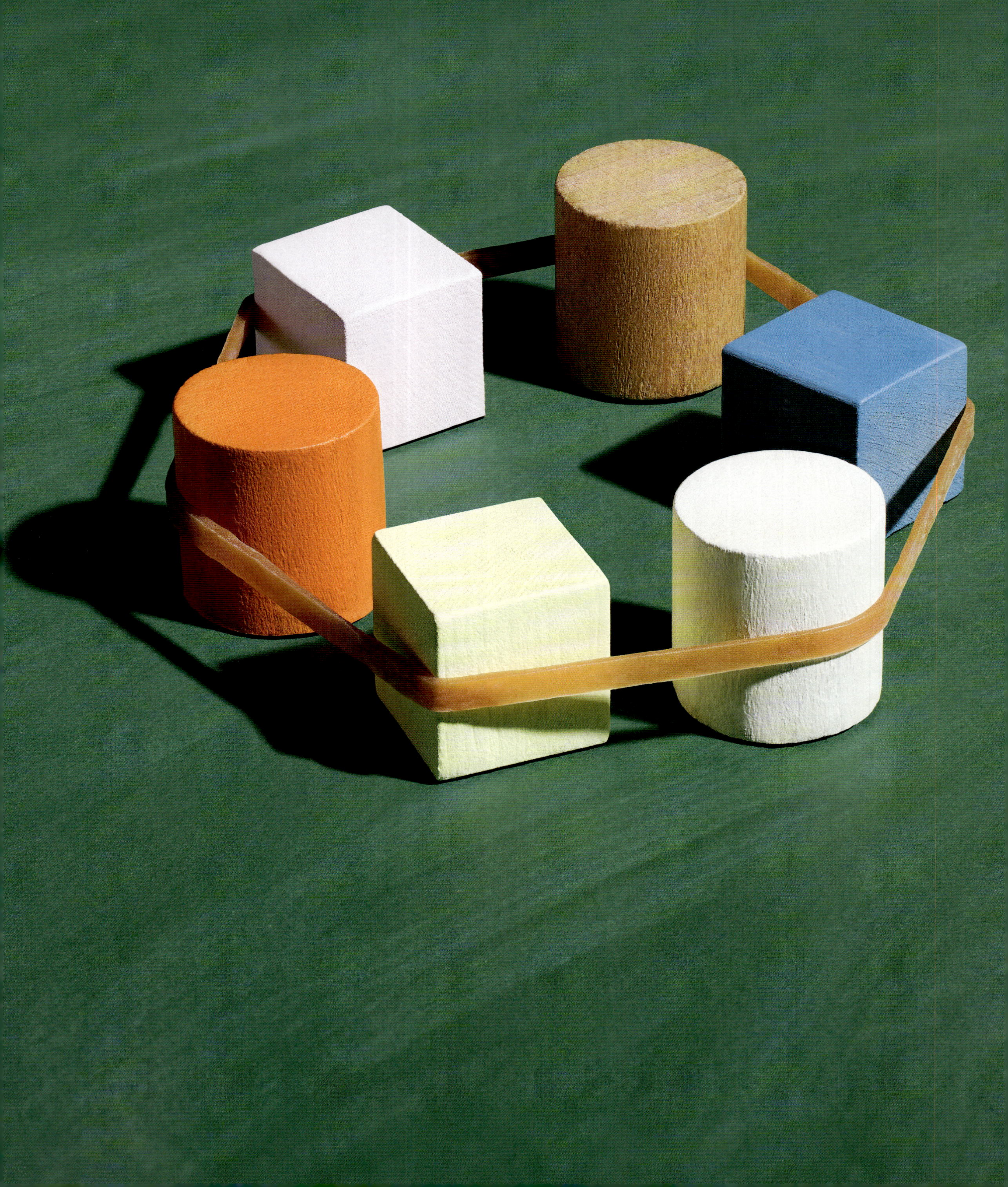

(below)
CREATIVE PLAY
Creative play transforms imagination into something tangible. It includes making, composing, designing, building, writing and performing—any act in which new ideas take shape through active engagement.

"We have taught ourselves that play is the opposite of work, but actually play is productive, play is learning; it is not a waste of time."

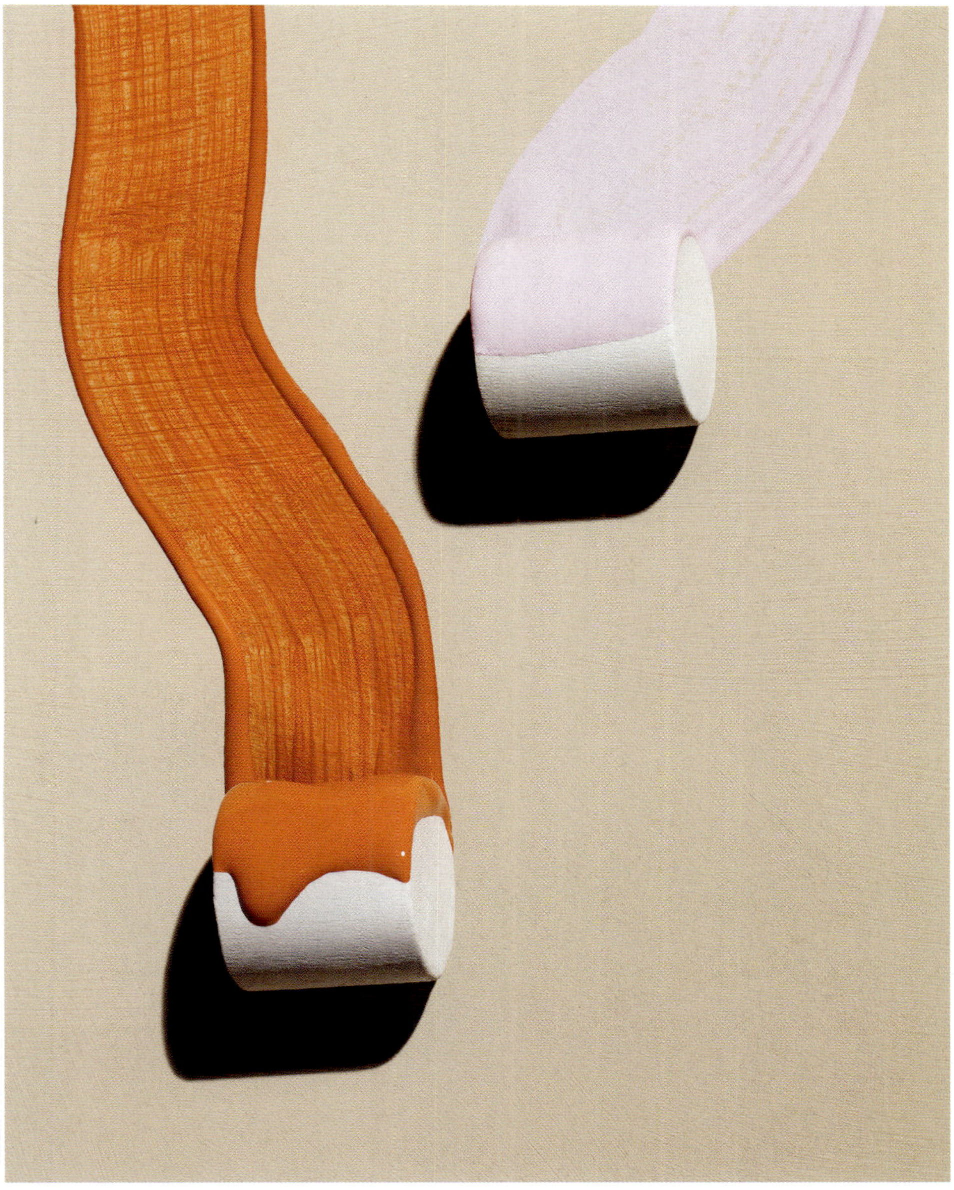

researcher Peter Gray would answer by taking us back to the 16th century, when the Protestant Reformation taught us to believe in the moral virtue of work and that play, by contrast, is the breeding ground of sin. And then you throw capitalism into the mix which calls for more production, more consumption: that's what defines success in the capitalist dream, right? Then you add in the compounding effects of automation and AI. Of course play isn't celebrated in a world that prioritizes those things.

EPH: Has digitization played a role?

MS: We can't prove causation, but our screens do seem to be factor in why we're not playing. Scrolling on your screen disguises itself as play because you lose track of time, and it feels fun in the moment. But it has long-term detriments in terms of our attention span and our loneliness. If we're scrolling, we're not connecting with each other on a human level.

EPH: What kind of society would we have if we all played more?

MS: Play dissolves our differences and reminds us of what we have in common. Our world is so polarized, but play brings us together and is one of the most powerful ways to create a better society. Play lowers our inhibitions—I want to shout that from the rooftops. If you disagree with someone and go play with them, you'll see the humanity in one other. It can also help combat the trends that we're talking so much about right now—loneliness, disengagement, burnout—because play brings us back to that deep intrinsic drive to do something for a sustained period of time that makes the time pass more quickly.

EPH: What should adults do to help recover their love of play?

MS: We help adults rediscover their natural spark—their thing that makes them most curious and fully alive—and then think about small ways to reintegrate that into their life. The first step is to think back to your earliest memory of play: What was that thing you loved to do before the world told you who to be? Second, based on that, what do you love to do now—is there something that you've forgotten about and haven't done for ages? Third, nothing ever works when we try to create massive changes all at once. So we say that 30 seconds is enough. See if you can add a burst of play into your morning or evening routine, based on those two things you reflected on. What's great about play is that it's self-reinforcing, so as soon as you give yourself that permission, it will keep you coming back for more.

COMPETITIVE PLAY

Competitive play is shaped by the pursuit of challenge, performance and achievement. It engages the desire to test limits, refine skills and strive toward measurable goals. Those who like to compete access the energy and exhilaration of play through games with rules, structure and scoring.

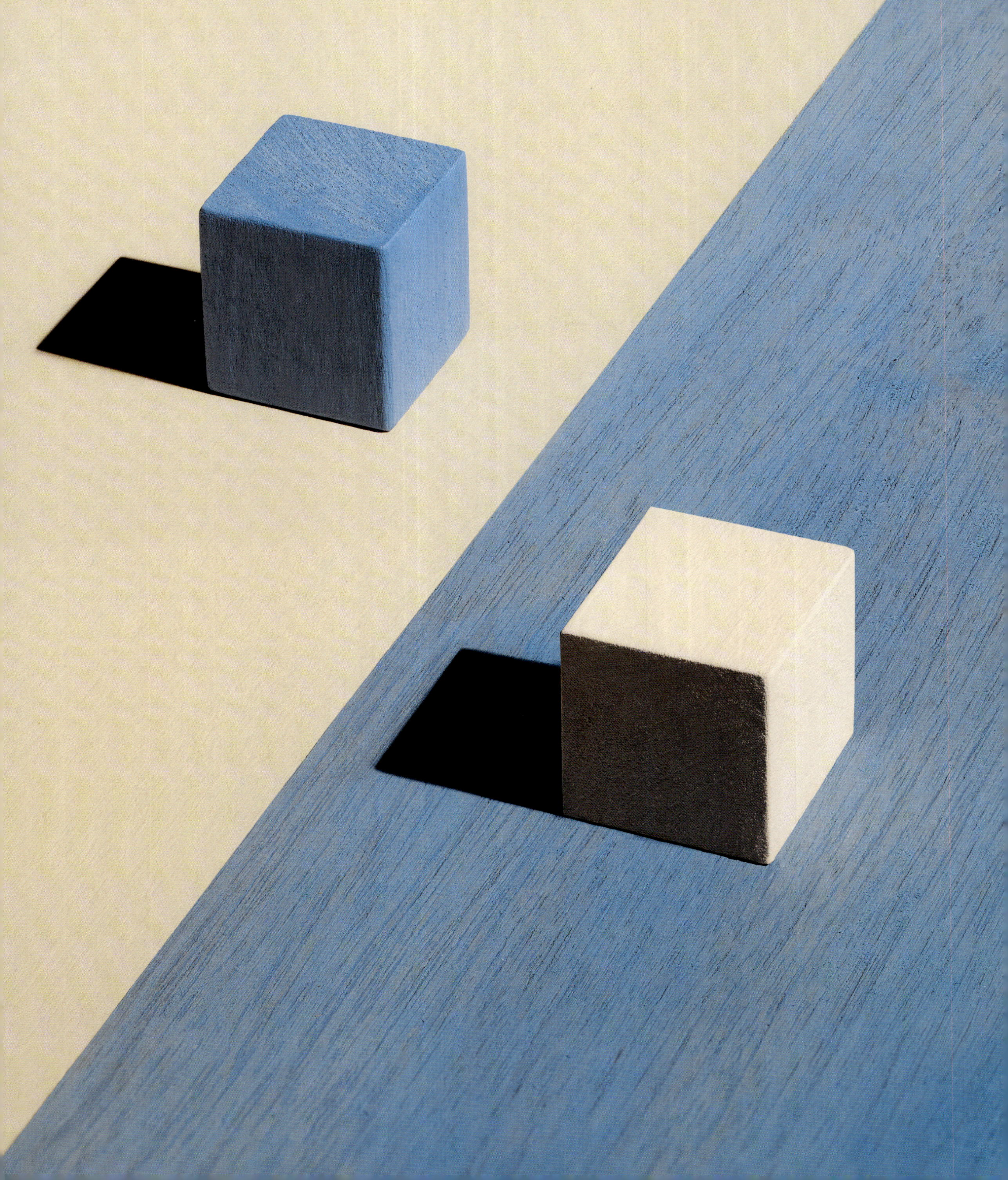

IV

Directory

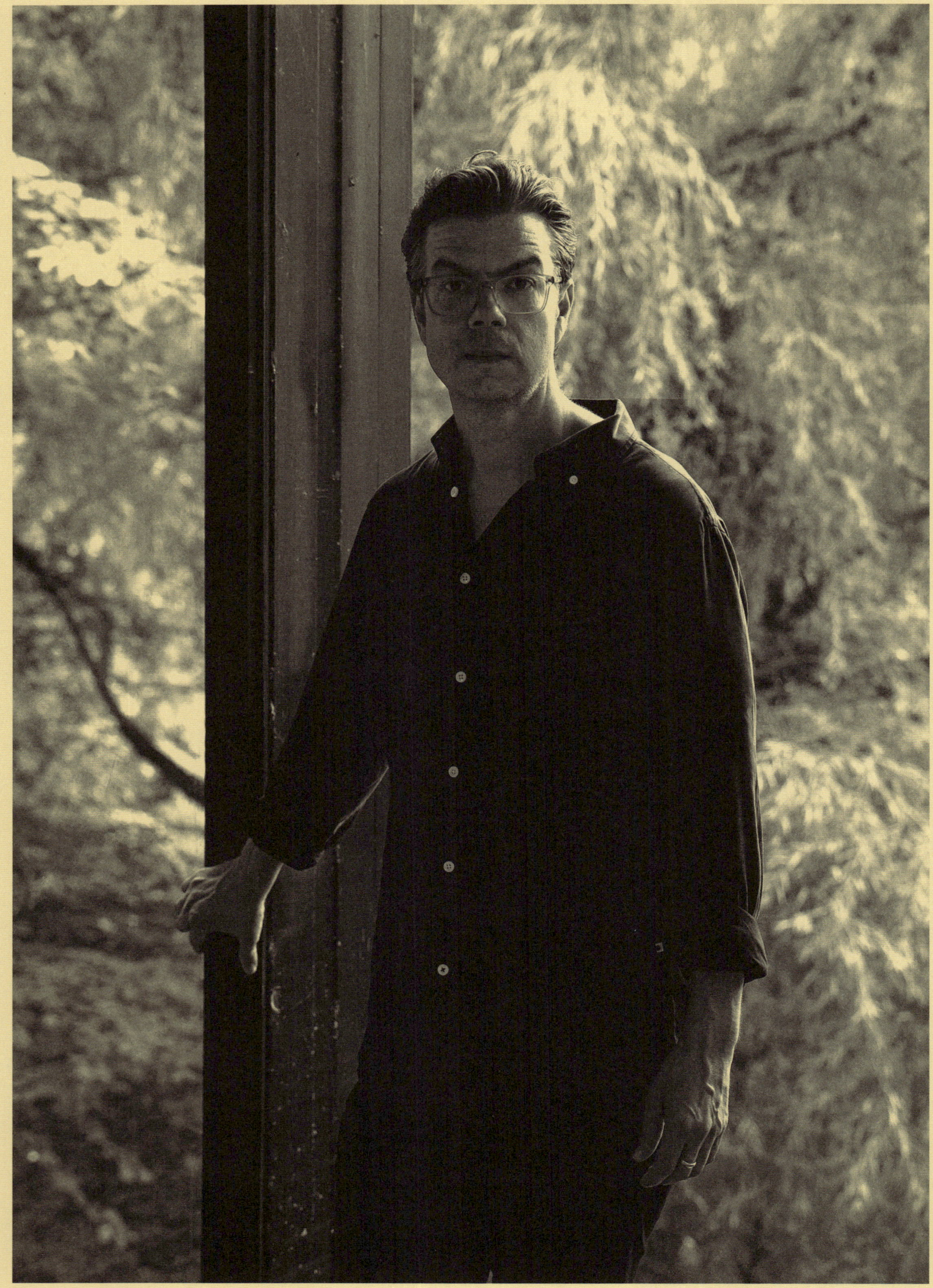

Photo: Beowulf Sheehan

Words:
Natasha Stallard

Novelist BEN LERNER reflects on the art—and artifice—of the interview.

Ben Lerner—the poet and author of *Leaving the Atocha Station*, *10:04* and *The Topeka School*—has long been interested in the blurred lines between fact and fiction. His fourth novel, *Transcription*, opens with a deceptively simple premise: The narrator drops his phone in the sink, leaving him without a recording device for an interview with his mentor, Thomas, a 90-year-old writer, theorist and filmmaker. What follows is a metafictional, midlife exploration of how our identities and experiences are mediated through art, technology and family.

NATASHA STALLARD: You've described yourself as an "accidental novelist," and how generative it can be to write in one form and then find it belongs to another. *Transcription* starts with the form of the interview. Where did the novel emerge from?

BEN LERNER: There's a moment in the dialogue with Thomas where they interrupt each other and the lines almost start to form a poem out of the fragments of their speech. I had written a few experimental dialogues, and I was interested in that phenomenon—the way a poem could form out of the rapid juxtaposition of two speakers.

But there are many different points of origin. I interviewed a hero of mine, the poet Rosmarie Waldrop, for *The Paris Review*. As with many publications, you have a long conversation and it's edited a lot—you move things around and you add things later. I was struck by how I'd had this emotionally intense experience of interviewing this elder woman who I love, and then there was this document. The document had its own kind of authenticity, but it was less and less an actual transcript of the experience.

NS: *The Paris Review* format is interesting because they're quite open in the introduction about how interviews take place over various conversations and have been edited and revised.

BL: Totally. I'm also interested in what transcripts *can't* capture. When you see a conversation that's transcribed, it can often be all the words that were uttered, but it's lost the texture of the experience—because of intonation and the unaccountable effects of presence and room tone and just the energy of people who are present. Then at other times transcripts mysteriously do capture things that are lost in other kinds of recording.

NS: After the narrator drops his phone in the sink, he lies to Thomas about not having a recording device. Lying is an activity that occurs across your novels. Why is that?

BL: I think the question of why he does not just say, "This is really embarrassing, I broke my phone," is not a question the book answers. It could be that he's reckoning with Thomas' mortality—the idea that this would be the last conversation, the exit interview. Or regressing in the presence of a mentor.

I remember, as a little kid, telling totally implausible lies that I would stick to until the bitter end. I broke a window once with a baseball and someone saw me do it, but I stuck to the lie for weeks and weeks. And lies in fiction are interesting because they represent a problem or impasse for the narrator, but also, on some plane, refer to the act of fiction-making and reading fiction to begin with.

NS: You had heart surgery in between writing and publishing this novel. What has that experience been like for you? And how are you now?

BL: I'm okay. There's some quite complicated health stuff related to this that kind of never goes away, but I feel good. *10:04* uses an epigraph about how everything is the same but a little different. And that's how it was after the surgery—the book was the same book I'd written, but *I* was a little different. In a way, that's a great position from which to edit, although I don't recommend having heart surgery to be able to have fresh eyes on your writing.

Words:
Daphnée Denis

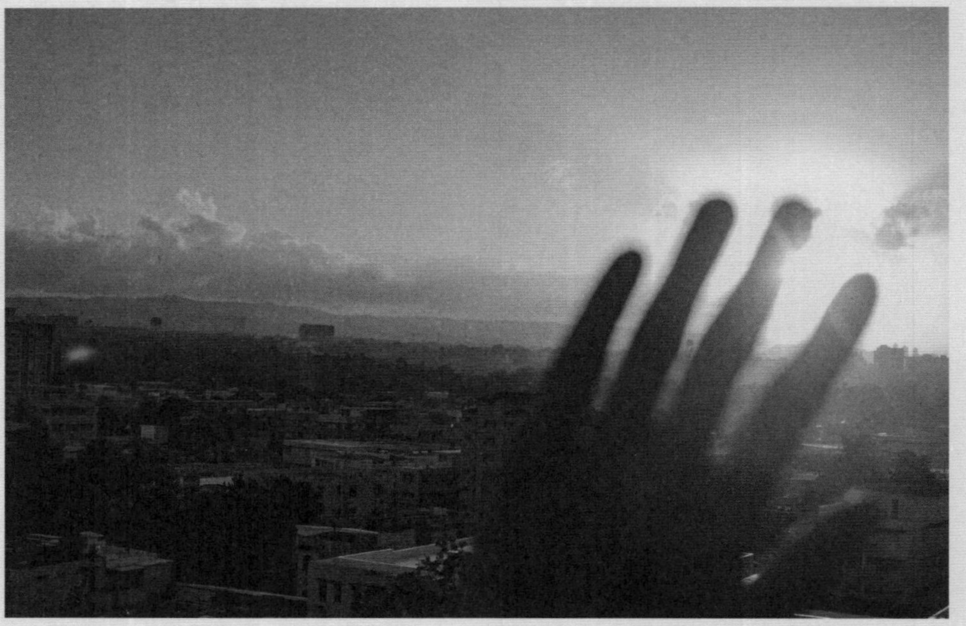

A dispatch from Puerto Rico.

It's a Monday evening in Río Piedras, the student neighborhood of Puerto Rico's capital, San Juan. Far from the beaches and tourist attractions, the district—which houses the largest campus of the University of Puerto Rico, or "la yupee" as locals call it—is surprisingly desolate. Despite its colorful murals, the empty streets feel eerily still, like a ghost town. But on one building, a portrait of the late master percussionist Tito Matos hints that life isn't far away.[1] On this island, music never is.

Just a few blocks away, El Boricua, a student hangout turned cultural institution, hosts its weekly night of plena, one of the Afro-descendant genres of music native to Puerto Rico. It's a place where loneliness dissolves into the amaranthine light of sunset: People pour out onto the streets, as professional musicians and amateurs gather outside the bar, singing and playing handheld drums called panderos, as well as güicharos—gourds scraped rhythmically to produce a dry, rasping pulse vital to many Latin American musical forms.

Known as the "people's newspaper," plena covers a large range of topics, from love to daily gossip, but at its core, it's about identity and resistance. The island of Boriquén, as Puerto Rico was originally named by the Indigenous Taínos, is often referred to as the world's oldest colony. First occupied by the Spanish, it's currently a commonwealth of the United States: Boricuas must abide by US laws but can't vote for the president. Music—salsa, plena, bomba, rumba and even reggaeton—is one of the ways Puerto Ricans assert their culture.

Tonight at El Boricua, the crowd, mostly regulars, hums along to the choruses of the songs, often joining the artists on stage. Soon, they start singing "La Borinqueña," the revolutionary hymn of the land. The music echoes across the empty streets, reminding the neighbors—and ghosts—of Río Piedras of what Puerto Rican pride sounds like.

(1) Matos, who died in 2022 at the age of 53, was considered by the Smithsonian Institution to be one of the finest requinto players of his generation. He learned much of his craft not in Puerto Rico but in New York, studying under plena masters who had emigrated there in the 1940s and '50s.

Photo: Adriana Parrilla

GARDEN

Words:
Poppy Okotcha

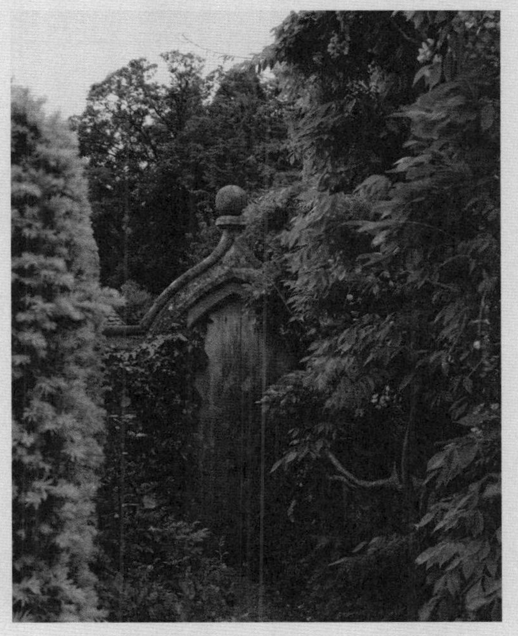

A guide to the garden in fall.

Fall is often overlooked in the garden. It may lack summer's easy charm, but it can be just as satisfying, equally as beautiful and deeply rewarding. A sustainable garden benefits enormously from thoughtful fall work, much of which involves knowing what not to tidy away. And we humans benefit too—autumn gardening offers a slower, grounding rhythm that helps carry us through winter's darker months.

Planting spring bulbs, for example, is one of the season's essential jobs. Bulbs provide an important nectar source for pollinators when they emerge in early spring, and there is something comforting about knowing future color is hidden beneath the soil during winter. Garlic, broad beans, winter hardy peas and green manures can also be sown in the fall, and if you have a greenhouse, kale, chard and lettuces can be planted (or moved) to overwinter with some protection.

It's also important to consider wildlife. Rather than cutting back herbaceous perennials completely, leaving stems standing creates overwintering habitats for insects and seed sources for birds. Plants such as mint, lemon balm, echinacea and even annual flower stems can all remain through winter. In areas that have to be cleared, I gather dry stems into bundles tied with twine and place them around the garden, where they provide shelter while adding rustic character. Fallen leaves should be treated as a resource rather than waste: Left to decompose, they become leaf mold, a rich compost that improves soil structure and moisture retention.[1]

As daylight hours shorten, plants begin to slow their growth and redirect energy into roots, bulbs and storage tissues—the natural process that prepares them for winter dormancy. Fall gardening supports this process of drawing in and preparing for winter's cold, so that plants and life can reemerge in abundance come spring. By working with the season, gardeners can create resilient spaces that sustain their corner of the natural world—and themselves—through winter and into spring.

(1) The practice has ancient roots. In *De Agri Cultura*, written around 160 BC and considered the oldest surviving work of Latin prose, Cato the Elder recommends composting ilex and oak leaves.

Photo: Joyce and Andres de Lange

CHESS BOXING

A cerebral game interspersed with combat.

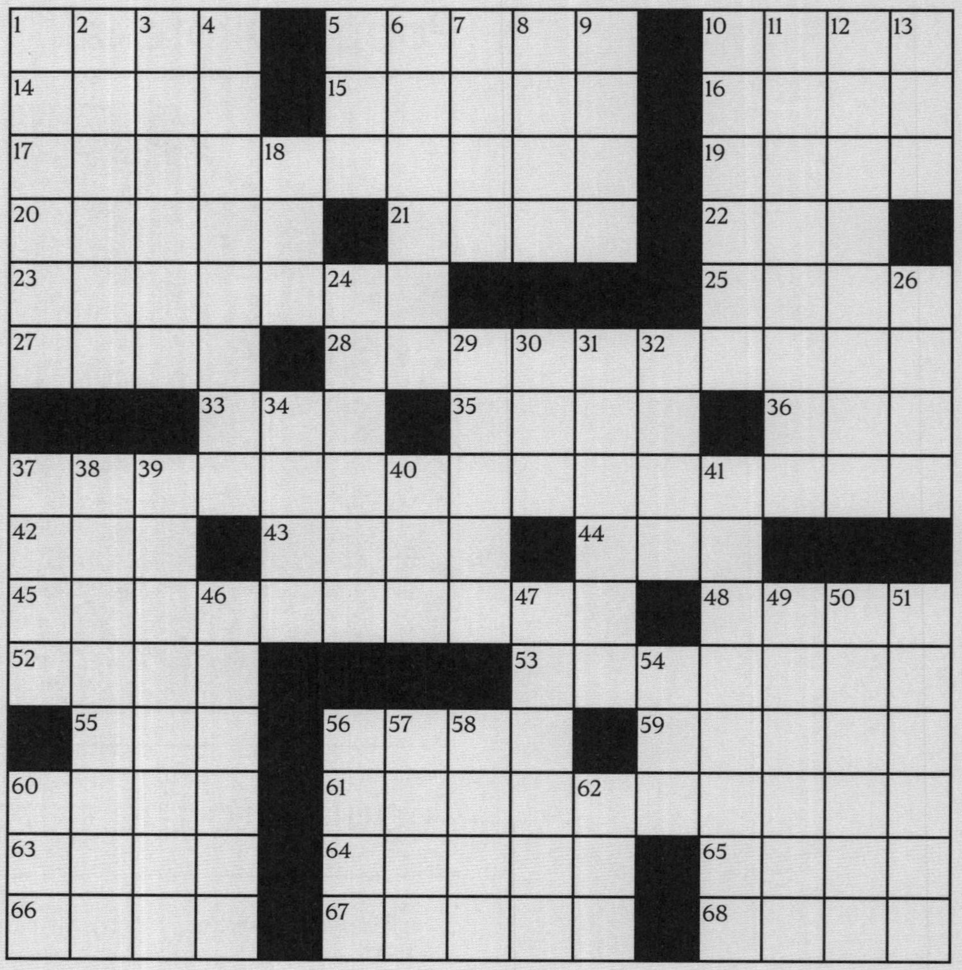

ACROSS

1. Ginormous
5. Savory jelly
10. Heroic Stark of fantasy lit.
14. Tenerife, por ejemplo
15. Large plant-eating mammal
16. Setting for "The King and I"
17. Game in which players leap about a chalk grid attacking each other with karate?
19. Sacred
20. Large meat-eating mammal
21. Gosling on film
22. Fruity drink
23. Attempting to slim down, in a way
25. Country icon McEntire
27. Painter Magritte
28. Game in which would-be real estate tycoons push each other from a ring?
33. Upper limit
35. Prep school on the Thames
36. Regret
37. Tile-laying game in which players assault each other with high kicks?
42. Building extension
43. Actor Morales
44. W.W. II arena
45. Poker variety focused on disarming one's opponent?
48. Narrow amount to win by
52. Würzburg "very"
53. Home of the Braves
55. "There's ____ in 'team'"
56. Lacking rainfall
59. Classical performance hall
60. Art Spiegelman's Pulitzer-winning graphic novel
61. Game in which detectives use their opponents' force against them?
63. Online publication with the motto "Cure ignorance"
64. It might be helpful to read clue 6 Down this way
65. Reclined
66. H.S. equivalency exams
67. Takes a breather
68. SF franchise set in "The Grid"

Crossword: Mark Halpin

DOWN

1. Champion
2. Glowing
3. "Just Do It," e.g.
4. Obsolete music player
5. Bow
6. Something found in tubs, but not tubes?
7. Feel sorry for
8. Early empire builder
9. "Walking in Memphis" singer Marc
10. B-flat equivalent
11. Part of Western Sahara aka "River of Gold"
12. Official color of an Ivy League university
13. Comedian Poehler or Sedaris
18. Hindu honorofic
24. Husband in Hidalgo
26. Sailors' assents
29. News outlets, film, etc.
30. Ear-related prefix
31. Vegetarian's credo
32. "I've got this!"
34. Blown away
37. Black, green, etc.
38. Estrange
39. Norway's national dog
40. '60s war zone, in brief
41. Minor
46. Van Gogh subject
47. Worked through a disagreement
49. Like most Bluetooth headsets
50. A little flat?
51. Irish equivalent of "Edward"
54. "That's extremely amusing!" online
56. Slightly open
57. Govern
58. Marriage vows
60. Make faces
62. Vinyl alternatives

TABLE

Words: Ruby Tandoh

On the strange seduction of figs.

Around this time of year, trees proffer some of their finest—and most challenging—fruits. It is as though they have been watching us prove ourselves: We started the year slowly, with entry-level clementines, building through to strawberry season. By late summer, we progressed to picking roadside blackberries through thorns—a rotten-berry roulette. We ate ripe plums with their occasional burrowing grubs. And now there are figs, the most grown-up fruit of all.

A fig is not technically a fruit, but a perversion of a bundle of tiny blooms. The body you see—the teardrop of green or brown or wine-purple skin—is a vessel for flowers. These grow inward from the spongy subcutaneous matter of the fig. They seek its depths, and because they are never exposed to the sun, they stay embryonic and even jellylike, forming what registers to us as sweet flesh, flushed pink like a berry. When truly ripe, which they seldom are if you buy

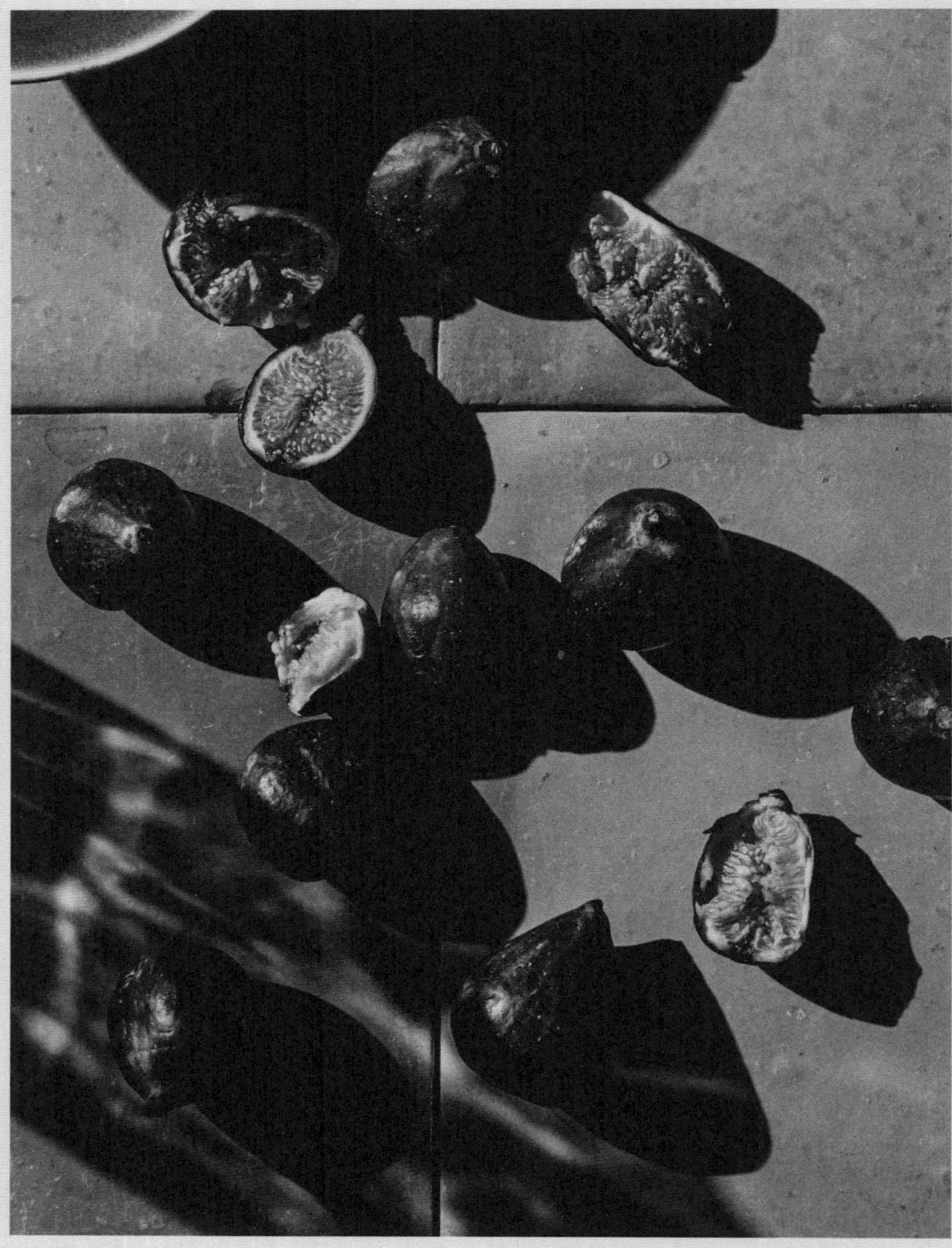

imported ones from a grocery store, figs are thick with intoxicating perfume. In fact, some people believe that it was a fig, not an apple, that was the original forbidden fruit. Other fruits have a salutary air about them but a fig, in no uncertain terms, is a potent and ancient symbol of sensuality—the sex organ of the tree.[1]

There is an element of doubt each time you bite into a fig. An apple will reveal its wormhole to you as a warning; a fig keeps its secrets hidden. Certain varieties, mainly Smyrna figs—the tan-leather dried ones—are pollinated by tiny wasps that crawl inside the fruit to lay their eggs. The upshot is a pollinated fig. The downside for us is the knowledge that this flesh was once home to innumerable bugs. Thankfully, this doesn't apply to all figs, but knowing that even one variety grows this way is enough to put some people off figs for life.

If you're able to get over your squeamishness, the fig offers riches. Italian chef Giorgio Locatelli calls them "the fruits of Paradise." The impulse for the fig novice is to cook them, perhaps grilling and serving them with honey and ricotta. This is good, but try the opposite: Put the figs on ice. Their squishy, multitudinous buds turn into cool, firm flesh resembling gorgeously marbled Wagyu beef. It still isn't a beginner's fruit, but serve these iced figs with some fresh mint or a few drops of Cointreau, and you have mastered the fruiting year.

(1) Despite the sensual associations of the fig, its leaves have long been linked with modesty and concealment. Following a decree issued in 1563, fig leaves were added to nude sculptures across Rome, inspired by Adam and Eve's use of fig leaves to cover themselves in the Bible. The practice later gave rise to the phrase "fig leaf," now used to describe an inadequate attempt to conceal something embarrassing.

Photo: Christopher Simpson

Words:
Tom Faber

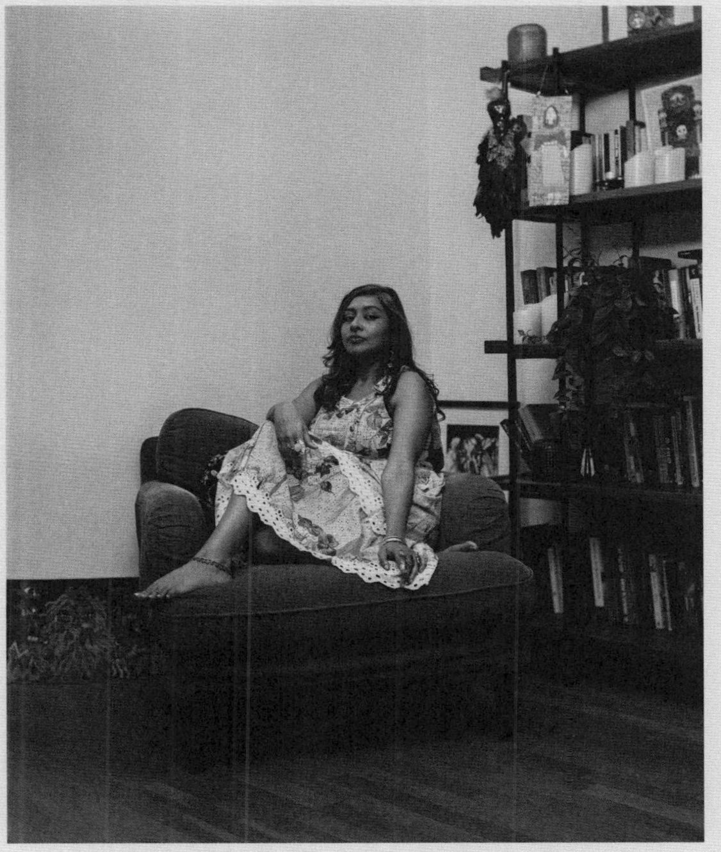

Narrative designer MEGHNA JAYANTH on writing for video games.

As a narrative designer, Meghna Jayanth is responsible for crafting the overarching narrative of a video game, writing dialogue and collaborating with coders and animators to ensure the storytelling is aligned with how players interact with the game's world. Jayanth is also an outspoken political voice in the industry: Her forthcoming game *All Will Rise* is about taking a billionaire to court for destroying a river. She speaks from her home in London.

TOM FABER: How is the process of writing a game different from writing a novel?

MEGHNA JAYANTH: One difference is that games are really collaborative. There are so many people required to make a game, from coders to art directors to animators. The role of the writer is that you're both a collaborator and a conduit. It's not just about writing words. It's about articulating a vision, figuring out what we're trying to say

Photos: Anselm Ebulue

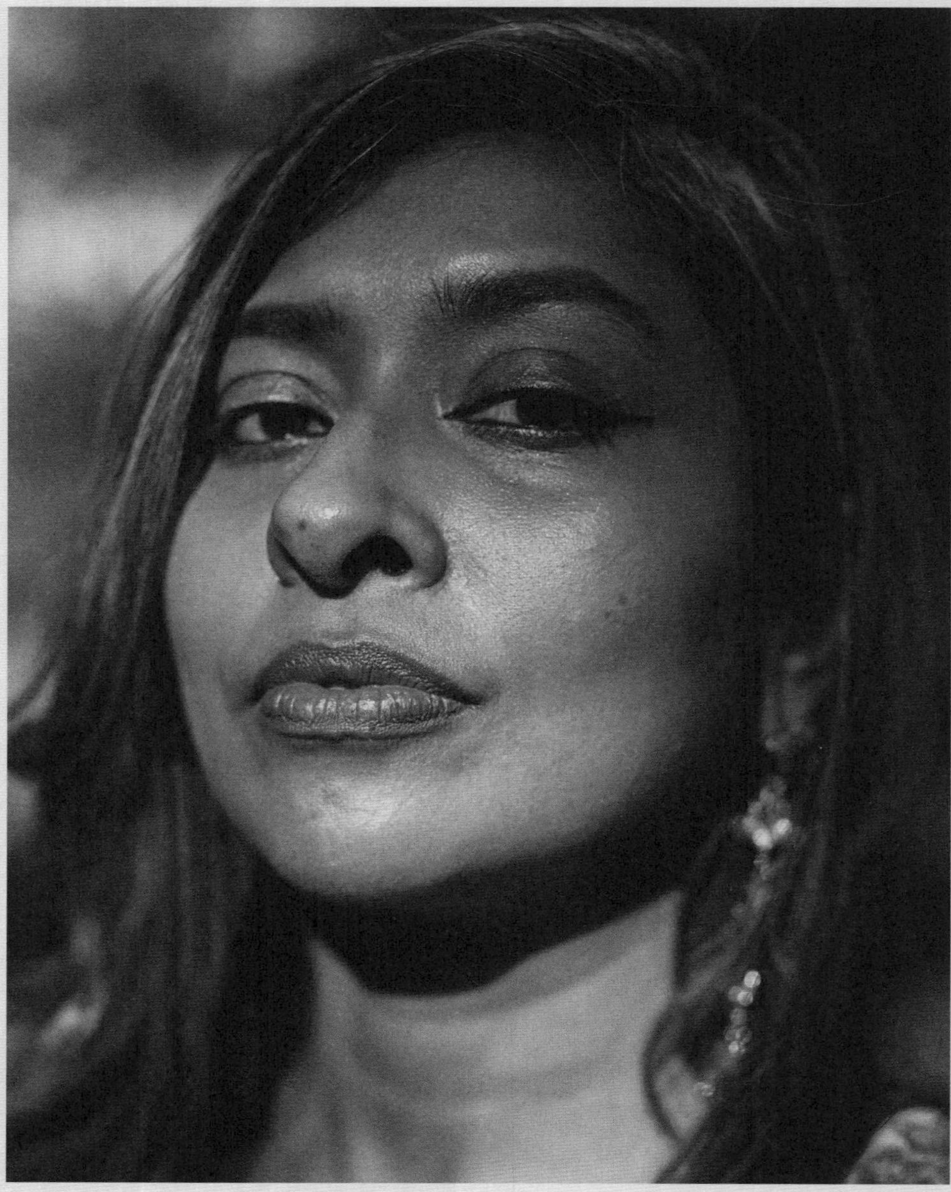

with our mechanics, and thinking more broadly about how meaning is created for the player.

Game writing also has to be alive to the mechanics of a game, in the same way that playwriting is alive to the constraints of the theater. You're not thinking about creating one story; you're creating an engine that can tell multiple stories. You have to let go of that authorial control and be more in conversation with the player. We're designing pleasurable agency rather than a linear story.

TF: Does game writing feel like self-expression for you?

MJ: Absolutely. Every game is personal, and you're spending three or four years on it, so it's a bit like doing a PhD. It has to start with something that you really want to convey to a player, and hopefully it's deep and important enough that it can carry you through four years.

TF: You have often worked on socially conscious games, or games that prominently feature underrepresented voices—both of which are still rare in gaming. What are your thoughts on that?

MJ: Whether we like it or not, the video game is the dominant cultural form of our time. I do think it's really important not to get stuck in what's pushed by the mainstream, or what gets funded. Personally, I feel the world is burning, and I don't see a point in doing anything creative that doesn't have some meaning to it.[1] But also, the social commentary needs to cohabit with a sense of fun, joy and expressiveness. My games are fun and silly, but they have a bit more of a moral soul to them.

(1) Jayanth's other games include *80 Days*, a steampunk reimagining of *Around the World in Eighty Days*, and *Thirsty Suitors*, a surreal story about the South Asian diasporic experience and battling one's evil exes.

FILM

Words: Simran Hans

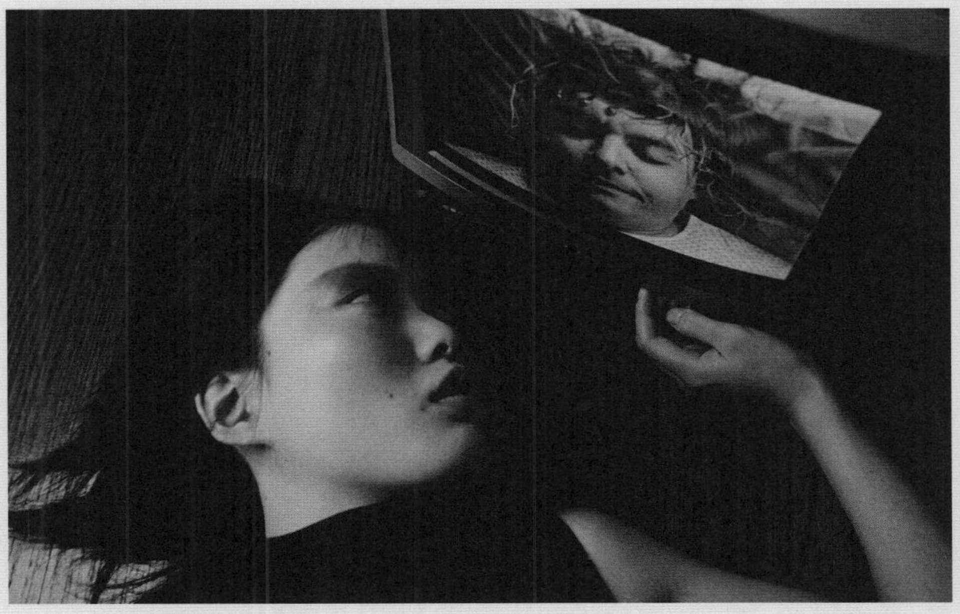

A critic's guide to watching a movie.

Here's how *not* to watch a film: in the background while doing something else; with one eye on the clock to determine how long is left; after you've read lots of reviews.

Of course, I'm guilty of all of these things—of watching and getting distracted, of instinctively reaching for my phone—but it wasn't always this way. In my 20s, I worked as a film critic for a newspaper. I would spend Mondays and Tuesdays in Soho, in London, notebook on my lap as I scrawled illegible notes in the dark. It didn't especially matter whether I liked the films (often, I didn't). I would have to find something to say about them by Wednesday's deadline.

The critic's job is to try to understand the film's substance—what the film is trying to say, and whether it's saying it clearly. But it is also their job to give voice to the feelings stirred and questions raised when encountering something for the first time. As Richard Brody, film critic at *The New Yorker*, put it, "When writing reviews, critics are in the position of the public."

But you don't have to be a critic to watch like one. The watching, I learned, was just as important as the writing. Watching is noticing. To notice, you have to concentrate, and to concentrate, you need to be immersed. And watching a film in a single, uninterrupted sitting is the simplest and most intuitive way to drop into another world. Most of us have been chasing this feeling since childhood—the delicious sensation of having lost track of time.

Giving yourself over to the film in this way allows you to get closer to it. From this somewhat cozier vantage point, it's easier to scrutinize and draw meaning. How would you describe the tone? Is the world-building convincing? What details are taking you out of the narrative?

Everyone deserves to enjoy art in their own way, but that enjoyment is often deepened when you have worked out, on a gut level, what it is trying to do. Advertising moguls and tech companies have tricked us into believing that joy feels like the dopamine hit of passive scrolling; that as long as we're having fun, it doesn't have to be that deep. But there is power—and importantly, pleasure—in thinking about something, talking about it, and turning over its merits.

Our attention span, like my own diminished one, is a muscle, but I am trying to actively retrain it. Because, at the end of the day, the best way to watch a film is to actually *watch* it.

Photo: Paul Westlake

Words:
Emily Nathan

JEREMY DELLER on the power and limits of art.

The British artist Jeremy Deller has built a career on staging events that sit somewhere between history lesson and public spectacle: a brass band performing acid-house anthems, a reenactment of the Battle of Orgreave, a procession that turns a city street into a surrealist "self-portrait."[1] His work rarely declares itself to be political, yet it returns, again and again, to the emotional life of politics—nationalism, memory and the strange choreography of crowds.

If there is a consistent idea running through his practice, it is a modest one: Art won't change the world, but it can, at least for a moment, shift the mood and recalibrate how people move through space—together, apart, in friction, in alignment.

EMILY NATHAN: You've said you're not a political artist, yet your work often brushes up against politics. How do you decide what to engage with?

JEREMY DELLER: I'm not a politician, so I just swim around in it like everyone else. When it comes to my work, it really depends on the project. Sometimes I can make work about something that's been bothering or intriguing me for years. Other times it's a commission; institutions really love anniversaries. In those cases, you try to steer opportunities toward what genuinely interests you, so it's practical in that sense. Making work is a negotiation. You try to go where your interests are, but you also go where people invite you to go.

EN: Participation is central to many of your projects. Has that relationship changed in the age of constant digital documentation?

JD: When you do a public event these days, thousands of photographs are generated, and I see maybe a fraction of them. In a way, the public now archives the work for you; they document it on your behalf.

I think this is just a natural progression; it's how we've evolved. People today feel like something isn't real unless it's filmed: that it's proof you were there, proof of life, almost. I can't blame people for documenting the work—these events are often full of moments you'd

Photo: Joshua Monaghan

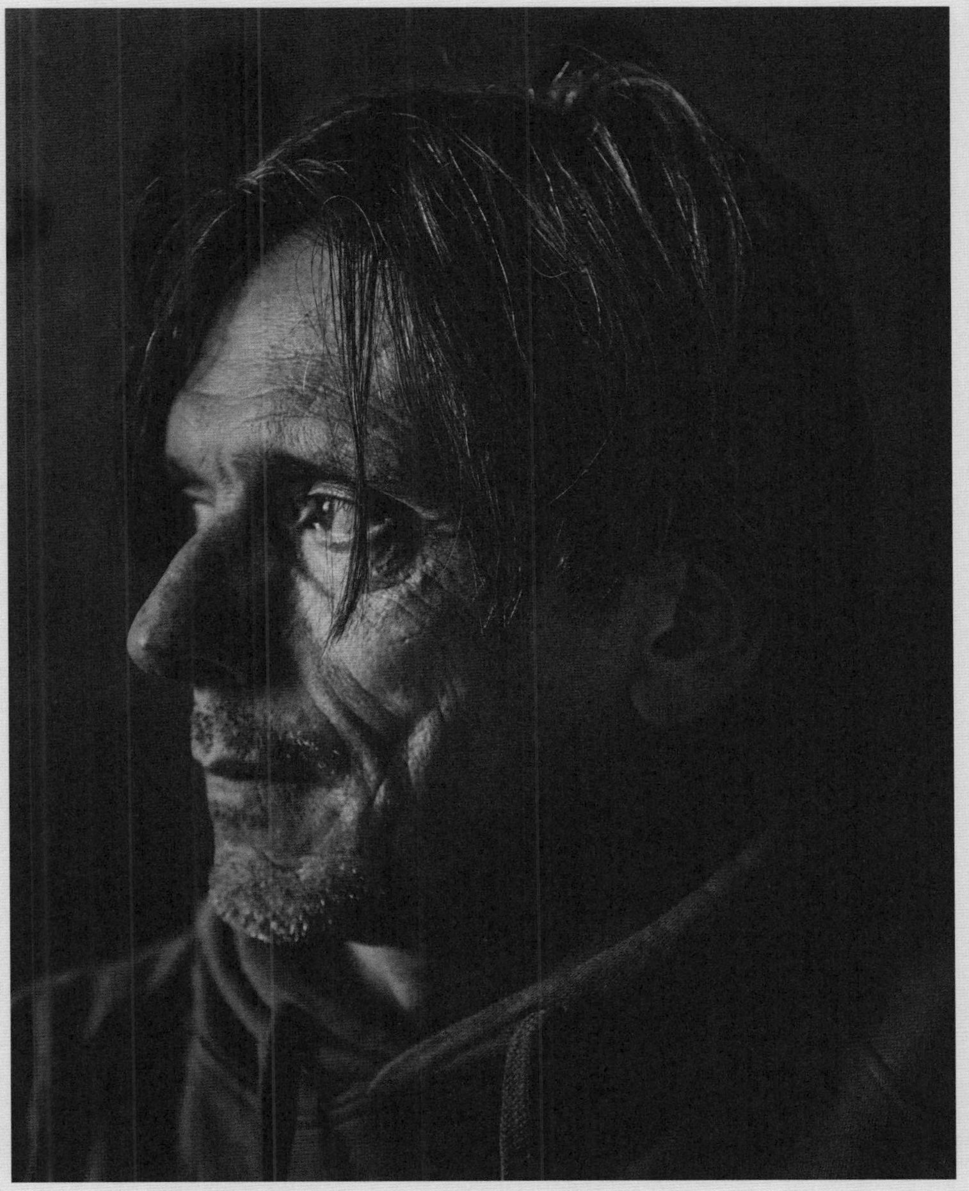

want to capture—so I'm responsible too; it's a kind of invitation.

EN: What are you working on now?

JD: I'm editing footage from public events I did last year, including *The Triumph of Art*. I'm trying to make a multiscreen installation that conveys what it felt like to be there, which is harder than I thought. One camera operator didn't record any sound, so I have some silent footage, which complicates things. But I'll have to make something of it. The installation will first be shown in Iceland in May—prints in one room, film in another. It might be a disaster; it's too early to tell.

EN: You once suggested that art might save us individually, but it can't save the world. Do you still believe that?

JD: Yes. I don't think we should look to artists to change the world. If that's our job, we haven't done a very good one—just look around and see where we are today. Changing the world is an enormous task, so it's quite impossible. I believe, though, that you can change reality for a time. You can change moments. Some artists have changed how we see the world. They've changed the atmosphere—and that counts for something. But they haven't stopped wars.

EN: Your work often operates on a plane that feels like parody or satire. What's your relationship to optimism and cynicism?

JD: Outside my work, I'm quite cynical and pessimistic. The truth is, I make art to make myself less like that. Art keeps me engaged and hopeful, and it's a very personal activity in that sense. Working with the public helps; it brings me into contact and connection with people. I think that human exchange counteracts the cynicism, for me.

(1) The Battle of Orgreave was a violent clash between police and striking miners in South Yorkshire on June 18, 1984, during the year-long miners' strike. It became one of the defining images of Prime Minister Margaret Thatcher's campaign to close Britain's coal mines and weaken the unions.

CREDITS

COVER:	PHOTOGRAPHERS: STYLIST: ARTWORK & SET DESIGN: HAIR & MAKEUP: PRODUCER: MODEL:	Alejandro Arrias & David Bravo Manu Mendi Jhonson Camilo Victor Maresco Laura Meijueiro Rui Huila at Uno Models Rui wears a suit by BIBENCIA and a shirt by BRUNO LANGARICA BLANCO.
P.13		Anna wears a dress and bracelet by MAISON MESA and shoes by CAMPER.
P.14		Rui wears a sweater by ARKET, trousers by MANS CONCEPT MENSWEAR and shoes by CAMPER.
ALWAYS GO TO THE FUNERAL:		Image from Alternative Perspective Series, 2019.
THE FLOW STATE:	PHOTOGRAPHY ASSISTANT: STYLING ASSISTANT:	Antonio Quiroga Luis Carmona & Raul González
KYLE KUZMA:	PHOTOGRAPHY ASSISTANT:	Oscar Jordan
SPECIAL THANKS:		Mako Ayabe Espacio La Candelaria Gomi & Sen at Furry Weekend Atlanta Sadler's Wells Theatre Twentieth Century Society Marta Zuliani

STOCKISTS:
A — Z

A	AMOMENTO	shopamomento.com
	ANGEL SCHLESSER	angelschlesser.com
	ANTIK BATIK	antikbatik.com
	ARKET	arket.com
	ATHOCE	@athoce.seoul
B	BIBENCIA	bibencia.com
	BRUNELLO CUCINELLI	brunellocucinelli.com
	BRUNO LANGARICA BLANCO	@langarica.studioo
C	CADUCIFOLIUM	@caducifoliuum
	CALZEDONIA	calzedonia.com
	CAMPER	camper.com
	CARL HANSEN & SØN	carlhansen.com
	CARLOTA BARERRA	carlotabarrera.com
	CHANEL	chanel.com
	CHROME HEARTS	chromehearts.com
	COMMISSION	commission.nyc
	COS	cosstores.com
D	DOBLAS	carlosdoblas.com
E	ERNESTO NARANJO	ernesto-naranjo.com
	EXPORMIM	expormim.com
F	FERRAGAMO	ferragamo.com
G	GRYTHYTTAN STÅLMÖBLER	grythyttanstalmobler.com
H	HABEY CLUB	habeyclub.com
	HERMÈS	hermes.com
	HOUSE OF FINN JUHL	finnjuhl.com
I	ISSEY MIYAKE	isseymiyake.com
J	JACQUEMUS	jacquemus.com
	JIMMY CHOO	jimmychoo.com
K	KAPITAL	kapital.jp
L	LIMO	bylimo.es
	LORO PIANA	loropiana.com
	LUIS BERRENDERO	luisberrendero.com
M	MAISON MARGIELA	maisonmargiela.com
	MAISON MESA	maisonmesa.com
	MANÉ MANÉ	manemane.es
	MANS CONCEPT MENSWEAR	mansconceptmenswear.com
	MEMORY.NYC	@memory.nyc
	MIU MIU	miumiu.com
O	OMEGA	omegawatches.com
P	POST ARCHIVE FACTION	postarchivefaction.com
	PRADA	prada.com
R	RICHARD MILLE	richardmille.com
S	SANDRO	sandro-paris.com
	SPORTMAX	sportmax.com
	STRING FURNITURE	stringfurniture.com
T	TINA FREY	tinafreydesigns.com
Y	YUJI	yujiofficial.kr
Z	ZEGNA	zegna.com

POINT OF VIEW

As Told To: Julia Webster Ayuso

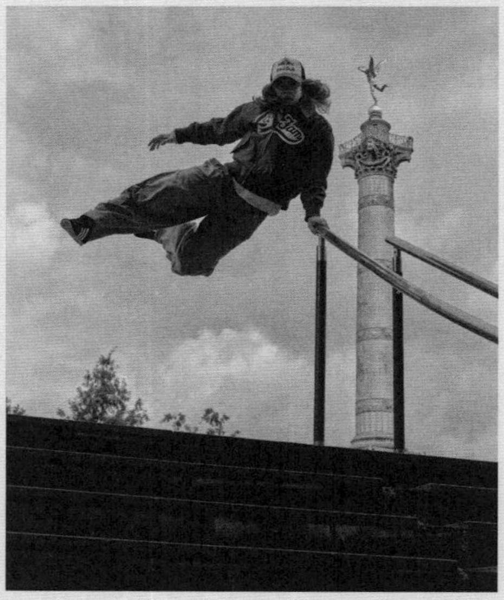

Paris from the perspective of parkour athlete and freerunner LILOU RUEL.

I'm at the Bassin de l'Arsenal, near the Place de la Bastille in Paris. I did a shoot for Red Bull near here in 2024—I did a backflip from one of the quays along the Seine onto one of the barges you can see right there. It was a pretty crazy moment; the Parisians were going wild.

That was just before the Olympics—a few weeks later, I was taking part in the opening ceremony. I was one of seven masked torch bearers who carried the Olympic flame through the streets and across the rooftops of Paris in front of billions of viewers. It was one of the most defining moments of my life.

Whenever I'm in Paris, I like to go up to the rooftops, which are well known by the parkour community because they're surprisingly easy to access. Once you're up there, it's magnificent—the zinc roofs reflecting the sun; the orange chimney pots.... It's usually very flat, so not as dangerous as you'd think, and it's also not particularly slippery, so it's ideal for parkour. You can watch everything happening below, but nobody can see you. You feel like you're alone in the world.

It's also in Paris that I made history in my sport. The world's best parkour athletes come to the suburb of Évry to attempt the Manpower Gap, a jump between two rooftops 4.5 meters [15 feet] apart, with a 16-meter [50-foot] drop below. Four years ago, I decided to be the first woman to attempt it. I did a year of physical and mental preparation, with much soul-searching along the way. Then, on May 2, 2022, I stood at the edge of those 16 meters and launched myself into the air. I landed on the other side without injury and an absolutely insane rush of adrenaline.

In parkour, the city becomes your playground. With every step you take, you discover different possibilities, different challenges. Your eyes unconsciously search for these different features in the urban environment. There's an infinite number of possibilities; you just have to use your imagination and rediscover that childlike spirit. It's an enjoyable way of seeing the world—you're always in the moment.

—

—

Photo: Edouard Jacquinet